THE PENTECOST REVOLUTION

Related available works
by the same author

SECRETS OF THE DEAD SEA SCROLLS
THE AUTHENTIC NEW TESTAMENT
THE PASSOVER PLOT
THOSE INCREDIBLE CHRISTIANS
THE POLITICS OF GOD

THE PENTECOST REVOLUTION

The story of the Jesus Party in Israel, A.D. 36 - 66

Hugh J. Schonfield

MACDONALD · LONDON

First published in 1974 by
Macdonald and Jane's
St Giles House, 49/50 Poland Street, London W.1.

Printed in Great Britain by
Tonbridge Printers Ltd., Peach Hall Works, Tonbridge

ISBN 0 356 04698 2

DEDICATION

To my dear wife for so devotedly aiding and abetting me in the preparation of all my books, and to the University of Boston, Mass., for generously and courageously determining to collect and preserve them.

CONTENTS

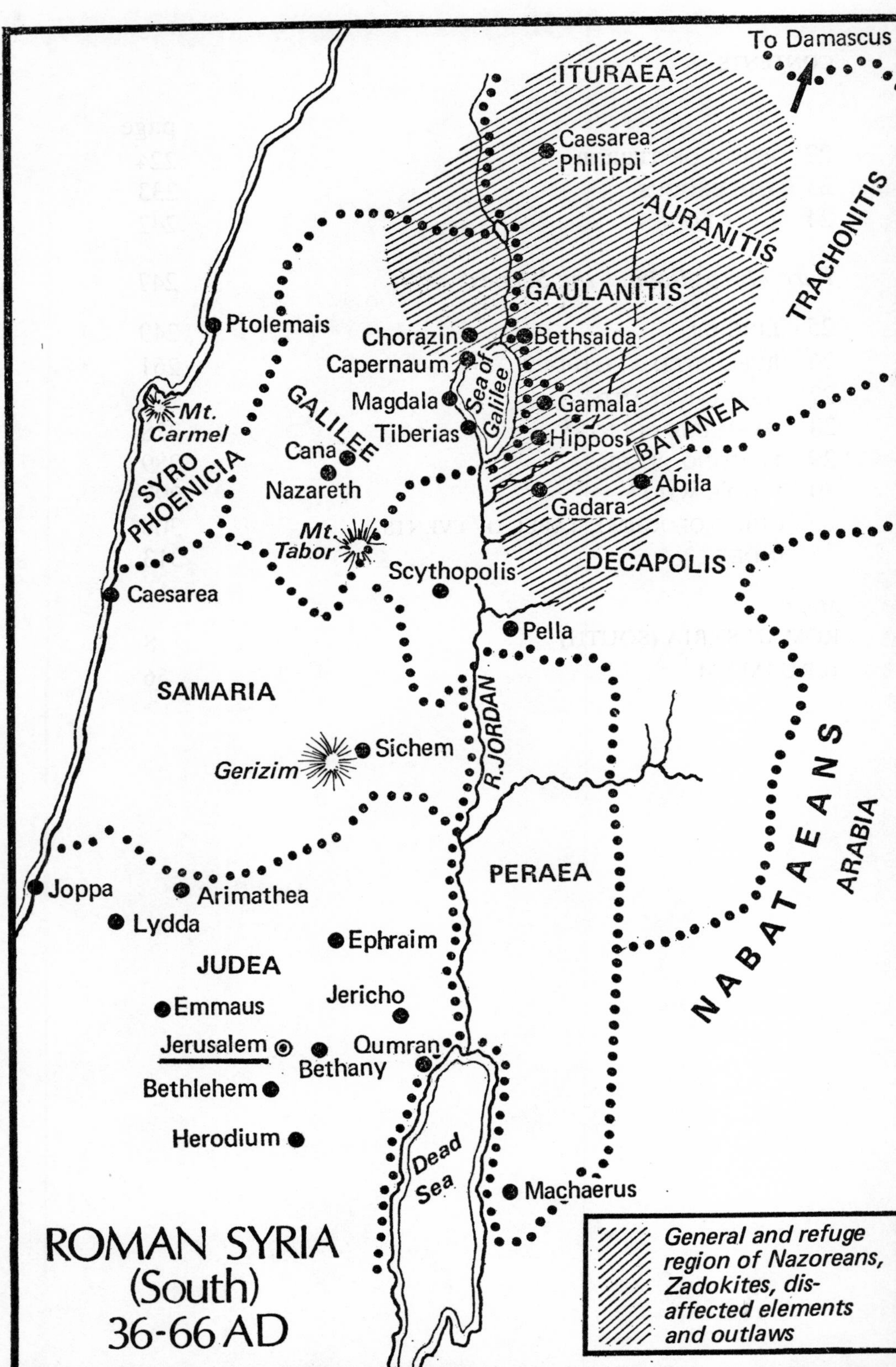

To Damascus
ITURAEA
Caesarea
Philippi
AURANITIS
TRACHONITIS
GAULANITIS
Ptolemais
Chorazin
Bethsaida
Capernaum
Sea of Galilee
Magdala
Gamala
GALILEE
Mt. Carmel
Tiberias
Hippos
BATANEA
SYRO PHOENICIA
Cana
Nazareth
Abila
Gadara
Mt. Tabor
DECAPOLIS
Scythopolis
Caesarea
Pella
SAMARIA
R. JORDAN
Sichem
Gerizim
NABATAEANS
ARABIA
PERAEA
Joppa
Arimathea
Lydda
Ephraim
JUDEA
Jericho
Emmaus
Jerusalem
Qumran
Bethany
Bethlehem
Herodium
Dead Sea
Machaerus
ROMAN SYRIA (South) 36-66 AD
General and refuge region of Nazoreans, Zadokites, disaffected elements and outlaws

INTRODUCTION

A great transformation has been taking place in the understanding of Christian Beginnings. This is of so consequential a nature that it could not be expected to be officially confirmed by any section of the Christian Church, which has to think in terms of the effect on the rank and file of believers. Yet very largely the transformation has been due to the diligence, integrity and objectivity of Christian scholarship, assisted by the discovery of fresh material such as the Dead Sea Scrolls.

The nineteenth century witnessed an enormous advance in archaeology, notably in what were called Bible Lands, and the literary as well as monumental finds in Mesopotamia, Egypt and Palestine radically changed thinking about the Scriptures, the manner of their composition and their value as historical records. Independent of their spiritual worth there could now be applied to them the same criteria as with other relics of antiquity. They could no longer be treated as sacrosanct, to be received as factually true in every detail. Resistance to the secular treatment of the Bible was considerable, especially as regards the New Testament, since the truth of the principal dogmas of Christianity was now open to challenge, as it appeared to conservatives, by the arrogance of fallible mortals.

Fortunately, the majority of Christian scholars were not deterred from pursuing their investigations, and a fruitful era opened for the study of the New Testament documents in an endeavour to determine their quality and reliability, to reach back to their sources, and to ascertain what was primary and what was secondary in their texts.

These activities necessarily demanded high qualifications of learning, and therefore denied to the general public an adequate realization of what progress was being made. Consequently, as some of the results were disclosed they hit sharply and created confusion and offence, since the minds of laymen had not been prepared for them. The clergy who might have helped were more reluctant than they should have been to act as a means of communication, and those who did commit themselves to pronouncements often failed to grasp that an insufficient ground work of education had been laid to cushion the shock of what they stated. It is understandable that scholars should be preoccupied with communicating their researches to one another in their own academic fashion; but it is to be deplored that so few of them have been concerned with the need for public enlightenment, particularly when their labours deal with matters which materially affect questions of belief. If humanity is to advance, the means must be found of imparting information to the greatest possible number. The aim must be to enrol the vast majority as students in the university of mankind.

In the domain of research into Christian Origins vast changes have been in progress, both in attitudes and in achievements. Those changes were already remarkable when I entered this field half a century ago. One of my advisers in those days, Professor Burkitt of Cambridge, put it mildly when he wrote: 'We look at the earliest Christianity, the data given us in the New Testament, as a *problem* [his italics], in a way that seems to me new. We are able, in fact are compelled, to look at Christian Beginnings objectively, as no previous generation of Christians, sincere or nominal, were ever able to look at them' (*Christian Beginnings*, p. 40).

What he was indicating was that the documents, more especially the Gospels and the Acts of the Apostles, could no longer be treated as authentic records which reported what had actually happened, but as expressions of what at a later time, stretching into the second century A.D., it was desired to convey had happened. We had objectively to take account of the motivations of the writers in connection with circumstances which had materially altered, and which affected both the manner of presentation and the content of what was set down. We had to recognize that the past had been shaped to present needs, and patiently endeavour to learn what could be gleaned of earlier elements which in turn might lead us towards conclusions on which we could depend.

Certainly the capacity for objectivity had increased substantially fifty years ago; but it had not by any means been easy to achieve. Many had hoped that their studies would confirm that the Church was fully justified on the evidence in holding that the Jesus of history had answered to the Christian delineation of him, and that his first followers had endorsed such delineation. The evidence, however, would not do what was demanded of it, and for the more theologically-minded this occasioned a grave mistrust of the historical method of approach. After a process of demythologizing there seemed to be very little left, and for some accordingly it was virtually written off that the Jesus of history was discoverable. The Church's insight had therefore to serve as an inspiration in its own right. This attitude, much too pessimistic as it transpired, gave encouragement to sceptics at the other extreme, who were very willing to vote Jesus out of existence as a creation of Christian legend.

In fact, to a marked extent the quest of the historical Jesus had succeeded. Only what was disclosed about him did not sufficiently conform to the likeness of Christian piety and adoration. And rather than acknowledge him in the dimensions that were appropriate it seemed preferable to affirm that we were confronted with the Great Unknown.

The quest was on the road to success in both negative and positive respects. Negatively, it acknowledged that there was much in the Jesus story that was of later contrivance. There had been imposed upon the presentation of him and his teaching a great deal that was alien and devoid of historicity. There were anachronistic, apologetic and anti-Jewish tendencies. The new approach to the Gospels and Acts disclosed that they reflected many later developments and interpretations. Underlying the documents were certain earlier sources which to an extent could be defined and reconstructed. A freedom had been exercised to bring variously together sayings and actions, so that it was a problem to ascertain what were the original circumstances (*sitz im leben*) in which a saying or teaching of Jesus had been delivered. There was uncertainty about dates and sequences. There was an influence of prophetic interpretation on the description of events, so that in some instances details had been invented to comply with supposed prophetic requirements. There were indications that the Evangelists had altered or discarded material in their sources which did not suit them, and therefore there existed the possibility that they had omitted more than could be observed that was contrary to the impression of Jesus they wished to convey. The gain on the negative side was that to a considerable extent there was removed from the portrait of Jesus the extravagances and embellishments of later over-painting.

Turning to the positive aspect, while in point of detail there remained very much less of the Jesus of history this in itself could tell us a great deal more. Many of the contradictions and inconsistencies conveyed by the Gospels had disappeared. Jesus was no longer enveloped in an aura of the unearthly, and emerged as a man of strong personal feelings, convictions and purposefulness. Unmistakably he was a Jew, a religious nationalistic Jew, who believed himself to be the Messiah his people were awaiting. It became possible, therefore, to carry out experimentally with the aid of available resources a fresh assessment of him. One of the pioneers in this field in the present century was Robert Eisler, followed by Brandon and Carmichael. My own contribution was made in *The Passover Plot*.

The quest, which for a time had seemed to peter out, was reactivated by the finding of the Dead Sea Scrolls and the excavations at Masada. Suddenly there was a wealth of fresh material dating from before the destruction of Jerusalem in A.D. 70 and having an evident relevance to Christian Beginnings. There loomed up in this literature the personality of the mysterious True Teacher, or Teacher of Righteousness. There were expressions and ideas which had parallels in the New Testament. Much more could be learnt of Messianic thinking and activities among the Jews current in the first century of the Christian Era. New light was thrown on the Essenes and Zealots.

The discoveries directed fresh attention to the character and fortunes of the original Jewish followers of Jesus, the so-called Jewish-Christians. One scholar, J. L. Teicher, jumped to the conclusion that the Scrolls were Christian Ebionite documents, and more recently Father O'Callaghan has believed that minute fragments found in Cave 7 at Qumran were remains of scrolls of New Testament books, Mark, James, and I Timothy, and possibly the Acts, Romans, and II Peter. Neither of these contentions could be established; but the general effect of the impact of the new discoveries has been a notable movement of research workers into the area of the Jewish background of Christianity.

For many centuries the chief concern of Christians with post-Biblical Jewish literature had been to seek evidence that Judaism was inferior to Christianity and hostile to it. Subsequent to the Reformation, however, the Rabbinical literature began to be studied as a means of assisting the understanding and interpretation of the Gospels. Yet down to the beginning of the twentieth century there were only a few specialists in this field, both Jews and Christians. On these authorities the majority of scholars had been accustomed to depend for their information and references. The great work of Strack and Billerbeck was particularly important. In the nineteenth century another aspect of Jewish studies had also developed, partly as a result of new manuscript finds. Editions and translations were made of the ancient Jewish Apocrypha and Pseudepigrapha as a revelation of the climate of Jewish thought in which Christianity was rooted. The name of R. H. Charles stands out in this connection.

There is no need here to enlarge upon the various directions and contexts in which relations between Christians and Jews have radically improved. But it is pertinent to appreciate that the change has been quite revolutionary. Christian warming towards the understanding of Judaism has been reciprocated by a greater interest in Jesus on the part of Jews. The outcome has been that valuable collaboration in research has become practicable, and this in turn has made clear that the Gospels and Acts had furnished an inaccurate and prejudiced representation of the historical circumstances. The false impression which had endured for centuries and brought untold suffering to the Jewish people could at long last begin to be rectified. But this could not have happened were it not for the modern objective approach to the study of Christian Beginnings.

It took a great deal of courage, first of all to acknowledge that in many matters the chief documents of Christianity were unreliable, and then to face up to the necessity for looking very differently at how Christianity had come into being. It was not only what was told of Jesus that had to be subjected to penetrating investigation, but also what was reported of the foundation of the Church. It had to be set aside that the Christian religion had started with the outpouring of the Holy Spirit at Pentecost following the Resurrection and Ascension of Christ. The old division of early Ecclesiastical History into Apostolic, Sub-Apostolic and Patristic Ages no longer held good. New divisions marking stages of development were called for which were much closer to the reality. As a new religion, partly based on Pauline teaching, Christianity had progressively come into existence between A.D. 75 and 150. How this came about I have described in my book *Those Incredible Christians.* It was not easily acceptable that Jesus and his first followers had not only been Jews, but had remained Jews. There had been nothing known about Jesus by the original apostles which necessitated the creation of a new religion.

Where the testimony of the Gospels and Acts suggested that two religions were in conflict – Christianity and Judaism – this had to be thrown overboard as prejudiced and untrue as regards the position in Palestine before A.D. 70. What the Evangelists had done was to transfer to the past the characteristics of a subsequent period. They wrote up the story of Jesus and his followers in a manner agreeable to the circumstances of their own time, and falsely conveyed that the Faith to which they subscribed had been in evidence from the very beginning, demonstrated by Jesus and endorsed by apostolic teaching. Surviving information which told a different story was largely altered or suppressed.

Increasingly it could be discerned that the shaping of the Christian religion had been a secondary development, which in no small measure had been brought about by the consequences of the Jewish war with the Romans. An earlier phase of Christian expression of quite another order had operated before A.D. 66.

Thus the pursuit of objectivity and realism dictated a movement away from preconceptions based on or influenced by concern with Christianity as a religion and a concentration on its original aspect as a Messianic movement within Judaism. Scholarship, accordingly, has been coming to recognize that a correct approach to Christian Beginnings must be made through Jewish channels, spiritual and historical, not neglecting those Jewish sects of adherents of Jesus in the early Christian centuries which were branded by the Catholic Church as heretical.

The quest of the 'Early Church' is by no means a new one, and it had run on somewhat parallel lines to the quest of the historical Jesus. The irreducible minimum of knowledge was that there had sprung up after the death of Jesus a Jewish organization centred on Jerusalem which claimed him as the Messiah and the prophet foretold by Moses. This organization was commonly described as Nazorean. It might fittingly be called an Israel Loyalist Movement, since it emphasized loyalty to God and His Law and devotion to the king of Israel of God's choice. The king, namely Jesus, after having been raised from the dead was now in heaven, but would soon return to earth in judgment to punish the wicked and deliver the faithful remnant of his people from their enemies and oppressors. Thereafter he would reign over a world converted to knowledge of God and obedient to His commandments.

Moreover it was certified that the leader of the Nazoreans for about a quarter of a century had been a younger brother of Jesus named Jacob, known as the Just. In the English New Testament he is called James, and Paul describes him as 'the Lord's brother'. While the Acts and Pauline epistles suggest his importance, the Nazorean and even ecclesiastical literature gives him much greater prominence and authority. It appears that Jacob was an ascetic Jew admired for his devotion to the Jewish Faith and almost venerated by the Jewish populace as their champion. This could not have been the case unless the Party of Jesus had taken a position of involvement, and indeed danger, in relation to the fortunes of their nation, and commended itself as heralding the imminent Messianic redemption of Israel. The longing for that redemption, and the ways in which it expressed itself, was fully portrayed in the pages of the histories of Josephus. What demanded clarification was the relationship between Nazorean affairs and Jewish history of the period.

The difficulty in obtaining a coherent picture was immense. So much had been lost, perverted or suppressed. In one way or another a large slab of history, covering the most exciting and vital features of Christian Beginnings, had sunk beneath the surface of remembrance as though by volcanic action, leaving through legends and traditions only some tantalizing projections still visible.

A certain amount of reconstruction on the available evidences had been practicable before the contribution of the Dead Sea Scrolls and other fresh resources. I had myself published a book on the subject entitled *Saints Against Caesar* (Macdonald, 1948). But it has been most valuable to have S. G. F. Brandon devoting himself more recently to the same theme in *Jesus and the Zealots.*

The recovery of a whole library of pre-70 Hebrew manuscripts belonging to an Essene type of Jewish sect has been a tremendous gain. In many ways they illustrate the environment of thought in which Nazoreanism had subsisted. Unfortunately, the references and allusions in the Scrolls were often cryptic and ambiguous. What could be agreed by scholars was that the Qumranites had been active at least until the Jewish War with the Romans. The sect had therefore been contemporary with the Zealot Movement initiated by Judas of Galilee, the Baptist Movement of John the son of Zechariah, and the Movement centred on Jesus the son of Joseph. The connections between them had therefore to be re-explored. Every scrap of information old and new had to be assembled and pieced together. Fresh questions had to be asked and possibilities entertained. What has stood out is that the story of the original Jesus Movement is even more a part of Jewish history than it is of Christian history.

The scope of inquiry has broadened out tremendously. The issues to be covered include those of geography and chronology as well as of religious, social and political history. Much of what has to be considered and discussed will be unfamiliar to the general reader. And therefore in the approach of this book I have aimed at imparting essential information in a manner which could most readily be understood.

What I am now making public are the results of my own endeavour to crash the time-barrier in an attempt to recover as much as possible of the lost record of Christian Beginnings in their native Jewish environment. It has been an adventurous undertaking, because although my explorations have already extended over fifty years, and I had come to a number of tentative conclusions, I could not know in advance whether these would hold good when put to the test of an orderly narrative where every circumstance had to find its natural place and explanation. Neither could I guess what new points might crop up to change or confirm previous findings. In fact I had to discard very little, and was rewarded by many fresh insights and some quite exciting discoveries.

It has been fully borne out that we have entered a new era which is bound to be very disturbing to those who have pinned their faith on the veracity of the New Testament version of the Christian story. Much will have to be reformulated and reappraised, and what the outcome will be cannot be predicted with any assurance. Yet it must be better to adjust, however painfully, than to try to hold on to concepts, however precious, which truth demands should be abandoned. I am confident that a spiritual gain and enlargement awaits those who must undergo this travail. Already there are signs of this in a new apprehension of the Messianic.

But while what I have set down has an obvious bearing on modern belief it has been my primary concern to furnish sensitively and also realistically a portrait of a quite extraordinary Movement in the setting of its own period and location. For the Jewish people the time was perhaps the strangest in the history of any nation, dominated as it was by the obsession that this was the climax of human history, the closing phase of an age-old struggle between the forces of Light and Darkness. Every event was to be observed prophetically and apocalyptically as marking some aspect of the conflict, some pertinent stage in the advance of the Last Days towards the moment when the righteous would be vindicated and the evildoers would be overthrown. The personalities and sects of the period which come into the story were responding to its atmosphere. They were both created by the contemporary situation and making their own impact upon it. It is vital to understanding that we should see them in their context.

One of the aspects I have featured is the reaction of the ordinary people to the state of affairs. We are very conscious today of popular feeling and the way it expresses itself, the hasty and often unreasoning judgment of what presents itself as a wrong, the instinctive drawing together in crowds for comfort and strength, the proneness to resort to violence when faced with obstruction or refusal of redress, the panic effects of fear, the readiness to listen to demagogues, and also the profound courage to challenge arbitrary power, and the simple devotion to principle. The voice of the people is not the voice of God; but sometimes what the people feel is closer to the heart of a matter than the complex reasoning of the more sophisticated.

The ordinary people, artisans and peasants, play a large part in our story. The pages of Josephus the Jewish historian bear continual witness to the effect upon them of the grievous circumstances in Palestine in the dark days he had to describe and at the most crucial period he had personally witnessed. The Gospels and the Acts also testify to the involvement of the masses in the situations depicted.

To interpret Christian Beginnings rightly there has to be an empathy with the Jewish people in a great time of trial and of expectation. We have to share their sufferings, their bewilderment, their anger and desperation, and also their hopes for the future. Here neither science nor theology is of sufficient service. The manifestations which made their appeal to the people were mainly inspired by men of the people. The outpouring of the Holy Spirit in all ages has pre-eminently been a working-class phenomenon, and it is the ordinary people who, more psychically, are aware that 'the times they are a'changin' '.

It was the 'Wind of God' which tore into those who first mustered under the banner of the slogan 'No Ruler but God'. It was the 'Wind of God' which shook the soul of John the Baptist and took possession of the Galilean carpenter Jesus. It was the 'Wind of God' which turned on the Apostles and compelled them to prophesy. Like strong drink it created a euphoria, put fire in the belly and loosened the tongue. Those who were 'lit up' were emboldened to vocal witness beyond normal capacity and released from all abashment in the presence of princes. With more feeble minds it could have side-effects in producing a babel of tongues and incoherent utterances; but chiefly it conferred a sense of exaltation and positivity. There was an apocalyptic realization of the imminent overturning of the existing order and its replacement by the ideal society of the Kingdom of God. It is because of the fervent Messianism which gripped and convulsed the Jewish populace in the period we are to cover, and because the Nazorean Movement was so exuberantly connected with it, that I have entitled this volume *The Pentecost Revolution.*

It had impressed itself on me that, valuable as it has been for scholars to pursue particular lines of inquiry and research, certain indispensable insights could only be obtained by a dramatic reconstruction of the sequence of events, by telling a whole story which was descriptive of the actual conditions and evocative of the atmosphere of the period. To this end it has to be recognized that what we had to reach into was the reactions of the people in general to developments as they occurred. I had worked on these lines with considerable success for many years, not always to the liking of pundits and the more conservatively orthodox. It was not easy for them to entertain a view of Jesus and his followers that was not wrapped up in a mystique which was held to be indispensable. Nevertheless, my contentions were able to get through to multitudes thanks to the media of press, television and radio, which were not only more news conscious but more in contact with what people wanted to know. The climate of opinion is now, I am sure, much more ready to seize upon the relevance to modern needs and conditions of what these pages will relate.

If the Nazorean initiative in ancient Israel has a hero, that role must be assigned neither to Peter nor to Paul, but to Jacob (James), the brother of Jesus. It is interesting that in the recovered *Gospel of Thomas* the disciples ask Jesus who will be great over them when he has left them. Jesus replies, 'In the place to which you will go [i.e. Jerusalem], you will go to Jacob the Just, for whose sake heaven and earth came into being.' Of him it was said elsewhere that the Scriptures prophetically bore witness to him as they had done to Jesus as Messiah. He was deemed to be the Suffering One spoken of in Isaiah as 'My servant Jacob'.

Jacob is revealed, not as a Christian bishop, but as vicegerent of the Messiah, head of a government of loyalist Israel in opposition to the 'apostate' government largely composed of the Sadducean hierarchy. He is the protector and champion of the Jewish people in face of their enemies and oppressors. Only this saintly but very determined personality could have held together the very mixed and diverse ingredients of the Nazorean Movement, embracing Zealots, Pharisees, Essenes, and others. It is brought out that the original 'Christians' with the Apostles and Elders constituted a religio-political 'People's Party' within the Jewish economy, with the seat of its government on Mount Zion in the ancient City of David.

The history of Christian Beginnings comes out very differently to what has commonly been taught. Therefore, in preparation for the narrative entitled 'Drama in Progress' which covers the theme of this work and occupies Part Two, I selected a number of consequential subjects for particular exploration. These are distributed between Part One and Part Three. Here we get away from a 'Christian' approach, and seek for leads and clues – sometimes in strange places – which will assist us in the task of reconstruction. Certain points I have made are novel and may be found illuminating. Part One, 'Setting the Stage', furnishes indispensable background information, while Part Three, 'Behind the Scenes', takes up lines of inquiry which are pertinent to aspects of the historical events.

Possibly because I am an enthusiast, and deeply concerned with seeking to learn what was the truth about Jesus and his Jewish followers in Israel before Christianity existed, I have difficulty in imagining a casual approach to the subject. The challenge is so great that it calls for effort to come to grips with the problems and issues which have to be faced. But I have purposefully refrained from being too academic, and at all times I have been mindful of the requirements of the general reader.

In Part One, and at the close of Part Three, I have applied myself to the vital matter of chronology. It has been a serious hindrance to apprehension of the historical circumstances that there has had to be so much dispute about the dating of key events in the Christian story. I have brought forward criteria which enable us to relate Nazorean to Jewish affairs much more confidently. We can now perceive interactions, which previously were obscure or unrecognized, with very great gain to our understanding.

The topography, especially of Jerusalem, is also of consequence. Many of the events with which we have to deal are tied in with the layout of the city. Fortunately we are assisted by the descriptions of

Jerusalem before the Jewish War given by Josephus, and by the results of archaeological excavations. For several years work has been going on to the south-west and south of the Temple plateau. Thanks to the helpfulness of Professor Yigael Yadin, my wife and I have inspected the sites for the purposes of this book, and have also studied the area of the Ophel where the Nazorean headquarters was situated. It is hoped that in the not distant future major excavations will be conducted there as well.

Thus in one way and another I have spared no effort that would be conducive to bringing to life the period with which this volume is concerned, and have striven to throw light in an efficient manner on the fortunes of the first followers of Jesus in their native Jewish environment. My indebtedness to other pioneers in this field is very great, and I believe that together we have redeemed the historical approach from the slurs cast upon it by those who have not wished to allow that it had an important and constructive contribution to make in its own right.

The sources to which I am particularly indebted are given in the text and notes. But I would specially acknowledge my obligations in respect of major translations I have used. For the Old Testament quotations I have largely employed the Revised Standard Version, while for the New Testament I have used my own rendering from *The Authentic New Testament* (Dennis Dobson). For the writings of Josephus and Philo I thankfully make acknowledgment to the translators of the Loeb Classical Library editions, and to the publishers, Heinemann and Harvard University Press. The reader is thus directed to authorities which can readily be consulted. This applies also to quotations of the Zadokite literature, where I have principally cited the translation by G. Vermes, *The Dead Sea Scrolls in English* (Penguin Books, 1962).

HUGH J. SCHONFIELD
Pentecost, 1973

Part One

SETTING THE STAGE

CHAPTER 1

THE LAST TIMES BEGIN

To understand the times of which we are writing, their extraordinary personalities and events, we have continually to remind ourselves that for multitudes in the Holy Land these were the Last Times.

We must not approach them with a cold logic or an alien attitude; for if we do our interpretations will bear little resemblance to the reality. Much of what occurred could not have happened except in response to the hopes and fears, the urgencies and pressures, of a period of intense emotional disturbance generated by the conviction that the sands were fast running out in the hourglass of destiny. Ahead lay Judgment Day, and beyond it the bliss of the Kingdom of God on earth. But 'That World'[1] would be attainable only by the righteous, and to prevent more than a few from getting there the People of God were now being subjected to the fiercest beguilements and bombardments of the forces of Evil.

The reactions varied according to individual character and inclination, and even social status. There were scoffers, particularly among the upper classes, for whom the End-Time imagination had all the marks of mania and ignorant folly; but they could not avoid being involved in its consequences and effects. A whole nation was increasingly in the grip of persuasions which defied reason, and looked to the miraculous to overcome obstacles of a magnitude to deter the sober-minded. By such fanaticism the Jews were prodded and goaded into war with the Romans, assured by the militant that the Kingdom of God could be taken by storm and that the destruction of sinners must now begin.

Also among the believers that the Last Times had come were those who counselled patience and personal preparation for the moment chosen by God for His signal intervention. But their influence could not stem the tide, or cope with the aggravations caused by the malpractices of Roman governors and Jewish aristocrats. The more we study this category of believer, which included Jesus, the more evident it is that their contribution arose from and was shaped and inspired by contemporary convictions and expectations. Part of our approach, therefore, has to be to release ourselves from any supposition that what they represented was something that lay outside and was independent of the peculiarities of the special situation to which they responded in their own fashion.

When we have got over that hurdle – and it is no easy one to negotiate – we shall more readily be able to notice significant indications which distinguish what reflects the time from what was imposed by later teaching.

We begin, then, with the question, how did it come about that the first century A.D. was so strongly held to be the Last Times?

Part of the answer lies far back in the period when Palestine was under Persian rule, and came strongly under the influence of Iranian-Babylonian religious thought. The concept of a Cosmic Drama came to the fore, in which through a succession of Ages the Forces of Light and Darkness were contending with each other with varying success, and which looked to a Final Age in which Light would ultimately triumph. While Judaism could not embrace a dualistic concept of Deity, the idea of the Drama fired prophetic imagination, and fitted in well with Jewish hopes of an era in which Israel would be redeemed and the world under God would live in peace and justice.

Thus there developed among the Pious (the Chasidim) a doctrine of the Two Spirits linked to the Two Ways[2] of the Deuteronomic Code which achieved full expression in subsequent apocalyptic literature.

The greater the sufferings of the Jews, and heathen pressure upon them to forsake their ancestral faith, the more evident it became that the Forces of Evil were exerting themselves to gain the victory. This could only mean that the Enemy (Belial and his minions) realized that this might well be their last chance. The Drama must therefore be approaching its climax; and it behoved the faithful to intensify resistance by unswerving loyalty to God and His Law, accepting persecution and isolation as the price to be paid for winning through to a share in the bliss of the Age to Come, which clearly could not be very much longer delayed.[3] Indeed, the Saints could perform an atoning work for the people and the land, acceptable to God, so that He might advance the Day of Deliverance.

But these considerations did not by themselves sufficiently pinpoint the times, and a new industry and technique of interpreting the Scriptures was called for to secure greater clarification and capacity to read the Signs. This development was foreshadowed, among other writings, in the book of Daniel, composed about 166 B.C., in the midst of the terrible experiences of the attempt by Antiochus IV to abolish the practice of the Jewish religion.

The book is set in the period of the Medo-Persian conquest of Babylon, nearly four hundred years earlier, and Daniel's visions 'foresee' the course of events culminating in the present catastrophe. The outcome cannot therefore be precisely revealed to the supposed author. He is told: 'Go your way, Daniel, for the words are shut up and sealed until the Time of the End. Many shall purify themselves, and make themselves white, and be refined; but the wicked shall do wickedly; and none of the wicked shall understand; but those who are wise shall understand' (xii. 9–10). It is the task of 'the wise', the skilled (*maskilim*) of the real author's own time, to comprehend the enigmatic intimations of the visions.

Daniel, like *I Enoch*, was a product of the Chasidim (the Assideans of the book of Maccabees). This body of pious Jews appears to have arisen towards the close of the third century B.C. in an attempt to counteract the inroads of Hellenism which increasingly had made an impact on Jewish life and thought since the conquests of Alexander the Great. The more the trend developed the more did the Chasidim, who included many of the priests, move towards the organization of a distinct group within the nation to preserve its spiritual and moral values. Later, around the middle of the second century, there came a development which dedicated part of the movement to a near-monastic existence (the Essenes), while another part remained in more immediate contact with public affairs and sought to move the people away from the enticements and turpitudes of Hellenized society (the Pharisees). These are rough approximations, because the process of alignments was more complex.

The visions of Daniel are fairly circumstantial and relatively easy to follow in secular history when they deal with what in fact was the past at the time the author was writing. It is when he looks to the real future that he has to be rather vague and employ numerical riddles. What he seems to anticipate is that the present tribulation would continue, and that it would be the last great struggle before God would inaugurate His Kingdom on earth, when the world would be ruled by the people of the Saints of the Most High. The dominion of the warring 'Beast' Powers would be taken away, and replaced by the *homo sapiens* 'Son of Man' Power represented by the Saints.

The great epoch of anti-God imperialism until the manifestation of the Kingdom of God would occupy seventy weeks of years from the date of the decree (i.e. of Cyrus) to restore and build Jerusalem (ix. 24ff). The period is an awesome whole of seventy times seven, not an exact chronology as it was taken to be later. It is like the occasion when Peter asks Jesus whether he is to forgive his brother seven times, and Jesus replies: 'I do not say to you seven times, but seventy times seven' (Mt. xviii. 21ff).

The Jews had not devised for themselves a chronological system like the Greek Olympiads and the Founding Date of Rome. It was an act of the heathen, resented by the pious, when they were expected to adopt the Seleucid Era (corresponding to 1 October, 312 B.C.), called by the Jews *minyan shetarot*, Era of Contracts. It may well have been in token of their opposition that the Chasidim set up their own system of calculation from the Creation by Jubilees (seven times seven years), such having an authority in the Law of Moses. This was based on a lunar calendar, emphasizing Sabbaths and New Moons, and fixing the principal Feasts, and was adhered to by their successors, other than the Pharisees, who opted for a more accurate lunar-solar system. Thus one of the highly prized documents of the Essene-type groups was the book of *Jubilees* written about a quarter of a century after Daniel.

Perhaps it is with reference to the insistence on use of the Seleucid Era in Palestine that Daniel makes Antiochus 'think to change the Times and the Law' (vii. 25). However that may be, it is evident that Daniel expected the Kingdom of God to be established at no remote date, but immediately after God's judgment of the Seleucid monarch, who by converting the Temple at Jerusalem into a shrine of Zeus Olympios had set up *the abomination that makes desolate*. The term *shiqutz shomaim* parodies the title *baal shamaim*, 'Lord of Heaven', applied to Zeus.

In Daniel four kingdoms precede the advent of the Kingdom of God, the Babylonian, the Medo-Persian, the Macedonian, and the Seleucid. They appear first in the dream of Nebuchadnezzar (ii. 31ff) of a great image with a head of gold, breast and arms of silver, belly and thighs of iron, and feet part of iron and part of clay. Then a stone is cut from a mountain without human agency and falls on the *feet* of the image: with this the whole idol disintegrates. The interpretation that follows is quite clear. The stone is the Kingdom of God which destroys the imperialisms of mankind when it strikes at the Seleucids.

'In the days of those kings the God of heaven will set up a kingdom which shall never be destroyed, nor shall its sovereignty be left to another people. It shall break in pieces all those kingdoms and bring them to an end, and it shall stand for ever' (ii. 44).

The contribution of Daniel to Jewish eschatology (the lore of the Last Times) was of the highest importance. Its terms furnished the currency for later Messianic study, the Fourth Beast, the Seventy Weeks, the Stone, the Son of Man, and the Abomination of Desolation.[4] When the coming of the Kingdom of God did not materialize as anticipated by Daniel his terminology was not discarded; it became subject to fresh interpretations in the conviction that the application of the dreams and visions was to events still to be fulfilled.

What is so significant is that a Last-Times state of mind had been created which had a powerful effect on subsequent Jewish history for the next quarter of a millennium, and which through evangelical Christianity has remained influential down to the present day.

It particularly concerns us here that from the time the Romans under Pompey intervened in Jewish affairs in 63 B.C., Daniel's Fourth Kingdom was increasingly identified with Rome. The might of Rome seemed to answer more explicitly to the description that it was 'different from all the rest, exceedingly terrible, with its teeth of iron and claws of bronze; and which devoured and broke in pieces, and stamped the residue with its feet' (vii. 19). Surely then, it was argued, the Romans must be the last dread enemy of the Saints, and the Seventy Weeks must be taken literally to mean that the Last Times would begin 490 years after the decree of Cyrus to restore and build Jerusalem.

The date of the decree is known: it was 538 B.C. The terminal year of the Seventy Weeks would thus be 48 B.C. This was in fact the year in which Pompey was killed as he landed on the shores of Egypt. Not long after this the *Psalms of Solomon* makes reference to the events of 63 and to Pompey's death, in language that shows that the Roman occupation of Jerusalem and penetration into the Temple was regarded by the Saints as a punishment for Israel's sins, and that Pompey's end was a judgment on him for his sinful arrogance.

> In the insolence of the sinful man, he cast down with battering rams the strong walls and Thou didst not restrain him. And the Gentile foreigners went up on Thy altar and were trampling on it with their shoes in their insolence. For the children of Jerusalem had polluted the Holy House of the

Lord; and they were profaning the offerings of God with wickedness. . . . Thou hast made Thy hand heavy, O Lord, upon Israel by the bringing in of the Gentiles; for they have mocked and not pitied, in anger. . . . But Thou, O Lord, delay not to recompense them upon their own heads: to cast down the pride of the dragon to contempt. And I delayed not until the Lord showed me his insolence smitten on the mountains of Egypt; and despised more than him that is least on land and on sea: and his body coming on the waves in much contempt and none to bury him. Because He had rejected him with scorn, for he did not consider that he is a man. And the end he did not regard; for he said, I will be lord of land and sea: and he knew not that the Lord is God, great and mighty and powerful, and He is King over Heaven and over Earth. . . . (*Ps. Sol.* ii).

However, we should not make too much of the date 48 B.C. since we do not know what reckoning was followed by the Jewish interpreters in calculating the seventy weeks. What we can discover is that from about this date onwards there was a growing conviction that the Last Times had begun. Thus John the Baptist and Jesus could proclaim, 'The time has ended, and the Kingdom of Heaven is at hand' (Mk. i. 15; Mt. iii. 2). For how long the Last Times would continue was unknown; but when by the third quarter of the first century A.D. the Kingdom of God had still not appeared, the Saints – both the Christians and the Zadokites of the Dead Sea Scrolls – found it necessary to explain that in the wisdom and mercy of God the Last Times had been prolonged.

Particular excitement developed in the reign of Herod (37–4 B.C.), made king of the Jews by the Romans. To his subjects he was a foreigner, 'the Edomite', a puppet of the Romans, who had started his sanguinary career when in command in Galilee by destroying the Jewish marauding bands led by their chieftain Hezekiah. As king, having superseded the Hasmoneans, he was in constant fear of plots against his life and throne, and things became so bad that he converted the country into a police state with spies and informers planted everywhere, and denied to his subjects the right of free speech and assembly.

Herod had many qualities of greatness, and in other circumstances he might have commanded not only the loyalty but the affection of his people. But in addition to court intrigues he was up against something with which he could not cope, a religious fervour in which nationalism was blended with an emotional response to Last-Times preaching, for which the Pharisees were partly responsible. This expressed itself in detestation of the pomp and pride of heathen culture, resentment of foreign domination, and the nourishment of Messianic hopes. The king might make his country more powerful, create fine cities and edifices, plan a glorified Temple as one of the wonders of the world; but he could do nothing right in the eyes of the sullen populace and their spiritual guides.

The gulf between monarch and the puritanical masses widened, so that he was seen and forced to behave as the bloody tyrant he had no wish to be. Herod, who in his own way was a devout Jew, simply could not understand the animosity of the Pharisees and other sectarians, who encouraged underground movements and prayed continually for the coming of the Son of David, the Messiah.

We are required to look at the situation from the viewpoint of the opposition, of which we have sufficient record.

Writing about a quarter of a century after Herod's death, the author of the *Testament of Moses* thus describes his reign:

> And an insolent king will succeed them [i.e the Hasmoneans], who will not be of the race of the priests, a man bold and shameless, and he will judge them as they deserve. And he will cut off their chief men with the sword, and will destroy them in secret places, so that no one may know where their bodies are. He will slay the old and the young, and he will not spare. Then the fear of him will be bitter unto them in their land. And he will execute judgments on them as the Egyptians executed upon them, during thirty and four years, and he will punish them (vi. 2-6).

The same writer seems to have regarded the War of Varus against the Jews, who revolted after Herod's death in 4 B.C., as signalizing the last phase of the Last Times. 'And when this is done the times will be ended, in a moment the (second) course will follow, the four hours will come' (vii. 1). After this God will arise and punish the Gentiles, and destroy their idols, and Israel will be exalted (ch. x).

Among others, as late as the latter part of the first century A.D., those who were related to Jesus were putting out stories hostile to Herod. They declared that robbers of Idumea, attacking Ascalon, led Antipater (father of Herod) captive from the temple of Apollo. Antipater's father had been a minister in the temple, and since the priest would not pay the ransom for his son he was trained up in the ways of the Idumeans. Thus Herod was of alien and idolatrous origin, and no true Jew. They also said that to conceal his ancestry Herod when he became king had burnt the archives which recorded the genealogies of the noble Jewish families.[5] There was no truth in the libel, or in the Rabbinical one that Herod was a slave, and son of a slave.[6]

The vilification of Herod crops up in the Gospel of Matthew in the account of the massacre of the babes of Bethlehem. This was a Messianic version of similar stories told currently about the infancy of Abraham and Moses, also used in a saga of the nativity of John the Baptist. According to this legend there was talk that John the infant son of the priest Zechariah was destined to be the Messiah, and Herod therefore massacred the babes of Bethlehem. But, forewarned, John's mother Elizabeth had fled with him into the wilderness, and Zechariah was then slain for refusing to disclose his son's whereabouts.[7]

Another anti-Herodian story apears in the Old Russian version of the *Jewish War* by Flavius Josephus. While this cannot be attributed to Josephus himself, as proposed by Eisler, it is worth quoting in part because it conveys something of the atmosphere of the period.[8] A discussion of the priests is reported, dated in 31 B.C. The date is significant because the story immediately precedes what must have been regarded as one of the Signs of the Times, the great earthquake which devastated Judea in which, as Josephus relates, thirty thousand people and multitudes of cattle perished. Among buildings which suffered were those of the Essene settlement at Qumran, which caused the site to be abandoned for a good many years.

At that time the priests mourned and grieved one to another in secret. They durst not do so openly for fear of Herod and his friends. For one Jonathan spake, 'The law bids us have no foreigner for king. Yet we await the Messiah, the meek one, of David's line. But of Herod we know that he is an Arabian (*sic*), uncircumcised. The Messiah will be called meek, but this man has filled our whole land with blood. Under the Messiah it was ordained for the lame to walk, and the blind to see, and the poor to become rich. But under this man the hale have become lame, the seeing are blinded, the rich have become beggars. What is this? or how? Have the prophets lied? . . . Not as under Nebuchadnezzar and Antiochus is it. For then the prophets were teachers also of the people, and they made promises concerning the captivity and the return. And now – neither is there any of whom one could ask, nor any with whom one could find comfort.'

But Ananus the priest answered and spake to them, 'I know all books. When Herod fought before the city wall, I had never thought that God would permit him to rule over us. But now I understand that our desolation is nigh. And bethink you of the prophecy of Daniel; for he writes that after the return the city of Jerusalem shall stand for seventy weeks of years, which are 490 years, and after these years shall it be desolate.' And when they had counted the years, there were thirty and four years [still remaining]. But Jonathan answered and spake, 'The number of the years is even as we have said. But the Holy of Holies, where is he? For this Herod he [i.e. Daniel] cannot call the Holy One – him the bloodthirsty and impure.'

But one of them, by name Levi . . . overcome with shame, fled to Herod and informed him of the speeches of the priests which they had spoken against him. But Herod sent by night and slew them all,[9] without the knowledge of the people, lest they should be roused; and he appointed others. And when it was morning the whole land quaked.

Earthquake, famine, war and oppression, which marked the reign of Herod, seemed fittingly to signalize that the Last Times, if they had not been reached, were assuredly imminent. The conviction, certified by the searchers of the Scriptures, stimulated sectarian activity. On the one hand it intensified Messianic expectation, while on the other it allied itself with militant anti-Herodian and anti-Roman resistance movements. Loyalty to God and His Law became the order of the day, manifesting itself in intense religious devotion, fasting and prayer, and serving also as a rallying slogan for the downtrodden and disaffected.

Henceforth, and particularly at the popular level, all events, all history would be coloured by Last-Times imaginations and their psychological effects. Life could not be ordinary and humdrum when lived under the shadow of impending Judgment and invested with apocalyptic significance. A terrific strain was imposed on human relationships within the family and the nation, with individuals and groups reacting to the circumstances in ways that would be fantastic in normal conditions, but which in the emotional stress of the times appeared quite natural and appropriate. It is in this light, and not in that of rational sobriety, that we must view all that happened, and the character and behaviour of certain individuals who appeared on the scene.

NOTES AND REFERENCES

1. Otherwise called 'the World to Come', the ultimate Age in which the Kingdom of God would be realized on earth, the Millennium. At the beginning of the Age, according to views which developed, the righteous of all former Ages would be raised from the dead to share in its bliss, and the living righteous, including those of the Gentiles, would equally enjoy the felicities of the redeemed and regenerated earth with its centre in the New Jerusalem.
2. The Two Spirits, of Light and Darkness, and the Two Ways, of Life and Death, Blessing and Cursing (Deut. xi. 26; xxx. 15–20). The Levites of the

Zadokite Community proclaimed these alternatives to all who wished to enter the New Covenant.

3. This was the view of the Zadokite-Essenes, and the same objective inspired Paul (Phil. iii. 10–14). Hence the Children of Light contended with the Children of Darkness, and Christ was opposed to Belial.
4. These terms are featured in early Christian teaching. But by this time the Stone and Son of Man images had been applied to Jesus. He is the stone laid in Zion (Isa. xxviii. 16; I Pet. ii. 6), the stone rejected by the builders (Ps. cxviii. 22; Mt. xxi. 42). In the Gospel apocalypse those who are in Judea are directed to flee to the mountains when they see the Abomination of Desolation, spoken of by Daniel, standing in the Holy Place (Mt. xxiv. 15–16).
5. Julius Africanus, *Epistle to Aristides,* cited by Eusebius, *Eccl. Hist.* I vii.
6. According to the Talmud, Herod had been a slave in the house of the Hasmoneans (*Baba Bathra,* fol. 3b).
7. For details see Schonfield, *The Lost Book of the Nativity of John* (1929), and more briefly *The Passover Plot.*
8. The various interpolations in the text of the Old Russian Josephus are given and discussed by Robert Eisler in *The Messiah Jesus and John the Baptist:* they are also reproduced in Thackeray's translation of the *Jewish War* (Loeb Classical Library). There is reason to believe that these insertions were the responsibility of a Christian judaizing movement in the Middle Ages, which in northern Italy got the name of Josephinists, and had affiliations with kindred sectarians in the Balkans, Lithuania, and South Russia. They were partly inspired by Jewish Karaite teachers in Vilna, Kiev, and elsewhere.
9. The Talmud tells that Herod put to death all the rabbis of his time, except one whom he blinded (*Baba Bathra,* fol. 3b–4a). It is possible that this tradition was the source of the interpolator's story we have quoted.

CHAPTER 2

EVIDENCE IN CHIEF

Initially in its native habitat Christianity was identified closely with the struggle of the Jewish people spiritually and pragmatically to achieve fulfilment of its destiny. We have to draw a sharp line of distinction between what Jesus and his Jewish followers represented and the character and content of the Christian religion as it progressively evolved. We have to detach ourselves completely from the view that the latter gives us direct access to the former, and consequently we must revise the judgments and beliefs that have been current for many centuries.

When the authors of the Gospels and the Acts created their narratives they were thinking very much of contemporary Christian needs in the latter part of the first century and the beginning of the second century A.D. By reason of the outcome of the Jewish war with the Romans there had been a considerable separation of the Church at large from its Jewish environment. The old Nazorean-Christian community at Rome had virtually been wiped out by the Neronian persecution after the Great Fire of A.D. 64, and in the West the churches were now predominantly Gentile. Yet they still preserved features of Jewish theology and messianism, and thus occupied a kind of no-man's-land which made them neither Jews nor Gentiles, regarded with dislike and suspicion by both. A defence-mechanism came into operation which hit out in both directions, over-playing repudiation of the Jews to procure Gentile tolerance, and attacking Gentile idolatry – including the divinity of the emperor – which made it appear that Christians were crypto-Jews.

The Gospels and the Acts appreciably reflect the situation we know from the historians to have existed in the closing years of the reign of Domitian. This emperor had a morbid fear of the Jews and their messianic predictions, and was convinced that the Christians, who not being Jews ought to have stuck to their ancestral Roman or Greek religion, were plotting against him.[1]

We learn from Eusebius, partly reporting Hegesippus, that Domitian gave orders for the seizure of all descendants of King David to avert the possibility of another Jewish revolt. Among those arrested were two grandsons of Judas the brother of Jesus; but they were released as peasant simpletons from whom no danger was to be anticipated.[2] A few years later, in Trajan's reign, the aged Simeon, a first cousin of Jesus and leader of the Nazoreans, was also apprehended, tortured and executed.[3] It was in this period, between A.D. 90 and 110, that the Gospels of Matthew and Luke and the Acts of the Apostles were written.

Another echo of the situation meets us in the position in which the historian Flavius Josephus found himself. In spite of attempts by Jewish nationalists to discredit him after the war because he had defected by going over to the Romans, he had stood high in favour with Vespasian and his son Titus. But he was again in danger because of Domitian's terrors. Josephus had just completed his *Antiquities of the Jews,* in which he had sought to show his pride in the history and contribution of his people, and even treated more fairly than in the *Jewish War* the causes of the revolt. Suddenly there was published another history of the war by Justus of Tiberias, which accused Josephus of having been responsible for the participation of the city of Tiberias in the revolt. This might convey that Josephus was not sincere in his allegiance to Rome, and he hastened to reply with an autobiography largely rehearsing his activities in Galilee where he had been the Jewish commander at the beginning of the war. Here he stressed that he had fully realized what would be the outcome of the revolt, and therefore had done his best to curb the hotheads at very great personal risk.

At the conclusion of the *Life*, apparently drafted prior to a second impression of the *Antiquities*, issued in the thirteenth year of Domitian (A.D. 93–4) but not published until after A.D. 100, the author tells how Domitian had added to his honours. 'He punished my Jewish accusers, and for a similar offence gave orders for the chastisement of a slave, a eunuch and my son's tutor. He also exempted my property in Judea from taxation, a mark of the highest honour to the privileged individual. Moreover, Domitia, Caesar's wife, never ceased conferring favours upon me. Such are the events of my whole life; and from them let others judge as they will of my character.'

Here we should note that in the *Jewish War*, which in the Greek edition was published between A.D. 74 and 78, written when Josephus had been represented by the Jewish rebels as a fellow-conspirator in order to destroy him, he carefully had made no allusion either to John the Baptist or to Jesus. Even in the *Antiquities* the account given of John is quite innocuous, and conveys no suggestion of the messianic character of his preaching. Josephus only says that Herod Antipas feared that the crowds which flocked to John might be tempted to engage in some form of seditition.

The passage about Jesus which appears in the *Antiquities* has long been considered a Christian forgery, as a whole or in part. The passage did not appear in the copy of Josephus known to Origen late in the third century, and is first quoted by Eusebius in the fourth century. An argument against it is that the passage breaks the continuity of the text. We cannot rule out that something was said, because in the *Antiquities* (XX. 200–203) Josephus speaks of the execution by the Sanhedrin of one named Jacob 'the brother of Jesus who was called Christ'.[4] But it would be most unlikely to be in terms that suggested a favourable attitude to Jesus as Messiah. Josephus well knew how eager his enemies would be to pounce on anything of the kind.

When the *Jewish War* was published the Christians in Italy must have been disturbed by the silence of Josephus, and it is possible that one of a number of reasons for the writing of Mark's Gospel, at about this time, was to make good this omission. When the *Antiquities* appeared it suggested itself that there was now needed a Christian document on more historical lines than Mark and Matthew, which no less had an apologetic purpose and included an account of Christian beginnings. The need was filled by the production of Luke-Acts.

The author states in the Foreword to the first part of his work: 'Since it is the case that many have endeavoured to draw up an account of those matters held by us to be fact, exactly as they transmitted them to us who initially were eye-witnesses and bearers of the message, I have thought fit myself, as I have carried out a thorough investigation of all the circumstances from their beginnings, to set them down for you consecutively, most excellent Theophilus, that you may realize how well-founded are the things of which you have been informed.'

There are various evidences which suggest that Luke made use of the works of Josephus, and it may well be that the two-part Luke-Acts was inspired by Josephus' two-part book *Against Apion*, published around A.D. 100.

Both sections of this work of Josephus are dedicated to the author's latest patron Epaphroditus, held to be the distinguished grammarian and book collector of that name. The first part begins, 'In my history of our Antiquities, most excellent Epaphroditus, I have, I think, made sufficiently clear to any who may peruse that work the extreme antiquity of our Jewish race.' He goes on to state that the design of the work is 'to correct the ignorance of others, and instruct all who desire to know the truth concerning the antiquity of our race'. The second part opens with the words, 'In the previous book, my most esteemed Epaphroditus, I demonstrated,' etc. When we turn to Luke-Acts we similarly find part one (the Gospel) addressed to the most excellent Theophilus, and part two (the Acts) begins, 'In my previous treatise, Theophilus, I covered everything that Jesus did and taught down to the time . . . he was taken on high.'

The Theophilus of Luke may well be fictitious – the name simply means God-lover – since it is difficult to believe that at this time a Christian author would have had a wealthy patron. The presumption is that Luke took his cue from Josephus. There was a Theophilus son of Annas who was the Jewish high priest at the time Josephus was born, which may have suggested the name.

We shall be considering further the question of Luke's use of Josephus. But before this we must say something about Josephus as a historian. For the period with which this volume is principally concerned, falling between A.D. 36 and 66, our chief witnesses for what was happening in Judea are Josephus and Luke. Consequently we must know how far their testimony is dependable.

Josephus, born of a priestly family in A.D. 37 or 38, was at least a native Jew and had personal knowledge of what was going on for part of the period in which we are interested. The *Jewish War* was composed originally in Aramaic, and this version has not survived. One of its objects was to deter those in the East, notably Jews of Babylonia, from opposing themselves to Roman might. Some changes were no doubt made in the Greek text, and it evidently had the approval of the author's imperial patrons who had conducted the war.

Josephus comes down heavily on the Jewish militants and messianists, whom he describes as brigands and impostors. We have therefore to recognize that he was writing with a very strong prejudice. He was not a man of the people: he was an aristocrat. Moreover, he had visited Rome before the war, been received at Nero's court, and had been greatly impressed by Roman pomp and might.

As a historian Josephus was very much of an amateur when he

wrote the *Jewish War*, with the result that the work is very uneven. When he could he availed himself of written sources to which he had access, such as the history of Herod's reign by Nicolaus of Damascus, and the *Commentarii*, the official war despatches of Vespasian and Titus. He supplemented his information by discussion and correspondence with his friend Agrippa II, notes of his interrogations of prisoners taken in the war, and conversations with eminent Jews who had fled to the Romans.

But where Josephus had no detailed sources at command he leaves great gaps, and compensates by devoting far too much space to matters having little bearing on his theme. Of the seven books into which the *Jewish War* is divided, almost the whole of Book One and the first quarter of Book Two are taken up with the reign of Herod the Great and his successor Archelaus. The record is then extraordinarily thin for the whole period from the deposition of Archelaus in A.D. 6 to the coming of Ventidius Cumanus as Procurator in A.D. 48. Josephus jumps from the governorship of Coponius (A.D. 6–9) to that of Pontius Pilate (A.D. 26–36), completely missing out the intervening governors, the last of whom, Valerius Gratus, was procurator of Judea for eleven years.

In Pilate's term of office only two incidents are dealt with, the affair of the Roman standards and the affair of the seizure of the Temple treasure to build an aqueduct. For the latter there is no indication of date. The next incident mentioned is the attempt by Gaius Caligula to have his statue erected in the Temple (A.D. 39–40). Josephus then switches to Rome to describe the part played by Agrippa I in making Claudius emperor when Gaius was assassinated, for which he was rewarded with the kingship of Judea. Nothing is related of Agrippa's reign (41–4) except his construction of Jerusalem's third wall. No reference is made to the disturbed conditions in Judea in the governorships of Cuspius Fadus and Tiberius Alexander (44–8), and the story of the circumstances leading up to the war does not really get going until the administration of Ventidius Cumanus (48–52), by which time Josephus was about twelve years of age.

As we have observed, Josephus says nothing about John the Baptist and Jesus, yet he was not averse to speaking about Jewish movements, since he speaks of the Pharisees and Sadducees, and at much greater length about the Essenes for whom he had a high regard. Of Judas of Galilee he has only this to say, 'The man was a sophist who founded a sect of his own, having nothing in common with the others,' a statement he had to correct in the *Antiquities*. The *Jewish War* is therefore of only minor assistance when we are seeking to learn as much as possible of Jewish affairs in the time of Jesus and the immediate Nazorean movement which sprang up after him.

Before writing his *Antiquities* many years later Josephus had opportunity to quest for more information, and in this work he did endeavour to rectify some of his omissions and to correct mistakes. But even so for the period which saw the beginnings of Christianity the history is still very weak and patchy. We do, thankfully, obtain some additional knowledge about nationalist and messianic activities, but there is still too little precision about dates and events where we need these most. Either Josephus could not get the information, or he did not care to record it. On the whole, the *Antiquities* is much more useful to us, and some of its deficiencies can be remedied. At least we have a fairly reliable outline of developments to assist reconstruction.

We return now to Luke. With his work too it is important to know from what sources he obtained his information; and it is also of consequence to discover how he used them. He declares in his Foreword that he had 'carried out a thorough investigation of all the circumstances from their beginnings'. This is an impressive claim, and he would certainly appear to have made no small effort, involving considerable reading. But he too was an amateur, with rather less qualifications than Josephus. He was not genuinely concerned with reporting what took place, except to the extent that would achieve the effect at which he aimed.

On the Christian side, for the Gospel section, he had Mark before him, possibly Matthew, but in any case a source on the teaching and some of the activities of Jesus also employed by Matthew, the Q document. Perhaps the 'many' of his Foreword, who had previously covered the ground, implies certain other written sources. For much of the earlier part of the Acts, relating to the Christian movement in Judea, the style and language suggests a written source, originally in Hebrew or Aramaic. We learn from Epiphanius that the Ebionite-Nazoreans had their own Acts of the Apostles, together with a work called the *Ascents of Jacob*. The contents of these books infuriated Epiphanius, since they gave a very different picture of early Christian affairs to what was in Luke's Acts.[5] Epiphanius elsewhere gives us the information that the Jews of Tiberias in the fourth century had in their archives the Hebrew *Matthew,* the Hebrew *Acts,* and a Hebrew *Book of John,* apparently a form of the Revelation in the New Testament.[6] A Jewish tradition suggests that these works were composed by Simeon son of Cleophas, martyred at the beginning of the second century.[7]

Much of canonical Acts is devoted to the career of the Apostle Paul. Here the author might have had access to some of the Pauline epistles, and chunks of his material come from a *Diary* document written in the first person plural by someone who had accompanied Paul on some of his travels. This individual may well have been the Doctor Luke mentioned in the later epistles, a circumstance which gave rise to the view that it was this Luke who had written the Gospel and Acts. Yet clearly the actual author was living at a much later date, when Paul's Luke, if he was still alive, would have been approaching ninety years of age.

So much then, briefly, for Luke's Christian sources. Most of them are not extant, and we can only judge how he handled them from what has survived, chiefly Mark, and as regards the Q document by comparing Luke's employment of it with Matthew's. Without going into details, it is evident that Luke subordinated his sources to his own requirements in the manner in which he wished to tell his story. In the Acts it is observable that Luke's account of Paul's post-conversion movements and of the controversy over the condition of admission of Gentile believers does not agree with what is related by Paul in his epistles. Luke does much to soften the harsh edges.

The whole two-part work has an apologetic tone. Luke is at pains to demonstrate that Roman officials had not been opposed to Christians as such, and had been extremely fair to Jesus and his followers, exonerating them from all subversive intentions. Indeed, the principal Christian emissary, Paul, had been very proud of his Roman citizenship. Everywhere, whether in Judea or in other parts of the Empire, it was the Jews who had been hostile to the movement and its founder, stirring up trouble and bringing lying accusations.[8] Far from being enemies of the human race, as was alleged by the ignorant, Christians had laboured for the salvation and good of the Gentiles at great personal risk and sacrifice. In accepting the message of Jesus they had not been required to undergo circumcision or follow the customs of the Jews' religion.

Highly distasteful as this special pleading is, it can at least be understood in the circumstances in which the Christians were placed at the time Luke-Acts was written. Accordingly, in utilizing the work we must allow for its bias in the same way as we have to do with the writings of Josephus. In both cases we are warned that in certain specific connections of great consequence these witnesses must be treated as hostile and prejudiced. It has to be our obligation, in the interest of truth, to do justice to those who have been traduced, and fully to recognize that what we are being given is an extremely one-sided story.

Luke, like Josephus, is most effective where he employs documentary sources, though he too no doubt omits things he does not wish to speak about or which would give a different impression. Similarly, as regards affairs in Judea, Luke's narrative has a substantial gap. Nothing is said of the native Nazoreans from the death of Agrippa I (A.D. 44) to the last visit of Paul to Jerusalem (A.D. 58), a crucial interval of fourteen years, during which, as we learn from the *Antiquities,* there was a great deal of messianic and Zealot activity, and ruthless efforts were made by the Romans and pro-Roman authorities to suppress every manifestation of a rebellious spirit. The Nazoreans must have been among the victims of the repressive measures. Luke says nothing about this, and makes no mention of the worsening situation under Cumanus, Felix and Festus. To an extent we can compensate for Luke's deficiencies; but it is no use pretending that what he offers us is a faithful representation of Christian beginnings.

Because Luke has read some non-Christian authorities, notably Josephus, he makes a display of his historical knowledge. In his Gospel, alone among the Evangelists, he tells of the census carried out by Quirinius, and lists the rulers flourishing at the time when John the Baptist began to preach, dating this event in the fifteenth year of Tiberius Caesar. He introduces Pilate's slaughter of the Galileans in the Temple, and relates that when Pilate discovered that Jesus was a Galilean he sent him for trial to Herod Antipas, tetrarch of Galilee. In the Acts, to cite only Palestinian matters, he puts into the mouth of Gamaliel reference to Judas of Galilee and Theudas, the latter anachronistically. He mentions the famine in the reign of Claudius, and the manner of the death of Agrippa I. He has a Roman officer in Jerusalem suppose Paul to be a notorious Egyptian false prophet, leader of terrorist bands of Sicarii. His story includes notables like the governor Felix and his wife Drusilla, Agrippa II and his sister Berenice, and the governor Festus.

All these touches have the intended effect of impressing on the reader that the author knows what he is talking about. We would be more impressed if we were not in a position to observe that Luke is ready to put anything to use that will lend more verisimilitude to his narrative and convey that he is a writer of standing. We noted in the last respect his device of the dedication to a presumed illustrious patron. In the first respect we may begin with Luke's borrowings from the Old Testament for his nativity stories.

The account of the birth of John the Baptist and of Jesus draws upon the stories of the birth of Samson and the prophet Samuel. An angel announces to the mother of Samson that she is to have a child. His mother, however, is barren, as with John's mother, and her son is to be a nazirite from birth, as with John. Luke's song of Mary, or more accurately Elizabeth, takes its language from the song of Hannah mother of Samuel (I Sam. ii. 1–10), and he too is dedicated to the Lord from birth. The child is brought to the Sanctuary to be accepted by the aged priest Eli. In Luke Eli is replaced by the aged Simeon, the name possibly being derived from the venerable Simeon son of Cleophas martyred not long before Luke wrote the Gospel. The prophetess Anna of Luke takes her name from Samuel's mother. When Luke writes that Jesus 'increased in wisdom and stature, and in favour with God and man' (ii. 52), he is quoting directly from what was said of Samuel (I Sam. ii. 26), and thus betrays his source. So it is plainly demonstrable that Luke partly created his story out of this Old Testament material. And if Luke could use biblical sources in this way, he could as readily employ others which served his purpose. In other words, Luke was not averse to resorting to fiction when he lacked facts, or thought that his authority as an investigator would be enhanced.

The works of Josephus were an ideal hunting-ground. This has been illustrated in *The Passover Plot*, but a reminder of what the present writer noted there may not be out of place.

There was nothing related of Jesus before his public life began. It was tempting, therefore, to put in a story of the hero at the age of twelve. The inspiration came from Josephus, who in his *Life* had written, 'While I was still a mere boy, about fourteen years old, I won universal applause for my love of letters; insomuch that the chief priests and learned men of Jerusalem used constantly to come to me for precise information on some particular of our ordinances.' Bombastic on the part of Josephus; but here was the germ of a tale to convey the qualities of the young Jesus.

In Josephus Luke found an account of how Archelaus had gone to Rome to be confirmed as king of the Jews by Augustus, and how the Jews had sent a deputation to Rome to beg that he should not be made their king. Archelaus got his sovereignty, but only as ethnarch, with the promise that if he ruled well he would be made king. But he proved to be a cruel tyrant, and was deposed in the tenth year of his reign (*Antiq.* XVIII). Luke worked this bit of history into the parable of the pounds (Mt. xxv. talents), where his version relates that 'a nobleman went into a far country to receive a kingdom and then return. . . . But his citizens hated him and sent an embassy after him, saying, "We do not want this man to reign over us." When he returned, having received the kingdom . . . [he gave orders] "But as for these enemies of mine, who did not want me to reign over them, bring them here, and slay them before me" ' (Lk. xix. 11–27).

Josephus had related that 'it was the custom of the Galileans at the time of a festival to pass through the Samaritan territory on their way to the Holy City. On one occasion . . . the inhabitants of a village called Ginae . . . joined battle with the Galileans and slew a great number' (*Antiq.* XVIII. 118). Here was another interesting story, which would give a realistic touch to the journey of Jesus to Jerusalem via Samaria. So we read, in Luke only, that Jesus 'sent messengers ahead of him, who went and entered into a village of the Samaritans, to make ready for him; but the people would not receive him [i.e. coming from Galilee], because his face was set to go towards Jerusalem' (Lk. ix. 51–6). The stormy sons of Zebedee want to call down fire from heaven to consume the inhospitable Samaritans.

The last touch is from the story of Elijah in the Old Testament, and like his borrowings from the accounts of the birth of Samson and Samuel our author found inspiration also in the Elijah-Elisha stories (cp. Lk. iv. 25–7). From this source came the idea of the raising of the son of the widow of Nain, again uniquely in Luke (vii. 11–16).[9]

It will suffice to furnish one further instance of Luke's technique. He elaborates the curing of the centurion's servant by mentioning that the Roman 'loves our nation'. The officer asks that Jesus would give a command for his servant to be healed, 'for I also am a man set under authority'. The best known Roman official who had befriended the Jews was the legate Petronius, who risked his life to stop the scheme of the mad emperor Gaius to set up his statue in the Temple. Significantly, Petronius explains to the people, 'For I am under authority as well as you' (*J.W.* II. 195; Lk. vii. 1–10).

We are warned, therefore, that Luke was something of a novelist, working into his narrative colourful touches derived from his reading, for which there was no warrant in the Christian documents at his command.

But even with the Christian sources we may suspect some switching around on Luke's part. There is reason to believe that the words which he alone attributes to Jesus on the cross, 'Father, forgive them; for they know not what they do,' were borrowed from the dying speech of Jacob the brother of Jesus.

On the whole, then, when we examine our chief witnesses who profess knowledge, the one of Jewish affairs in Palestine and the other of Christian affairs, we are conscious of grave defects. Both with Josephus and Luke we have to dig into their testimony with full consciousness of their shortcomings to try to extract what more accurately reflects what took place. We have to be sceptical about what they want us to believe, and at the same time seek through them to recover what they would deny to us. Fortunately in this pursuit we have other aids to put us on the right track. Even if we cannot obtain full enlightenment there is now emerging a picture very different to what we may have imagined and which is much closer to the reality.

NOTES AND REFERENCES

1. See Suetonius, *Domitian*, in *Lives of the Caesars*, and Schonfield, *Those Incredible Christians.*
2. Eusebius, *Eccl. Hist.* III xx.
3. Eusebius, *op cit.* III xxxii.
4. A variant version of the Josephus passage on Jesus has recently come to light. The accounts of Jesus as the Wonder-worker in the Slavonic text of the *Jewish War* are interesting, though without historical value. For a different view see Eisler, *The Messiah Jesus and John the Baptist.*
5. Epiphanius writes: 'They have other Acts which they call those of the Apostles, among which are many things filled with their impiety, whence they have incidentally supplied themselves with arms against the truth. For they set forth certain Ascents and Instructions forsooth in the *Ascents of Jacob*, representing him as holding forth against the Temple and sacrifices, and against the fire on the altar, and many other things filled with empty talk, so that they are not ashamed in them even to denounce Paul in certain invented utterances of the malignant and deceitful work of their

false apostles' (*Panar.* xxx. 16). Some remains of the *Ascents* are preserved in the Clementine *Recognitions* (1. 66–71). The Ascents were the steps leading up to the inner area of the Temple, on which according to the story a public disputation was held between the Nazoreans and the chief priests.

6. Epiphanius, *op. cit.* xxx. 3–6.
7. See Schonfield, *According to the Hebrews* (1937).
8. Cp. Acts xiii. 43; xiii. 50; xiv. 19; xvii. 5; xvii. 6; xviii. 12.
9. Cp. I Ki. xvii and II Ki. iv.

CHAPTER 3

TIME FACTORS

In these preparatory surveys there is another angle which it is essential to consider. To obtain a proper understanding of the significance of events it is obviously important to be able to relate them to what was going on at the time. One of the difficulties with our sources is that they are frequently vague as to when things happened. A statement such as 'about this time' might represent a difference of months or years. If we had more exact knowledge this could have a bearing on why something occurred.

A simple example arises in connection with the settlement at Qumran. Examination of the buildings revealed great cracks across them due to an earthquake, which caused the settlement to be abandoned. Through Josephus we can determine that this was in 31 B.C. The numismatic finds establish that the site was restored and reoccupied at the beginning of the reign of Archelaus, and we can link this with the messianic and nationalistic outbursts which followed the death of Herod the Great. Possibly also this connects with one of the Qumran texts which conveys that because of the imminence of the Last Times the Zadokite Community removed from the wilderness of the peoples (in the north) to the wilderness of Jerusalem (in the south).

There are many events in the life of Jesus and in the Nazorean story which we would like to date as exactly as possible; but we have a difficulty in doing so because the records have not furnished a sufficient intimation, such as the year of an emperor's reign or the month and year of one of the eras in use. Occasionally we are fortunate. The Acts reports that from Athens the apostle Paul travelled to Corinth, where he was brought before the proconsul Gallio. But no date is given. However, among inscriptions recovered in the vicinity of Corinth, capital of the Province of Achaia, was one which not only referred to Gallio as proconsul, but also mentioned when he took office, corresponding to A.D. 51. The incident in the Acts therefore took place between July, A.D. 51 and June, A.D. 52. This is of great assistance in dating other events in Paul's career.

The problem of fixing a chronology of the life of Jesus has been the cause of endless discussion, chiefly because it was thought necessary to take account of data which were partly contradictory. Instead of treating the appearance of a star shortly before the birth of Jesus, according to Matthew, as part of the apparatus of messianic legend, the phenomenon was accepted as literally true, and many have been impressed by the discovery made by Kepler of a conjunction of planets which might have occasioned the phenomenon, and which would fix its date as 7 B.C.[1] Herod the Great had died in 4 B.C., and since Matthew says that after the Wise Men's visit he killed the infants of Bethlehem that were under two years of age a date about 7 B.C. would thus seem appropriate.

But if, as Luke says, Jesus was about thirty years of age when he began his ministry then he would need to have been baptized by John the Baptist not later than A.D. 24. And, according to Luke, the Baptist did not begin his preaching before the fifteenth year of Tiberius Caesar, which was not until A.D. 28 or 29 when Jesus would have been nearly thirty-five.

We can compare this with Josephus with whose writings Luke was familiar. Josephus states that Philip the tetrarch died in the twentieth year of Tiberius, which was A.D. 34 (*Antiq.* XVIII. 4). There is no possibility of reconciling the information conveyed by Matthew with what is proposed by Luke. The gap is further widened by the assertion of Luke that Jesus was born at the time of the census carried out when Quirinius was legate of Syria. This we know to have taken place in A.D. 6–7 after the deposition of Archelaus as ethnarch. So there is a difference of approximately twelve years between Matthew's dating of the birth of Jesus and Luke's.

The question then is, are we to take seriously the statement of Luke that Jesus began his ministry when he was about thirty years of age? He might well be basing himself on the Old Testament, where it is said (II Sam. v. 4) that David was thirty years old when he began to reign. It would be well not to rely too much on Luke on this point. But even if he was loosely correct, if Jesus was not born before A.D. 6 he could not have been baptized by John until at any rate A.D. 34. We have to note that Luke does not suggest that Jesus was about thirty years of age in the fifteenth year of Tiberius, say A.D. 28-9, but that it was at this time that John began to preach. John's Gospel may appear to support the view that the ministry of Jesus began almost immediately after the Baptist started to preach, because that Gospel places the cleansing of the Temple by Jesus almost at the outset of his public life instead of at the end of it. When Jesus says, 'Destroy this temple, and in three days I will raise it up,' the Jews respond, 'It has taken forty-six years to build this temple, and will you raise it up in three days?' (Jn. ii. 19-20). The reconstruction of the Temple was initiated by Herod the Great in 19 B.C., and forty-six years thereafter would be A.D. 28.

But it simply will not do that Jesus had already begun his ministry in A.D. 28 or 29. If the cleansing of the Temple in fact took place at the end of Jesus' activities John's dating would not be relevant, and if he was born in A.D. 6 he would not have been more than twenty-three years of age in A.D. 29. A much weightier reason for rejecting this date is that John the Baptist, whom Jesus survived, was not executed – as we shall see – until A.D. 35. None of the information given about the length of the public life of Jesus indicates that it lasted seven or eight years.

Following Luke's birth date, however, we could place the baptism of Jesus in A.D. 34, shortly before John was imprisoned, which would seem much more likely.

We come then to the length of the public life of Jesus, and to the date of the crucifixion.

Mark's Gospel conveys that three spring-tides have to enter into our calculations of the duration of the ministry. There is the reference to Jesus plucking ears of corn (ii. 23), to the feeding of a multitude who were seated on green grass (vi. 39), and of course the final Passover was in spring. Indications of this sort are extremely useful. On Mark's evidence, with which that of John can be brought into line, the ministry of Jesus must have occupied about two years. Tentatively dating its commencement in A.D. 34, the baptism of Jesus would have been shortly before the Passover of that year, and the crucifixion would have taken place at the Passover of A.D. 36. This was the last Passover at which both Pontius Pilate and Caiaphas were in office, the former as Roman governor of Judea and Samaria and the latter as Jewish high priest.

The evidence for A.D. 36 is overwhelming on historical grounds, and this date alone concurs with what the Evangelists agree upon, that Jesus began his public life shortly before John the Baptist was imprisoned by Herod Antipas and terminated it a few months after John was executed.

It has been said by baffled authorities that the year of the crucifixion presents a virtually insoluble problem.[2] And indeed it does if it is insisted that the credit of the Evangelists has to be saved by ignoring history and trying to reconcile the conflicting testimony of Matthew and Luke. Not only do we have the difficulties we have already considered, we also have the opposing views of the Markan and Johannine records. The former claims that the Friday on which Jesus was crucified was the first day of the festival of Passover (Nisan 15), while the latter declares that it was the eve of the festival (Nisan 14). Since the New Moon of Nisan, which governed when the fourteenth and fifteenth of the month occurred, was fixed by ocular observation, sighting did not necessarily agree with the astronomical new moon. We have the possibility of one day's difference at the beginning of the month, and the added complication of whether the Friday of the crucifixion was the fourteenth or fifteenth. That the Passover for Zadokites would have fallen on a Wednesday is a red herring in this connection. All astronomical calculations are necessarily inconclusive, and it is vain to propose certain years, 29, 30 or 33 on the ground that in those years the fourteenth could have fallen on a Friday astronomically. All that we can rely on is that the crucifixion took place on a Friday at the time of the Passover and we must employ safer criteria for determining the year.

These criteria are fortunately available, and they throw a great deal of light on circumstances mentioned incidentally in the Gospels. We can, and we must, fix the year of the crucifixion of Jesus, because it has a bearing on the whole course of events in early Christian history down to the fall of Jerusalem in A.D. 70.

We are afforded valuable assistance by two systems of regularly recurring occasions, the Jewish Sabbatical (seventh) Year and the Roman Census Year.

Under the Mosaic Law the soil had to lie fallow every seventh year. The ground was not tilled, and crops taken from it whether of grain or fruit were only those which grew of themselves. For a largely agrarian population this meant that food supplies, apart from what was imported, depended very much on what had been stockpiled immediately before the Sabbatical Year. The peasantry would suffer great hardship if drought, blight or locust invasion had prevented an adequate storage of produce. A great famine comes into Luke's story of Paul, because we are told that shortly before the accession of Claudius as emperor (A.D. 41) prophets came down from Jerusalem to Antioch foretelling this dearth. 'And the disciples determined, everyone according to his ability, to send relief to the brethren in Judea; and they did so, sending it to the Elders by the hand of Barnabas and Saul' (Acts xi. 27-30).

Another effect of the Sabbatical Year was that the Jewish rural population would largely be free from labour, and therefore at liberty to flock in crowds to hear some preacher or nationalist leader, or engage in political demonstrations and protests. At this period, particularly, the Sabbatical Year turned the thoughts of the people to deliverance from foreign domination and oppression by some of their own rulers.

Thanks to Josephus and Rabbinical literature we can know which years from the death of Herod the Great to the Fall of Jerusalem were Sabbatical Years. And these years always began on the first of the Jewish month Tishri[3] (falling in September). According to the *Seder Olam* the services of the Temple ceased in the year following a Sabbatical Year, actually on the ninth Ab in the summer of A.D. 70[4]. Thus September 68 to September 69 was a Sabbatical Year, and we can work out an exact table of the seven-year cycle retrospectively.

There was great public agitation and nationalist disturbances in the year following the death of Herod the Great, and we are not surprised to discover that the year 3-2 B.C. was a Sabbatical Year.

The worth of this guide can be further illustrated from the following example. It was the custom for the Royalty Law with other passages from Deuteronomy to be publicly read in the Temple on the first day of the festival of Tabernacles which followed the termination of the Sabbatical Year. The Mishnah informs us that this was done by King Agrippa, and that he wept when he reached the words, 'You are not to set a foreigner over you who is not your brother,' because he was partly of alien descent. But the congregation cried out to him, 'You are our brother! You are our brother! ' (*Sotah* vii. 8).

Now the year from September A.D. 40 to September A.D. 41 was a Sabbatical Year. This incident would therefore have taken place at the Feast of Tabernacles in October A.D. 41.

This in fact was the only such occasion during the brief reign of Agrippa (A.D. 41-4). Gaius Caligula had been assassinated in January of 41, and was succeeded as emperor by Claudius whose friend Agrippa was. Claudius rewarded him by conferring upon him the throne of Judea. In A.D. 46, just before the next Sabbatical Year, there was the great famine in Judea referred to in the Acts, which must have caused the greatest misery since in 47-8 no crops could be sown. Josephus records that Helena queen of the Adiabene, a convert to Judaism, assisted with relief by expending vast sums to bring grain from Egypt and figs from Cyprus (*Antiq.* XX. 51-3).

We have, then, in the Sabbatical Year cycle a most effective instrument for dating events affecting early Christian and contemporary Jewish history. The only Sabbatical Year falling within the ministry of Jesus was from September A.D. 33 to September A.D. 34. In this period the crowds were free to flock from all parts to hear John the Baptist, and the spirit of revolt was abroad. The indications then are that Jesus went to the Jordan to be baptized early in A.D. 34; and not long after this John was thrown into prison by Herod Antipas, chiefly because the tetrarch, who was on the eve of war with the Arabs, was afraid of a Galilean revolt inspired by the Baptist's preaching. Freedom from agricultural labour meant that multitudes of the peasantry could cause trouble if stirred up by the Zealots. It was a significant moment for Jesus to proclaim in the synagogue, 'The Spirit of the Lord is upon me, because he has anointed me to preach good news to the poor. He has sent me to proclaim release to the captives . . . to set at liberty those who are oppressed, to proclaim the acceptable year of the Lord' (Lk. iv. 18-19).

But we also have another cycle to assist us with our dating of events, namely the periodic Roman Census in the eastern Provinces. This took place every fourteen years.

The first census taken in Palestine was in A.D. 6-7, which brought Judas of Galilee to the fore; and the whole process has been illuminated by papyri discovered in Egypt. It began with an official proclamation instructing persons away from their native localities to return there for the purpose of the census. The census-takers then moved in with their papers. Each householder furnished particulars in such terms as these: 'I, so-and-so, son of so-and-so, aged x years, straight nose, black hair, scar on right cheek, register myself with so-and-so, my wife, aged x years.' Then followed details of property possessed, land, cattle, etc. When all the papers had been collected and examined the tax assessment in each case was worked out, and this held good from the ensuing year until the next census. A census announcement of A.D. 104

has been found, and census papers of A.D. 34-5, and possibly of A.D. 20-1.

Again we are enabled to tabulate the census years, which were so offensive to Jewish national sentiment, partly because the numbering of the people was contrary to Jewish Law, and partly because it was regarded as a mark of enslavement to an alien heathen Power. The Zealots proclaimed the slogan, 'No Ruler but God', and the census year and the year immediately following in each period, when the hated tax-collectors went round demanding payment of the new assessment, were times of great civil disturbance. The provincial governors, whom Augustus called 'his leeches', continually tried to line their own pockets by extorting more than was due, and their minions followed suit in their own interests.

Through the pages of Josephus we can ascertain that certain manifestations of revolt and messianic fervour which he records in fact coincided with the periodic census. We have particularly to note that census years partly overlapped with the Jewish Sabbatical Year once in every two cycles, so that the issuing of census papers was to an extent facilitated by it. September A.D. 33-4 was a Sabbatical Year; but A.D. 34-5 was also a census year. When such coincidences occurred popular repercussions were to be expected.[5]

In A.D. 35-6 the first taxes of a new assessment were being collected. This would explain the hostility towards the tax-collector Zacchaeus at Jericho (Lk. xix. 1-10), and the topicality of the question put to Jesus in Jerusalem, 'Shall we pay tribute to Caesar?'

A notable event which can confidently be assigned to A.D. 36 was the appearance among the Samaritans of a messianic leader, expected by them as the Taheb. They crowded to Mount Gerizim to witness the recovery of the sacred vessels believed to have been buried there by Moses. Pilate took alarm, and sent cavalry and heavily-armed infantry to attack and disperse the Samaritans, putting to death many of their chief men who were captrured (Josephus, *Antiq.* XVIII. 85-7).[6]

This crowning act of ruthlessness by Pilate was at once brought to the attention of the legate of Syria, who ordered the governor to go to Rome to answer the charges of the Jews and Samaritans against him. Pilate must have left Judea towards the end of A.D. 36. During the ten years of his administration he had frequently acted ruthlessly and in a high-handed manner, and his crucifixion of Jesus as a claimant to be king of the Jews at the Passover of A.D. 36 was a relatively minor incident.

When we come to the ordered narrative in Part Two of this volume there will be more to be said of these matters, and we shall also be dealing with the effects of the cycle conjunctions of A.D. 47-9 and of A.D. 61-3. Here, however, it is vital to seek confirmation that the year of the crucifixion of Jesus was indeed A.D. 36. We are enabled to do so with the help of Josephus because the Gospels are quite clear that the death of John the Baptist preceded that of Jesus. We have only to ascertain when John was executed.

The evidence is not new: it has been presented several times during the past century by scholars of repute.[7] It has not received general acceptance because it is in conflict with certain statements in the Gospels, whose veracity had to be upheld. But no amount of erudition has been able successfully to reconcile their differences, and the honest have admitted defeat. It is time, however, to cease treating legend as fact, and to pay closer attention to historical factors which yield positive results and which show that there was a high degree of accuracy in certain primitive recollections underlying the Gospel accounts of the public life of Jesus.

The ostensible cause of the Baptist's arrest was his denunciation of Herod the tetrarch, in true Zadokite fashion, for having taken his brother's wife while his own was still living. Josephus devotes quite a long section to the business and its outcome (*Antiq.* XVIII. 109-19). The wife to be replaced by Herodias, whom Antipas had met in Rome and who was married at the time to his half-brother Herod, was the daughter of the Nabataean monarch Harith IV (Aretas), who reigned from 9 B.C. to A.D. 40. She got wind of her husband's design, and when he returned from Rome she asked permission to go to Machaerus, a castle on the border between the territory of Harith and that of Antipas. From there she reached her father in Nabataea. He already had a land dispute with Antipas, and was now so angry at the insult to his daughter that he determined to go to war. Antipas was forced largely to denude Galilee of troops in order to meet the Arabian threat. And anxious not to risk a rising of his subjects he arrested John and took him in chains to Machaerus.

It seems probable that John was imprisoned for much of A.D. 35 and executed before the end of the year. His beheading, according to the Gospels, took place on the occasion of Herod's anniversary banquet, and among those present were the chief commanders of the tetrarch's forces (Mk. vi. 21). When battle was joined with the Arabians the army of Antipas was heavily defeated. The Jews declared that this was a judgment of God upon him for killing John the Baptist.

Smarting under this defeat, Antipas wrote to Italy to inform the emperor Tiberius of what had happened. In due course the emperor, incensed at the hostilities on which Harith had embarked, wrote to Vitellius the legate of Syria ordering him to declare war on Harith and either capture him alive and send him in chains to Rome, or send his head. Not long before, or soon after receiving these instructions, Vitellius was involved with the protests of the aggrieved Samaritans, and had sent his friend Marcellus to take charge of the government of Judea and Samaria from Pilate, who was ordered to proceed to Rome to give an account of his conduct.

Vitellius then went himself to Jerusalem, and judging by his actions the people there were in a state of great unrest. In Book XVIII of the *Antiquities* Josephus says that Vitellius came to Jerusalem at the Passover. But scholars believe this to have been a slip on the part of the historian, because in an earlier reference to the same visit he does not refer to any festival. He is confusing the legate's first visit with a second which was at the Passover of A.D. 37, when he was accompanied by Herod Antipas.[8]

On this first visit – perhaps in September of A.D. 36 – Vitellius deposed Caiaphas as high priest, remitted to the citizens the taxes on the sale of agricultural produce, and agreed that the high-priestly vestments and ornaments should be kept by the priests in the Temple. Before this they had been in the custody of the Roman garrison in Fort Antonia, which released them to the priests before the festivals and took them back afterwards. This had long been a Jewish grievance.

Either at Jerusalem, or on his return to Syria, Vitellius got his orders to attack Harith. For this purpose he assembled two legions of heavily-armed infantry, with cavalry and lightly-armed infantry in support. The army was ready and on the march before the end of the winter of 36-7, and Vitellius went up again to Jerusalem together with Antipas to offer sacrifices at the Passover of 37, presumably for the success of the expedition. On this occasion Vitellius made another change in the high priesthood, deposing Jonathan son of Annas whom he had appointed a few months previously and giving the office to his brother Theophilus. Vitellius had only been in Jerusalem four days when he received notification that Tiberius had died on 16 March and had been succeeded by Gaius. He therefore made the people take an oath of allegiance to the new emperor, and since he now required a mandate from Gaius to pursue the war with Harith he recalled his forces and himself returned to his headquarters at Antioch.

It is therefore in the context of the historical events and circumstances we have described that we have to place the ministry and crucifixion of Jesus. If he was executed at the season of the Passover, the year which best agrees with the evidence is A.D. 36. And what is more, we no longer see the death of Jesus in isolation, but in the context of conditions which have an important bearing on what took place.

From this fixed point in time, with the help of our seven- and fourteen-year cycles and all the other resources now at our command, we can follow subsequent developments more intelligibly and realistically. To the factors which have been brought to our attention we are able to add the vital contribution of chronology. (Other factors are considered in Part Three.) Once we are put on the right track we become aware of many things which previously had not been seen to be relevant. Pieces of the puzzle fall into place, and scattered fragments of tradition help to build up a coherent picture. What emerges may not in many respects accord with what we have imagined; but the new insights, the compulsion to look at things differently, should beneficially increase our understanding.

TABLE OF CYCLES

	Sabbatical Year	*Roman Census Year*
	B.C.	
Sept.	3-2	
	A.D.	
	5-6	
		A.D.
		6-7
	12-13	
	19-20	
		20-21
	26-27	
	33-34	

Sabbatical Year	*Roman Census Year*
B.C.	A.D.
	34-35
40-41	
47-48	
	48-49
54-55	
61-62	
	62-63
68-69	

NOTES AND REFERENCES

1. This was a conjunction of Jupiter and Saturn in the sign of Pisces, which occurred in May, October and December of 7 B.C.
2. Thus Manson in *A Companion to the Bible,* 'The date of the Crucifixion presents an unsolved, probably insoluble, problem.'
3. This was the official New Year's Day, *Rosh Hashanah.*
4. *Seder Olam,* ch. xxx, ed. Neubauer. See S. Zeitlin, *Megillat Taanit as a Source for Jewish Chronology and History in the Hellenistic and Roman Periods* (1922). The *Megillat Taanit* (Scroll of Fasts) in fact lists dates in the year on which there should be no fasting. since they commemorated propitious events in Jewish history from Maccabean to Roman times.
5. We may note that the Second Jewish Revolt under Bar-Cochba began in a Roman Census Year (A.D. 132–3), which was immediately preceded by a Sabbatical Year.
6. Josephus does not fix the year and season exactly; but it is difficult to believe that the affair of the Samaritan Messiah can have taken place until A.D. 36 was far advanced. It was particularly due to the protests of the Samaritan Council to Vitellius that Pilate was ordered to Rome. Pilate cannot have long delayed to obey this order, and by March A.D. 37 the emperor had died.
7. Among others, by Theodor Keim, Schenkel, Hausrath, and Kirsopp Lake.
8. See Feldman's note on *Antiquities* XVIIII, 90, vol. ix. p. 65, of the translation of Josephus in the Loeb Classical Library edition. When Vitellius paid his first visit to Jerusalem he had already sent Marcellus to take temporary charge of Jewish affairs after he had ordered Pilate to go to Rome. It is incredible, therefore, that this visit should have been at the Passover of 36 when Pilate did not leave Palestine until at least six months later. If there was a feast at the time of the legate's visit it must have been one of the autumn festivals, possibly Jewish New Year's Day in September, which would have been an appropriate occasion for returning the high priest's robes to Jewish custody and appointing a new high priest.

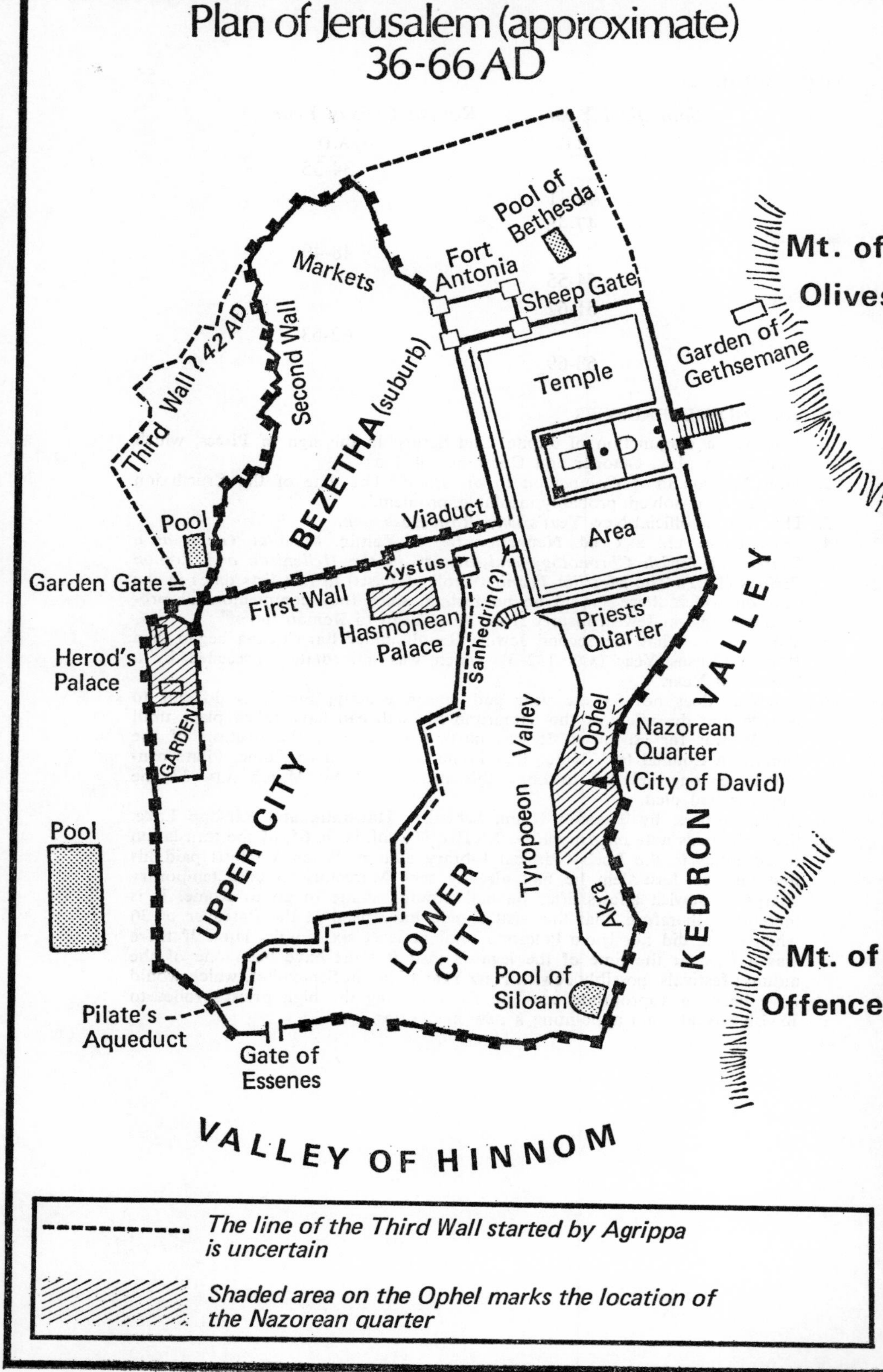
Plan of Jerusalem (approximate)
36-66 AD
Pool of Bethesda
Mt. of Olives
Fort Antonia
Markets
Sheep Gate
Third Wall ? 42 AD
Second Wall
Garden of Gethsemane
Temple
BEZETHA (suburb)
Viaduct
Area
Pool
Xystus
Garden Gate
First Wall
Hasmonean Palace
Sanhedrin (?)
Priests' Quarter
Herod's Palace
GARDEN
KEDRON VALLEY
Ophel
Nazorean Quarter
(City of David)
Tyropoeon Valley
UPPER CITY
Pool
LOWER CITY
Akra
Mt. of Offence
Pool of Siloam
Pilate's Aqueduct
Gate of Essenes
VALLEY OF HINNOM
The line of the Third Wall started by Agrippa is uncertain
Shaded area on the Ophel marks the location of the Nazorean quarter

CHAPTER 4

REMEMBERING ZION

For the final chapter of Part One we must turn to the topography of Jerusalem, because many of the events with which our narrative in Part Two will be occupied took place in and around the city. Some of them cannot rightly be understood without familiarity with its aspect. We have to become acquainted with its layout and contours, with the position of certain buildings, and with the character of its various sections. Over and above we have to be continually conscious that this teeming city, standing upon its rocky hills, was the spiritual and political metropolis of Israel, a chosen centre of worship as well as a seat of government. Jerusalem had a history reaching back into remote antiquity a thousand years and more before the foundation of Rome, and was representative of a world vision extending far into the future.

The visitor to Jerusalem today can still respond emotionally to what Jerusalem signifies, especially to Jews, Christians and Muslims. But while it is a city in the same place as of yore, and certain landmarks have survived, it wears hardly at all the appearance it presented in the first half of the first century A.D.

The destruction wrought by the forces of Vespasian and Titus in the Jewish war with the Romans left Jerusalem and its Temple in ruins. But a greater change was brought about by Hadrian in the second century when he built on the site a new city called Aelia Capitolina. Not only was this smaller in extent: it was laid out on a different plan with a north-south instead of an east-west axis. Hills were reduced, and valleys were filled in with debris. Part of Jerusalem on the south-west now lay outside the city walls. The Temple area remained, but it was now occupied by a heathen shrine dedicated to Jupiter Capitolinus. In the midst of the forecourt was erected an equestrian statue of the emperor.

Further considerable alterations were made in the Omayyad period. Arabs, Franks and Turks left their impress. As a distinguishing feature the Dome of the Rock stood on the Temple platform, and the present city walls were the contribution of Suleiman the Magnificent in the sixteenth century. It has to be said that some of the Christian holy places in Jerusalem have no genuine connection with the circumstances they commemorate, and Jesus never carried his cross along the Via Dolorosa.

How then can we recapture the look of Jerusalem in the period we are to cover in our history? Partly we can do so now as a result of the archaeological excavations which have been undertaken over the past century and more, and which are being continued energetically in the neighbourhood of the Temple area.[1] But fortunately there is also available a general description of the city as it was in the first century furnished from personal memory by Josephus in the Fifth Book of the *Jewish War* (136-247). This can be accepted as substantially accurate and has proved of great service to modern archaeologists. From other sources we can supplement certain points. The total picture is not as complete as we could wish; but by using our imagination we can conjure up a quite impressive visual image.

For our purposes it will be enough if we can convey an overall impression, so that we have in mind the relationship of different parts of the city. We shall seek to illustrate the bearing of topography on particular happenings, and dwell on certain features which aid our understanding of events.

It was in the period our history will cover that Jerusalem achieved in antiquity its greatest extent and the height of its glory. The housing situation had become acute, and the city had spilled over on the north beyond its walls. Because of the lie of the land this was the only area in which it could effectively expand. A well-to-do suburb with villas and gardens was formed and given the name of Bezetha, but was commonly described as the New City. To give it some further protection from attack in addition to the Second Wall it was partly enclosed by a new wall (the Third Wall) commenced on the orders of King Agrippa I in the brief period of his reign (A.D. 41-4) when Judea was temporarily once more under Jewish government. Jesus, of course, did not witness this development; but the northern expansion in his time had already brought much closer to the city limits the place where he was executed and buried.

Roads communicated with Jerusalem at different points; but we shall make our own approach from the east, not only because this afforded the most striking view of the Temple, which faced eastward towards the Mount of Olives, but also because the roads from Jericho and Bethany reached the city on this side.

The aspect was awe-inspiring on the eastern side because the city here stood on a hill formation running north and south with its ramparts on the edge of a sheer drop into the ravine of the Kedron Valley which lay between Jerusalem and the Mount of Olives. The valley was much deeper than it is now, but there was access to the Temple across it. Behind the wall here was the artificially levelled platform of the Temple Mount enclosed by high porticoes, and standing up in the midst on another platform was the Temple itself, its towers and upper part visible across the divide. With its white marble walls and gilded roof the effect it gave of beauty and majesty, especially in the morning sun, was profound.

We could enter Jerusalem north of the Temple by the Sheep Gate; but instead we make our way through olive orchards, with the Garden of Gethsemane (Ge-shemanim)[2] nearby, and proceed south down the Kedron Valley. On our left we pass fine funerary monuments – still surviving – and looking up at the city we can see houses along the top of a slightly lower hill. This is very exciting for us, for up there is Mount Zion, the site of the original Jebusite fortress which became the City of David. When we are in Jerusalem we shall be able to observe that in spite of alterations made by the Hasmoneans, who reduced the hill in order to give a better view of the Temple from within the city, it presents a singular feature. The hill juts towards the south in a spur bounded by the Kedron Valley on one side and the Tyropoeon Valley inside Jerusalem on the other. From its shape it was known as the Ophel (the Protuberance). Here and not on the more lordly western hill – as later supposed by Jews and Christians – was the real Zion, which plays an important part in our history. On its rocky face towards the south-east are the great cave tombs of the royal House of Judah, including that of David (Acts ii. 29).

We come to the ancient Spring of Gihon, and recall that King Hezekiah cut a tunnel through the rock to bring its waters within the city to the Pool of Siloam. Across the valley on our left is another hill since known as the Mount of Offence because King Solomon is supposed to have sacrificed there to heathen gods. Among the protecting towers of the city in this neighbourhood had been that of Siloam. According to Luke xiii. 4 the tower had fallen in the time of Jesus, killing eighteen people. The fall is linked in Luke with the slaughter of Galileans in the Temple on the orders of Pontius Pilate. This points to an insurrectionary activity (cp. Mk. xv. 7), which could have been connected with the protest against Pilate's use of the Jewish sacred funds (the *Corban*) to construct another aqueduct to Jerusalem from Solomon's Pools. There was a demonstration then, as related by Josephus (*Antiq*. XVIII. 60-2) in which many Jews perished. Was the tower at Siloam seized by the rebels on this occasion, and assaulted by the Romans? We may never know.

Just beyond the Pool of Siloam the wall of the city runs west above another ravine, the Valley of Hinnom, where refuse was burnt, and which gave its name to Hell (*Ge-Henna*). We enter Jerusalem at its south-eastern angle where the valleys of Kedron and Hinnom meet, and where they are joined by another valley winding upwards through the city and almost bisecting it. This was the Tyropoeon, the Valley of the Cheesemakers. At its foot and climbing up the lower slopes of the hills on either side were the crowded tenements of the poor in a veritable rabbit-warren of narrow stepped streets and alleys. Those who were rather better off occupied the higher levels. This general area was called the Lower City, overlooked on the Ophel spur by the Akra (the Citadel). Almost the whole of this zone was devastated and changed, and lies outside the present city walls to the south-east.

As we now ascend the Valley of the Cheesemakers we look up on both sides to tier upon tier of houses and streets, some of the latter representing various trades. There are sections favoured by Jews from other parts of the world, who have their own synagogues and maintain here their own community life. The Lower City as a whole is a distinct enclave. If we go up the hill to the left, on the western side, there runs along its slopes the aquaduct constructed by order of Pontius Pilate to bring water into the city from Solomon's Pools near Bethlehem. It created an uproar when he employed the sacred treasure of the Temple for the purpose. An interior wall on this side blocks off the Upper City. If we were to go up the hill on our right we would find another wall covering the approach to the Akra. At the northern end of the Ophel is the quarter of the priests.

The Ophel and its immediate neighbourhood is of particular interest for us, for here as we shall discover was the centre of Nazorean activity. Though since reduced in height, its contours below the south-eastern section of Suleiman's wall of today should be more sacred to Christians than many of the places within what is now the Old City to which they make pilgrimage. At ground level there is not much to indicate that here was Zion; but from the air it is much more discernible.

If we mistake not it was in this sacerdotal vicinity that there stood the home of John the Jewish priest, otherwise known to us as the Beloved Disciple, the house with the upper room to which Jesus came to celebrate the Passover with his disciples before he suffered,[3] the house which was afterwards his mother's home and the headquarters of the Nazorean movement. We learn from the Acts (vi. 7) that a great company of the priests, residing on the Ophel, joined the disciples.

What could be more appropriate than for the Messiah, the Son of David, to crown his witness in the City of David! Was it not written, 'I have anointed My king upon My holy hill of Zion' (Ps. ii. 6)? But no shrine has been placed here by the devout, since the site of the house with the upper room is shown wrongly on the west of the city. Perhaps it is well that this is so.

From our itinerary we may already have remarked that it was the eastern side of Jerusalem with which Jesus was familiar. The roads from Jericho and Bethany, the Mount of Olives, Gethsemane and the Kedron Valley, the Pool of Siloam, and of course the Temple, all figure in the Gospel story. So it would be natural also, as well as prophetically in keeping, that Jesus should have gone among the poor of the Lower City and ascended to the historic Akra and the Ophel. Beyond the Temple, and also on the east, he knew the Pool of Bethesda near the Sheep Gate. There was nothing to attract him to the western half of Jerusalem, for reasons that will appear. He came there only at the end, as a prisoner.

It will be necessary for us in our tour to visit the western sector of the city, but we do not propose to do so directly. The character of the Upper City is very different, more in keeping with Greece and Rome than with Judea. It has its own *agora,* a kind of market-cum-forum, good streets lined with high class villas, and an abundance of trees, gardens and fountains. To reach this opulent neighbourhood, however, we shall make a detour, following the street of the Valley of the Cheesemakers as it inclines upwards towards the north, and then branches off to the west. Before us on our right the Temple Mount comes quickly into view and down beside it the building devoted to the repository of archives, bonds and contracts. Broad steps lead up from the valley to give access to the Temple on the western side by an arched staircase. Ahead of us the valley is crossed completely by a viaduct which directly links the Temple area with the Upper City.[4]

Beyond, Jerusalem opens out. We are in the civic sector. Here is the building where the Jewish Council (the Sanhedrin) holds its sessions, combining the functions of Law Court and Town Hall, and on the left is the Xystus. Formerly this was an athletic arena, but at this time it is doing duty as a place of public meeting to which citizens are summoned to hear official speeches and proclamations. Further marks of an alien culture are encountered to the north-west, the theatre and hippodrome, to delight the Gentiles and hellenized Jews, but anathema to the devout patriot. It had been the pleasure of Herod the Great to make his capital vie in grandeur and amenities with any city of which the Roman Empire could boast.

There is no need for us, except as sightseers, to occupy ourselves with this part of the city. It was enclosed on the west and north by the Second Wall, and northwards stretched the New Town, while on the eastern side were to be found the woolshops, the smithies and the clothes-market.

Our way from the civic centre takes us due west at the northern foot of the Upper City, following the line of the First Wall which cut right across Jerusalem from the Temple Mount to the western entrance to the city at the Gennath or Garden Gate, near what is today the Jaffa Gate, where the Second Wall joined the First. This was the gate through which Jesus was led to execution on Golgotha, an eminence outside the city towards the north. In immediate proximity to the gate, and standing high above it, were two quadrangular towers called Phasael and Hippicus, and nearby was a third tower called Mariamme. All three were constructed by Herod the Great, and Josephus has left a full description of them (*J. W.* V. 164-71).

Between Phasael and Hippicus we ascend to that part of Jerusalem which may be termed Government Hill, the northern face of the Upper City. All along here were the palaces of the rulers and nobility. The first, occupying a vast area, was the magnificent Palace of Herod, at this time the residence of the Roman governor on his visits to the capital. It contained large banqueting halls, offices, and bedrooms for a hundred guests. At the rear of the state rooms were circular cloisters opening one into another and adorned with lawns and fountains. The gardens had long walks shaded by trees, and were enriched with ornamental waters and an abundance of statuary. Part of the main structure was the praetorium with its courtyard where Jesus was brought for trial.

As we return eastward at this higher level towards the Temple along a finely paved road other fine edifices stand out. There is the Palace of the Hasmoneans, and equally close to the Temple the Palace of the High Priest. The viaduct across the Tyropoeon Valley, under which we passed previously, connects with the road we are following and affords direct access to the Temple Mount without need to mingle with the populace. The exalted with their retinues and escorts can proceed to the Sanctuary right over their heads.[5] Troops can also march along here to Fort Antonia at the north-west corner of the Temple area.

Our eyes are now upon the Holy House which we can see standing up in all its beauty in the midst of its enclosure. We enter by a western gate, and find ourselves in a vast piazza paved with stones of different colours. The great platform running north and south is surrounded by high porticoes with flat roofs supported by tall corinthian columns. The portico on the south side known as the Royal Porch has three rows of columns. The whole enclosure is the Court of the Gentiles to which everyone has access, and in the shade of its colonnades one can listen to teachers or take part in discussion, or one can just gossip with friends. The portico on the east bears the name of Solomon's Porch. Above the junction of the south-western walls of the enclosure, visible only from the outside, there is a projecting feature where a trumpeter takes his stand to summon the people to worship at the hours of prayer. The sound carries right down the valley in the midst of the city.

But we have come to see the Holy House itself. This faces towards the east and rises up in the midst of the general court on higher platforms within another enclosure pierced with gates. The walls of this enclosure have colonnades on the inner sides, and on the outside is a terrace raised above the Court of the Gentiles with a balustrade on which inscriptions in Greek, Latin and Hebrew warn non-Jews that entrance to the interior is forbidden.

We can proceed, therefore, only with our Jewish friends, but may describe what we see. The most imposing entrance is on the east. The gate here is of glowing burnished Corinthian bronze, and is known as the Beautiful Gate, forming a two-leaved door above a flight of twelve steps. This introduces us to the outer court of the Sanctuary itself, called the Women's Court because apart from chambers at its corners a section is set aside for female worshippers. The priests do not have to pass through this court or the Court of the Gentiles outside: they are able to reach their stations by underground passages communicating directly on the south with their own residential quarter on the Ophel.

On the eastern side of the Women's Court we reach another level. The central gate is at the top of a flight of fifteen steps which form a semicircle. On these steps during the services the choir of Levites chant the hymns to the accompaniment of stringed instruments.

At the head of the steps the Nicanor Gate gives access to the inner court, of which the first section is the Court of Israel and then beyond it the Court of the Priests. We shall not penetrate further; but we would next reach a large open space where the sacrifices and libations are offered. Then at last on a still higher platform approached by more steps rises the House of God itself, flanked by towers and roofed with cedar beams overlaid with gold.

The entrance of the Holy House is covered by a curtain. There is a vestibule inside, and then another curtain screens the room where stands the great golden seven-branched candlestick, the altar of incense and the table of the shewbread. Behind this room a more splendid curtain covers the inmost chamber, the Holy of Holies, which is completely bare except for a flat-topped outcrop of rock. Into this eloquent silent unadorned shrine the high priest enters in all solemnity only once a year on the great Day of Atonement.

Quietly we return to the Court of the Gentiles; but now we make our way northward along its western side. We can observe that a great deal of construction work is going on, which will be occupying some 18,000 skilled workmen for many more years.

The last building we look at is the massive fortress of Antonia, with its four towers, standing at the north-west corner of the Temple Mount. The fortress, linked on the west with the Second Wall covering the northern approach, was designed as a protection to the Temple, and had been rebuilt by Herod the Great. It occupies a high rock whose sheer face has been covered with smooth stones to prevent any enemy climbing up. The whole great structure with interior courtyard is completely self-contained, with its own reservoir and ample accommodation for officers and men.

To quote Josephus, 'At the point where it impinged upon the porticoes of the Temple, there were stairs leading down to both of them, by which the guards descended; for a Roman cohort was permanently quartered there, and at the festivals took up positions in arms around the porticoes [i.e. on their roofs] to watch the people and repress any insurrectionary movement' (*J.W.* V. 243-4). Thus the Antonia was a continual reminder to the Jewish people of their subservience to a heathen Power.

Our itinerary has, I hope, brought realistically before us the appearance of Jerusalem in the first half of the first century A.D., so that we can visualize the position and character of some of its principal features. We shall have need of this information to clarify many of the matters to be related.

But there should also have been brought home to us something which the histories have not sufficiently emphasized. The valley of the Street of the Cheesemakers represented not only a natural division within the city, it constituted largely a spiritual and political division. Those on the eastern heights served the God of Israel alone, while those on the western hills also served Caesar and Mammon. Zion stood for complete devotion to the Torah and national independence. When the break with Rome came, coins of the Revolt bore the legend 'For the Redemption of Zion' and 'Freedom of Zion'. On the opposite hills from the Upper City northwards there was compromise. The cultures and philosophies of the Roman Empire blended with the Jewish, and there was little desire here to throw off the alien yoke. It was significant that when, in the period we shall be covering, the royal family of Adiabene was converted to Judaism and Queen Helena and her son Monobazus built palaces at Jerusalem, they did not set them among those of the hellenized aristocracy of the Upper City, but in the heart of nationalist Jerusalem on the Akra. Several members of this family took part in the revolt on the side of the rebels.

It was on the eastern side and in the depths of the Lower City that the Fourth Philosophy of Judas of Galilee had its supporters.[6] Here, in and below the ancient City of David, the Nazoreans were to obtain multitudes of recruits. On the Ophel Jesus had spent his last evening with his disciples, and in after-years from this eminence, looking across the Valley of the Kedron, they trusted to witness his descent from heaven on the Mount of Olives according to the word of the Prophet Zechariah (xiv. 4).

The contrasts within the city, as seen by those on the east side, serve to illustrate sayings of Jesus which were first set down there. 'Those who are gorgeously apparelled, and live delicately, are in royal palaces' as in the Upper City (Lk. vii. 25). The rich man of the parable of Dives and Lazarus 'was clothed in purple and fine linen, and fared sumptuously every day' (Lk. xvi. 19). Fancy having plenty to eat *every day!* In the World to Come, of course, everything will be different. Then the poor beggar will be comforted and the rich man tormented. But there is still a Tyropoeon Valley. 'Between us and you there is a great gulf fixed.' Jesus says that 'it is easier for a camel to go through the eye of a needle than for a rich man to enter the Kingdom of God.'

Jesus says, 'Blessed are ye poor; for yours is the Kingdom of God. Blessed are ye that hunger now; for ye shall be filled. Blessed are ye that weep now; for ye shall laugh . . . But woe unto you that are rich; for ye have received your consolation. Woe unto you that are full; for ye shall hunger. Woe unto you that laugh now; for ye shall mourn and weep' (Lk. vi. 20-5). Jesus says that the way to Destruction is by a wide gate and broad avenue (as in the Upper City), while the way to life is by a small opening in a narrow alley, hard to find – as in the Lower City (Mt. vii. 13-14).

The rich and aristocratic of the Upper City might affect to despise the denizens of the Lower City; but they also feared them. They could luxuriate in their lordly palaces and pleasant gardens remote from the congested hovels, the stench and squalor, at the bottom of the valley, only because they were under the protection of Roman arms.

When we let the topography of Jerusalem speak to us, it conveys to us much more vividly the environment in which Christianity had its beginnings. We get the feel of the city in which localities reflect the human moods and contrasts. With this illumination we are more realistically and accurately instructed in the significance of what will be brought before us as our history unfolds.

NOTES AND REFERENCES

1. Following the Six-Day War of 1967 excavations have been proceeding in the area immediately west and south of the Temple Mount under the auspices of the Israeli Institute of Archaeology at the Hebrew University, Jerusalem, and the Israel Exploration Society. Progress Reports by B. Mazar have been published. By courtesy of Professor Yigael Yadin I went over the sites systematically in November 1972, as part of the preparation for this book.
2. The term means the Fat, or Fertile, Valley, to which reference is made in

Isa. xxviii. 1 and 4. The Syriac rendering of Matthew, *Gusemani,* supports the reading *Ge-shemanim,* as in Isaiah.

3. Further information will be found in Schonfield, *The Passover Plot.*
4. The remains are known from their discoverer as Wilson's Arch. South of it may be seen the eastern spring of Robinson's Arch; but it is now known that the latter was not part of a viaduct which crossed the valley; it was a means of descending into it.
5. See the plan of Jerusalem on p. 56, and note 4 above.
6. See Part Three, Chapter 25.

Part Two

DRAMA IN PROGRESS

CHAPTER 5

UNDER PONTIUS PILATE

Anyone acquainted with the deep attachment of the Jewish people to their Faith, which fostered in them a strong sense of national pride, could have informed the Roman Governor of Judea and Samaria that trouble was to be expected in the years corresponding to A.D. 34 and 35. The Jewish Sabbatical Year would then overlap the Roman Census Year for the first time since Pontius Pilate took office.[1]

Perhaps Pilate was warned; but despite earlier experiences of Jewish solidarity in defence of their 'absurd superstitions', and the clashes in which this had involved him, he had no expectation that this subject people would engage in any major hostile adventure. They had no national leader and no military organization. Any incidents which might occur could readily be dealt with by the troops at his disposal.

Pontius Pilate had come to Judea in A.D. 26 full of arrogance and self-importance, with none of the finesse of a career diplomat, determined to perform his functions for Caesar, and to stand no nonsense. Behind him doubtless stood the ambitious and antisemitic L.Aelius Sejanus, who at this time virtually ruled the Roman Empire in the name of Tiberius. The character of Pilate is described by Philo of Alexandria in his *Embassy to Gaius*, quoting and probably working-up a letter from Agrippa I to the Emperor Gaius dating from A.D. 40. Pilate is depicted in this near-contemporary source as 'naturally inflexible, a blend of self-will and relentlessness, a man noted for vindictiveness and furious temper'. When he was finally called to account in A.D. 36 the charges against him were consistent with the reputation he bore, 'briberies, insults, robberies, outrages and wanton injuries, executions without trial constantly repeated, ceaseless and supremely grievous cruelty'.[2]

The first act of Pilate when he arrived at Caesarea on the coast, the regular place of residence of the Roman governors of Judea, was to send a new garrison to Jerusalem. The soldiers would have been on duty at Herod's Palace on the west of the city and chiefly at the fortress of Antonia at the north-west corner of the Temple Mount.

Previous governors had deferred to Jewish religious scruples, but not Pilate: his troops were permitted to take with them their standards probably bearing embossed portraits of the emperor. Since Caesar was an object of worship this flouted the Jewish law against graven images. Josephus says that the troops arrived under cover of darkness, and the citizens of Jerusalem only became aware of what had happened the next morning. It is to be presumed that the standards were seen on the walls of the Antonia when the Temple was opened for the morning service, and that it was the profanation of the sacred precincts which so aroused Jewish ire. Those flocking in from the country were immediately apprised, and soon a swelling concourse was on its way to Caesarea to call upon Pilate to have the standards removed. The action appears to have been spontaneous, and without violent intent, many imagining that a genuine mistake had been made by the new governor due to ignorance.

The Jews were speedily disillusioned. Insolently, Pilate kept them for five days without an answer. On the sixth they were summoned to the great stadium at Caesarea, where they found themselves ringed by three lines of Roman soldiers. From his tribunal the governor signalled to the troops to draw their swords, and threatened that the demonstrators would be cut down without mercy if they refused to receive the emblems of the emperor's divine authority. Whereupon, says Josephus, the people flung themselves on the ground in a body and bared their necks, crying that they would rather be slaughtered than transgress their laws. This was an unexpected development, and blustering Pilate dared not carry out his threat. He agreed to have the standards removed.

From this day, however, the Jews knew the kind of man they had as governor. And Pilate, smarting under the insult to his pride and prestige, registered that he had a score to settle which he was determined to repay with interest.

It is unfortunate that we have so little information about the period of Pilate's administration. Agrippa's letter to Gaius suggests a long series of misdeeds and harsh measures. Yet Agrippa cites only one incident, one that was pertinent to the purpose of his letter. This particular incident is not mentioned by Josephus, who gives only two instances of Pilate's actions in the *Jewish War*, and two more in the later *Antiquities*, if we include the reference to the execution of Jesus. The latter is in any case certified by the Gospels and Tacitus. Thus from these sources we have a total of only five specific incidents, and all but the first, which we have described, must be assigned to dates several years later than A.D. 26.

The particular example of Pilate's behaviour referred to by Agrippa can only have occurred after the governor had been in office for some time, because the complaining citizens of Jerusalem proposed to send an embassy to Tiberius. This Pilate was afraid of, says Agrippa, because the envoys could expose the long record of his previous misconduct. Brandon, who discusses at length the known incidents, is prepared to accept that all except the initial one of the standards were subsequent to A.D. 31, the year in which Tiberius at last acted against Sejanus and had him executed.[3]

In Part One it is pointed out how little Josephus has to say in his first work, the *Jewish War*, about events in Judea prior to A.D. 48.[4] One reason could be that he was anxious to emphasize that one of the factors which brought about the Jewish revolt was the turpitude and mismanagement of the later Roman governors. Pontius Pilate seems to have been nearly as bad as any of these. But if Josephus had said this, and furnished evidence, it might have been asked why, in this case, had the Jews not revolted a generation previously? Josephus did give more information in the *Antiquities*, but that was nearly a quarter of a century later when he had another aim in view.

All our information brought together, including that of Mark and Luke, and of course Philo, conveys that Pilate's administration was characterized by animosity towards the Jews, by gross turpitude and ruthlessness, which aroused the ire of the people at a time when they were most liable to be disaffected and open to anti-Roman stimulus. This time was represented by the Sabbatical Year of 33-4 followed on by the Roman Census Year. From what we know of Pilate the census was probably conducted harshly, and the tribute imposed from A.D. 35 collected in a violent manner. The Gospels refer to the tribute, but Josephus, though he must have known about it, chooses to ignore it. Altogether we must conclude that from A.D 33 to 36 conditions in Palestine were much more turbulent and the provocations much greater than has been allowed. They must have been worse than is conveyed by the few events of which we have record. Only so can there be justification of Agrippa's specification of 'briberies, insults, robberies, outrages and wanton injuries, executions without trial constantly repeated, ceaseless and supremely grievous cruelty'.

The arrest and execution of Jesus was therefore but one incident out of a large number, though for the Gospel writers it was all important. They were also concerned, for reasons sufficiently explained, to minimize the culpability of Pilate and magnify the responsibility of the Jews. Their records reflect the attitudes, polemics and apologetics of the late first and early second century. A presentation, with many contradictory elements and embellishments by one and another Evangelist, was built up after the Fall of Jerusalem and given circulation in the Roman Empire. As the story of Jesus emerged its value as history was much reduced, yet it did retain some links with reality from older sources and recollections. We have to seek to get behind these interpretations of the Evangelists, and take account of things they hint at or allude to which they do not develop.

Initially, here, it is desirable to look at the later events during Pilate's period of office as listed in our sources, without pre-judging either the order in which the events took place or the question of what relationship one might have with another.

1 Pilate set up in Herod's Palace at Jerusalem some gilded shields dedicated to the emperor 'to annoy the multitude' (letter of Agrippa to Gaius quoted by Philo).

2 Pilate constructed a new aqueduct to bring water to Jerusalem, applying to the cost some of the sacred funds of the Temple. The Jews of Jerusalem demonstrated against him and shouted abuse. Anticipating trouble, Pilate introduced into the crowd soldiers disguised as civilians with orders to beat the rioters with cudgels when he gave the signal. Many people died either from the blows or from being trodden down in the stampede to get away (Josephus).

3 On the occasion of some disturbance by Galileans at Jerusalem action was taken by Pilate which 'mingled their blood with their sacrifices'. In connection with this report mention is made of the fall of the tower at Siloam killing eighteen persons (Luke).

4 A rising of some kind occurred at Jerusalem in which blood had been shed. Certain Jews implicated were seized and held in prison. With them was one called Barabbas (Mark).

5 Jerus of Nazareth was arrested at Jerusalem as a mover of sedition and claimant to the Jewish throne. It would appear (so John's Gospel) that many of the citizens had gone out to greet Jesus as king when he entered the city shortly before the Passover. He was tried by Pilate and crucified.

6 A man came to the Samaritans calling on them to follow him to Mount Gerizim, where he would reveal the sacred vessels believed to have been buried there by Moses. The progress of the multitude was blocked on Pilate's orders, and they were attacked by his troops. Many were killed and some of the more prominent and influential Samaritans were captured and executed (Josephus).

Each of these items may represent a separate incident. On the other hand it is possible that 2, 3 and 4 reflect aspects of one event, or that 3 and 4 should be taken together, or alternatively 4 and 5. The Samaritan affair, 6, is clearly distinct, and this must be held to be the last in point of date, since it was the final cause which decided the legate of Syria, Vitellius, to order Pilate to proceed to Rome to answer the charges brought by the Samaritans and Jews against him.

All the events would seem to have taken place within four or five years, between A.D. 31 and 36. They witness collectively to a rapidly deteriorating situation, aggravated by Pilate's spiteful and domineering personality.

But we must also see that the treatment to which the people were subjected, and the violations of their religious principles, would have stimulated the conviction that these were the Last Times and intensified Messianic expectations. The more militant, like the Galilean Zealots, stood ready to exploit any development that gave promise of speeding up the deliverance of Israel.

We have explained how the Sabbatical Years released multitudes from agrarian labour to flock around those who proclaimed the coming of the Kingdom of God, and we also learn how those who followed Judas of Galilee and Zadok reacted to the first Roman census.[5] When these periodic events came together, as they did at this juncture, all the ingredients were present, even without Pilate, for explosive occurrences. His vindictiveness and ruthlessness added fuel to the flames.

The Gospels, while preoccupied with what they wish to represent as the story of Jesus, have yet preserved traces of circumstances they make no attempt to emphasize and which would tell a rather different tale. From them we have obtained items 3, 4 and 5 in our list. But we also get glimpses of other reflections of the contemporary situation.

John the Baptist tells the tax-collectors to exact no more than the correct tribute, and the soldiers that they should do violence to no man, or accuse anyone falsely. The people are in expectation, and everyone is wondering whether John could be the Messiah (Lk. iii.

12-15). This happens with Jesus also (Mt. xii. 23), and he is frequently hailed as Son of David. Some of the citizens of Jerusalem are convinced that Jesus must be the Messiah (Jn. vii. 42). There are passages in the Sermon on the Mount which allude to Roman oppression. In Galilee the people want to compel Jesus to become their king (Jn. vi. 15). As Jesus goes to Jerusalem with the Galilean pilgrims it is assumed that the Kingdom of God is about to be achieved (Lk. xix. 11). Salome, the wife of Zebedee, claims for her two sons the seats on the right and left of Jesus in his kingdom (Mt. xx. 21). Jesus promises the Twelve that they will sit on thrones judging the twelve tribes of Israel (Mt. xix. 28). We have references to the tax-collector Zacchaeus and the question to Jesus about payment of the tribute to Caesar. The synoptic Gospels state that Jesus rode into Jerusalem in the character of Messiah, while John says that crowds issued from the city to welcome him as king (Jn. xii. 12-13). Instructions are given by the authorities that the whereabouts of Jesus should be reported, so that he can be arrested (Jn. xi. 57). All Jerusalem was seething (Mt. xxi. 10). Among the chief rulers are those who believe Jesus to be indeed the Messiah (Jn. xii. 42). The authorities decide to seize Jesus by stealth, and not on the feast day, because they fear a tumult by the people (Mk. xiv. 1-2).

When we study these and other intimations they emphatically convey to us not only the state of mind of the Jewish people, but a climax to the activities of Jesus charged with political dynamite. Is Pontius Pilate going to sit still in Herod's Palace and do absolutely nothing about this grave threat?[6] From all we know of him this is unthinkable. Look what he did later to the Samaritans at Mount Gerizim! We would naturally expect to read in the Gospels how Pilate, believing that an insurrection was brewing, sent his troops to disperse the people and seize or kill Jesus, of a battle in the Kedron Valley and on the lower slopes of the Mount of Olives.

The incidents on record reveal a progressively worsening relationship between Pilate and the inhabitants of Jerusalem. They watch his every move and assail him with abuse, staging massive protests which result on occasion in violence and bloodshed as the exasperated and vindictive governor hits back. Our chapter on topography at the end of Part One helps to throw light on what was going on. There was a state of hostility between the Lower City and the Upper City.

Quite clearly, as the Gospels allow, the common people of Jerusalem regarded Jesus as emphatically on their side. If the Evangelists had set down that Pilate, by some stratagem or display of force, had succeeded in getting Jesus into his power, but that then the people in their thousands had flocked to the governor's residence to clamour for his release, their account would have been in harmony with the people's known attitude. But that they should be represented as shouting to their enemy to crucify their champion is utterly incongruous. Only persons antagonistic to the Jews, writing long afterwards to placate the Romans and for Gentile believers unfamiliar with Pilate's character and the history of his administration, could have been guilty of striking such a grossly false note. For Christian spokesmen still to talk of popular disillusionment, and of fickle mobs, is in this instance absurd.[7]

Even Josephus, who was proud of being a Jew, could for his own ends suppress anti-Roman evidence. He informs us that to defray the cost of his aqueduct Pilate used 'the sacred treasure known as *Corbonas*'. But he neglects to say how the governor got possession of these funds. How did he compel the chief priests to hand over the treasure from the Temple of which they were the custodians? Are we learning otherwise of the same event when Luke's Gospel refers to those Galileans whose blood Pilate mingled with their sacrifices? Have we an echo of what had happened on this occasion when the jittery high priest Caiaphas, according to John's Gospel, expresses the fear that if the people acknowledge Jesus 'the Romans will come and take away our place and our nation'?

These are the kind of questions which confront us when we seek to discover what really took place in relation to Jesus.

Everything we know of the situation contributes to the conviction that the Gospel account of the Passion is in many respects biased and artificial. No one seems to be acting in character. Pilate is unlike his real self. The chief priests and scribes, for all that they may have had reason to press for the crucifixion of Jesus, could never have come to the scene of execution and mocked the victim. The Jewish populace, if it was in fact they who attended the trial – which there is every reason to doubt[8] – would have been clamouring for the release of Jesus, not for his death.

It has rightly been pointed out by scholars that some bits of genuine history and tradition have been woven tendentiously at times into a fabric consisting of strands of Old Testament passages held to be prophetic of what occurred. Papias, circa A.D. 140, stated that Matthew had composed the Oracles (relating to Jesus) in the Hebrew language, and that 'everyone explained them to the best of their ability'. We are aware from Justin Martyr and others that such *testimonia*, utilizing the Greek Septuagint version of the Old Testament, were considerably added to by Christians, especially to confute the Jews.[9] The Passion narratives rest on the 'discovery' and interpretation of what were deemed to be relevant Old Testament texts. In quite another sense than the prologue of John's Gospel 'the Word was made flesh'. Now that we have the explanatory commentaries on the Bible furnished by the Dead Sea Scrolls, we are in a much better position to apprehend that a method of interpreting the Scriptures prophetically in relation to the Time of the End was in vogue, which in the hands of Gentile Christians went to extreme lengths, so that texts became the fathers of bogus history.

Yet the prospect of disengaging fact from fiction is not completely bleak. There are things which feature in the Passion narratives which cannot have been invented, even if some of them have been perversely employed. For example, the individual called Bar-Abbas, or in the Hebrew Gospel Bar-Rabban, cannot have been conjured up out of any presumed prophecy. He may well furnish one of the clues to a more factual account of what transpired.

NOTES AND REFERENCES

1. See Table of Cycles, pp. 54–5.
2. Philo, *Embassy to Gaius*, xxxvii. 301–3. Christian divines have for many centuries been familiar with this source, but until modern times have taken very little pains to correct the image in the Gospels of a weak and pliant Pilate, who exonerated Jesus and sought to save him from the Jews. Such are the effects of theological prejudice.
3. See Brandon, *Jesus and the Zealots*, pp. 75–7. According to the *Embassy to Gaius*, four of the Herodian princes wrote to Tiberius about Pilate's action regarding the shields, and the emperor replied promptly and emphatically the same day as he received the communication, ordering Pilate to have the shields removed to the Temple of Augustus at Caesarea. This suggests that Tiberius had fully resumed control of affairs of state, as happened in A.D. 31.
4. See Part One, Chapter 3.
5. See Part One, Chapter 3, pp. 50–1, and Part Three, Chapter 25, p. 253ff.
6. Of course, when the triumphal entry of Jesus into Jerusalem took place Pilate may still have been at Caesarea where he normally resided. In that case he might only have heard of the action of Jesus in the Temple on the day after the event when a message could reach him from the Roman commander at the Antonia fortress which overlooked the Temple area.
7. It might have favoured the Gospel version if it could be claimed that the

Jewish populace was very ready to obey the behests of the chief priests. We have evidence, however, that the ordinary people were antagonistic to the Sadducean hierarchy as high-handed, decadent and tolerant of Roman government. Even the Acts of the Apostles allows that the Jews of Jerusalem were against the chief priests and on the side of the followers of Jesus (Acts v. 25–6).

8. See Schonfield, *The Passover Plot*, Part One, ch. xi.
9. See Rendel Harris, *Testimonies* (2 vols.), and Lukyn Williams, *Adversus Judaeos*.

CHAPTER 6

BARABBAS

In Mark, the earliest of the Gospels, Barabbas (i.e. Bar-Abba or Bar-Rabban) is introduced into the trial of Jesus before Pilate in these terms: 'And there was one named Barabbas, in bonds with those who had made insurrection, those who in the insurrection had committed manslaughter' (xx. 7). Since these men were supposed to have slain other persons the presumption is that they were awaiting trial and not serving a prison sentence. In this case the insurrection must have been very recent, and they were being kept in the dungeons pending the imminent arrival of Pilate in Jerusalem from Caesarea. It would appear that two of them, regarded as among the ringleaders, were the so-called 'brigands' who were crucified with Jesus. They were not just robbers, since they had taken part in an insurrection, and consequently those they had killed may well have been Roman soldiers. Barabbas, for some unexplained reason, is distinguished from the others, and the suggestion has been made that he was not known to have killed anyone himself. He might even have been a perfectly innocent bystander caught up in the fighting.[1] We may dismiss the changes in Matthew, Luke-Acts and John. For Matthew, Barabbas is a notable prisoner, Luke makes him a murderer, and John a brigand.

But what of this Jewish insurrection, what was its nature and when did it occur? The Gospels give no indication. But Luke at an earlier point speaks of a report made to Jesus of Galileans whose blood Pilate had mingled with their sacrifices, where there is also mentioned the fall of the tower at Siloam killing eighteen persons. The tower was a strong fortification at the south-east corner of the wall of Jerusalem, covering the Pool of Siloam and entrance into the city via the Tyropoeon Valley. It is certainly not likely to have collapsed by itself, and would have been kept in regular repair.[2]

Since there is reference to the Galileans being engaged with their sacrifices we may infer that the incident took place on the occasion of a Jewish festival. The circumstances could relate to the protest described by Josephus when Pilate seized the sacred funds to build the aquaduct; but this is by no means certain. There is also difficulty in linking Luke's story with the insurrection in which Barabbas was involved. Yet not only has this been proposed; it has been claimed that the rising concerned took place in Passion Week, and that it had to do with Jesus the Galilean.

This last view has had strong and erudite advocates.[3] It conceives that there was compressed into Passion Week a full-scale struggle between the Jews and the Romans. It will have begun, according to the theory, with Jesus and his supporters occupying the Temple, the Roman garrison at the Antonia being too weak to interfere. Galilean forces mustered on the Mount of Olives moved down the Kedron Valley and seized the tower at Siloam, easily taken because it was not strongly manned since no attack was expected. The aim of the manoeuvre would be to occupy the Lower City and the Akra, with the rebels increasing their strength by a sympathetic rising, and then join up with those already in possession of the Temple Mount. Thus with great rapidity, as a result of surprise, the whole of Jerusalem east of the Tyropoeon Valley would be in the hands of the revolutionaries, and they would virtually be in an invulnerable position.

It would appear to be suggested that it took Pilate no more than three days to muster a large force equipped with siege engines and get them to Jerusalem. Beyond the bounds of probability the Romans were immediately successful. We are not offered much in the way of details of what is called 'the Roman counterstroke'. It is to be presumed that one body of Roman troops advanced from the west and joined up with the besieged Roman garrison in the Antonia, and then fell upon the rebel Galileans and those who made cause with them in the Temple when the Passover lambs for their requirements were being slaughtered. Thus the blood of the Galileans was mingled with their sacrifices. In the meantime another Roman force with siege engines and, one would imagine, accompanied by cavalry, had got round the north of the city outside the walls, routed the ill-organized and ill-equipped rebels on the Mount of Olives, brought the engines down the Kedron Valley, and in next-to-no-time had battered down the strong tower at Siloam which in its fall killed eighteen of the defenders.

But what of Jesus? What was he supposed to be doing while events were getting quite out of control? While the massacre in the Temple is taking place he is found with his disciples quietly celebrating the Last Supper in some remote house away from the fighting. Then they go to Gethsemane, where a Roman cohort with the constabulary of the high priest led by the traitor Judas finds them and Jesus is arrested. It is ignored that with the Kedron Valley now in Roman hands the chances that Jesus could have reached Gethsemane were slim, and he would much more likely have gone somewhere else.

This version of the circumstances makes excellent reading, but it will not stand up to serious examination. There is neither the time nor the likelihood for such a major occurrence. What Luke has said about the slaughter of the Galileans and the fall of the tower at Siloam, if it has historicity, must relate to some prior event of a less complex character. It is to be noted that in Luke the report is given to Jesus of what has taken place while he is on a journey to Jerusalem well in advance of Passion Week. The conflict could have arisen in the course of the Roman census of A.D. 34-5, since it is known how bitterly the Galilean Zealots in particular were opposed to the levying of a tribute. They may well have staged a demonstration at a festival in Jerusalem in that period.

But then, what of the insurrection in which Barabbas and others were seized? Was this another and more recent happening of which we are denied the details? We might say that it is idle to speculate were it not for the fact that underlying the conception of which we have given the gist is a most interesting passage relating to Jesus, interpolated with a number of other striking insertions in the Old Russian text of Josephus' *Jewish War*. We reproduce here the relevant part of the chief reference to Jesus.

> And many of the multitude followed after him and hearkened to his teaching; and many souls were in commotion, thinking that thereby the Jewish tribes might free themselves from Roman hands. Now it was his custom in general to sojourn over against the city upon the Mount of Olives; and there, too, he bestowed healings upon the people.
>
> And there assembled unto him of ministers one hundred and fifty, and a multitude of the people. Now when they saw his power, that he accomplished whatsoever he would by a word, and when they had made known to him their will, that he should enter into the city and cut down the Roman troops and Pilate and rule over us, he heeded not.
>
> And when thereafter knowledge of it came to the Jewish leaders, they assembled together with the high priest and spoke: 'We are powerless and too weak to withstand the Romans. Seeing, moreover, that the bow is bent, we will go and communicate to Pilate what we have heard, and we shall be clear of trouble, lest he hear it from others, and we be robbed of our substance and ourselves slaughtered and our children scattered.' And they went and communicated it to Pilate. And he sent and had many

of the multitude slain. And he had that wonder-worker brought up, and after instituting an inquiry concerning him, he pronounced judgment: 'He is [a benefactor, not] a malefactor, [nor] a rebel, [nor] covetous of kingship.' [And he let him go; for he had healed his dying wife.]

[And he went to his wonted place and did his wonted works. And when more people again assembled round him, he glorified himself through his actions more than all. The teachers of the Law were overcome with envy, and gave thirty talents to Pilate, in order that he should put him to death. And he took it and gave them liberty to execute their will themselves.] And they laid hands on him and crucified him according to the law of their fathers.

The text here follows the translation of Robert Eisler.[4] The square brackets enclose what he believed to be late Christian additions. After the words, 'And he [Pilate] had that wonder-worker brought up, and after instituting an inquiry concerning him, he pronounced judgment', we should read on, 'He is a malefactor, a rebel, covetous of kingship. So they laid hands on him and crucified him *according to the law of the emperors*'. The italicized conclusion is correctly supplied from a Roumanian manuscript.

What this passage does is to furnish a variant of the Gospel story, which – if it has a basis in fact – would go far towards explaining Mark's allusion to a rising, and much else that creates a difficulty in the Gospel presentation.

The multitude of Galileans who accompany Jesus, and share in acclaiming him as king when he approaches Jerusalem, believe that he has the power to liberate Israel from the Romans. Josephus furnishes other instances of this kind of credence in the period leading up to the revolt of A.D. 66. The people therefore call upon Jesus to enter the city as their leader, cut down the Roman troops, and become their ruler.

Jesus, who is convinced that he is the Messiah but opposes militancy, rejects the proposition. His understanding of the Messiahship answers to the prediction of the Prince of Peace, as developed in the *Psalms of Solomon*, and he will not involve his people in war.[5] The chief priests, however, knowing that Jesus has been acclaimed as king, and taking alarm at his actions in the Temple, are fearful that a rising will ensue even without his consent. Lest they be thought guilty of complicity they hasten to send word to Pilate of the potentially dangerous situation. Accordingly, the governor readily gives orders for the multitude to be dispersed. In the process there is fighting and many are killed.

Jesus, the presumed instigator of insurrection, is seized, interrogated, and condemned to be crucified.

So far as it goes the account makes sense and is fully in keeping with contemporary conditions and Pilate's known behaviour. And what the Gospels themselves relate would not exclude what the Old Russian Josephus represents. The Evangelists could have included this additional information without violence to their narrative, except that it would mean surrendering their anti-Jewish attitude. It is common ground that Jesus did appear at Jerusalem as king, acclaimed by multitudes as such, that the chief priests feared a popular rising in his favour and accused him to Pilate, and that the governor condemned Jesus to be crucified. We also have the reference in Mark to an insurrection, which in Luke becomes 'a certain sedition made in the city' (xxiii. 19).

The question is, how did the additions to the *Jewish War* originate? They were partly brought to scholarly attention in the West in the last decade of the nineteenth century; but the collation and translation of the Slavonic texts did not become available before the work of Professor Alexander Berendts and his colleague Konrad Grass, and of Professor V. N. Istrin, from 1906 to 1921. The labours of these pioneers, and others, were completed by the exhaustive researches of Dr Robert Eisler in the following decade.

The thesis which Eisler sought to establish was that, aside from certain recognizable Christian interpolations, the additions could have derived ultimately from genuine Josephan material. He claimed that they had formed part of the first Greek draft of the historian's book *On the Capture of Jerusalem*, a work later revised and reissued as the *Jewish War*. The contents of the passages, however, do not seem to warrant this conclusion. The interests of the writer, and some of the things he says, suggest that he is not Josephus, and that he is crediting the historian with opinions and information alien to his outlook and knowledge. Following what Eisler himself has adduced in a thorough quest for confirmation of his thesis, it seems probable that the additions are the work of a sectarian Byzantine Christian of the tenth or eleventh century A.D. The resultant expanded version of the *Jewish War* was later altered by an orthodox Christian copyist to make it acceptable to the Church. The fresh interpolations, as Eisler saw, can be readily recognized.

But in pronouncing against the Josephan authorship we are not saying that the additions are to be dismissed in their entirety as no more than medieval inventions. Their author could well have used sources of information which are not now extant. Several early Nazorean documents were still available in the Byzantine Empire, some of them in Jewish hands. There had been a substantial find of Dead Sea Scrolls at the beginning of the ninth century, which through the Jewish sect of Karaites came into circulation to an unknown but not negligible extent. They had a large community at Constantinople. From Byzantium much of such material found its way into South Russia, including the expanded Greek text of the *Jewish War*, and contributed through Slavonic translations to the development of a widespread Judaizing heresy which the Church found difficult to combat. One of the centres of activity was Kiev.[6]

All in all, we must allow that ancient traditions of historical importance relating to Jesus and his followers survived well into the Middle Ages, and we may hold that such are reflected in some of the additions in the Old Russian Josephus.

The position we shall take, then, is that the account of what happened as we have quoted it, neglecting the orthodox alterations, could well rest on sources which had preserved genuine information. It bears the marks of authenticity in the light of what we know of the state of Jewish affairs, and explains a great deal that the Gospels allude to or have represented in a prejudiced manner. Among other things this different story permits much more sense to be made of the Barabbas incident, and this also tells in its favour.

It was apprehended already by Eisler that the rising in favour of Jesus, promptly put down by the Romans, could be the very same sedition to which Mark refers which caused the arrest of Barabbas and the others.

> The support which he (Barabbas) received from the high priests and their mass of followers, strongly suggests that he was a well-known partisan of the hierarchy, the son of an *Abba* (Father) or *Rabba* (Master), both words designating a venerable doctor of the law, connected not with the rebels, but with their opponents, who in the mêlée had been captured along with them and was now destined to share their punishment. If it was a case of mistake on the part of the Roman guard, such as would often occur in every tumult of this kind, then Pilate, yielding to the voice of the people, might well have liberated him 'for the feast,' i.e. with such dispatch that the innocent man might still take part in the Passover celebration. But to pardon a known and condemned rebel was notoriously beyond the

power of a Roman governor, and by doing so he would have been guilty of an invasion of the prerogative of the emperor such as the suspicious Tiberius would have been the last to tolerate. No one, in fact, has hitherto succeeded in discovering an illustration in Jewish or pagan writings of the alleged Jewish custom of obtaining pardon for a prisoner at the Passover.[7]

Let us see if we can take this argument further. On information sent to Pilate by the chief priests of the threat of a seditious outbreak in favour of Jesus as king of the Jews by the multitude camped on the Mount of Olives for the impending festival, he in true character as well as duty dispatches troops to disperse the demonstrators and seize the ringleaders. In some Gospel manuscripts the one we know merely as Barabbas is named Jesus. He might have chanced quite innocently to be on the spot at the time, as Eisler proposed, or he may even have been there intentionally to rebuke or warn the people (cp. Lk. xix. 39). Finding a distinguished person (Mt. xxvii. 6) with the 'rebels' called Jesus, the Romans may have believed they had captured the one they had been told about. It was useless for him to deny that he was the man responsible, and with others who had resisted in arms he was dragged off to await trial and sentence.

When the news reached the Jewish Council there was great concern. Knowing Pilate, it would be difficult to convince him of the innocence of the prisoner. They would have to establish that this was a case of mistaken identity, and the only effective way to do it would be to produce Jesus the Nazorean.

After Jesus had left the Temple for the last time his whereabouts were unknown. How thankful and relieved then were the chief priests and elders when Judas came to them with his offer of betrayal. With his co-operation the civil guard was sent in force to Gethsemane to make sure of seizing Jesus at night with the minimum of publicity. A confession was obtained from him that he claimed to be the Messiah, the king of the Jews. An indictment was drawn up accusing him of 'subverting the nation, forbidding payment of tribute to Caesar, claiming to be Messiah, a king' (Lk. xxiii. 2). The prisoner was rushed before Pilate first thing in the morning so as to anticipate the passing of sentence on Barabbas. The governor, seeing he had the man really wanted, and with the servants and henchmen of the chief priests clamouring before him, made a virtue of necessity and released the innocent but luckless Jesus Barabbas. Not so the two militant demonstrators who were also in custody: they were condemned to be crucified with Jesus the Nazorean.[8]

Of course this is only conjecture; but it does present a more reasonable and likely account of what took place. Eisler, as we have noted, thinks that Jesus Barabbas could have been a well-known partisan of the hierarchy, son of an eminent doctor of the law. Pursuing this suggestion, the identity of this 'distinguished' man may be discoverable.

The name we know him by comes to us in two forms, Bar-Abba and Bar-Rabban. Both are descriptive and give the quality rather than the name of the parent of this Jesus. Now the presiding officer of the Jewish Court administering the Mosaic Law and dealing with matters of ritual was the high priest. But he was given a deputy who could preside in his absence, and who bore the title of *Ab* (Aramaic, *Abba*) *Beth-Din,* Father of the Court of Justice. This official also had the honorific description of *Rabban* (Master). We find attributed to Jesus the saying, 'Be not ye called Rabbi, for one is your Master, even Christ. . . . And call no man Father upon the earth; for one is your Father, which is in heaven' (Mt. xxiii. 8-9). The saying is associated with the Scribes and Pharisees who 'sit in Moses' ' seat, and may in its original form have had reference to the High Court officer called Father and Master. By courtesy of the Sadducean majority in the Sanhedrin the office of deputy of the high priest was assigned to one of the Pharisee members, who were in the minority. According to Rabbinical tradition the office had been conferred at about this period on the leading Pharisee Gamaliel, who was the first to be addressed as Rabban.

Was Jesus Bar-Abba, or Bar-Rabban, in fact a son of Rabban Gamaliel? Naturally this is speculation. But it can be urged that it is somewhat strange to find this eminent Pharisee, known to be strongly opposed to heterodoxy, speaking up later for leniency to be shown to Peter and John, and citing with reference to Jesus cases of religiously inspired revolutionary activities which proved abortive. He calls for the release of the disciples by the Council on the grounds that if their activities are of men it will come to naught; 'but if it be of God, ye cannot overthrow it' (Acts v. 34-40). Indeed, the Nazoreans, as their tradition declares, claimed Gamaliel as a secret sympathizer, who apprised them of measures against them contemplated by the chief priests. Was the Rabban seeking to save the Apostles out of gratitude, remembering that he owed his own son's life to the Jesus whose followers they were? Had Jesus the Nazorean not in the nick of time been arrested and crucified, it would have been his own Jesus who suffered on the cross.[9]

The documents in which confidence has been reposed are themselves so inadequate, partial, and of such dubious historicity, that there is need and every justification for a search for enlightenment through deductions from all the data that can be assembled and explored.

If we have to be critical, we have also to be adventurous, and not neglect clues because they reach us through unfamiliar channels. In the absence of any single reliable authority the whole of our enterprise has to be one of imaginative reconstruction, but one which does not do violence to evidence on which we can fairly depend.

NOTES AND REFERENCES

1. This view was expressed by Robert Eisler in *The Messiah Jesus and John the Baptist* (Methuen, 1931). We return to it later in the chapter.
2. During the war with the Romans the defenders mined under the wall of Fort Antonia towards the attackers' earthworks. By igniting the timber in the tunnel the Roman earthworks collapsed. Later, when the Roman assault on the Antonia developed, even the siege engines made little impression on the wall. The fortress only fell because of the previous mining beneath it by the Jews (Josephus, *J.W.*, V. 469–72; VI. 26–8). The fall of the tower at Siloam may similarly have been due to undermining by the Jews of Jerusalem in the outbreak to which Luke is alluding, bringing down the structure on those who set fire to the timber props.
3. See Eisler, *op. cit*, pp. 500–10. He is largely followed by Joel Carmichael, *The Death of Jesus*. The author had the privilege of knowing Robert Eisler personally for twenty years. He was a man of widespread interests and great erudition, with a fabulous memory, being ready to tackle almost any subject. He had a child-like innocence and curiosity; but when he had got hold of an idea he would brook no contradiction of it, and pushed his often brilliant insights too far.
4. The reader who wishes to study this and other additions in the Slavonic Josephus will find them readily in H. St John Thackeray's translation of the *Jewish War* in the Loeb Classical Library edition, where they are printed as an Appendix to the third volume.
5. Many of the Pharisees rejected the idea of a Warrior Messiah. See Schonfield, *The Passover Plot*.
6. For obvious reasons it is impossible to go into the mass of details assembled by Eisler in his researches, and his book must be consulted accordingly.
7. See Eisler, *op. cit*, p. 473ff.
8. While the present writer's contentions in *The Passover Plot* remain valid for him as regards its main thesis, there is room for the circumstances here indicated. The Passion story is invested with even more realism and significance. On the Barabbas question, Joel Carmichael, *The Death of Jesus*, largely depends on Eisler.
9. Interestingly, in Christian sectarian and Muslim sources we find a garbled tradition that someone who looked like Jesus was arrested and crucified in his stead. See Schonfield, *According to the Hebrews* (Duckworth, 1937).

CHAPTER 7

THE SEETHING CITY

An important ingredient in our approach to what followed the crucifixion of Jesus and his fellow-sufferers has to be a mental transference to the scene, so that in seeking to recreate it we are sensitive to the feelings and reactions of the Jewish people as well as of the disciples. The Gospels do not present us with a balanced historical description of the circumstances. They present us with a cultic drama, which utilizes certain valuable recollections, but employs them in a manner that will contribute most effectively to convey a certain impression. They concentrate on a hero who is tremendously alone in his last hours, deprived of the support of God and man, and jeered at by multitudes of his own race. The very earth shudders at what is happening, and the sun hides itself from the sight. The tragedy is pitiful and tremendously moving. The suffering is real enough; but we are all the time aware that much of what is being put before us is fictitious, an artistic creation, a kind of Miracle Play, designed to appeal both to our sympathy and prejudices. The authors, however, are not simply using their imagination. Much of what they relate is woven out of passages of the Scriptures, interpreted as having been fulfilled in the Messiah's Passion, which thus is given a unique significance.

We have to free ourselves from the spell cast upon us by the Gospels, and almost bludgeon our way towards the reality with which they are so little concerned.

What does not ring true, when tested by the criteria we are able to apply as a result of scholarly researches, we have boldly to set aside. This holds good for the total circumstances described, and affects all the participants and not only the central figure. We have to recapture understandingly the conditions and motivations as these are revealed by historical investigation, and be capable of entering into the whole emotional environment. Here more is required than studious analysis and erudition. The historian needs the equipment of other disciplines, but he also needs the qualities of the journalist and reporter. In what he is covering he must be right in the thick of things, observing, questioning, getting different viewpoints, alive to atmosphere.

It is incongruous that, after all the excitement in Jerusalem in Passion Week, to which the Gospels bear witness, everything suddenly falls completely flat. The disciples of Jesus are of course shocked and miserable, and remain in hiding fearful of arrest, but otherwise this first day of Passover in A.D. 36 is apparently a quiet peaceful Sabbath day. One wants to scream at the Evangelists, 'Don't you realize what it means to these hundreds of thousands of Jews that yesterday out there beyond the walls men have been crucified by the Romans, and in particular one whom multitudes had believed was their expected king! Can you be so utterly indifferent to these unhappy people's feelings?'

Public executions were no novelty to the inhabitants of Jerusalem; but no one before had been crucified as King of the Jews. To every Jew, no matter where he stood politically, this went to the heart. The whole city must have been seething on that Sabbath day.

We have been apprised in our sources of sensational events which preceded the arrest of Jesus, of anticipations whether welcomed or feared that a Messianic rising was imminent. There had been demonstrations, and even in all probability a show of militancy. Dispositions had been made by the authorities to deal with the threat of a clash between the Zealot partisans and the Roman forces. The danger had been created by the activities of the Galilean prophet Jesus, who had given clear evidence that he believed himself to be the Messiah. There were those who were convinced he would perform a miracle to deliver Israel from Roman rule.

Afraid of a popular outbreak if Jesus was arrested openly at the time of the feast, the Sanhedrin responsible for keeping order had been able to avail themselves of a tip-off which enabled them to seize Jesus by night. Indicted as a rebel against Rome, self-confessed Messiah, king of the Jews, he was rushed before the governor Pilate early in the morning. At his trial those who clamoured for his crucifixion were not the Jewish people, who were in total ignorance of what had happened. They were the largely Gentile servants and henchmen of the chief priests mustered by their masters to do their bidding. The proceedings took place in the Upper City at Pilate's residence on the extreme west. The Jewish populace of the Lower City in the remote south-east was not alerted, and the cowed disciples were in concealment behind barred doors.

We need not pursue what followed at the Herodian Palace,[1] except to note the glee of the Roman soldiers in arraying Jesus as a mock king after he had been flogged. 'Here's your king! ' proclaims Pilate malevolently to the official representatives of the nation, and for their greater discomfiture insists that the titulus on the cross of Jesus shall read 'Jesus the Nazorean, King of the Jews'. Thus the brutal Roman showed how he hated and despised those he had so grossly misgoverned during his ten years of office.

When news did reach the people of the crosses set up on Golgotha, and some of them went in misery to the scene, they witnessed not only the agony of the victims, but the words which so insultingly spelled out the death of the hopes so many had cherished. Was there never to be an end of the tribulation of Israel? Wailing and beating their breasts they came away.

This was indeed a black and bleak commemoration of the freedom of Israel from bondage. Grief was mingled with rising anger. We may believe that not only Pilate was cursed and abused, but also the chief priests and Council. Yet what could be done? No appeal could be made to Tiberius, since Jesus had revealed himself as king, and that was high treason against the emperor.

But early in the new week strange reports were circulating in the streets and markets. It was being whispered that the body of Jesus had disappeared from the tomb in which it had been laid, one constructed by the pious senator Joseph of Arimathea. Some women who had been followers of Jesus had discovered the tomb open and empty. This was a fact which had been verified. Who had removed the body? Perhaps the Galileans had done it so that they could re-inter the corpse of Jesus in his native land. If so, it was a dangerous and foolhardy exploit. Others suggested that the Romans might have been responsible, so that there would be no remains of the Nazorean to inspire others to revolt.[2] It was impossible to find an answer to the puzzle while the festival was in progress, and at the end most of the pilgrims, including the Galileans, had streamed away from the city, returning to their respective homes.

But another idea might have been voiced among the devout. While on the cross, it was said, Jesus had called upon the prophet Elijah. Had God answered that call and taken His servant on high as the great prophet had been carried aloft in a fiery chariot? It was taught by the Pharisees that just as Moses had disappeared from Egypt and had later reappeared to free his people from slavery, so would the Messiah disappear and appear again to save Israel.[3]

It was an idea that could bring a measure of consolation to the pious and credulous, but for most, especially the ardent nationalists, such a notion was an acceptance of defeat. They wanted action, not a juggling with texts that caused failure and suggested knuckling under for an indefinite period. The young men would have grown old, and still nothing might have happened to throw out the Romans. All right, there could be a miracle! But it was better to believe that God helps those who help themselves.

That self-help might explain the mystery of the empty tomb did not, it would seem, suggest itself even to the disciples. It was not guessed that there could have been an attempt to revive Jesus, which necessitated that he should still be alive when taken down from the cross. How this may have been planned with Joseph of Arimathea I have narrated elsewhere.[4] The body of Jesus would then have secretly been taken from the tomb on Saturday night, and not returned to it when it was found that he was too far gone to recover. On this view, when Jesus had expired, his corpse was hastily buried in a new grave whose whereabouts, like that of Moses, was never subsequently revealed.

Puzzled and disturbed, Jerusalem on the surface slowly quietened down when the shock had been absorbed, as so many other shocks had had to be in these grievous times. But an undercurrent remained, both of bitterness and speculation. Among the masses there was anger with the chief priests, especially with the high priest Caiaphas, for what they had done. They were lackeys of the Romans, concerned to safeguard their wealth and privileges. They were corrupt, unworthy servants of God, anti-messianists who accepted foreign ways and tolerated heathen rule. Saints and militants alike agreed that wickedness in high places was one of the great obstacles to redemption.

But in another quarter, hostile to the Jews, there were repercussions of the recent events in Jerusalem. The Messianic Hope strongly awakened by Jesus, and having an immediate appeal to Fourth Philosophy advocates such as the Zealots and Baptists, had stirred the Samaritans.[5]

Josephus has given an account of what took place (*Antiq.* XVIII. 85-7). Among the Samaritans a prophetic personality appeared, whom the historian chooses to regard as a rogue. He called upon the people to accompany him to Mount Gerizim, 'which in their belief is the most sacred of mountains', where he undertook to reveal to them the sacred vessels Moses had buried there. There was great excitement as the word went round, and more and more Samaritans streamed towards Tirathana, the village chosen as assembly point. Many, as it would appear, carried weapons.

News of the formidable gathering reached Pilate, who was governor of Samaria as well as Judea. Having just suppressed one potential revolt at Jerusalem occasioned by the Galilean prophet Jesus, claiming to be king of the Jews, he was now to his great annoyance confronted with another madman. He may well have thought that there was some connection between the two episodes, and that they were part of a common hostile design. Again he acted promptly and ruthlessly. A force of cavalry and heavy-armed infantry was rushed to the foot of Mount Gerizim to block the crowd's advance. Not to be thwarted, the Samaritans full of religious fervour pressed forward. Josephus indicates that there was a pitched battle in which a number of Samaritans were killed and the rest put to flight.

'Many prisoners were taken, of whom Pilate put to death the principal leaders and those who were most influential among the fugitives.'

The wrathful and aggrieved Samaritan Council thereupon sent a deputation to Vitellius, legate of Syria and Pilate's superior, who was probably at his seat at Antioch. They charged Pilate with the unprovoked slaughter of innocent victims, claiming that they had not assembled as rebels against Rome, but as refugees from the governor's persecution.

Vitellius, who by this time must have had enough of hearing of the governor's aggravations and misdeeds, decided to take firm action. If things went on like this the whole Province might become disaffected and endanger Roman rule and revenues, circumstances which Tiberius would not tolerate. The legate therefore sent his friend Marcellus to Jerusalem to take charge of Jewish affairs, while he ordered Pilate to return to Rome to answer to the emperor for what was charged against him by the Jews and Samaritans.

Pilate never resumed his post and on the emperor's death in March, A.D. 37, a new governor was in due course sent by his successor. We should therefore date the Samaritan incident in A.D. 36, in all probability – as we shall suggest – early in the summer of that year.

Josephus has furnished only a rough and not quite exact account of what this affair was all about. The Samaritans, like the Jews, were in expectation of the coming of a prophet like Moses. For them Gerizim was the holy mount of blessing. The true Temple could therefore only be established on Gerizim, and the Temple set up at Jerusalem was an act of Jewish apostasy. All had gone well for Israel in the days of Joshua until the time of the high priest Uzzi. Then had come evil times, the *Fanuta*, the turning away of God's favour, and these had continued. In Uzzi's day the sacred vessels had been secretly hidden on Mount Gerizim, and these would be brought to light at the *Rahuta*, the era when God's favour would be restored. The event would be indicated by the advent of the *Taheb*, the Restorer. Through him the genuine Law given to Moses would, so to speak, be re-given and universally acknowledged, and the faithful would enter into the promised bliss.[6] That a claimant to be the Taheb should have appeared at this juncture is eloquent of the widespread conviction at this time that the Last Days had come, a conviction to which Jesus had also responded.

Traditionally, the festival known as the Feast of Weeks, Pentecost, the fiftieth day after Passover, commemorated the giving of the Law to Moses on Sinai. It may well have been believed by the Samaritans, therefore, that the Taheb would manifest himself at Pentecost. The prophet who called the people to Mount Gerizim was evidently representing himself to be he. The festival, as we shall discover, had a special significance for the Zadokite-Essenes, and this has a bearing on why it was at Pentecost that the disciples of Jesus experienced the outpouring of the Holy Spirit.

There is a strong probability, accordingly, that the Samaritan incident took place towards the end of May or in early June of A.D. 36, and this would fit in with the other date indications; for it must have been well into the summer of that year when Vitellius, after representations to him by the Samaritan Council, put Marcellus in temporary charge of affairs.

Pilate had made powerful Jewish as well as Samaritan enemies, but had it not been for this fresh outrage coming so swiftly on the heels of others he might still have continued in office. In the event the Jews had their religious enemies to thank for his removal.

Nevertheless, Marcellus must have reported to Vitellius that considerable unrest in Jerusalem remained. Relief that Pilate had been sent to Rome allowed it to be supposed, as indeed was the case, that the legate of Syria was extremely anxious to moderate anti-Roman feeling. This was an occasion, therefore, to press for various measures which would mitigate the severity of Roman rule, especially in matters affecting Jewish religious sentiment. In the circumstances Vitellius thought it well to visit Jerusalem in person. We have seen the reasons for believing that the visit took place towards the end of August or in early September.[7]

The actions of Vitellius at Jerusalem speak for themselves. He was determined to be conciliatory. Josephus says (*Antiq.* XVIII. 90-5) that the legate remitted to the inhabitants of the city all taxes on the sale of agricultural produce. He also agreed that the vestments of the high priest and all his ornaments should be retained in the Temple in custody of the priests, as had been their privilege before.[8] It had been a strong Jewish grievance that the sacred robes in which the high priest officiated were held, between festivals, by the Roman guard in Fort Antonia. It had been one matter for the vestments to be laid up there in the time of the Hasmonean rulers, who were both high priests and heads of state, and quite another when the two offices were separated under Herod the Great. He had maintained the practice to give him a hold over his subjects, 'so that they would never rise in insurrection against him'. The Romans when they took over no doubt had the same idea; but what might be just tolerated under a Jewish king was intolerable when the custodians were heathen. Their retention of the garments was an insult to Almighty God.

This concession pleased both priests and people. But one other may be attributed to popular insistence. Vitellius deposed Caiaphas as high priest. However, it would neither be politic nor financially desirable to offend the rich and powerful house of Annas. Therefore he replaced the son-in-law of Annas by one of his sons called Jonathan.

Thus it transpired that the crucifixion of Jesus did not go entirely unavenged. Within a few months both the individuals primarily responsible, the Roman governor and the Jewish high priest, were divested of their authority. The deeply aggrieved Jewish populace was partly appeased.

NOTES AND REFERENCES

1. The circumstances have been described by the author in *The Passover Plot,* and the question of Barabbas has been dealt with in the previous chapter.
2. These of course are not verifiable suppositions. But then neither is the story in Matthew that it was held among the Jews that the disciples had stolen the body of Jesus to support their claim that he had risen from the dead. No doubt such an argument was used in later controversy, and Matthew counters it with the tale of a guard put on the tomb which would

have prevented access to it by the disciples. The other Gospels know nothing of any measure of this kind, which is highly fanciful. What may actually have happened has been fully considered and discussed in *The Passover Plot,* and has since been fictionally treated by Frank Yerby in his novel *Judas, My Brother.*

3. The Midrash *Shir haShirim Rabba* on Cant. ii. 9, 'My beloved is like a roe or a young hart,' comments: 'A roe appears and is hid, appears and is hid again. So our first redeemer [Moses] appeared and was hid, and at length appeared again. So our last redeemer [the Messiah] shall be revealed to them, and shall be hid again from them . . . and shall be revealed again.' The Targum on Micah. iv. 8 paraphrases, 'And thou, Messiah of Israel, who art concealed on account of the offences of the congregation of Zion, to thee shall the kingdom come.' The idea of the Messiah being caught up to heaven had one of its derivations in Daniel's vision of the Son of Man borne on clouds into the presence of the Ancient of Days, so as to receive his kingdom. A legend was current that Menahem, descendant of Judas of Galilee, was taken to heaven in his infancy as Messiah, and such a legend also appears in the Revelation (xii. 5). See Schonfield, *The Lost Book of the Nativity of John* (T. & T. Clark, 1929).
4. See Schonfield, *The Passover Plot,* Part One, chs. xii-xiii. I there put forward the view that Jesus had expected to survive crucifixion, and had planned with Joseph of Arimathea for a drug to be administered to him while on the cross which would give the appearance of death. Later his body would be removed from the tomb by Joseph so that he could be revived. This plan had not been made known to the disciples.
5. See Part One, Chapter 3.
6. See Gaster, *Samaritan Eschatology*. I have paid many visits to the Samaritans and studied their traditions, and was instrumental in building them a school for their children at Nablus, at the foot of Mount Gerizim.
7. See Part One, Chapter 3, p. 53, and note 8 on p. 55.
8. In *Antiq.* XV. 405, Josephus had said earlier that Vitellius did not authorize the handing over of the vestments until he had consulted the emperor by letter, and that Tiberius had granted the request. It would certainly have been appropriate that the transfer should be made at the time of the Jewish high festivals in the autumn, especially before the Day of Atonement.

CHAPTER 8

BETWEEN TWO FEASTS

If our dating of the Samaritan incident is correct it was at this very season, the festival of Pentecost of A.D. 36, that the Spirit of God came upon the followers of Jesus in Jerusalem, and they began to prophesy. What had led up to this manifestation? Here many problems arise which do not belong exclusively to history. But those that relate to human behaviour, to individual reactions, are capable of substantial understanding.

The belief that Jesus had risen from the dead and had ascended temporarily to heaven governs the transformation that took place. But the emergence of this conviction is by no means the whole explanation of the circumstances. There is much more that calls for investigation on a less exalted plane, and we must not fight shy of such research. The writer has argued in *The Passover Plot* that the disappearance of the body of Jesus from the tomb can reasonably be accounted for without resort to the idea of resurrection. But it has to be accepted that the disciples did believe that he had risen from the dead and had been taken up to heaven. Our concern is with how the conviction arose; and in this connection we must make clear exactly what resurrection meant. We are not entitled to be evasive by reference to some phenomenon of quite another order.

Resurrection is not the same thing as spirit or soul survival of death. It has nothing to do with wraiths, ghosts or spirit materializations.

Resurrection means the 'getting up' of one who has been lying down as a corpse, the reanimation of a dead body, so that the individual breathes and moves and has all his physical functions restored. It is as the awakening from sleep or coma. Jewish resurrection teaching was quite definite about this, and the Gospel stories of the raising from the dead of the widow of Nain's son and of Lazarus conform to it. As regards the doctrine in general the only allowable difference between life as experienced in the present world and life as it would be experienced in the world to come (the Messianic Age) was that the restored body would be endowed with greater permanence, even conceivably with immortality.

In spite of certain eastern myths the idea of resurrection was alien to the thinking of the Graeco-Roman world. When Paul spoke of it in Athens his contentions were received with polite incredulity. He was prepared to concede, however, that the resurrection body, though quite definitely a body, would be of a new order, not flesh and blood, akin to that of the angels.[1] This view gained ascendancy in the Church, but it met with a great deal of resistance for a long time. As regards Jesus, the Gospels on the whole reflect what resurrection signified unequivocally, when they make the 'risen' saviour display his wounds, invite the disciples to touch and handle him, and call for food which he proceeds to eat. He does everything conceivable to demonstrate that he is solid flesh and bone.[2]

We are therefore not to speak of any 'resurrection' of Jesus unless we mean the reanimation of his physical body after death. Certain theologians may want to treat the references to the open and empty tomb as secondary; but they are in fact basic. The tomb by the manner in which it was closed had to be opened from outside, by rolling back the stone that covered the mouth. The only entertainable possibilities were that either men or angels had opened it; the object being to remove the body for attempted resuscitation or other purpose, sinister perhaps, or to enable a physical person, already reanimated, to emerge.

Paul gives a list of 'seeings' of Jesus. Luke and John add others. These only 'witness' to resurrection if it was the physical Jesus restored to life who was claimed to have been seen. Paul could not see Jesus in this manner, only in vision, since prior to the apostle's conversion it was held that he had ascended to heaven. His body was no longer on earth. Thereafter, pending the Messiah's return, it was only in dreams and visions that he could appear to his followers. In some of these he would be seen in heaven, sitting or standing at the right hand of God. Paul's experience might confirm to him that the report of the resurrection was true; but it did not qualify as proof of the order asserted by the 'seeings' of others which he lists, presumed to have taken place before the Ascension.

When the resurrection proposition won acceptance there could be argued in its favour that it represented a Messianic necessity which previously had been discerned by very few, one of whom was Jesus himself. There had been some glimmerings of it in Essene speculation, where the accent was on Assumption; but there was nothing to cause it to be stressed or pursued until the circumstances of the unexpected death of the Messiah called forth a revelation. Once this solution of the puzzle had registered it was quite surprising how much evidence of its correctness could be discovered in the Scriptures. Jesus, it was said, had himself disclosed all the relevant passages. As might be expected in connection with the Son of David the Psalms of David were found especially eloquent prophetically. The texts 'foretold' not only the sufferings of the Messiah, but also his triumph over death.

It was written: 'The Lord said unto my lord, Sit thou at My right hand, until I make thine enemies thy footstool. The Lord shall send the rod of thy strength out of Zion: rule thou in the midst of thine enemies' (Ps. cx. 1-2). 'The right hand of the Lord is exalted. . . . I shall not die, but live, and declare the works of the Lord. The Lord hath chastened me sore: but He hath not given me over unto death. . . . The stone which the builders refused is become the head of the corner' (Ps. cxviii. 16-23). 'I have set the Lord always before me: because He is at my right hand I shall not be moved. Therefore my heart is glad, and my glory rejoiceth: my flesh also shall rest in hope. For Thou wilt not leave my life in the grave; neither wilt Thou suffer Thine holy one to see corruption. Thou wilt show me the path of life: in Thy presence is fulness of joy; at Thy right hand are pleasures for evermore' (Ps. xvi. 8-11).

Such ideas were unknown to the original apostles, simple fishermen from the Sea of Galilee and the like. Initially, when the empty tomb was reported, this only conveyed that others unknown had removed the body of Jesus for some purpose of their own. To their grief and despair, having trusted that Jesus was the one who would deliver Israel, there was now added the misery that the master's remains were in alien and perhaps hostile hands, and there was not even left to them the comfort of being able to mourn at the place where he was laid to rest.

There was nothing to keep these Galileans in Jerusalem. When the Passover ended they went home. Those who were fishermen returned to their trade. The Fourth Gospel says that they were Simon Peter, Thomas Twin, Nathanael of Cana, John and Jacob the sons of Zebedee, and two others, presumably Andrew and Philip, the latter hailing from Bethsaida. But someone else was with them, the one called 'the disciple whom Jesus loved'. Who was he, and why had he left Jerusalem?

We learn a good deal about this anonymous individual from the

Fourth Gospel and Christian tradition. He appears first as a disciple of John the Baptist, when he became acquainted with Andrew the brother of Peter. When Jesus went to John the Baptist to be baptized, and the Baptist discerns in him the one he has been announcing as his successor, our man with Andrew sought Jesus out the next day and spent a night in discussion with him. They came away the next morning convinced that Jesus was the Messiah. It is to be inferred that the Beloved Disciple continued with Jesus for some time; but he belonged to Judea, and when Jesus concentrated his activities on Galilee he returned to his home in Jerusalem. There is no further reference to him until the Last Supper at Jerusalem. He is found then (Jn. xiii. 23) in a favoured position, leaning on the bosom of Jesus. This suggests that it was in his house that the celebration was being held, which would explain the strange story in the other Gospels of an unknown person, evidently greatly trusted by Jesus, with whom Jesus had secretly planned to keep the Passover at his house (Mk. xiv. 12-16; Mt. xxvi. 17-19; Lk. xxii. 7-13). That the Beloved Disciple had a house in Jerusalem is conveyed by the incident at the crucifixion when Jesus asks him to care for his mother as his own mother, and he takes Mary into his home (Jn. xix. 26-7). That house, which must have been quite large, became the subsequent first headquarters of the disciples in Jerusalem (Acts i. 13-14). The Beloved Disciple would appear to have been a man of note and means. He was well-known to the high priest, possibly a relative (Jn. xviii. 16), and there are strong indications that he was himself a priest.[3]

Thus far on three occasions the Beloved Disciple and Peter are brought together. The first is purely introductory, when Andrew and the Disciple have been with Jesus, and the former fetches his brother Simon. The second is at the Last Supper, when Peter signals to the Disciple to ask Jesus who is going to betray him. The third is when the Disciple procures Peter's entry into the courtyard of the high priest's palace. We come now to a fourth occasion after the crucifixion (Jn. xx), when Mary Magdalene comes to Peter and the Disciple with the alarming news that the body of Jesus is missing from the tomb. The two men run to the sepulchre, and the Disciple, who may have been younger than Peter, outdistances him and arrives first. He stoops and looks into the tomb, but does not enter. We may attribute his reluctance to his being a priest afraid of incurring defilement. Peter has no such scruples. He goes in and finds the tomb empty. Thereupon the Disciple also enters, 'and he saw, and believed. For as yet they knew not the scripture that he must rise again from the dead.'

We have the claim here, and it is an important clue, that the one whom we may now speak of as John the Priest was the first to hold the conviction of the resurrection of Jesus. What had disposed him to entertain this belief, which had not entered Peter's head or that of Mary Magdalene?

What we learn of the Beloved Disciple suggests that he was a young man of good education with a strong leaning towards Messianism and mysticism. He had joined the circle of John the Baptist, and it is reasonable to suggest that like the young Josephus, also of priestly stock, he had studied with the Essenes. It is significant that in the Fourth Gospel much more is made of a take-over by the Jesus movement from the Baptist movement, and that this Gospel has closer affinities than any of the others with the ideas and language of the Dead Sea Scrolls. Likewise we find in the Fourth Gospel a greater insistence on the need of the Messiah to fulfil the Scriptures, and there is brought much more into prominence a Heavenly Man (Son of Man) doctrine. Some of the same things that are characteristic of the Fourth Gospel are also characteristic of the book of Revelation.

The ramifications of the Baptist movement are intriguing. It seems to have had some connection both with the Zealots and the Zadokite-Essenes. By tradition, the Mandaeans of today, who call themselves Nazoreans, are representative of that ancient baptizing movement whose hero was John the son of Zechariah of the priestly family of Abijah. The Mandaean literature and liturgy reveals many similarities of teaching and belief to what we find in the Dead Sea Scrolls.[4] So we may deduce that there was an inter-relationship between those who followed the several expressions of the Way. Essentially, the groups were on the same side: they were the Elect comprehensively, whatever might be their differences of emphasis and attachments to particular personalities deemed to fulfil their messianic expectations. We are compelled to give these intimations full weight when we consider how these Nazoreans, whom we think of as the original Christians, came to create their own party.

It was a man who was a bridge figure on whom it first dawned that Jesus as Messiah had risen from the dead. The confusing accounts in the Gospels reflect a situation which is not fully disclosed.

But there has not been wholly eradicated that Peter and others of the Twelve had been extremely dubious of John the Priest's interpretation of the phenomenon of the empty tomb, and that they returned to Galilee still unconvinced. Mary Magdalene's assertion that she had seen and spoken to the risen Jesus was dismissed as the wishful thinking of a woman who was mentally unbalanced. Indeed, only the Fourth Gospel speaks of her experience. Neither the other Gospels nor Paul make any reference to it. The Beloved Disciple does so because she was on his side.

The story of the Beloved Disciple going to Galilee with those who went back there suggests that he was continuing his efforts at persuasion, and endeavouring to get them to return to Jerusalem. We have the extraordinary account of the unknown man on the lake shore identified as Jesus by the Beloved Disciple, and credited by Peter solely on John's pronouncement. Informed that the man was Jesus, none of the disciples dared to ask him, 'Who are you?' (Jn. xxi. 12). A kind of parallel in Matthew admits that some doubted (Mt. xxviii. 17).

Luke's Gospel gives another hint of Peter's disbelief. At the Last Supper Jesus had said to him, 'Simon, Simon, behold, Satan has desired to have you, that he may sift you as wheat: but I have prayed for you, that your faith will not fail: and when you are converted, strengthen your brethren' (Lk. xxii. 31-2). We have something to the same effect in the lakeside story in the Fourth Gospel, where Jesus three times asks Peter if he loves him, and bids him take care of his followers ('feed my sheep'). Then it comes out that the devoted Peter has become jealous of John. 'Then Peter, turning round, sees the disciple whom Jesus loved following. . . . Peter seeing him says, Lord, what about him?' Jesus virtually replies, 'Never mind about *him*. You follow me.'

Early in the Acts of the Apostles we find Peter working in harmony with a certain John, who is presumed to be the stormy son of Zebedee, usually mentioned with his brother. But Luke may be mistaken, and the John concerned may really have been John the Priest of Jerusalem, whose house had become the headquarters of the disciples. It is conceivable that, both as regards belief in the resurrection of Jesus and the organization of the Nazorean community, John the Priest played a much greater part than it was desired subsequently to acknowledge.

The situation demanded a man of John's calibre and associations, who believed himself to be guided by the Essene 'Spirit of Truth' as one of the 'Sons of Light'.[5] We can discern this, however, only because we have the Fourth Gospel, incorporating the personal remembrances of the Beloved Disciple himself when he was a very old man living far away from Jerusalem at Ephesus in Asia Minor.

It is unfortunate that we have to struggle so much to obtain even an approximate idea of what was going on. Much material has been lost as well as destroyed, and much that has endured is garbled and perverted. Only by a resolute attention to detail and by ranging over a vast amount of evidential data does there emerge an assurance that we have in our grasp what must be fairly close to the reality. Many puzzles nevertheless remain, for lack of any sources which will throw light on them. One of these concerns the Nazorean triumvirate. In the synoptic Gospels they are Peter, with Jacob and John the sons of Zebedee. But when Paul writes of the pillar apostles of his time the names are the same, but at least one of the three is a different individual. Jacob now is not the son of Zebedee, but the brother of Jesus, and it may well be that the John of Paul is also not the son of Zebedee but John the Priest. There are other evidences of a Galilean tradition in opposition to a Jerusalem tradition, which crop up in the accounts of the resurrection and ascension of Jesus.

Thus there have come down to us elements of different versions of what occurred between Passover and Pentecost. The official line, representing the Jerusalem tradition, emphasized the new beginning, brought about by the transference of the centre of activity from Galilee to the metropolis. This is particularly reflected in Luke-Acts. Luke accepts to know nothing of any forsaking of Jerusalem by some of the apostles. None of them had even temporarily returned to Galilee. On the instruction of the risen Messiah they stayed in the city, and having witnessed his ascension they were continually in the Temple, praising and blessing God.

But recollection was not wholly stamped out. Memories remained of initial doubts and difficulties, of some inducement having been required to convince Peter and others who had gone home to Galilee still grieving that they should return to Jerusalem, in so many respects an alien environment. They were plain country folk with an outlandish northern accent, unused to life in a great city. Nothing short of conversion to belief that in conformity with a Messianic necessity Jesus had risen from the dead and ascended to heaven could have brought them to forsake Galilee and take up residence and begin a fresh life among the Judeans.

Recognition of how very much the Galilean fishermen were themselves fish out of water in Jerusalem raises the gravest doubts that the apostles could have devised and carried out the measures of organization that appear almost instantaneously to have come into effect. This kind of engagement was beyond their experience and competence. It is indicated in the Acts that the apostles did not take readily to the chores of a settled and substantial community (Acts vi. 1-6). We must hold, therefore, that they entered into a pattern which others were responsible for creating. The character of it, as conveyed by Luke, is akin to that of the Essenes.[6] And this tends to confirm what we have proposed, that there was a tie-up with established communities of other expressions of the Way, and that John the Priest had something to do with this.

What we are offered in the Acts is a very sketchy and over-simplified description of the circumstances with many legendary features. Much of the book reads like selected stories from history retold for children. None the less there are indications of many things which are not being related.

Besides John the Priest there is another individual who is a key figure, Jacob the brother of Jesus, who became head of the Nazorean Community. Paul mentions an appearance to him of the risen Jesus; but Luke says nothing about this or of how he came to a position of authority. We have to turn to other sources for this vital information. *The Gospel of the Hebrews* tells us that Jacob had sworn not to eat or drink until he was assured that Jesus had risen from the dead. After the resurrection Jesus had come to Jacob and called for a table and bread to be brought. He said the blessing, broke the bread, and offered it to Jacob, saying, 'My brother, eat thy bread, for the Son of Man is risen from among them that sleep.'[7]

The *Gospel of Thomas*[8] (Saying 11) informs us that 'the disciples said to Jesus, "We know that you will go away from us. Who will be great over us?" Jesus said to them, "In the place to which you have gone [i.e. Jerusalem], you will go to Jacob the Just, for whose sake heaven and earth were created." ' We have here a Hebraic tradition that the apostles were instructed to place themselves under the leadership of the Messiah's brother at Jerusalem. Jacob, as reported by Hegesippus, was a lifelong nazirite like John the Baptist, who followed the ascetic Essene way of life, and consequently he could be another link between the Galilean apostles and the groups of the Saints at Jerusalem. Luke allows that after the ascension of Jesus from the Mount of Olives the apostles were together in the house with the upper room, the house which we have suggested was the home of John the Priest on the Ophel, and that with them were the women who had followed Jesus and also his mother and his brothers (Acts i. 13-14).

It is significant that the Acts emphasizes the importance of Jerusalem because it would be to the Mount of Olives that Jesus would return from heaven 'to restore the kingdom to Israel'. This arose from interpretation of ancient prophecies.

There is no reason to doubt that after it was agreed that Jesus had risen from the dead and ascended to the right hand of God many claimed that they had seen him in one fashion or another before his ascension. This was only natural. But the impression we receive is that it was the contention on doctrinal and prophetic grounds, which called for an acute Essene type of exegesis, 'that the Messiah ought to have suffered these things, and to enter into his glory' (Lk. xxiv. 26), that induced the 'seeings', and not the other way round. There was an admitted 'slowness of mind' initially to credit the thesis of the Messiah's resurrection, which took hold largely through John's intuition and sophisticated reasoning. The Galileans dearly wanted it to be true, and they yielded thankfully, though not too readily, to the arguments of those whose superior knowledge they respected. The Spirit came when a common fervour of belief had been generated, and 'unanimity' had been achieved, when the disciples were of one heart and mind.

The revelation counted for so much, the transformation it caused was so great, the relief was so tremendous, that it induced a fervour and exuberance bordering on hysteria. The disciples, we are told, acted as if they were drunk, singing and declaiming, intelligibly and in gibberish. A truth had been vouchsafed to them they could never have arrived at of their own accord: they were transported, ecstatic. The *Paraclete* (Comforter, Adviser) in the guise of John had done his work. Like a rushing wind, like burning flames, the Holy Spirit was poured forth. It was just as the Prophet Joel had described.[9] The inhabitants of Jerusalem, and the pilgrims come from many lands for the Pentecost, were startled and began to catch fire themselves as the waves of emotion reached and engulfed them.

There were wild scenes in the Lower City, people crying, praying, hugging, kissing. 'That same day there were added to the disciples about three thousand souls' (Acts ii. 41).

NOTES AND REFERENCES

1. See I Cor. xv., also Mk. xii. 25.
2. This is further emphasized in non-canonical sources. In the *Gospel of the Hebrews* it was written, 'And when he [Jesus] came to Peter and those who were with Peter, he said to them, Lo, feel me and see that I am no bodiless spirit. And forthwith they touched him and believed' (quoted by Jerome, *Of Illustrious Men,* 16). Origen found a similar passage in *The Doctrine of Peter*. Ignatius, *To the Smyrnaeans,* writes, 'I know and I believe that he [Jesus] is in the flesh even after his resurrection.' Ignatius was under the influence of the Fourth Gospel.
3. Both the Gospel and the Revelation show great familiarity with the Temple and its ritual. That the Beloved Disciple had been a Jewish priest was stated by Polycrates, Bishop of Ephesus at the end of the second century, in a letter to Victor, Bishop of Rome (Euseb. *Eccl. Hist.* V. xxiv). See Schonfield, *Those Incredible Christians,* ch. xii.
4. See usefully the notes in Theodor H. Gaster, *The Dead Sea Scriptures in English Translation* (Doubleday Anchor Books, 1956).
5. John's Gospel (xvi. 13) makes Jesus say that 'the Spirit of Truth will guide you into all truth'. In the *Community Rule* among the Dead Sea Scrolls the Spirit of Truth is the guide of the Children of Light. In a midrash it is taught, 'To that generation [in Egypt] Thou didst send redemption through two redeemers, as it is said (Ps. cv. 26), "He sent Moses His servant and Aaron whom He had chosen." And also to this generation (of the Last Times) He sendeth two, corresponding to those other two. "Send out Thy Light and Thy Truth" (Ps. xliii. 3). "Thy Light," that is the Prophet Elijah of the house of Aaron. . . . and "Thy Truth," that is Messiah the son of David. . . .' (*Midr. Tehill.* xliii. 1). The Elijah figure of John the Baptist is described as 'a burning and a shining light' (Jn. v. 35), while 'grace and truth came by Jesus the Messiah' (Jn. i. 17). The prologue to the Fourth Gospel, however, makes Jesus the light as well, in keeping with the doctrine that the Messiah was both priest and king. See further, Schonfield, *Secrets of the Dead Sea Scrolls*, ch. ix.
6. See below, Part Two, Chapter 9.
7. Quoted from the *Gospel of the Hebrews* by Jerome, *Of Illustrious Men,* 2.
8. *The Gospel of Thomas* is not strictly a Gospel, but a collection of sayings and teachings of Jesus recorded by the Apostle Judas Thomas, according to a Coptic manuscript found at Nag Hammadi in Egypt among a number of Gnostic books. Portions of the same work in an earlier Greek text had come to light previously in Egypt at Oxyrhynchus at the end of the nineteenth century and early in the twentieth. The work is believed to have preserved certain Jewish-Christian traditions.
9. Joel ii. 28–32 (Acts ii. 17–21), and see below, Chapter 9.

CHAPTER 9

THE PENTECOST REVOLUTION

The Acts of the Apostles is the only book in the New Testament to furnish some account of the genesis of the Nazorean Party, and therefore it is of great service. The author, writing early in the second century A.D., must have had access to sources of information, still extant at that time, which had preserved recollections of Nazorean history in the period before the Jewish War with the Romans. These sources were at least in part documentary. But whatever they may have been, and we can hazard some guesses, Luke employed only what would suffice for the purpose he had in view, chiefly to describe how the Gospel had come to the Gentiles by means especially of Peter and Paul. We are not being offered a history of the Nazorean Party in its formative years, but rather an edifying and apologetic story which would serve as an introduction to Christianity. We can thankfully avail ourselves of certain illuminating particulars; but we need to put a greal deal more flesh on these bare bones, and address ourselves more directly and much more comprehensively to the task of reconstructing the character and fortunes of the Jesus movement in Judea.

The second and third chapters of the Acts are largely taken up with speeches put into the mouth of Peter as chief spokesman for the followers of Jesus. These harangues were composed by the author to convey ideas and sentiments he considered to be appropriate, availing himself of an accepted licence exercised by historians to make their accounts more vivid and circumstantial by creating orations for prominent persons to deliver. The Greeks loved making speeches, and set much store by the rhetorical quality of such artificial addresses. Josephus pandered to this taste in his own writings, and Luke modelled himself a good deal on this authority.[1]

The words we are reading, therefore, are substantially those of the narrator who, while he may be seeking to put himself in the position of the speaker, is also making him the mouthpiece of views which it was deemed he should correctly have held. He could, indeed, be credited with sentiments and doctrines he had never entertained, and would in actuality have strenuously repudiated.

The two speeches of Peter, to which we have referred, continually betray the ideas of the Church half a century and more later, and have only the most tenuous links with reality. The composer was quite incapable of speaking as a Jew to Jews. Had he been able to do so, the opportunity would not have been neglected in the Pentecost speech to bring out in relation to Jesus the significance of the festival. Pentecost, the Feast of Weeks, was the festival of first-fruits in the Hebrew calendar. In proclaiming the resurrection it would have been pertinent to speak of the Messiah as 'the first fruits of them that slept'. If Paul could use this telling symbol (I Cor. xv. 20), so could Peter. Pentecost also commemorated the giving of the Law to Moses on Sinai, and it could be affirmed that the Messiah had come in fulfilment of the promise to Moses, to confirm the covenant between God and His people. Something of this is suggested in the second speech (Acts iii. 21-6), but this was not on the occasion of Pentecost. Appreciably the speeches lack the Jewishness that would have lent them verisimilitude. This is typical of Luke, who thinks it will pass for Jewish if he employs Old Testament language. And no doubt for non-Jewish readers he was right.

But we have another concern – that Luke is not giving us a true insight into what had been happening at Jerusalem – and we only get from him certain useful pointers which we have to develop for ourselves. The probabilities are that he could not have thrown much more light on the situation even if he had wished to do so, because it was one of which neither his sources nor he himself would take cognizance.

It is not explained to us why the Nazorean Party should have originated at Pentecost. It was certainly fitting, as we have pointed out. But another factor could have been in evidence having to do with what we touched upon in the last chapter, that the new initiative was given an impetus from existing Fourth Philosophy partisans in Jerusalem. These elements – Pharisees, Essenes, Baptists and Zealots – who alike awaited the 'consolation of Israel' and the coming of the Kingdom of God, must have been greatly exercised by the activities of Jesus and the events of Passion Week. They may further have been affected by the convictions of John the Priest in respect of the common knowledge that Jesus' body had disappeared from the tomb.

We would expect that the cause of Jesus as Messiah would bring in recruits from those bodies who believed that the Last Times had come. Among the original disciples were some drawn from these groups. It is most significant that from its foundation the Nazorean Party exhibits a strong resemblance to Essenism, in both form and manners, and to a considerable extent in ideas and practices. So much so, that fourth-century investigators of Christian Beginnings could hold that the Essenes of Judea and the Therapeutai of Egypt were the early Christians. Also, like the Baptists, the Nazoreans emphasized baptism for the remission of sins, which was made a requisite of membership.[2]

But now we are put much more in the picture by the information furnished by the Dead Sea Scrolls of the importance of Pentecost for the Zadokite-Essenes. It was already known from the book of *Jubilees* (vi. 15-22) that this festival was held in special regard. According to the author of this work the Feast of Weeks had been celebrated in heaven from the day of Creation until the time of Noah, when it began to be celebrated by Noah and his descendants after the Flood. Thus Pentecost for the Essenes was the festival of the Renewal of the Covenant between God and man. The celebration came to be marked by a distinctive ritual among the Zadokite-Essenes. On this day a general assembly of members was held, when their status was reassessed, and on the same occasion new applicants for membership took an oath to observe the Covenant of the Law.

We cannot do better here than to quote Vermes on the solemnity of the Pentecost Assembly.[3]

> The most important of their festivals was the Feast of Weeks [i.e. Pentecost], the Feast of the Renewal of the Covenant. Its ritual is described at the beginning of the *Community Rule* and in an unpublished section of the *Damascus Rule*. Opening the ceremony, the Priests and Levites offer blessings to God and those entering the Covenant with them reply 'Amen, Amen.' The Priests go on to recall the past favours of God and the Levites follow them with a recital of Israel's transgressions. This culminates in a public confession, 'We have strayed! We have disobeyed!' etc., after which the penitents are blessed by the Priests. Then the Levites pronounce a long curse on the 'lot of Satan', and with the Priests they solemnly adjure all those whose repentance is incomplete not to enter the Covenant. 'Cursed be the man', they say, 'who enters this Covenant while walking among the idols of his heart. . . . He shall be cut off from the midst of the Sons of Light and . . . his lot shall be among them that are cursed for ever' (*Community Rule*, 1–11).

The concluding paragraph of the description says: 'Thus shall they do, year by year, for as long as the dominion of Satan endures. The

Priests shall enter first, ranked one after another according to the perfection of their spirit; then the Levites; and thirdly, all the people one after another . . . that every Israelite may know his place in the Community of God according to the everlasting design' (*Community Rule* II; cf. *Damascus Rule* XIV).[4]

It is to be noted that at the close of Peter's Pentecost address, in response to the people's appeal, he calls upon them to repent and be baptized in the name of Jesus for the remission of sins, urging them to 'Save yourselves from this untoward generation' (Acts ii. 38-40). The Pentecost ritual of the Essenes is clearly based on the account in Deuteronomy of the blessings and curses of the Covenant recited to the people of Israel on Gerizim and Ebal, and this reinforces our suggestion that the incident of the Samaritan *Taheb* also took place at Pentecost, for his appearance could only mean that the era of God's favour had at last returned.[5]

In the light of the information we have gleaned from the Dead Sea Scrolls we can now see that the inauguration of the Nazorean Party at Pentecost was not fortuitous. It was the Essene day of solemn renewal of the Covenant, a day when the people were admonished to repent and enrol themselves with the Elect of God, a day, therefore, when the call to give allegiance to Jesus as the Messiah would make a very strong appeal. There was an emotional stimulus inherent in this festival, magnified by Essene custom, which, playing upon the disciples through those connected with them, contributed to fostering an atmosphere both of concord and lively expectation. Essene inspiration designated Pentecost as the day when a signal Divine manifestation might be looked for.

Such a manifestation did take place, according to tradition in the coming of 'the Spirit'. The indications are that the phenomenon was that of *khamsin,* the sirocco.

We are to imagine that June day before Pentecost as being remarkably hot, still and oppressive, the sun glowing in a dull yellowish sky. Those who have experienced the prelude to a sirocco of particular intensity know how it causes headaches, nerviness and mental tension. Few would have slept well that night. Then at the dawning of the festal day, when the disciples were together for the early prayers and praises such as were typical of the Essenes, the storm broke. The psychic effects are stressed by Luke, but the physical description answers to the sirocco. 'Suddenly there came a whistling out of the sky as of a tearing furious blast of wind that filled the house where they were sitting' (Acts ii. 2).

One kind of sirocco, writes W. M. Thomson (*The Land and the Book*), is 'accompanied with vehement wind, which fills the air with dust and fine sand. I have often seen the whole heavens veiled in gloom with this sort of sand-cloud, through which the sun, shorn of his beams, looked like a globe of smouldering fire. It may have been this phenomenon which suggested that strong prophetic figure of Joel, quoted by Peter on the day of Pentecost: "Wonders in the heaven above, and signs on the earth beneath; blood, and fire, and pillars of smoke; the sun shall be turned into darkness, and the moon into blood." The pillars of smoke are probably those columns of sand and dust raised high in the air by local whirlwinds, which often accompany the sirocco.'

No less apt is the sirocco imagery of the psalmist. 'The voice of the Lord is powerful; the voice of the Lord is with force. The voice of the Lord breaketh the cedars; yea, the Lord breaketh the cedars of Lebanon. He maketh them also to skip like a calf; Lebanon and Sirion like a young buffalo. The voice of the Lord cleaveth the flames of fire. The voice of the Lord sets the desert awhirl; the Lord setteth awhirl the desert of Kadesh' (Ps. xxix. 4-8).

The storm released the overcharged feelings of the disciples. They were conscious of an enormous relief. The sirocco had answered to their own condition. They had endured a time of acute misery and distress when hopes had been dashed to the ground by the death and disappearance of Jesus. This had been succeeded by the transporting joy of faith that God had raised him from the dead and wafted him to heaven to receive the kingship he would soon display in majesty on his return to earth.

In token of this truth God had now sent the Ruach, His holy Wind. It was a sign and a portent: they became ecstatic, and broke forth into crying, singing and declamation, as if they were drunk. And drunk indeed they were, with the wonder of it all, with the glory of it all.

It was the exuberance and the positiveness of their testimony to the solution vouchsafed to them of the mystery of the missing Messiah, which as much as any words electrified the multitudes of Jews from many lands participating in Jerusalem in the rejoicings of the Feast of the First-fruits. On them too 'the sign' of the incidence of the sirocco had made its impact.

In modern parlance many were 'turned-on' and joined the community of believers. The Pentecost Revolution had begun. The one declared to be the awaited Son of David and the Son of Man, who was now at the right hand of God, had become the catalyst of a new coalition of loyalist Israelites, separated from and in opposition to the sinners and apostates in high places.

Over Pentecost, it is reported, membership of the Nazorean Party jumped from 120 persons to something like 3,000. 'And all that believed were together, and had all things common; and sold their possessions and goods, and distributed them to all, as everyone had need. And they, continuing daily with one accord in the Temple, and partaking of food from house to house, took their meals with gladness and singleness of mind, praising God, and having favour with all the people. And the Lord added daily to the Community those who should be saved' (Acts ii. 44-7).

So it is disclosed, incidentally, that the populace of Jerusalem – supposedly having demanded the crucifixion of Jesus seven weeks previously – were in the strongest sympathy with what the movement represented. In fact they had been so all along.

What was proclaimed from the Scriptures as having come to pass did not seem to the common people in the least incongruous or far-fetched. Was it not declared by the devout that these were the Last Times? The miracles of the past must surely be repeated today! When people are desperate, they do not argue like lawyers. They simply react. And these were Jews, whose whole history was a record of miracles. Josephus furnishes evidence enough of the temper and credulity of the people, shared in their own manner by the Samaritans, which finally persuaded them that with Divine aid they could overthrow the Romans, however formidable was their military power.

Assuredly we must concede that for a great many Jews, among them members of all the eschatological groups, the Nazorean Party must have had convictions with which they could readily identify. It must have incorporated a great deal of their ideology. If the Church of later times had been given all the facts it might well have had great difficulty in recognizing its forerunner as truly Christian. In many respects the Gospels and the Acts have attempted to put the Christian clock back more than half a century.

We would not think of as particularly Christian a Jewish movement which had no trinitarian doctrine, which accepted Jesus as the Messiah descended from David, but did not ascribe to him deity or even divinity, and held him simply to have been a man sent and endowed by God. Neither would we regard as Christian in any orthodox sense a community which was zealous for the Law of Moses, practised circumcision, worshipped in Temple and synagogue, and was animated by expectations of Israel's national deliverance. Yet this was actually the position of the apostles themselves and those who joined them. We would only say that we have here an undoubted Jewish sect which acknowledged Jesus as Messiah, from which Christianity derived certain of its beliefs and practices.

In the same way, as we have indicated, we have to see the Nazoreans (incorrectly described as Jewish-Christians) as drawing upon and having features in common with the contemporary expressions of eschatological Judaism. The likenesses we find in the New Testament to the language and ideas of the Dead Sea Scrolls are straws in the wind. The literature of the so-called early Church embraced many of the Jewish sectarian books, and Dr Charles in his editing of the Jewish *pseudepigrapha* showed conclusively how much more the New Testament writers utilized these resources than is allowed for in Christian exegesis. Similarly, it has not been sufficiently appreciated to what extent the New Testament reflects the Jewish liturgy. A translation of the New Testament which was accompanied by references and quotations covering all the Jewish non-Biblical sources would astonish Christians and give them a very different perspective.[6]

Certainly, if the Evangelists had not been so anxious to impress on the past the stamp of the attitudes and beliefs of their own period much more of its true image would have come through.

That image had nothing to do with the birth of a new religion distinct from Judaism. The movement created at Pentecost was an expression of Israel's faith in its own future in reliance on Divine promises certified by its Scriptures. The expectation was already strongly present that the time of fulfilment was imminent. It had inspired the formation of bodies of penitents and devotees, and influenced the banding together of freedom-fighters. The advent and mysterious departure of Jesus now permitted the Messianic Hope to focus on a name of deliverance, of God's salvation, Joshua, the name of that successor of Moses who of old had led Israel into the Promised Land.

What was now told to the people explained the secret of the empty tomb. They could readily respond to the announcement that Jesus had escaped extinction by his enemies by a miracle, and been taken to heaven by God, whence he would speedily return to save Israel and execute judgment on the heathen and evil-doers. But also popular ire was intensified against the Romans and their minions for crucifying the Messiah. Associations like that of the Essenes had preached withdrawal from public affairs: they concentrated on a segregated dedication to the observance of the Torah. The Nazorean Party took over a great deal of their thinking and organization and boldly went out to the people. A revolutionary situation was created, because now opposition to the common enemies was for the first time being coordinated.

NOTES AND REFERENCES

1. See above, Part One, Chapter 2. Luke makes Peter address fellow Jews as if he were not himself a Jew, mostly employing the second person plural. But Peter does make reference to the tomb of David which was in close proximity to the place where he is speaking (Acts ii. 29).
2. Baptism 'in the name of Jesus' calls for explanation since it is not generally understood. We learn from Rabbinical sources of baptism 'in the name of' (*Yebam,* fol. 45b). Thus a proselyte was baptized 'in the name of a proselyte', a woman 'in the name of a woman'. 'In the name of' thus represents 'in the capacity of'. To be baptized in the name of Jesus signified 'in identification with Jesus' as an adherent of Jesus. The implication of the Hebraism was afterwards lost (cp. Mt. xxviii. 19).
3. Vermes, *The Dead Sea Scrolls in English,* p. 44. See also Black, *The Scrolls and Christian Origins,* p. 92.
4. Vermes, *op. cit.* p. 31. It is an interesting point that the Essene calendar fixed the celebration of Pentecost on Sivan 15, and it always fell on a Sunday, the first day of the week. It was on a Sunday that the resurrection of Jesus took place according to the Gospels.
5. See above, Part Two, Chapter 7, pp. 92–4.
6. In my own translation of the Christian Scriptures, *The Authentic New Testament,* I did furnish in the notes a considerable number of such references. A comprehensive record would of course be very costly and its compilation require a team of scholars. But it would be an extremely valuable undertaking.

CHAPTER 10

THE FIRST CLASH

There had been no formal inauguration of the new movement in Jerusalem. It had sprung into existence spontaneously in an outburst of emotionalism and enthusiasm. But among those who were at the centre of it, and those of different affiliations who had responded to the stirring Pentecost call, were individuals who could quickly create an orderly coherence. The patterns of structure were already there and could readily be adapted to the requirements of the new circumstances. Recruits also brought in the doctrines and ideas which were characteristic of the groups to which they had belonged or still belonged. The emerging Nazorean Party was heterogeneous in complexion, with elements representative of a diversity of attitudes and associations. It embraced patient pietists and political militants, reformers and revolutionaries. This was bound in the future to give rise from time to time to internal frictions; but what was held in common was strong enough to enable them to be overcome; and in due course the establishment of an effective government would permit a firm control to be exercised.

A factor which contributed to resolving differences was the sense of a united front against a mutually abhorred regime, the dominion of Satan, embracing both the Roman occupying power and Jewish authorities subservient to it. The movement stood for the total liberation of Israel, spiritually and politically, and consequently manifested certain reflections of xenophobia and class-war.

We have several times emphasized the physical and ideological cleavage in Jerusalem between the Lower City and the Upper City, between the Jewish masses and their rulers. But ingrained habits of belief are so hard to break that it is necessary to stress this dichotomy again. The Jewish Council, or Great Sanhedrin, exercised under the Romans powers of government in the area of domestic and religious affairs, which though restricted were still considerable. Its membership was largely furnished by adherents of the Sadducean Party, consisting of the chief priests and representatives of the leading families with which they were often allied in marriage, with the high priest as president. But there also served on this body a certain number of prominent Pharisees, who could act as something like a left-wing opposition. The Council accepted allegiance to Rome, and the Roman legate of Syria at this time appointed the high priest. Scandalously, bribery sometimes played a part in this appointment. Thus the Council was regarded by the Jewish people as heavily compromised, and acting for the enemy. It was also a grievance that many of these wealthy aristocrats were tolerant of alien ways of life, as well as being haughty, overbearing and avaricious.

The Jewish people were rarely on the side of their hierarchy. They gave them support only when they made some kind of stand against further Roman infringements of civil and religious rights. Mostly they were hostile to their own ruling clique. Even Luke with all his prejudice and apologetic misrepresentation in the Acts has in places to admit this. As conditions progressively deteriorated so did relations between populace and hierarchy. The Talmud had put on record a chant of abusive denunciation of the great families:

Down with the Boethusians!
Down with their bludgeons!
Down with the Ananites!
Down with their viper hissings!
Down with the Kantherites!
Down with their libels!
Down with the house of Ishmael ben Pheabi!
Down with their blows with the fist!
They themselves are high priests;
Their sons are treasurers;
Their sons-in-law are captains of the Temple,
And their servants strike the people with staves.[1]

The Jewish people of Jerusalem were strongly on the side of the followers of Jesus. They were pro-Messianism, and the Nazoreans stood for the Messianic redemption of Israel. The Nazoreans cared for the poor, the needy, and the oppressed: they associated with them, and most of the members came from the ranks of the ordinary people. Furthermore, they were devout and staunch observers of the Law of Moses, and in no way tainted with heathen customs and habits.

If we fix this firmly in our minds once and for all we shall not be misled by the falsifications which appear in the New Testament, or confused by statements, sometimes close together, which contradict one another. What we have represented occasionally comes out where earlier sources used by the Evangelists were allowed to stand instead of being adjusted to agree with the impression they wished to convey.

To the hierarchy it must have been a cause of grave concern that a danger which they believed had been overcome when Jesus was executed not only still existed but had acquired increased vitality. It was one thing for the people to respond momentarily, as they were ever prone to do, to the outpourings of some fanatic, prophet, or charlatan, who promised them freedom. It was quite another, however, when an organized body of propagandists was formed capable of building up a large-scale threatening movement. A new party favoured by the Zealot guerrillas and the Jerusalem 'underground' was going to be much harder to deal with.

The worst feature of what was reported was that the new movement was centred on a man who was dead, but who was now proclaimed by his followers to be alive in heaven, directing activities from the skies in the capacity of the Messiah he had claimed to be. There was no limit to the nonsense the superstitious populace would swallow; but it was alarming nonsense. What was more, the movement was playing on the hostility of the people towards their rulers by charging them with having slain the Lord's anointed. The spokesmen of the movement were apparently so sure of mass support that they had no hesitation in boldly preaching their doctrine in the Temple porticoes.

Already there was talk of miraculous cures, all the attendant phenomena of unreasoning religious fervour. They had even got hold of one of those fake cripples begging at the Temple gates, and were parading him as an example of a lame man the use of whose limbs had been restored in the name of Jesus. So could they claim fulfilment of the word, 'Then shall the lame man leap as a hart, and the tongue of the dumb shall sing' (Isa. xxxv. 6). And this would lend credence to what was further stated by the prophet: 'Say to them of fearful heart, Be strong, fear not: behold, your God will come with vengeance, even God with a recompense; He will come and save you. . . . And the ransomed of the Lord shall return, and come to Zion with songs, and everlasting joy upon their heads: they shall obtain joy and gladness, and sorrow and sighing shall flee away.'

How easy it was to dupe the untutored masses by quoting Scripture so that they would be ready for any vain adventure and expect Divine interventions on their behalf! That was not the way things worked in these days. The most helpful weapons now were cunning and diplomacy, sacrificing something here to gain a little more there. But the people just could not grasp this. They were impervious to intelligent argument, and could only clamour for their rights, however nebulous these were under Roman rule. Such privileges as could be claimed rested on agreements concluded with the Imperial government, and depended on good relations and good order. The fools simply would not see how much worse their position would be were it not for the influence and continual watchfulness of the hierarchy and aristocracy.

The atmosphere on the Ophel was very different. There those who had worked with Jesus in Galilee were in their glory. The incredible had come to pass. It had not been like this in the north where the crowds had flocked to Jesus but few had actually joined him. Now every day there were recruits to the cause, hundreds of them, thousands. It was hard to keep count. They brought their savings, their treasured possessions, even their household goods, and laid them at the feet of the apostles. Down in the Lower City it was an effort to move through the narrow twisting streets because of the press of people. They cried, called out blessings, threw garments on the ground for the holy ones to walk on. They touched them, held napkins against them, to gain some virtue for their sick and diseased. Claims of cures were announced, magnified, multiplied.

At the big house of John the Priest it took several young stalwarts to expel the throng at night so that the doors could be shut. The courtyard was piled high with offerings. Dwelling after dwelling was brought into requisition as their inhabitants were enrolled. Some sold buildings and lands and handed over the proceeds. Others came with title-deeds and had the ownership transferred to the Community of the Messiah. 'For Jesus,' they said. 'For our king,' they said.

It was much too cramped in the Lower City for large gatherings. Here, in contrast to the Upper City, open spaces were few. Only the Temple with its great outer court and porticoes could accommodate the throng. There the spokesmen harangued the crowds. All timidity, all fear, had vanished. The former grieving and defeated disciples were thrilled and exalted, carried away by their new-found power and authority. They had found their voices too. The 'Spirit' put words in their mouths.

Amazingly everything had changed. It seemed unbelievable; but it had to be believed. Looking at this sea of eager faces the evidence was there before their very eyes. Who could have imagined it? There was this beggar man beside them, hopping about bawling Hallelujahs. The people knew him. They said he had been lame from birth. Peter and John had been accosted by him at the Beautiful Gate as he held out his hand for alms. Peter had said something to him. It might have been, 'Jesus says you can walk.' Perhaps he could. Perhaps it was a miracle. Anyway there he was now, able to use his feet and giving his testimony, adding to the people's excitement. There was a great rush to Solomon's Portico where the apostles were speaking.

It was near evening. The crowds had to be got out and the great gates shut. Many were already leaving, and the Temple police came along to hustle them on their way. But some would not budge, and since the apostles were the cause, and acting upon instructions, the Captain of the Temple took them into custody.

The reason for the arrest given in the Acts is that the Sadducean hierarchy objected to the public preaching of the resurrection of the dead, with Jesus offered as proof of this doctrine. The official interrogation the following day did not, however, concern itself with this issue, which was a bone of contention between the Pharisees and Sadducees. Instead the Court dealt with the means by which the cripple had been cured. Since no law had been broken, there was nothing for it but to release the prisoners with an injunction that they should cease their propaganda about Jesus. This they flatly rejected. The Acts makes the point that the chief priests would dearly have loved to inflict punishment, but were forced to take account of the temper of the people.

The Nazoreans had scored a tactical victory which increased their influence. Their message began to bring into the movement people from neighbouring towns and villages. About five thousand more adherents, says the Acts, had resulted from the public meetings in the Temple. If we are to credit the figures we are given the Nazorean Party was well on the way to being the largest association in the country, but as we have pointed out many of those who joined retained their previous sectarian identity. A notable recruit was a well-to-do Levite from Cyprus named Joseph, who became prominent in the movement. He was promptly dubbed 'the Encourager' and thereafter appears in the records as Barnabas.[2] The Acts contrasts his wholehearted generosity in giving every penny the property he sold had realized with the behaviour of one Ananias and his wife Sapphira, who when they disposed of their property for the benefit of the movement retained part of the price obtained and pretended to have received a lesser sum. As an awful warning they suffered 'death at the hand of Heaven', struck down by act of God for their deceit. 'Great awe seized the whole community as well as those who heard all about it' (Acts v. 11).

This is the story as it has reached us; but we are tempted to wonder whether the unlucky couple were not summarily dealt with by Zealot extremists. Otherwise their punishment was far beyond their deserts. Even the Essenes, harsh as they could be in many matters, prescribed only a moderate penalty in such circumstances.[3]

With the knowledge we have of the temper of the Zealots, and the ramifications of their 'underground' partisanship, we are obliged to consider their infiltration of the new movement. Many Zealots could espouse in sincerity the cause of Jesus as the legitimate king of Israel; but others would be quick to see that the Nazorean Party's popularity with the masses presented a golden opportunity to make use of it for their own ends in striking at the authorities. Suspicion of this would explain the further action of the threatened hierarchy in re-arresting Peter and John as the apparent ringleaders. The Acts claims that the senate of Israel, the whole of the Great Sanhedrin, a muster of the chief priests and their eminent relations, was convened to deal with the menace. But when the officers went to fetch the prisoners the birds had mysteriously flown. 'During the night,' says the Acts, 'an angel of the Lord had opened the prison doors and led them out.' How the rescue was contrived must be a matter for speculation; but it looks as if the 'underground' had got to work. Either the jailers were sympathizers or yielded to threats. The jail was the civil prison, and not therefore under Roman guard.

To continue with the Acts: 'When the Captain of the Temple guard and the chief priests heard of the escape they were quite at a loss how it could have happened. Then someone came and informed them, "The men you put in prison are actually standing in the Temple speaking to the people." So the Captain of the Temple guard went with his officers and fetched them, but without using force, for they were afraid they might be stoned by the people' (v. 24-6).

The Sadducean hierarchy, we are told, were anxious to make an example of the prisoners and have them executed (though on what grounds is not stated), to prevent a sedition of more formidable proportions. But on this occasion the apostles had a champion in the prominent Pharisee Rabban Gamaliel. Whether being a Pharisee he had a hearty dislike of the Sadducees, or had other motives such as we have conjectured,[4] he rose up to request a private deliberation without the presence of the prisoners. He then urged the need for extreme caution. After all, if the new movement was not inspired by God it would fizzle out and come to nothing as other messianic initiatives had done. The best course, therefore, was not to act precipitately, but to await events.[5] The hierarchy was not so sure that strong action was not called for; but they could recognize that it could be dangerous to themselves and their position to provoke an open conflict in the present circumstances. Accordingly, having recalled the prisoners, the Court ruled that they be flogged, given a further warning, and set at liberty.

This outward show of magnanimity did not reflect the true feelings of the hierarchy. They were in no way mollified, and could with great difficulty restrain their animosity. It simply meant that they saw the wisdom of biding their time, and striking at the movement when conditions should be more propitious. As it happened, they did not have too long to wait. In the meantime 'God's message spread, and the number of disciples in Jerusalem was greatly augmented. Quite a considerable body of the priests gave their allegiance' (Acts vi. 7).

This almost casual reference to a fresh body of adherents is of consequence, and indeed significant. It confirms that the religion of the Nazoreans was Judaism in a form which emphasized strict attachment to the Mosaic ordinances. If it had not been so the movement would not have attracted Zealots, Pharisees, Essenes, and many of the priests. What distinguished the Nazoreans was faith in Jesus as God's appointed Messiah. We must not interpret such belief in terms of a new religion, carrying with it acceptance of doctrines peculiar to the later formulation of Christianity.

The Jewish priests who joined the Nazorean Party remained Jewish priests, continuing the performance of their duties in the Temple. But in these days there was a widening gap in the relationships between the rank and file of the priesthood and the wealthy hierarchy. Many of the priests were poor: they were debarred from all secular employment and depended for their support on their share of the prescribed tithes. A large number of them were quartered in the area immediately south of the Temple on the Ophel, and therefore in close proximity to the centre of Nazorean activities. At various times, going back more than two hundred years, it had been faithful priests who had attacked the laxity and hellenic ways of the great high priestly families. Their initiatives had helped to promote Chasidism, and not a few had joined the Zadokites. Some of the priests were descended on the paternal side from the itinerant clan of Rechabites, who refrained from all intoxicants.[6] It was natural now that many should favour the new movement.

Thus a great company of the ordinary priests made their own gesture of protest against the haughty Ananites and Boethusians, and expressed their solidarity with those who were opposed to them. The defection did not go unnoticed, and ultimately led to reprisals.[7]

In this atmosphere of unrest and tension the summer of A.D. 36 passed. A process of alignment was developing in Jerusalem. There was no plan afoot for any organized outbreak; but there was a drawing together of those who ranged themselves on one side or the other within the nation, the pro-Messianists and the anti-Messianists. There was a watchful assessment of relative strength.

When Pilate had departed, to everyone's great relief, an uneasy vacuum was created. Vitellius, the Roman legate of Syria, when he came to Jerusalem was very sensitive to public feeling and anxious to take the heat out of the situation. As we have already shown, the measures he adopted speak for themselves, one of them being to depose Caiaphas as high priest and confer the office on his brother-in-law Jonathan son of Annas.[8]. No new governor had been appointed before Tiberius died in March, A.D. 37, a fact that was very consequential for the Nazoreans. It produced a kind of interregnum in which the new high priest could exercise a certain measure of power ostensibly in the Roman interest.[9]

NOTES AND REFERENCES

1. *Pesach.* fol. 57a.
2. The Greek *paraklesiōs* here implies giving aid, which agrees with the reference to Joseph's support of the cause. The derivation of Barnabas from *Nebuah,* 'prophecy' or 'exhortation', is forced. *Nedabah,* however, conveys the idea of liberality (cp. the Jewish names Nadab and Nodab). The Hebrew root is *nua,* translated in the Greek Septuagint by *paraklesis* (Jer. xvi. 7, and cp. Job. xliii. 11 and Isa. li. 19). The full nickname Bar-Nadabas has been abbreviated to Bar-Nabas, like the contraction of Silvanos to Silas. Among the high priests we find an Ananias Bar-Nedebaios.
3. The *Community Rule* of the Zadokite-Essenes provides that if anyone has lied in matters of property, 'he shall be excluded from the pure Meal of the Many for one year, and shall do penance with respect to one quarter of his food' (ch. vi). 'Death by the hand of Heaven', in the Jewish phrase,

did not necessarily exclude human agency. Cp. Josephus, *Antiq.* XVII. 285; XX. 186–7. There were those who were very ready to do the Lord's will by acting as executioners.

4. See above, pp. 87–8.
5. A similar passage appears in the Clementine *Recognitions,* Bk. I, ch. lxv. But there the references to Judas of Galilee and Theudas, as in the Acts, are omitted. According to Josephus, *Antiq.* XX. 97–8, the activities of Theudas were a decade later than the time at which Gamaliel is supposed to be speaking. In the *Recognitions* Gamaliel is described as a secret believer in Jesus who remained in the Sanhedrin on the advice of the Nazoreans so that he could warn them of designs against them or check the Council's intentions.
6. See Part Two, p. 222, and Part Three, p. 252. According to the *Yalqut* on Jer. xxxv. 12, Rechabites sometimes married the daughters of priests and their grandsons served as priests in the Temple.
7. See Part Two, pp. 206–7.
8. Josephus, *Antiq.* XVIII. 90–5, and see Chapter 11 below.
9. Towards the end of A.D. 36 and during the winter of 37 Vitellius could concern himself very little with Jerusalem, since, on orders from the emperor, he was busy getting an army ready to attack the Nabataeans on behalf of Herod Antipas.

CHAPTER 11

DEATH TO DISSENTERS

Where strong feelings are aroused and there is bitterness and resentment ugly things are bound to be said and done. The very smell of trouble attracts fanatics and agitators, and people are easily led to direct their animus against causes of grievance presented to them. It would be quite wrong to hold up the Jesus movement as a shining example of love in action. All was not sweetness and light in the Nazorean camp. The motley following of the Messiah included elements which were puritanical, aggressively nationalistic, and nonconformist, exhibiting much of the pettiness and irrationality of a downtrodden society. Of course there were also those with a simple goodness of heart and generosity of spirit. But we should not seek to invest the movement as a whole with qualities and virtues for the manifestation of which contemporary conditions offered little inducement.

From its inception the party embraced many foreign-born Jews. They had enclaves in Jerusalem where those from different areas of the Empire could find themselves at home among fellow-countrymen, and where they had their own synagogues in which they could meet. There was one for the North Africans – those from Libya, Cyrenaica and Alexandria – and another for the Asiatics – those from Lydia, Pamphylia and Cilicia (Acts vi. 9) – and similarly those from other regions. They were lumped together as Hellenists by the native-born Jews because they largely spoke Greek, and in the party, which a number of them had joined, there began to show itself a disposition to discriminate against them in the daily distribution of food. Native Jews should first be served, and the foreigners should have what was left over.[1]

It is in this context that the Acts introduces Stephen, as one of seven administrators – all with Greek names, and one of them a proselyte to Judaism hailing from Antioch – chosen at the insistence of the apostles to deal with this prejudicial treatment of Diaspora Jews.

Stephen, evidently, was an ardent propagandist and became involved in dispute with other Hellenists, not of the party. What he urged that aroused their hostility we are unable to know; but it may be inferred that his outlook was rather broad and universalistic. It would be unsafe to draw any positive conclusions from the speech composed for him in the Acts when he was hailed before the Sanhedrin by his irate opponents, but we may note in that speech a sudden change at the end from the first person plural to the second person. The charge that Stephen had declared that Jesus would destroy the Temple and change the Mosaic ordinances is, even in the Acts, attributed to false witnesses.

The fact that Stephen was a foreign Jew identified with the Nazoreans told very much against him, since the Council in this case did not have to be fearful of popular sympathy with the accused. The chief priests, possibly goaded by the unwisely outspoken Stephen, could vent their pent-up fury against the Nazoreans on one who was a welcome scapegoat. He was hustled away to be stoned, with the witnesses taking the lead in carrying out the execution. They laid their coats at the feet of a young man called Saul, who was a native of Tarsus in Cilicia, studying Jewish Law at the school of Gamaliel in Jerusalem. Saul, who was a Pharisee, would seem to have been in a state of blind rage bordering on insanity, ready and eager to take part in a wild attack of young bloods on the homes of Hellenists known to be Nazoreans or sympathizers.

'That same day,' says the Acts, 'there broke out a violent persecution of the community at Jerusalem, and except for the apostles they were all dispersed over the countries of Judea and Samaria. Pious men interred Stephen, and made great lamentation for him. Meanwhile Saul ravaged the community, entering house after house and dragging off both men and women to prison' (viii. 1-3).

We may grant that Saul took a prominent part in a hostile outbreak against a section of the Nazoreans, since as the convert Paul he says as much himself (Gal. i. 13). But it has rightly been doubted whether the circumstances were as Luke has represented them. How was it possible without official authority for a young firebrand like Saul to act as a police officer, rounding up Nazoreans and herding them into prison? Why were the leaders of the movement left untouched and only the rank and file affected?

It is likely that Luke's bald statement covers a progression of events, which began with a spontaneous and quite unauthorized demonstration against Hellenist Nazoreans by fellow Hellenists,

How the situation developed we shall have need to investigate; but before we can do this we must consider other evidence which bears upon it. This is found in the Clementine *Recognitions*. The work as it stands is not earlier than the third century, and is more generally known to us in an unsatisfactory Latin translation prepared by Rufinus of Aquileia in the fourth century. The value of the work, as with its companion, the *Homilies*, lies in partial dependence on earlier sources such as the *Preaching of Peter* and the *Ascents of Jacob*. The material importantly reflects elements of Nazorean teaching and tradition as represented by the extremist sect of Ebionites.

The version of the circumstances which concerns us occupies chapters liii to lxxi of the *Recognitions*. It makes no reference to Stephen and those who debated with him. Instead it is the Sadducean hierarchy which challenges the Nazoreans to a public disputation on the Messiahship of Jesus. Choosing what they consider a suitable occasion the Nazoreans accept, and it is arranged that the debate between the leaders on both sides shall take place on the interior Temple steps in the presence of the people.

Opening the attack, the high priest first objects to the emphasis on baptism 'as having recently been brought in in opposition to the sacrifices'. Thereafter, various points are raised by different persons, and these are answered in turn by the apostles. A certain Pharisee accuses Philip of putting Jesus on a level with Moses. Philip replies that Jesus must be considered to be greater than Moses since he was the Messiah as well as a prophet. Another intervention by the high priest attacks the teaching of Jesus because he had said 'that the poor are blessed, and promised earthly rewards; and placed the chief gift in an earthly inheritance; and promised that those who maintain righteousness shall be satisfied with meat and drink.'

The high priest then addresses himself to Peter, charging him with presumption, being an unlearned and uneducated man, in setting himself up as a teacher. In the course of his reply Peter attacks the sacrificial system. 'We have ascertained beyond doubt that God is much rather displeased with the sacrifices you offer, the time of sacrifices having now passed away. And because you will not admit that the time for offering victims is past, therefore the Temple will be destroyed, and the abomination of desolation shall stand in the Holy Place.' This greatly enrages the priests, and Gamaliel – claimed as a secret disciple – diplomatically intervenes with advice similar to what is reported in the Acts when Peter and John were before the Sanhedrin, and proposes to conduct the argument with the apostles himself the next day.

When the debate is resumed, Gamaliel is the first speaker, but on this occasion the spokesman for the followers of Jesus is his brother Jacob, who is head of the Community. His engagement in the argument continues for seven successive days and is so successful that all the people, the high priest included, are ready to be baptized.

At this juncture an enemy, clearly Saul, enters the Temple with a few men, and raises a tumult, reproaching and reviling the priests, and inciting every one to murder. Seizing a brand from the altar he begins to lay about him. Others are carried away by his madness.

> Much blood is shed; there is a confused flight, in the midst of which that enemy attacked Jacob, and threw him headlong from the top of the steps; and supposing him to be dead, he cared not to inflict further violence upon him. But our friends lifted him up, for they were both more numerous and powerful than the others; but, from fear of God, they rather allowed themselves to be killed by an inferior force than they would kill others. But when the evening came the priests shut up the Temple, and we returned to Jacob's house, and spent the night there in prayer. Then before daylight we went down to Jericho, to the number of five thousand men.

Jacob of course recovers, and the episode ends with the enemy – Saul – passing through Jericho on his way to Damascus in the belief that Peter had fled there. Saul misses the brethren, however, since at the time they were away from Jericho visiting the tombs of two of their number which miraculously whitened themselves annually.

There are obvious points in common with Acts v to vii. But since the *Ascents of Jacob* is not extant it is impossible to know how much of its contents have been reproduced and how much in the *Recognitions* has been based on or accommodated to the Acts. That there had been considerable adaptation is shown by the appearance in the *Recognitions* of reflections of advanced Christian teaching which we have not quoted in our outline.

We may accept, however, that the *Ascents of Jacob* dealt with a debate staged on the fifteen steps of the Temple between the hierarchy and the followers of Jesus, and that the principal spokesman on the Nazorean side was Jacob the brother of Jesus. The book probably ended in the manner suggested in the *Recognitions*. This view seems to be supported by Epiphanius who knew the *Ascents.* He says of it: 'They [the Ebionites] have other Acts which they call those of the apostles, in which are many things filled with their impiety, whence they have incidentally furnished themselves with arms against the truth. For they set forth certain Ascents and Instructions forsooth in the *Ascents of Jacob,* representing him as holding forth against both Temple and sacrifices, and against the fire on the altar, and many other things filled with empty talk, so that they are not ashamed in them even to denounce Paul in certain invented utterances of the malignant and deceitful work of their false apostles' (*Panar.* xxx. 16).

The *Recognitions* does make the point that the time for sacrifices has ended, and that because the priests will not admit this the Temple will be destroyed. In an earlier passage, perhaps taken from the *Ascents,* it is more positively said, 'It is Jesus who has, by the grace of baptism, put out that fire which the priest kindled for sins' (ch. xlvii). The Ebionite Gospel, cited by Epiphanius, put into the mouth of Jesus the words, 'I am come to abolish the sacrifices: if ye cease not from sacrificing, the wrath [of God] will not cease from weighing upon you' (*Panar.* xxx. 16).

There is some parallel here with the accusation against Stephen: 'This man never stops denouncing this Holy Place and the Law, for we have heard him say that Jesus the Nazorean will destroy this Place, and change the customs handed down to us by Moses.' We are reminded that according to the Gospels the apostles had been told by Jesus that the Temple would be destroyed, and that he was even accused of saying that he himself would destroy the Temple.

Evidently there was something emanating from a section within the Nazorean camp which false witnesses could construe in a sense hostile to the Temple cult. And it is clear that after the destruction of the Temple the views of this section became more emphatic and did indeed embrace antagonism to the sacrificial system.

The Ebionites appear in the early Christian centuries as an extremist ascetic branch of the Nazoreans, and we can now trace their derivation to the influence within the Jesus movement of the Zadokite-Essenes. The designation *Ebionim* means 'the Poor', and the term seems to have had reference to the Essene communal way of life, in which no member possessed anything of his own. The Poor regarded themselves as the Very Elect, who had freed themselves from every kind of contamination, including that of animal food. There were Baptists of the same persuasion, and John the Baptist was held up as one who was a strict vegetarian, as well as a teetotaller. In the Epistle of Jacob (James) mention is made of 'the Poor of this world, rich in faith, and heirs of the Kingdom God has promised to those who love Him' (Jas. ii. 5). To be mindful of the Poor was enjoined on Paul (Gal. ii. 10), and he was active in fund-raising on their behalf.

Since the discovery of the Dead Sea Scrolls we have learnt a great deal more about Zadokite-Essene reasons for condemning the contemporary custodians of the cult centre of Israel. The *Commentary on Habakkuk* attacks 'the last Priests of Jerusalem, who amass money and wealth by plundering the peoples' (ix). And in particular, 'the Wicked Priest . . . shall be paid the reward which he himself tendered to the Poor. For *Lebanon* is the Council of the Community; and *the beasts* are the Simple of Judah who keep the Law. As he himself plotted the destruction of the Poor, so will God condemn him to destruction. And as for that which He said [i.e. in Habakkuk)] *Because of the blood of the city and the violence done to the land*: interpreted, *the city* is Jerusalem, where the Wicked Priest committed abominable deeds and defiled the Temple of God. *The violence done to the land*: these are the cities of Judah where he robbed the Poor of their possessions' (xii).

Early in the study of the Scrolls, J. L. Teicher[2] contended that the recovered documents were to be attributed to the original Jewish-Christians. This opinion did not find favour; but it should not be completely rejected. The highest category of the Zadokite-Essenes was the Community of Holiness. Members in this category 'shall establish the spirit of holiness according to everlasting truth. They shall atone for guilty rebellion and for sins of unfaithfulness that they may obtain lovingkindness for the Land without the flesh of holocausts and the fat of sacrifice. And prayer rightly offered shall be as an acceptable fragrance of righteousness, and perfection of way as a delectable free-will offering. At that time, the men of the Community shall be set apart as a House of Holiness for Aaron for the union of supreme holiness, and a House of Community for Israel, for those who walk in perfection.'[3]

This passage in the *Community Rule* is very important. It conveys that the Very Elect were regarded as performing an atoning work, which did not require recourse to sacrifices and burnt-offerings. This had become necessary because the chief priests had defiled the Temple, and had polluted the sacrifices which consequently were no longer efficacious.

Teicher went too far in arguing that the Community of the Scrolls completely rejected the sacrificial system. What the Zadokite-Essenes contended was that as things stood the sacrifices had lost their atoning power. The true Sons of Zadok had therefore, as had been foreseen,[4] to provide an alternative means of propitiation by prayer and holiness according to the will of God.

Among the disaffected in Israel there were many grounds of antagonism towards the hierarchy, spiritual and political. Essenes, Pharisees and Zealots, all had cause of complaint, and the Nazoreans had the special grievance that the chief priests had compassed the Messiah's death. In general, however, as Brandon points out, the evidence of the Gospels and Acts exhibits Jesus and his followers as staunchly supporting the Temple ritual. But he allows that 'the episode of Stephen attests to the existence of an anti-cultic element in the primitive Christian community.'[5]

If we are to get somewhere near the truth of what took place we must additionally have regard to the tradition of the Mandaean-Nazoreans that at a date answering to A.D. 37 they suffered a persecution which caused them to flee from Judea and seek asylum in the Hauran. We discuss this in Part Three,[6] where we consider that we have a recollection here of the attack promoted by Saul of Tarsus to which in their different ways the Acts and the *Recognitions* refer. In the Ebionite story mention is made of a substantial body of disciples leaving Jerusalem for Jericho, close to which was the Essene settlement at Qumran. They would appear to have been making for the north through Peraea, to the Land of Damascus which figures in the Zadokite-Essene records. The Mandaean refugees are represented as escaping in the same direction. In the Acts we are told that Saul – armed with official authority to make arrests – himself set out for Damascus, where he was to encounter Ananias, a follower of 'the Just One', and after conversion to spend a period in Arabia. The *Recognitions* likewise reports that Saul passed through Jericho on his way to Damascus, believing that Peter had fled there.

From these various recollections we must now attempt to reconstruct the circumstances.

The sequence of events appears to have begun with argument in the

Hellenist synagogues, where Hellenist Nazoreans like Stephen were active propagandists. These Nazoreans favoured Essene views, and in the heat of debate used intemperate and inflammatory language about the hierarchy and the Temple cult. Congregants, among them Saul of Tarsus, hailed Stephen before the Sanhedrin, where his hostile outspokenness assured his condemnation. Following this, Saul and his associates went on the rampage. They did not attack the Nazorean Pharisees or the loyalist apostles of Jesus, but those on the sectarian fringe who appeared to be lending themselves to disruptive propaganda.

The Acts furnishes a more circumstantial account of the outbreak in Saul's (Paul's) defence of himself before King Agrippa at a much later date. There he says, 'I used myself to think it necessary to act in utmost opposition to the authority of Jesus the Nazorean,[7] which moreover I did in Jerusalem, and locked up many of the Saints [i.e. Essenites] in prison with a warrant I had from the chief priests. When they were sent to their death I pressed the vote against them, and had them punished repeatedly in all the synagogues, and compelled them to revile Jesus. Being mad with them beyond measure I even hunted them to towns across the border' (xxvi. 9-11).

There is some exaggeration here, but it can be accepted that the initial outbreak of violence by Saul and his associates was followed by a more thorough-going Gestapo-like apprehension and ill-treatment of Jewish sectarians, a number of whom were associated with the Jesus movement. This development could not have taken place without the assent of the chief priests, and the claim is made that Saul obtained their warrant to pursue his vendetta.

It looks as if the independent assault by a gang, possibly largely composed of Hellenist Jewish students at Jerusalem like Saul, had played directly into the hands of the Sadducean hierarchy. The chief priests, smarting from antagonistic utterances by their opponents, were furnished with an unexpected ally in the person of an ardent Pharisee. The chance was too good to be missed to deal a heavy body-blow at the most vulnerable part of the new coalition movement, and thus deprive it of power to become a serious menace to the position and privileges of the sacerdotal aristocracy. This was no persecution of Christians by Jews; it was an attempt within the Jewish polity to suppress what may be described as a dissident left-wing. This wing, having the ear of the people, was becoming dangerously vociferous about the infamy of the chief priests as polluters of the Sanctuary, and voices were even raised by extremists denouncing the sacrificial system and proclaiming the imminent destruction of the Temple itself. Such ideas fostered sedition and could lead from words to deeds. The hierarchy certainly had cause for alarm, and when the revolt did get going a generation later several of the chief priests were assassinated.[8]

A police-action, broadly to be described as anti-Nazorean, of the magnitude indicated is more likely to have been set in motion at a time when there was a reduction of Roman control, and when as a consequence the high priest and Sanhedrin were exercising greater civil authority and responsibility than was normal at this period. Such a situation, as we have shown, existed most conveniently in the winter of A.D. 36-7. The country was without a Roman procurator, and the Roman legate was engaged in preparations for war with the Arabs. Jonathan son of Annas was now high priest, and the lordly House of Annas had a score to settle with the Nazoreans.

Provided with a golden opportunity, the chief priests felt free to exploit the circumstances. If any questions arose they could claim that their action was concerned with the maintenance of religion and good order. Those being rounded up and dealt with were of a seditious type advocating novelties – to borrow a favourite expression of Josephus – which were subversive of all duly constituted authority. The Sanhedrin was in fact doing Rome a favour in putting down such elements.

However, the chief priests had not thrown all caution to the winds. In giving Saul his warrant they felt they had protection from a popular protest because odium would fall particularly on one who was a Pharisee unconnected with the hierarchy, and we gather from the Acts that they insisted that the principal apostles, whom the populace supported, were not to be touched.

Vitellius was very concerned that the inhabitants of Jerusalem should not be provoked against the Romans, and he cannot have been kept wholly in the dark about the punitive measures pursued by the hierarchy in their own interests on so considerable a scale. His displeasure seems to have been marked by the fact that when next he visited Jerusalem at the Passover of A.D. 37 he deposed Jonathan from office after he had been high priest for only a few months and appointed in his stead his brother Theophilus. Josephus gives no explanation of why Jonathan was superseded so quickly.[9]

NOTES AND REFERENCES

1. It was perhaps considered that all foreigners had money, since they could afford to travel, and many of the Hellenists must have been traders.
2. In a series of articles published in *The Journal of Jewish Studies.* See especially, 'The Dead Sea Scrolls – Documents of the Jewish-Christian Sect of Ebionites' (*JJS,* Vol. II, No. 3, 1951), and 'The Damascus Fragments and the Origin of the Jewish-Christian Sect' (*JJS,* Vol. II, No. 3, 1951).
3. *Community Rule,* ix (Vermes). Teicher inferred from the Scrolls that the sect did not eat meat. 'No consumption of meat means no sacrifice of animals. It is inconceivable therefore that the sect of the Dead Sea Scrolls should have had a class of sacrificing priests' (Teicher, 'Priests and Sacrifices in the Dead Sea Scrolls', in *JJS,* Vol. V, No. 4., p. 94). The prohibition, however, seems to have concerned the eating of raw flesh, not the eating of meat. The reference is to the Statutes in *Damascus Rule,* xii.
4. That the sacrificial system was abrogated at Christ's death is argued in the Epistle to the Hebrews, the work of a Hellenist follower of Jesus, possibly Apollos of Alexandria. In support of the argument Psalm xl. 6–8 is quoted (Heb. x).
5. Brandon, *Jesus and the Zealots,* p. 157.
6. See below, Part Three, Chapter 28, p. 285.
7. We have not considered here what was behind Saul's ire. Elsewhere I have suggested that he was a student of Jewish occultism, and had come to believe that he himself was destined to be the Messiah. See Schonfield, *Those Incredible Christians,* ch. v. and the supplementary study, 'The Christology of Paul', in the same volume.
8. Jonathan son of Annas was killed before the revolt, and during the revolt the younger Annas and Jesus son of Gamalas were done to death. See Josephus, *J.W.* II. 254–7; IV. 314–25.
9. The Zealots must have had strong cause to hate Jonathan, since some twenty years later he was assassinated by the terrorist Sicarii. It is of interest that Josephus reports that King Agrippa in A.D. 41 offered to restore the high priesthood to Jonathan who, however, diplomatically declined the honour (*Antiq.* XIX. 313–16). The real reason may have been his consciousness of the odium in which he was held by the people because of the pogrom against the Nazoreans four years previously.

CHAPTER 12

THE HOPE OF SALVATION

The persecution authorized by the high priest Jonathan was directed in particular, says the Acts, at those of 'the Way' (ix. 2; xxii. 4). No comment on this term is furnished. We find it in use, however, as a reflection of the position occupied by the eclectic dissenters. It was their claim that they were preparing the Way of the Lord as foretold by the prophets (Isa. xl. 3; Mal. iii. 1). This was the Way proclaimed in the Wilderness by the Baptists and Zadokites.[1] It was the true Way of the Law, and therefore the Way of Salvation. Only by faithfulness to the Way would Israel obtain deliverance.

Christians have thought of salvation as a right of admission to heaven by faith in the atoning work of Jesus Christ. But the idea of salvation meant originally escape from the coming judgment on the world and assurance of participation in the felicities of the Messianic Age, when the Kingdom of God would be established on earth.

Primarily salvation was related to the redemption of Israel through the agency of the Messiah, the ingathering of the faithful remnant, and the restoration of the nation's independence, so that it would fulfil its function as the guide and legislator of mankind.

The dissenters, battling with wickedness in high places and the general turpitude of the masses, had tended towards exclusiveness. Salvation was assured only to those who were obedient to the commandments of God, who turned away from evil, and thus constituted the Saints, the Elect, whose loyalty and suffering would be rewarded by their inheritance of the Kingdom. These would be spared in the Time of Trial that was imminent.[2] Their names were inscribed in the Heavenly Records, the Book of Life. The mentor of the Zadokite-Essenes was the True Teacher, and one with these qualifications would arise in the Last Times. In the Nazorean Party this personality was identified with the Messiah, Jesus being regarded as fulfilling all the offices of the Coming One as Prophet, Priest and King.[3] His name, signifying God's salvation, was thus pre-eminently that in which faith should be reposed for salvation. The concept of his atoning work was associated with this; but it did not initially change the nature of the salvation that was looked for. The conflict Paul was to have with the Central Authority of the Nazoreans was not about what salvation implied – the reward of reigning on earth with the Messiah in his kingdom – but about whether believing Gentiles were to be received as full members of the House of Israel without obligation to keep the commandments God had given to Israel.

A new situation began to be created by the persecution of a section of the Nazoreans. Instead of disrupting the movement and rendering it innocuous it had the effect of increasing its dimensions and influence. The refugees carried the Good News of the Kingdom further afield.

The Acts is chiefly interested in those who escaped to the north-west, though it describes the proclamation of the Message in Samaria. 'Those who were dispersed as a result of the persecution that broke out over Stephen travelled as far as Phoenicia, Cyprus and Antioch [i.e. in Syria], proclaiming the Message to none but Jews. Some of them were Cypriots and Cyrenians, who when they came to Antioch declared the Message to Greeks as well' (xii. 19-20). Clearly these refugees were Hellenists (Greek-speaking Jews), and the Greeks they addressed would have been Gentile 'God-fearers' on the fringe of Judaism, who attended the synagogues and had already abandoned idolatry. No general proclamation to non-Jews had yet been conceived, and the followers of Jesus were quite unaware of any such mandate as Matthew puts into the mouth of the risen Jesus, 'Go, therefore, and make disciples of all the Gentiles' (xxviii. 19).

The widening of the sphere of Nazorean activities initiated a new phase which called for a fresh assessment and organizational developments. But before we consider these it will be profitable to enlarge upon the attraction of the cause of Jesus for so many diverse types.

What the proclamation of Jesus as Messiah was doing was to invest with a sense of reality and immediacy hopes, anticipations and prophetic interpretations, which had lacked a convincing and acceptable personality to which to attach themselves. The synagogues of the Dispersion were at this time active centres of propaganda of Messianic ideas, proclaiming the coming doom of the existing world order and the advent from Israel of a righteous world ruler.[4] The Nazorean message that the Messiah had appeared, and was now in heaven awaiting the moment of his return to earth as Judge and King, afforded startling confirmation that events were moving rapidly and inexorably towards the predicted climax of the Ages.

Jesus thus served as a focal figure for all Last-Times devotees, as one who had set upon the purport of contemporary circumstances the seal of assurance of what they signified in terms of present distress to be followed swiftly by the deliverance of the righteous and wrath upon the idolaters and evildoers. Now all who had uttered their warnings could claim that their words had not been idle, once they could be convinced from interpretation of the Scriptures that Jesus was indeed 'he that should come'. The task of the Nazoreans was to demonstrate this and implant conviction that what Jesus had experienced answered to the predictions, including his death, resurrection and ascension. He, it was claimed, was that singular Son of Man, of whom it was written, 'Sit thou at My right hand until I make thy foes thy footstool.' By reason of this a line of communication extended from sky to earth through the operation of God's holy Spirit for the transmission of signals guiding the fortunes of the faithful and making known what would shortly come to pass.

The Nazorean movement was made impressive by its very positivity, and formidable by its believed command of supernatural resources which made it invincible and indestructible. A leader who was not on earth could not be arrested, imprisoned and executed. 'The Messiah having risen from the dead cannot be put to death again: death has no further power over him' (Rom. vi. 9). Furthermore, the Messiah's triumph over death guaranteed a similar victory for his followers, who were thus assured that even if they died before the Second Advent they would be quickened into new life to share in the joys of the Golden Age.

The present physical inaccessibility of Jesus was also of great service to the Nazoreans in another respect. He could not therefore be directly approached to state his views and define his doctrines. This meant that adherents belonging to various groups and persuasions could associate him with their own outlook, and accord him the place and titles which answered to their particular convictions. Even with the availability of many who had accompanied him while on earth it was only to a limited extent that it could be said that Jesus had categorically approved this and rejected that. The movement could thus embrace and bring within its framework a diversity of interests without need at first for a rigid orthodoxy.

We have remarked, among the mutually accepted features of the Party's position, an accent on present tribulation, since the forces of this world were inspired by Belial to lead Israel astray and to persecute those who were faithful to God and His commandments. There was no less emphasized the rewards of the Kingdom awaiting those who remained steadfast in affliction. It can well be appreciated what an appeal the themes of reward for the loyal and doom for the wicked oppressors made to the needy masses and to those souls who were moved to indignation by hedonism and corruption. Some might be militant, and others patiently quiescent; but they could all draw comfort from the knowledge that the evildoers would get their deserts while those who had suffered would have joy and gladness and an abundance of good things. Despite the Church's later accent on the other-worldly in a heavenly sense it was a prospect that moved the populace again and again in the course of its history, and inspired the peasant revolts, the chiliastic sects and New Society enterprises of one kind and another, down to the present day.[5] It gave encouragement to these shared beliefs that Jesus as a man of the people had endorsed them and in the capacity of Messiah had guaranteed their truth.

In the disputation we quoted from the *Recognitions* one of the criticisms made by the wealthy Sadducean high priest was that Jesus had said 'that the poor are blessed, and promised earthly rewards; and placed the chief gift in an earthly inheritance; and promised that those who maintain righteousness shall be satisfied with meat and drink.'

The Lukan version of the Beatitudes certainly makes Jesus declare to his disciples, 'Blessed are ye poor; for yours is the Kingdom of God. Blessed are ye that hunger now; for ye shall be filled. Blessed are ye that weep now; for ye shall laugh' (vi. 20-21). Matthew (v. 5) adds a verse from Psalm xxxvii: 'Blessed are the meek; for they shall inherit the earth.' This psalm was a favourite with the Saints, and we are fortunate enough now to have the Zadokite-Essene commentary on it, which is fully in line with Nazorean teaching. It comes out also in the *Testaments of the XII Patriarchs* (Judah. xxv. 4), where we read:

'They who have died in grief shall arise in joy,
And they who were poor for the Lord's sake shall be made rich,
And they who have been in want shall be filled,
And they who have been weak shall be strong,
And they who are put to death for the Lord's sake shall awake to life.'

It was the confidence that these expectations engendered which sustained the Nazoreans and nascent Christianity through all the vicissitudes which lay ahead, and enabled them to endure torture and death. They knew they would be raised from the dead, and live and reign on earth with the Messiah as kings and priests.[6]

The reference here is to the book of Revelation, dating from the last decade of the first century. From the same period comes the *Apocalypse of Baruch*, where it is promised that, 'The days will come, in which vines shall grow, each having ten thousand shoots, and on each shoot ten thousand branches, on each branch ten thousand twigs, and on each twig ten thousand clusters, and on each cluster ten thousand grapes, and each grape when pressed shall yield twenty-five measures of wine' (xxix. 5).

Now this very statement is quoted by the second-century Church Father Irenaeus from an earlier work of Papias, Bishop of Hierapolis, on the still earlier authority of 'the elders who saw John the disciple of the Lord', as having been made by Jesus himself, in a passage which continues: 'And when anyone of the Saints shall lay hold of a cluster, another shall cry out, "I am a better cluster, take me: bless the Lord through me." [In like manner the Lord declared] A grain of wheat shall produce ten thousand ears, and every ear shall produce ten thousand grains, and every grain shall yield ten pounds of clear pure fine flour . . .' And Papias adds that when the traitor Judas refused to credit this marvel, the Lord declared, 'They shall see who shall come to those times.'[7]

Rendel Harris suggested, no doubt correctly, that this superabundant fertility, described by *Baruch* and traced back to Jesus by Papias, depends on a haggadic interpretation of the blessing of Jacob by Isaac (Gen. xxvii. 28), where '*ribu* [ten thousand] of corn and wine' has been read instead of *rov* (plenty). Irenaeus, in introducing the reference from Papias, alludes to this blessing, pointing out that Jacob never obtained it in his lifetime. 'The predicted blessing, therefore, belongs unquestionably to the times of the Kingdom, when the righteous shall bear rule upon their rising from the dead; when also the creation, having been renovated and set free, shall fructify with an abundance of all kinds of food.'

The Nazorean eschatology, which pinned its faith on the return of Jesus from heaven to reign on earth, did not begin to be disputed until well into the second century, and even then was still held to be the true faith. In the *Dialogue with Trypho* Justin Martyr is questioned on this very matter. 'Tell me,' says the Jew Trypho, 'do you really admit that this place, Jerusalem, shall be rebuilt; and do you expect your people to be gathered together, and made joyful with Christ and the patriarchs, and the prophets, both the men of our nation, and other proselytes who joined them before your Christ came?' To this Justin replies, 'If you have fallen in with some Christians . . . who do not admit this . . . who say there is no resurrection of the dead, and that their souls, when they die, are taken to heaven; do not imagine that they are Christians. . . . But I and others, who are right-minded Christians on all points, are assured that there will be a resurrection of the dead, and a thousand years in Jerusalem, which will then be built, adorned and enlarged, as the prophets Ezekiel and Isaiah and others declare' (*Dial.* lxxx).

From the very beginning the followers of the Way, the Poor (as an ideological group or as the needy in general) had everything to gain from their devotion. It was written in the Psalms (Ps. lxix), 'The Lord heareth the Poor, and despiseth not his prisoners. . . . For God will save Zion, and will build the cities of Judah: that they may dwell there, and have it in possession. The seed also of His servants shall inherit it; and they that love His name shall dwell therein.'

The movement centred on Jesus as Messiah and, drawing to itself adherents from all the Fourth Philosophy groups, may well be termed Zionist. It took up all those passages of Scripture which promised the salvation of Zion and the coming to Zion of the king and redeemer (such as Ps. ii. 6; Isa. lix. 20, and Zech. ix. 9). In Zion would be deliverance. It also adduced the words of Isaiah, 'Behold, I lay in Zion for a foundation stone, a tried stone, a precious corner stone, a sure foundation: he that believeth shall not make haste' (Isa. xxviii. 16; I Pet. ii. 6-7). This stone was identified with Jesus as that which the builders rejected, which would be made the chief corner stone (Ps. cxviii. 22), and with the stone of Nebuchadnezzar's dream 'cut out of the mountain without hands' which broke in pieces the great image. This signified that God would set up a kingdom which would bring all others to an end and supersede them (Dan. ii).

Jesus had come to Zion as king, and had celebrated the Passover – festival of freedom – in the City of David on the Ophel. And here in Zion the Nazoreans had established their headquarters.

The persecution designed to curb the movement misfired and resulted in a wider circulation of the Message, something which, even if it had been contemplated, had not been planned at this stage. Already it had been heard and heeded beyond the boundaries of the Land of Israel. Fresh links were forged with existing sectarian communities, and new groups of believers were springing up to form a widespread network. The prophecy seemed indeed on the way to fulfilment that from Zion would go forth the Law, and the Word of the Lord from Jerusalem (Mic. iv. 2; Isa. ii. 3).

The exodus of refugees would appear to have been more considerable than the Acts suggests. Some were simply concerned to get to areas where the high priest's writ did not run or could not effectively be executed. Certain of the Hellenists seem to have decided to return to their countries of origin, and to have made for the sea ports, going down via Lydda to Joppa, or north to Ptolemais and Antioch to sail for Cyprus and Asia Minor. It is not improbable that at this time the Message was carried to Alexandria and Cyrenaica.

Ebionite and Mandaean traditions speak of a mass migration of some five or six thousand persons to seek asylum with friendly communities in the north-east. This considerable company crossed the Jordan near Jericho and travelled through Peraea to Batanea and Auranitis. It may be assumed that Saul's aim in setting out for Damascus was to pursue this body of devotees and apprehend as many as possible before they became dispersed. This would be more profitable than chasing all over the country for scattered individuals.

But things did not work out as planned. It was Saul himself who was arrested in his vengeful course by what some believe to have been a kind of epileptic fit in which he was blinded by a sudden light, and heard the voice of Jesus speaking to him. At Damascus the enemy was converted into the disciple, and began to proclaim Jesus as Messiah in the synagogues of the city. His sponsor in Damascus was a certain Ananias, who may well have been connected with the Zadokite-Essenes in this area. When there was heated controversy as a result of Saul's preaching, we may consider it likely that Ananias suggested that he sojourn for a time with one of the New Covenant communities long established in the north-east.[8] He states himself (Gal. i. 17) that he went away to Arabia. And since he subsequently returned to Damascus we may infer that this signified Nabataean territory in the eastern part of Auranitis.

NOTES AND REFERENCES

1. The prophecies were applied to the preaching of John the Baptist in the wilderness (Mk. i. 1–4; Lk. i. 76). The *Community Rule* of the Zadokite-Essenes instructs the members that 'they shall separate from the habitation of ungodly men and shall go into the wilderness to prepare the Way of Him: as it is written, Prepare ye in the wilderness the Way of the Lord. . . . this [Way] is the study of the Law which he commanded by the hand of Moses, that they may do according to all that has been revealed by His holy Spirit' (VIII).
2. The Dead Sea Scrolls make frequent reference to the Time of Trial, or Time of Testing, during which the wicked will persecute the righteous. The Revelation (iii. 10) also speaks of this Time. One of the sources of the concept is Dan. xii. 9–10, where we read, 'Go your way, Daniel; for the words are closed up and sealed until the Time of the End. Many shall be purified, and made white, and tried; but the wicked shall do wickedly; and none of the wicked shall understand; but the skilled shall understand.'
3. This conjunction had previously occurred in the person of the Hasmonean ruler John Hyrcanus I, whom many thought might be the Messiah. See Test. *XII Patriarchs* (Levi. viii. 14–15); Josephus, *J.W.* I. 68–9; *Antiq.* XIII. 300.
4. See Schonfield, *Those Incredible Christians,* chs. ii and iii.
5. See Cohn, *The Pursuit of the Millennium.*
6. Rev. vi. 9–10; cp. Dan. vii. 18. The Mosaic statement that Israel should be 'a kingdom of priests' has been varied to read 'kings and priests'. The Zadokite-Essenes seem not to have confined the description 'priests' to those of Levitical and Aaronic descent.
7. Iren. *Haeres.* V. xxxiii.
8. There are many likenesses to the thinking and terminology of the Dead Sea Scrolls in the Pauline Epistles. See also below, Part Three, Chapter 28. Curiously, in the account of the early history of the Zadokites there is reference to 'the Student of the Law who came to Damascus' and laid down the precepts they should follow. See Schonfield, *Secrets of the Dead Sea Scrolls* and *The Jew of Tarsus.*

CHAPTER 13

JACOB'S LADDER

With the conversion of Saul and the deposition of the high priest Jonathan the persecution petered out. Theophilus, the new high priest appointed by Vitellius at the Passover of A.D. 37, was no doubt advised by the legate that internal disturbances which fostered disaffection were not in the Roman interest. In any case Theophilus appears to have decided to proceed cautiously since he managed to remain in office for four very difficult years. Vitellius had been greatly concerned with popular unrest at Jerusalem the previous year, when he had sent Pilate to Rome and deposed the high priest Caiaphas. His policy of appeasement had since been further indicated by the fact that in obeying the orders of Tiberius to lead an army against the Arabs he had yielded to Jewish entreaties that the troops with their standards should not march through Judea. Coming again now to Jerusalem with Herod Antipas he had shown his respect by going up to the Temple and offering sacrifices to the God of the Jews. Josephus makes the unusual statement that when Vitellius arrived at Jerusalem 'he was greeted with special warmth by the Jewish multitude' (*Antiq.* XVIII. 121-3).

While in Jerusalem the legate received word of the death of the emperor, which had taken place on 15th March, and administered to the Jews an oath of allegiance to his successor Gaius Caligula.

For the Nazoreans a period of peace ensued. 'The Community throughout Judea, Galilee[1] and Samaria now enjoyed peace. Founded upon and motivated by the fear of the Lord and the exhortation of the holy Spirit it grew ever larger' (Acts ix. 31). Part of this development is attributed to the deacon Philip, who had proclaimed the Message in Samaria, and later, having gone south to Azotus (Ashdod), turned north again giving out the news in the towns of the coastal plain as far as Caesarea.

The communities which were formed as a consequence made it necessary for the apostles at Jerusalem to send Peter and John to confirm and instruct them. It was evident that for the future a great deal of pastoral work was going to be required, and that this called for a more clearly defined governmental structure. One of the lessons of the persecution was that the Party needed some tightening of its discipline. The formation of a Central Authority had to be envisaged, an Authority whose function and jurisdiction was as assured as that of the Sanhedrin itself.

The Party from its inception had been considerably indebted to the thinking and practices of the Essenes, and their experience was found extremely helpful as a model for the new structure. The Essenes had long had a network of communities, both urban and rural, with an administrative centre located at Qumran near the Dead Sea. Some information about the organization is furnished by Josephus; but with the discovery of the Dead Sea Scrolls we now have the sect's own documents giving many more details of its constitution and regulations.

Some uncertainty exists on particular points, but we may represent the position to have been approximately as follows. The body as a whole was composed of integrated but largely self-governing groups and camps. To form one of these the minimum number of full members must be ten, of whom one was a priest. The total of full members and probationers of all the communities was designated 'the Multitude', while the full members alone constituted 'the Many'. Those who belonged only to the Multitude could not eat with the Many, and the erring full member could be excluded from eating with the Many for specified periods according to the nature of the offence. For the gravest crimes, moral or spiritual, he could be excommunicated. In each local community 'an officer over the Many' examined every candidate for membership, but after the probationary period the novice was only admitted to the company of the Many if they voted for his acceptance.

Once a year, at any rate, on the feast of Pentecost the communities met in General Assembly. The affairs of the Many in each community were taken care of by a supervisor (*mebaqqer*) answering to the Greek *episkopos* (bishop). His duties included instruction of the congregation in the works of God. He was to 'love them as a father loves his children and carry them in all their distress like a shepherd his sheep'.

The Central Authority consisted of a body of elders, with an inner cabinet composed of three priests and twelve laymen. Collectively they constituted the General Council. Additionally there was a chief supervisor, who might be described as archbishop, who must be from thirty to fifty years of age and possess high qualifications. To him complaints were to be brought. There was also, with like age qualifications, a kind of high priest of great learning capable of giving final rulings. This priest could be regarded as the contemporary True Teacher (Teacher of Righteousness), supremely versed in prophecy and the interpretation of the Scriptures. It is a matter of dispute as to whether there was not also a third leader corresponding to the officer (*paqid*) of the local communities.

It is considered probable that at different periods of the history of the sect certain changes were made, which would account for variations in the descriptions furnished by the *Damascus Rule* and the *Community Rule*.[2]

The Nazorean organization did not call for such elaborate rules of admission, nor for a period of probation, nor for the strict disciplines of a monastic type of order. Later, however, the Ebionite wing was much stricter. For the Nazoreans there was no requirement to give up ordinary employment or to make over all possessions to the community. It sufficed that a candidate for membership was given some instruction, and having pledged allegiance to Jesus was immersed in water in token of repentance for former sins and in recognition of his identification with loyalist Israel. Thereafter he took part in the communal meetings. In order not to conflict with Sabbath attendance at the synagogue there was a weekly meeting on the first day of the week, the day associated with the Messiah's resurrection. The Sunday meeting was probably adopted from the Essenes, who honoured this day, the first day of Creation, and whose annual General Assembly was on a Sunday at Pentecost. Similarly the Nazorean love-feast on Sunday seems also to have come from the Essene Holy Meal of the Many, though also related by the followers of Jesus to the Last Supper and to his promise of return to establish his kingdom.[3] On the same day the affairs of the local community were considered and the needs of the poor and sick. The meal taken together was introduced, as in Jewish custom, by a thanksgiving (*kiddush*) over bread and wine.

One form of words used later on for the Thanksgiving (*Eucharist*) ceremony has been preserved in the *Didache* (Teaching of the XII Apostles).[4]

First concerning the cup: 'We give thanks to Thee, Our Father, for the holy vine of David Thy servant, which Thou didst make known to us through Jesus Thy servant: to Thee be glory for ever.' And concerning the broken bread: 'We give Thee thanks, our Father, for the life and knowledge which Thou didst make known to us through Jesus

Thy servant: to Thee be glory for ever. As this broken bread was scattered upon the mountains, but was brought together and became one, so let Thy Community be gathered together from the ends of the earth into Thy Kingdom; for Thine is the glory and the power, through Jesus the Messiah for ever' (ix. 2-4).

At first, as regards local communities, it seems to have sufficed to appoint one member as elder, whose duties answered somewhat to the Essene 'officer over the Many'. Later, with more developed organization, administrators (deacons) were also introduced, and local supervisors (bishops) were ordained by apostles under licence from the Central Authority. Such officials were in no sense clergy, but mature and reliable persons who were married men with families.[5] Duties of a social and charitable nature were also assigned to widows.

Much of our information comes from the Acts and Pauline Epistles, which largely relate to the communities established by Paul and his colleagues. But they cannot have differed radically from the general Nazorean arrangements.

As things stood around A.D. 38 to 39 circumstances had not yet arisen which demanded stringent control to maintain the unity and integrity of the Party. These did not begin to come about before the issue was raised of the terms of admission of converts from the Gentiles, and Pauline teaching threatened a split. When that happened the door was open for false teachers to propagate their doctrines in communities in lands too remote to be reached effectively by available field workers. Finally, with the destruction of Jerusalem and the cessation of an operative Central Authority, there was nothing to stop the growth of sectarian tendencies until a new Christian orthodoxy, having little in common with its predecessor, managed to establish itself. Even so, a struggle went on for centuries, notably between the new Catholic Church and those who sought to preserve or revive tenets characteristic of the original faith which had been superseded.

What was immediately needed was the creation of an acknowledged government of the Party, capable of bringing all local communities within a definite framework and possessing sufficient authority to deal with problems and complaints and lay down lines of policy. The very mixed composition of the Nazorean Party demanded that there should be a Council under a leadership acceptable to all sections.

A Council presented no great difficulty since there were models both in the Essene structure and in the Sanhedrin of the nation. It was considered, therefore, that it should be composed of seventy representative members to be termed Elders. Luke indicates that Jesus had chosen, after the twelve apostles, an apostolic body of that number (Lk. x. 1). Moses, of course, had had seventy elders to assist him with government (Nu. xi. 16-17), and the Sanhedrin accordingly consisted of this number of members. Luke is simply giving the sanction of Jesus in his lifetime to the Council the Nazoreans created. It may well be that the apostles and elders were normally engaged in field work and only met as a Council with legislative and juridical functions periodically. Very likely there was an annual General Assembly at Jerusalem at Pentecost.

As with the Essenes there would appear to have been instituted a Cabinet of fifteen, a group of twelve with three leaders, the latter also corresponding to the heads of the Sanhedrin, that is the high priest as *Nasi*, his deputy (*Sagan*), and the chief officer of the religious court (*Ab Beth-Din*). Our sources are rather confusing, because the twelve were identified later with the twelve apostles, and the three leaders with the Peter, Jacob and John who had been the closest companions of Jesus and belonged to the twelve. Again we may infer that the Nazorean structure which was created was later reflected in the Gospels in relation to the time of Jesus. Those whom Paul styles 'the pillars' (Gal. ii. 9) are also a Peter, Jacob and John, but the Jacob is not one of the sons of Zebedee, and very possibly the John also.[6]

The view we take is that the triumvirate at the head of Nazorean affairs consisted of Peter as general supervisor of all the communities, Jacob the brother of Jesus as *Nasi*, with John the Priest of Jerusalem as his Deputy. Peter was admirable as a propagandist, and he is shown in the Acts as largely engaged in pastoral work visiting and strengthening the communities. John the Priest was well qualified to deal with organization and points of doctrine, and could act as Deputy to the Nazorean *Nasi*, the supreme position accorded by common consent to Jacob the brother of Jesus. Jacob called the Just corresponded to the True Teacher of the Zadokite-Essenes, and is depicted as the wise interpreter of the Scriptures who presides over the Council and gives his rulings. It is pertinent that both Jacob the brother of Jesus and John who had been the Beloved Disciple are credited by tradition with having served in the capacity of high priest. The tradition could well have arisen from the fact that the offices they held answered to that of the high priest and his deputy in the Sanhedrin.

There seems to have been no doubt at all that there was only one man fitted to be head of the Nazoreans. The next younger brother of Jesus may have been about thirty-one years of age in A.D. 38. Jacob had the charisma that he was of the House of David and the closest blood-relative of the Messiah. In him the Messiah could be regarded as to a degree still physically present on earth. Jacob in this respect enjoyed increasingly the prestige of a Prince Regent.[7] But he also commended himself as a man of extreme Jewish piety, an ascetic, and a champion of the poor and oppressed. It was even said of him that, like Jesus, the Scriptures had prophesied concerning him. In the *Gospel of Thomas* when the disciples ask Jesus to whom they shall go when he has left them, they are told, 'You will go to Jacob the Just, for whose sake heaven and earth were created.'

As the years passed the spiritual stature of Jacob grew: he was widely venerated, and not only in Nazorean circles; and after his death legends sprang up around him. Indeed, there is some probability that certain sayings of Jesus in the Gospels actually originated with his brother Jacob.[8]

Most of the accounts of Jacob come from statements and traditions current in the second century A.D., including what we find in the Acts. The *Gospel of the Hebrews* told of the manner in which the risen Jesus had specially appeared to his brother, an appearance already attested by Paul (I Cor. xv. 7). The principal authorities on the leader of the Nazoreans are Hegesippus, Clement of Alexandria and Julius Africanus. But we have echoes and further references in the Clementine literature (quasi-Ebionite), and in the works of Origen, Eusebius, Jerome and Epiphanius (third and fourth century). It will be appropriate to quote some of these sources here.

'Peter, and Jacob and John [i.e. the sons of Zebedee], after the ascension of the Saviour, though they had been preferred by the Lord, did not contend for the honour, but chose Jacob the Just as Bishop of Jerusalem.' And further, 'The Lord imparted the gift of knowledge to Jacob the Just, to John, and Peter after the resurrection. These delivered it to the rest of the apostles, and they to the seventy of whom Barnabas was one.'[9]

Now Jacob, the brother of the Lord, who, as there were many of this name, was termed the Just by all, from the days of our Lord until now, received the government of the Community with the apostles. This apostle was consecrated from his mother's womb. He drank neither wine nor fermented liquors, and abstained from animal food. A razor never came upon his head; he never anointed himself with oil or used a public bath. He alone was allowed to enter the Holy Place. He never wore woollen, only linen garments. He was in the habit of entering the Temple alone, and was often to be found upon his knees and interceding for the forgiveness of the people; so that his knees became as hard as a camel's. . . . And indeed, on account of his exceeding great piety, he was called the Just [i.e *Zaddik*] and Oblias [i.e. *Ophla-am*], which signifies Justice and the People's Bulwark; as the Prophets declare concerning him.[10]

As Epiphanius picked up such information and somewhat embroidered it, it emerged that Jacob 'was of David's race, being the son of Joseph, and that he was a Nazorean [really nazirite]. . . . Moreover we have found that he officiated after the manner of the ancient priesthood. Wherefore also he was permitted once a year to enter the Holy of Holies, as the Law commanded the high priests, according to that which is written; for so many before us have told of him, both Eusebius and Clement and others. Furthermore, he was empowered to wear the high priestly diadem upon his head, as the aforementioned trustworthy men have attested in their memoirs.[11]

The legend that Jacob had officiated as high priest owed something, as we have suggested, to the position he came to occupy for the Nazoreans as the spiritual and political head of loyalist Israel, which made him in effect the high priest's counterpart and rival. This status may well have contributed eventually to his death at the instigation of the high priest Ananus.

The honorific title of *Zaddik* (the Saint, or the Just) invited comparison between Jacob and the famous high priest Simon the Just of the early third century B.C. whose memory was revered. Josephus says of him that 'he was surnamed the Just because of both his piety towards God and his benevolence to his countrymen' (*Antiq.* XII. 43). To him is attributed the saying, 'The world is sustained by three things, the Law, the Temple Service, and the practice of benevolence.'[12] Jacob appeared as another Simon the Saint, and it was related that he was so venerated by the people that when he went about 'they would crowd around him and strive to touch the hem of his garment.'[13] He is styled, 'the supreme Supervisor, who rules Jerusalem, the holy Community of the Hebrews, and the communities everywhere excellently founded by the providence of God,' and he is addressed as 'the Lord Jacob'.[14]

The other designation of Jacob, probably an original *Ophla-am*, alluding to his care for the people and his championship of their rights, was appropriately chosen in token of the circumstance that it was on the protecting ridge of the Ophel (*Ophla* in Aramaic), which defended the Lower City on the east, that Jacob had his official seat.

By the vast majority of Christians it is not known even today that Jacob the brother of Jesus was installed as the supreme ruler over all believers in Christ, and remained head of government for about a quarter of a century until his death. This is because the Acts is silent about his elevation. This silence of Luke, as many scholars have remarked, was not due to ignorance (cp. Acts xv) but to deliberate intention. For example, regarding the controversy at Antioch over the terms of admission of Gentile converts, where Paul had written that certain emissaries came to Antioch from Jacob (Gal. ii. 15), Luke will only say that they came from Judea (Acts xv. 1).

Luke's 'second treatise' was designed to represent the progressive universalization of the Gospel, especially in the Roman Empire, with Peter and others preparing the way for the call of the Gentiles carried out by Paul. He was at pains to make clear that the Jews were the opponents of this development and that Roman officials had been the best friends of the Christian cause. It did not at all suit the thinking of his time that the proto-Christians had been Jewish nationalists headed by an extremely devout Jew of the blood royal, who was also the brother of the Christ the Romans had crucified. The Church at Rome at the beginning of the second century, desiring to establish itself as the new Central Authority for Christians, built up Peter as the chief representative of Jesus, who had come to the West and had identified himself with the teaching of Paul.[15]

The choice of Jacob, however, had been a wise one in the formative period of the Nazorean Party, since he could hold together all its diverse elements as no other could. He followed strictly the Way of the Law. His nationalism pleased the Zealots, while his extreme asceticism commended him to the Ebionite-Essene wing. He enjoyed the respect of the Pharisees, and was beloved by the Jewish populace of Jerusalem.

It was well for the Nazoreans that they were enabled to consolidate at this time and define their governmental structure, because in Saul of Tarsus they had obtained a recruit of exceptional calibre and energy, who was destined to become a menace to their whole enterprise.

Saul did not appear again at Jerusalem until some three years after he had left it as the avowed enemy of the Nazoreans. His return can therefore be dated late in A.D. 39. After his experience on the road to Damascus, he tells us,

> I did not take immediate steps to consult any earthly authority. Neither did I go up to Jerusalem to interview those who were apostles before me. Instead, I went away to Arabia, and returned again to Damascus. Not until three years had elapsed did I go up to Jerusalem to report to Cephas, and I remained with him fifteen days. But I met none of the other apostles except Jacob the Lord's brother. . . . After that I went to the regions of Syria and Cilicia, and remained unknown by sight to the Christian communities of Judea. They only heard that 'he who formerly persecuted us now proclaims the faith he once attacked', and they praised God for me (Gal. i. 16–24).

For Paul's definite period Luke substitutes 'many days'. But we should prefer Paul's much earlier personal testimony, and allow that he was in Arabia for at least two years. We have suggested that he associated with a Zadokite community, which may have been recommended to him by Ananias of Damascus. Two years was the period of probation of the Zadokite-Essenes, who did not admit anyone to full membership until the third year. If Saul did stay in one of the sectarian camps in the Land of Damascus as a probationer, it would seem that either he had no intention of acquiring full membership, or that his views did not allow him to achieve it. We find a good deal of Essenite language and doctrine in his epistles. Of this time he wrote afterwards of the abundance of revelations he received, and of being caught up to the third heaven, to Paradise (the Garden), where he heard ineffable words which no human is permitted to utter (II Cor. xii. 1-4). Since Saul's conviction was that he had been appointed to preach to the Gentiles, this could well have brought him into conflict with his hosts.

Back in Damascus Saul was in further trouble. Luke talks of a Jewish plot to assassinate him, but Saul makes no mention of this. He relates that 'at Damascus the ethnarch of King Aretas picketed the city of the Damascenes to hem me in; but through a loophole I was let down the wall in a cage, and so escaped his clutches' (II Cor. xi. 32-3; cp. Acts ix. 23-5).

The King Aretas referred to was that Nabataean monarch Harith IV, who had defeated the army of Herod Antipas and whom Vitellius had been ordered by Tiberius to destroy. The order was on the eve of being put into execution when Tiberius died in March, A.D. 37. The new emperor Gaius Caligula rescinded it, and as a gesture of friendship on his ascension he leased Damascus to Harith. The city and its environs reverted to Roman rule on Harith's death in A.D. 40. It was only therefore between 37 and 40 that Damascus was under Arab government, and this confirms our chronology of events.

Luke reports that

> on arriving at Jerusalem Saul attempted to join the disciples. But they were all afraid of him and refused to credit that he was a disciple. Barnabas got in touch with him, however, and brought him to the apostles, and described to them how Saul had seen the Lord while on the road, and how he had spoken to him, and how at Damascus he had argued eloquently on behalf of Jesus. So then he was free to come and go with them at Jerusalem, and spoke eloquently on the Lord's behalf, particularly engaging the Hellenists in debate. But when the brothers became aware that these had designs on his life they brought him down to Caesarea and sent him away to Tarsus (Acts ix. 26–30).

Against Luke, who was anxious to show that Saul's credentials had been accepted by all the apostles, Saul insists that he reported only to Peter, and saw no one else except Jacob the brother of Jesus, who is thus indicated as already holding a position of particular authority. It may well be true that the former persecutor was shunned, and that he sought to give evidence of good faith by boldly debating with those foreign-born Jews who were previously active with him in attacking the Nazorean Hellenists. Their desire to destroy the defector would be natural. The Nazorean leaders would certainly not have welcomed the possibility that another outbreak against the Party would be triggered off by Saul's access of missionary zeal, and decided that the best thing to do was to get him quickly out of the country. They therefore had him seen off at Caesarea by boat back to his native Cilicia. In this way a fresh crisis was averted.

NOTES AND REFERENCES

1. Luke's Gospel had made the apostles stay on in Jerusalem after the death of Jesus, and in the Acts makes no previous reference to the existence of Nazorean communities in Galilee. Yet Jesus must have had a good many followers there. Luke's concentration on the westward movement of the Message has deprived us of important information.
2. See the discussion by Vermes in his Introduction to *The Dead Sea Scrolls in English,* and other authorities on the Scrolls.
3. The Zadokites had their 'Holy Meal of the Many'. An Assembly Banquet, foreshadowing the gatherings in the Messianic Era, is described in the *Messianic Rule,* where the Priest leader is the first to extend his hand over

the first-fruits of bread and wine, and thereafter the Davidic leader, the Messiah of Israel.

4. The *Didache* is considered to date from the early second century, but some of its elements are older. We note in this form of the Thanksgiving no thought of Jesus as divine, or any allusion to his atoning death.
5. Cp. I Tim. iii.
6. See above, Part Two, Chapter 8, pp. 102–5.
7. When Paul wrote to the Galatians of his doctrinal clash with the Central Authority, he is being deliberately offensive when he says of Jacob and his colleagues, 'As for those of repute – whatever they were makes no difference to me: God takes no one at face value – they imposed on me nothing additional' (Gal. ii. 6).
8. See below, Part Two, Chapter 21, p. 222.
9. Both statements are from Clement of Alexandria, quoted by Eusebius, *Eccl. Hist.* II. i. If Barnabas was one of the Seventy this would suggest that this body had not been appointed by Jesus in his lifetime, as stated solely by Luke. But since it was accepted that Jesus could speak from heaven to his followers on earth by revelation, some things received in this manner could easily be imagined later to have related to his lifetime and were thus given a place in the Gospels. Certain sayings of Jesus may have originated in this way.
10. Euseb. *op. cit.* II. xxiii.
11. Epiphanius, *Panarion,* lxxviii.
12. Mishnah, *Aboth.* i. 2. See further the *Jewish Encyclopaedia* (Funk and Wagnalls) under Art. Simeon the Just.
13. Jerome, *Commentary on Galatians,* i. 19.
14. *Epistle of Clement to Jacob,* preceding the Clementine *Homilies.* The Clement concerned is Clement of Rome, disciple of Peter.
15. See Part One, Chapter 2, p. 33, and Schonfield, *Those Incredible Christians.*

CHAPTER 14

THE STATUE

Luke's apologetic aim in the Acts, to present the Jews as hostile to the Christians, requires him as far as possible to convey that the Romans supported the Christians against the Jews. Consequently it does not suit his purpose to report circumstances which exhibit the Jews in a favourable light in relation to the Romans. Even so, it is surprising that he should say nothing at all of an event so signal and consequential that it could not fail to have a profound effect on all the followers of Jesus. This event was the design of the emperor Gaius Caligula to have a statue of himself in the guise of Zeus set up in the Temple at Jerusalem.

One of the repercussions was to identify the definition of a fantastically evil eschatological figure, the arch-enemy of the Saints, the Antichrist, who enters even into the Pauline documents as 'the Lawless One, the Doomed One, who opposes and elevates himself above everything regarded as a god or as an object of worship, so that he himself sits in God's Temple, claiming to be God . . . whom the Lord Jesus will consume with the breath of his mouth and annihilate with the radiance of his presence, that one whose coming is attended – in the way Satan works – by every kind of mendacious trickery practised on those who are perishing' (II Thess. ii. 3-10).

Ever since the days of Antiochus Epiphanes, 'the Manifest God', who had caused an altar to Zeus Olympios to be erected in the Temple at Jerusalem, the great sacrilege had been in the thought and anticipations of students of the Last Times. Daniel's dark description of the insolent and impious monarch who dared to contend with the Most High, his reference to 'the abomination that maketh desolate', and the intriguing numerals which dated the duration of the tribulations, were deemed to supply precise if baffling information as to when the climax might be expected. Now, and with startling suddenness, the major terms of the vision seemed as if they would correspond with actuality, due to the growing mental malady of Gaius Caesar.

The apotheosis of the emperors had begun in earnest in the reign of Augustus, though his predecessor Julius Caesar had been deified after his death by decree of the Senate, and even in his lifetime had been addressed as Jupiter Julius. For Augustus, acceptance of divinity became a matter of policy to secure the unification of the Empire and assure the loyalty of the provinces to Rome. Thus an Imperial Cult developed in which the worship of Rome and the divinity of Caesar were conjoined (*flamen Romae et divi Augusti*).

It was the eastern Provinces, with their tradition of monarchical deification, which were most forward in promoting the cult, which spread with great rapidity. But Egypt also was not slow to pay tribute; so that as far away as Ethiopia an inscription dated 7 B.C. could be directed to 'Caesar, who reigns over the seas and continents, Jupiter, who holds from Jupiter his father the title of Liberator, Master of Europe and Asia, Star of all Greece, who lifts himself up with the glory of great Jupiter, Saviour'.

Gaius Caligula, however, was the first of the emperors to take his divinity literally, instead of regarding the cult as a characteristic and useful expression of loyalty. To this obsession Lucius Vitellius, legate of Syria, contributed when, returning to Rome at the end of his term of office, he adored the emperor by prostrating himself on the ground, and would only appear before him with his head veiled.[1] Suetonius, who reports this, also tells how Gaius 'began to arrogate to himself a divine majesty. He ordered all the images of the gods, which were famous either for their beauty or the veneration paid to them, to be brought from Greece, so that he might take the heads off, and substitute his own. . . . He also instituted a temple and priests, with choicest victims, in honour of his own divinity. In his temple stood a statue of gold, the exact likeness of himself, which was daily dressed in garments corresponding with those he wore. The most opulent persons in the city offered themselves as candidates for the honour of being his priests, and purchased it successively at an immense price.'[2] The emperor's derangement went so far that he would invite the moon to cohabit with him, and pretend to hold converse with the statue of Jupiter Capitolinus.

How the design to have his statue erected at Jerusalem was put into the emperor's head is not completely clear. Neither is there exact agreement on the course events followed afterwards. The principal accounts are furnished by Philo, the Jewish philosopher of Alexandria, in his *Embassy to Gaius*, and by Josephus in his *Antiquities*. The former has the value of being contemporary and the work of one directly involved in what transpired at the Roman end. Philo headed the Jewish delegation from Alexandria which had been sent to Gaius to seek relief from Egyptian anti-semitism at the time the emperor's intention was disclosed, and without prior knowledge of the blow that was to fall. Nevertheless, from the two accounts the main features are sufficiently plain.

What had started things off was the hostility subsisting between the Gentile and Jewish inhabitants in towns where there were substantial communities of both. This was the case in many places along the eastern Mediterranean seaboard, and notably in Egypt in the great city of Alexandria. The causes of friction were radical religious differences which prevented integration and fostered civic jealousy and animosity. An incident at Jamnia in the Judean coastal region, and an outbreak of violence at Alexandria, gave opportunity to Jew-haters to feed the emperor's dementia by representing to him that of all his subjects the Jews alone refused to show their loyalty by paying him divine honours. Nothing would then content Gaius except the setting up in the Jerusalem Temple of a colossal gilded statue of himself.

Accordingly, the emperor sent Petronius to succeed Vitellius as legate of Syria (A.D. 39) with orders to have the statue made and convey it to Judea escorted by an army. If the Jews refused to accept it voluntarily force was to be employed to have it installed. Petronius set about his task, and while the construction of the statue was entrusted to skilled Phoenician craftsmen at Sidon he assembled a force of some two legions with auxiliaries and marched them to Ptolemais (Acco), apparently planning to have discussions there with the Jewish leaders about reception of the image. If the Jews rejected the emperor's commands the army would move on Jerusalem in the spring of A.D. 40 when the statue would be ready.

When the Jewish representatives arrived at Ptolemais and were apprised of Gaius' design their horror was unbounded. An unprecedented calamity now threatened the whole nation, for no Jews of whatever persuasion would submit to such violation of their fundamental faith. The dire news spread swiftly, not only to Jerusalem but to every part of the country, and the response was instantaneous. The Jews, high and low, rich and poor, men, women and children, poured out of every town and village, and in unarmed masses made their way to Ptolemais, startling and greatly disturbing the legate. It was clear that the emperor's orders could not be carried out without the wholesale slaughter of the population. Petronius temporized and went to Tiberias to test feeling there, but again he was besieged by clamouring and wailing multitudes. Members of the Herodian family urged him to write to Gaius telling him of the position. They suggested that he point out that because the populace had forsaken the countryside to make their appeal the crops would not be sown, and therefore it would be impossible to meet the payment of the Roman tribute. The only ones who would profit would be brigands. Apart from the reluctance of Petronius to make war on a whole nation which was not in arms, this contention seemed to make enough sense to justify writing to the emperor to change his mind.

We should observe here that with the Jews the year A.D. 40 to 41, from September of 40, would be a Sabbatical Year. Consequently, if no crops were sown in 39 to 40 the land would lie fallow for two successive years resulting in dearth on a vast scale. Whatever else might happen the collection of the Roman tribute would be impossible and revenue too would dry up.

The letter was forwarded to Gaius with the utmost speed, but the reply that came back insisted that Petronius proceed with the installation of the statue. At this time, in complete ignorance of the emperor's design, his old friend the Jewish prince Agrippa had come to court at Rome to pay his respects.[3] Gaius had made him heir of the tetrarchies of Philip and Antipas and honoured him with the title of king. When the emperor told him of his purpose and the trouble he was having with the Jews Agrippa simply could not believe his ears and fell sick with shock. When he had somewhat recovered he wrote to Gaius a long pleading letter explaining most carefully why the Jews could not receive the statue and that his persistence must mean the end of their friendship, since Agrippa at all costs to himself could not be a traitor to his people.

Gaius was so far moved by this communication as to give way reluctantly as regards erecting his statue in the Temple, but outside Jerusalem any persons were to have the right to set up altars and images in his honour. It is not certain whether the emperor had got as far as writing to Petronius to this effect before he received a further despatch from his legate which so enraged him that he changed his mind again. Due to the conflict of testimony we cannot be sure of the facts. It is evident, however, that Gaius did receive a request from

Petronius that he be authorized not to proceed with the project since it could only be pursued by waging total war on the Jews, and that this caused the emperor to rescind his word to Agrippa.

Josephus relates that Petronius had been so affected by the pleas of the Jews and their deep attachment to their faith that he took a risk which might well result in his own death. Apprising the concourse at Tiberias of his intention, he bade them depart and catch up on their agricultural work. 'As soon as Petronius had finished delivering this speech before the Jews, God straightway sent a heavy shower that was contrary to general anticipation. . . . Indeed, that entire year had been beset by so great a drought that it caused the people to despair' (*Antiq.* XVIII. 285). The downfall of rain was taken as an augury that all would be well.[4]

The response of Gaius was to accuse Petronius of taking bribes from the Jews and to recommend him to commit suicide for flouting his orders. Philo declares that it was the intention of the emperor to have another statue made in Rome, which would be conveyed to Judea on the ship by which he himself would travel after visiting Alexandria (*Embassy to Gaius,* 337-8).

But on 24th January, A.D. 41, Gaius was assassinated in Rome, and news of this reached Petronius twenty-seven days before the arrival of the emperor's letter, which bad weather had delayed in transit for three months. This remarkable circumstance was ascribed by the Jews to God's direct intervention to save His people and to honour Petronius for protecting them. If the design had gone forward not only would hundreds of thousands of Jews have perished in their homeland, but such a massacre would have followed in Egypt, Asia, Greece and Italy, that tens of thousands more would have been wiped out. As it was there were some incidents; but the death of Gaius and the prompt action of his successor Claudius prevented their development.

From the strange way in which things had worked out there were numerous Gentiles who now concluded that the Jews must indeed be under a special providence. Consequently there was a fresh inducement at this time for many to become God-fearers and attend Jewish worship.

We may have a hint of this in the Acts. It was at Antioch the Great, Antioch on the Orontes, that the first considerable adherence of Gentiles to the Messianic cause took place. Antioch was the official seat of the Roman legate of Syria, and here the deliverance of

Petronius and the salvation of the Jews must have created quite a stir. There was a large Jewish community in this Graeco-Roman city, which had been very forward in sending costly gifts to the Temple at Jerusalem. 'Moreover,' Josephus writes, 'they were constantly attracting to their religious ceremonies multitudes of Greeks, and these they had in some measure incorporated with themselves' (*J.W.* VII. 45). In other words these large numbers of Greeks had abandoned idolatry and become God-fearers, and attended worship in the Jewish synagogues. We may consider that the outcome of the affair of the statue was responsible for a considerable influx at this juncture.

The Nazoreans at Jerusalem received word that they too had obtained fresh recruits at Antioch, and Barnabas was sent to study the situation and report. What he found surprised and delighted him. But there was evident need of a teacher from a Greek environment who was of high intellectual standing. Barnabas bethought himself of Saul, and set out for Tarsus to seek him. He was fortunate, and for a whole year the two of them worked together at Antioch and became close friends. It was here that the name *Christiani* was coined, a term appropriately contrived in Gratin (mixed Greek and Latin).

It will agree best with the intimations in our possession if we date Saul's arrival at Antioch late in A.D. 41. Not only was this the last year Petronius was in office as legate of Syria; but in the same year the new emperor Claudius had conferred on Agrippa additionally the sovereignty of Judea. The proclamation of Jesus as a Jewish king would have sounded less strange to alien ears at this time than at any other.

Another pointer in the Acts, perhaps, is the story of the conversion of the Roman officer Cornelius at Caesarea, 'a centurion of the cohort known as *Italica*, pious and God-fearing with all his family, one who gave a great deal in charity to the people and looked continually to God' (x. 2).

The story is related at considerable and quite disproportionate length, and is designed to show how Peter became convinced that God-fearing Gentiles who accepted Jesus would also have a place in the Kingdom of God. It became the teaching of Judaism that the righteous of all nations would be granted this boon. But this matter was quite distinct from the question of the obligations of full proselytes, since Gentile God-fearers were not regarded as having become Jews. The full proselyte ceased to be a Gentile, and took on all the responsibilities of a member of the House of Israel. It was not considered by the Nazoreans that the Gentile God-fearers who accepted Jesus were to be deemed Israelites unless they embraced Judaism completely. It was only when Paul later challenged this that it became an issue for the Party.[5]

It may well be that we have in the account of Peter's activities furnished by Luke dependence on some lost Petrine document. The episode begins in the Acts with the apostle's visit to Lydda and Joppa, and tells of miraculous cures wrought at both places. The local colour and descriptions are good. In the second century a work was in circulation called *The Preaching of Peter.* This was a different kind of composition,[6] but it may have been created with knowledge that there had been an earlier book of this name.

In the euphoric atmosphere of A.D. 41 there was a disposition to entertain an expectation of all kinds of remarkable happenings, including the turning of many Gentiles to God. Some of the stricter Nazoreans might demur that Peter had broken the rules by entering a Gentile home and eating with the uncircumcized. But having received his explanation they were reasonably satisfied.

The whole affair of the statue had been startling. Suddenly the Jewish people had been confronted with a peril of such magnitude and horror that to meet it every section and persuasion had temporarily sunk their differences and animosities. The relief and rejoicing which took possession of the nation when the danger was so miraculously removed did not last for very long. Speedily the old antagonisms reappeared, and were accentuated by the interpretations which were put upon the significance of the extraordinary event.

For the Jewish hierarchy and aristocracy it registered a warning that good relations with Rome could not be relied upon. The whim or aberration of any emperor could place in jeopardy both freedom of faith and the continuance of national existence. Consequently it was imperative to have at court, both in Rome and elsewhere, as many friends as possible. It was also needful at home to be increasingly vigilant and to check as much as possible the growth of movements hostile to Roman rule.

In the extremist camp the effect was to intensify anti-Roman feeling. The sectarians hailed the circumstances as a notable Sign of the Times, which gave warning that world affairs were moving with increasing momentum towards the anticipated climax. It was most urgent, therefore, to be more diligent in devotion to God and His Law, and to sound out the call to national repentance. The Nazoreans, who came into this category, were naturally convinced that the return of Jesus would not long be delayed, and it behoved them to extend the sphere of their operations to reach with the Message all the Jews of the Dispersion. Preparations for this task began actively to be considered, and one of the requisites was to put in hand the writing of suitable literature to demonstrate from the Scriptures that Jesus was the Messiah and to give some account of his work and teaching. Small scrolls on these themes could readily be carried by travelling apostles, and groups would be put in possession of uniform basic material for their own propaganda.[7] We can see from the Dead Sea Scrolls that a scribal industry existed for multiplying copies of documents for circulation, and there were now in the Nazorean Party many priests and scribes.

The Zealots also were not idle. But there entered into their calculations another plan, to stimulate throughout the Roman Provinces the growth of anti-Roman feeling by means of emissaries who would seek to win the support of co-religionists to bring about the disruption of the Empire. Finance would be sought to obtain supplies of weapons to arm guerrilla forces in Israel, while subversive activities were conducted to promote disaffection among the peoples subject to Rome. When the time was ripe for revolt the military might which Rome could employ would thus be widely dispersed and deprived of effectiveness.

The repercussions varied, but they gave promise that the reign of Claudius would be marked by developments with which it would not be easy for Roman authority to contend.

NOTES AND REFERENCES

1. Suetonius, *Vitellius,* ii.
2. Ibid., *Gaius,* xxii.
3. While Tiberius was still living, Agrippa, who had made himself the friend of Gaius, unwisely in the hearing of his charioteer expressed to Gaius the hope that the emperor would soon relinquish his throne to him. His words were reported to Tiberius and Agrippa was put in chains. He was immediately released by Gaius on his accession and held in high favour. For the full story see Josephus, *Antiq.* XVIII. 161–255.
4. Josephus only refers to one letter of Petronius to Gaius from Tiberias,

and because of the allusion to the rain and agricultural work it must have been written very early in A.D. 40. But it would appear that Petronius sent a further letter later, the one which so enraged the emperor that he broke his promise to Agrippa. The Jewish Sabbatical Year began in September of A.D. 40.

5. See below, Chapter 17.
6. See M. R. James, *The Apocryphal New Testament.*
7. See below, Chapter 16.

CHAPTER 15

AGRIPPA

For the first time since the days of Herod the Great a Jewish king ruled the Land of Israel. When Claudius made Herod Agrippa ruler of Judea, Samaria and Caesarea in A.D. 41, this was reckoned as marking the fifth year of Agrippa's reign since he had already been a king for four years previously. Despite the fact that he was a scion of the detested Herodian family, most of the people were prepared to overlook his descent in their relief that there was no longer a Roman procurator in charge of their affairs. To the ardent nationalists the change made very little difference; for the king not only owed allegiance to the emperor, he openly proclaimed himself 'friend of Caesar and the Romans'. For the Nazoreans he was of course a usurper of the throne of David, and therefore an enemy of the cause of Jesus. But many of the moderates ranged themselves on the side of the sovereign, so that he not only received the full support of the hierarchy and the Sadducees generally, but also of numerous Pharisees.

The new king had greatly in his favour the fact that he had intervened personally on behalf of the Jews at considerable risk in his effort to persuade Gaius to drop his design of setting up his statue in the Temple. This already assured popular goodwill. Further, he had been manacled by Tiberius, and rather ostentatiously caused the gold chain with which he had been bound to be hung up in the Temple treasury as testimony that God raises the fallen. Chiefly, however, he obtained favour because he was determined to please, and because he was scrupulous in his observance of the Jewish religion.

Unlike the Roman governors, Agrippa elected to reside at Jerusalem rather than at ill-famed half-pagan Caesarea. In time to come they used this proverb, 'If any one should tell you that Caesarea and Jerusalem are both destroyed, do not believe him. But if he says, Caesarea is destroyed and Jerusalem inhabited, or Jerusalem is destroyed and Caesarea inhabited, then believe him; for it is written [Ezek. xxvi. 2], I shall be replenished now that she is laid waste.'[1]

In Jerusalem, as an act of benevolence, Agrippa relieved the citizens of the house tax. He also conferred the high priesthood on a family connection, Simon Cantheras son of Boethus, though he soon changed his mind. Many tales are told of the king's piety. It was customary for a funeral procession to give way to a wedding procession and both to a royal procession. But Agrippa once gave way to a wedding procession. He was asked what he saw in the bride to show her such condescension. His reply was, 'I wear a crown every day, but she only for an hour.'[2] At the festival of the first-fruits Agrippa shouldered a basket of fruit to carry into the Temple just like any of his subjects.[3]

The first year of the king's reign over Judea was the end of a Sabbatical Year, and at the beginning of a new cycle at the Feast of Tabernacles it was the usage that the portion of the Law relating to the king (Deut. xvii. 14-20) should be publicly read. The sacred scroll was handed by the high priest to the monarch, who received it standing, and – if he was of the House of David – read the passage sitting. Agrippa was commended because he received the scroll standing, and also read it standing. When he reached the words, 'Thou mayest not set a stranger over thee, which is not thy brother', he hesitated, and his eyes filled with tears, because though he had a Jewish mother he was partly of Idumean descent. But the congregation encouraged him, 'Be of good cheer, Agrippa!' they cried. 'Thou art our brother.'[4]

By such consideration for the tender religious susceptibilities of his people at a time when their feelings had been deeply lacerated the king wooed and won even some of the more fanatical. One of them, named Simon, while Agrippa was away from the city, had harangued a crowd, accusing the king of not leading a life of ritual holiness, and contending that on this account he should be excluded from the Temple. When Agrippa returned, he sent for the man, and invited him to sit beside him in the theatre. Then in a gentle voice he inquired, 'What is there done in this place that is contrary to the Law?' Simon could find nothing amiss, and begged his pardon, and was graciously dismissed with a present.[5]

Within a year, probably for reasons of state, Agrippa took the high priesthood from Simon, and proposed to give it to Jonathan son of Annas, who had held it in A.D. 37. But Jonathan had good reason not to wish to come again into prominence and tactfully declined, recommending instead his brother Matthias, whom Agrippa then appointed.

About this time C. Vibius Marsus was sent by Claudius as legate of Syria in place of Petronius with whom Agrippa had been on the friendliest of terms. Marsus was not enamoured at having a Jewish king within his jurisdiction, and was determined to keep a watchful eye on him. Indeed, he was probably given the office for this very purpose, as it did not suit Rome that the Imperial legate should be one who was hand in glove with the Jews and was prepared – as happened with Petronius – to take their part to the extent of temporizing instead of promptly executing the emperor's orders.

Marsus quickly made it evident that the measure of independence the king was permitted was severely restricted. When Agrippa embarked on the construction of a new city wall to protect the northern suburb of Jerusalem, known as Bezetha, the legate at once reported this to Claudius as a potentially dangerous move. The emperor accordingly wrote to Agrippa instructing him not to proceed with the wall, and he thought it best to comply without demur, though he was greatly chagrined.

This was not the only occasion of friction between the king and the legate. Agrippa was a typical Herodian in his love of display and his enthusiasm for lavish building projects. Just as he was eager to bind his Jewish subjects to him, so was he to gratify those who were Gentiles, and to be esteemed as a monarch of consequence. Holding court at Tiberias, he invited there the kings of Commagene, Emesa, Armenia Minor, and Pontus, as well as his brother Herod who ruled Chalcis. While these royalties were being handsomely entertained the legate arrived from Antioch. Agrippa went out to meet him, foolishly bringing all his guests with him. Josephus writes that 'Marsus was suspicious of such concord and intimate friendship among them. He took it for granted that a meeting of minds among so many chiefs of state was prejudicial to Roman interests' (*Antiq.* XIX. 341). He therefore sent privately to each of the kings requesting that they return home forthwith. Agrippa was deeply aggrieved at this injury to his dignity, and thereafter there was bad blood between him and the legate.

Again now the king changed the high priest, and Elionaeus son of Cantheras succeeded Matthias. Such speedy replacements, three different high priests in less than three years, were unprecedented, and Josephus offers no explanation. One possible reason is that the king was by nature prodigal with money and always heavily in debt,[6] and needed to replenish his coffers for his building schemes. The hierarchy was enormously wealthy, and Agrippa may well have used the high priestly office which was within his gift to obtain substantial donations as an alternative to increasing taxation.

Agrippa was very sensitive about standing well with his people. He was fully aware that being a Herodian and also a friend of Rome did not endear him to the rabid nationalists. There was an undercurrent of hostility, signified by the incident of the preacher Simon, and no doubt this was not an isolated case of openly expressed criticism. While we do not learn of any serious challenges to the king's authority, he had every cause to realize that he was sitting on a powder keg in occupying the throne.

Among the disaffected, as we have observed, would certainly have been the Nazoreans for whom Agrippa was a usurper – planted by the Romans in the position that now belonged to Jesus of the line of David as God-appointed king of the Jews. The Zealots too must have been no less inimical. Like Herod the Great Agrippa was in fear of plots, but felt strong enough to act decisively for his own security. The Acts records that 'King Herod [i.e. Agrippa] launched a savage attack on certain members of the Community. He beheaded Jacob the brother of John' (xii. 1). We may infer that these persons, and notably one of the firebrand sons of Zebedee, had conspicuously given vent to treasonable statements about the king. Beheading was the punishment for a political crime.

A story was later current that the man who stood guard over Jacob at the tribunal himself became a Nazorean when he heard the witness of the prisoner, and that both were condemned to death. On the way to execution he begged Jacob to forgive him; and after consideration Jacob replied, 'Peace be with you,' and kissed him. They were then beheaded together.[7]

The Acts continues, that Agrippa, 'finding that this pleased the Jews, proceeded to apprehend Peter, whom he imprisoned on arrest – the Feast of Unleavened Bread was then in progress – setting four squads of soldiers to guard him, purposing to bring him before the people after the Passover.'

Here we catch Luke again at his design to convey that it was the Jews rather than the Romans who were hostile to the Christians. The only Jews who could have derived any satisfaction from the execution of Jacob would have been the Sadducean hierarchy and aristocracy. The Jewish populace – ever on the side of the Nazoreans – would have been angry and disturbed. That there were reactions is suggested by the arrest of Peter at the time of the Feast of Unleavened Bread. The Passover was an annual reminder of the liberation of Israel from its oppressors, the season, therefore, when more particularly demonstrations against the yoke of Rome were to be expected. There must have been good evidence of disaffection which has been concealed from us for Agrippa to decide to take the risk of arresting Peter in order to deprive antagonistic elements of a leader around whom they might rally. The king must have been under strong pressure to take this bold deterrent action; but so notable and popular was the prisoner that the precaution was taken to have him very strongly guarded. Not only was Peter chained to two soldiers, but two others were in attendance, the four being changed for each three-hour watch.

Nonetheless, Peter's escape was effected. Luke of course will have it that this was due to a miracle, and his version of what happened reads as follows.

The very night before Herod was going to bring him up for trial, Peter was sleeping between two soldiers chained to them both, while warders posted at the door guarded the prison. Suddenly, however, an angel of the Lord stood by him, and a light shone in the cell. Tapping Peter on his side, he roused him and said, 'Get up quickly!' And his chains fell away from his wrists.

'Fasten your girdle, and strap on your sandals,' said the angel. And Peter obeyed.

'Now throw your cloak round you and follow me,' he told him.

He followed him out, and had no idea that what the angel had done had really happened: he imagined he was seeing a vision. When they had passed through the first ward and the second they came to the iron gate leading into the city, which opened for them of its own accord. They went out, and had gone the length of one street when the angel suddenly left him.

'Now,' said Peter when he had recovered himself, 'I know for certain that the Lord has sent his angel to extricate me from Herod's clutches and every expectation of the Jews.' Convinced of this, he went to the house of Mary, mother of John surnamed Mark, where a number were assembled in prayer. Knocking at the street door, a maid called Rhoda came to answer it. Recognizing Peter's voice, she was too excited to open the gate, and ran in to tell them that Peter was standing at the gate.

'Nonsense,' they said. But she insisted it was true. 'It must be his angel then,' they said.

Peter meanwhile kept on knocking. And when they did open up and saw him they were astounded. Waving his hand for silence, he described to them how the Lord had brought him out of the prison, and added, 'Give Jacob and the brothers the news.' Then he left and went elsewhere (Acts xii. 6–17).

The Jewish 'underground' would seem to have been at work, as once before when Peter and John had been shut up on the Council's orders.[8] That the rescue had been timed for the night Peter was to be brought up for trial is significant, since it illustrates that the nationalists had a very efficient organization and spy system. The incident is reminiscent of the fictitious exploits of the Scarlet Pimpernel during the French 'Reign of Terror'. And indeed many real-life stories of escapes in comparable circumstances are on record.

The miracle may be ascribed to brilliant planning, and helps to confirm that there was a close link between the Nazoreans and the independence movement promoted by the Zealots, as Brandon has effectively shown.[9] While the Nazorean government under Jacob the brother of Jesus was non-militant, there were numerous members of the Party – especially among the young – to whom the tactics of the Zealots made a strong appeal and who were ready to engage in dare-devil adventures. In this instance it is clear that Jacob and his colleagues were not involved and had no prior knowledge of what was intended. Peter requests that they be notified of his escape. Then he goes elsewhere, either into hiding or is secretly spirited out of the country.

We have all the time to accustom ourselves to a very different image of Nazorean affairs, certified to us by many indications, once we have understood the realities of the contemporary scene.

The sequel to what transpired on this occasion illustrates that Agrippa's fears were of a political nature. Peter's rescue so alarms the king that after having the guards interrogated, probably under torture, he gives orders that they be put to death. Such a drastic punishment would hardly be called for if the prisoner had been regarded as no more than a preacher of somewhat unorthodox religious views. The rescue, so boldly and cunningly contrived, revealed not only a security weakness but the possibility of organized conspiracy which put the king's life in peril. Some of the Jewish members of his retinue might be in league with the seditionists. Hastily, therefore, Agrippa removed himself from Jerusalem to the safer environment of Caesarea. There the population was predominantly Gentile, and the king had at hand a substantial body of troops.

How the situation might have developed it is idle to speculate, since Agrippa's reign was cut short by his sudden death in A.D. 44. Different versions of the circumstances are given by Josephus and the Acts; but they concur in claiming that he was struck down by the hand of God for failing to reject the flattery of non-Jews that he was more than mortal. On a public occasion at Caesarea the king appeared in brilliant raiment. Josephus says it was a robe of silver tissue which glittered in the rising sun. The largely pagan audience hailed him as a god, and at once because he did not promptly repudiate the notion he was seized with pain. Five days later he expired in agony. Various natural causes have been sugggested, including food poisoning. But it cannot be excluded that the long arm of the nationalist extremists had reached to Caesarea, and that Agrippa was wilfully poisoned.

The king left one son and three daughters. Young Agrippa, still only sixteen, was at Rome at the time. The elder girl Berenice was already married to Herod king of Chalcis. The two others Mariamme and Drusilla were respectively ten and six years of age. Most unpleasantly, when the king's death was known, his Gentile subjects at Caesarea and Sebaste heaped insults on him and his children in a lewd manner, and some of his troops deserted and went home. While he was living they could applaud and fawn upon him; but as soon as he was gone their hatred of the fact that they had been subject to a Jewish monarch immediately came out.

Claudius wished to put the young Agrippa on the throne of Judea. He was dissuaded, however, by his friends, who urged that this would not be conducive to the peace of the Empire since the burden of state was too heavy for such youthful shoulders to carry. Consequently, so far as Judea and its related territories of Samaria and Caesarea were concerned, the brief restoration of a Jewish monarchy was ended. Once again there was a Roman procurator, the governor appointed being Cuspius Fadus. As legate of Syria the emperor sent Cassius Longinus to replace Marsus.

Reversion to direct Roman rule was extremely galling to the Jews. Just for a moment they had been able to savour the sweets of at least quasi-independence. They had had a king of their own, even if he was a Herod. Now the general bitterness was great, and the extremists were not slow to profit from the prevailing unhappiness and discomfiture. False prophets, deluded madmen and guerrilla leaders were able to bid for considerable support, finding many to hearken to the most fantastic promises of signs that would demonstrate that God had not forsaken His people.

One self-styled prophet named Theudas led his dupes to the Jordan, promising that the river would divide and they would cross on dry ground as in the days of Joshua. Fadus sent a squadron of cavalry to put down what he regarded as an incitement to revolt. Many of the people were killed or taken prisoners. Theudas himself was captured, and his head was cut off and brought to Jerusalem as a warning.[10]

There were various outbreaks of violence, and Fadus had to act vigorously in a manner reminiscent of Pontius Pilate. Josephus mentions among the guerrilla leaders who were killed or exiled, Anibas, Amaramus, Eleazar and Tholomaeus, all of whom had been involved in armed attacks in the east and south. 'From then on,' says the historian, 'the whole of Judea was purged of robber-bands, thanks to the prudent concern displayed by Fadus' (*Antiq.* XX. 5).

One measure of the procurator was particularly resented. He required that the high priestly robes should again be in the custody of the Roman garrison in the Antonia fortress as formerly. Longinus, the legate of Syria, was in agreement with this demand, but was afraid it might provoke the Jewish people to rebellion. He therefore came to Jerusalem with a large force of soldiers. The Jewish authorities pleaded to be allowed to send a delegation to the emperor. This they were permitted to do only if the members of the embassy handed over their children as hostages. Fortunately for the Jews the delegation was successful due to the young Agrippa entreating Claudius to grant their request. Authority over the Temple and the selection of the high priests was now vested in Herod king of Chalcis and his successors. Exercising this mandate, Herod appointed Joseph son of Camei or Camith as high priest in place of Elionaeus.

The Nazoreans, for their part, were able to capitalize on the deep depression that pervaded the nation. They could urge, and evidently did, that the calamities rapidly succeeding one another were clear evidences of the speedy return of Jesus as Messiah triumphant. Luke might have enlightened us further had he been concerned to do so, but laconically in the Acts he adds this postscript to the account of Agrippa's death, that 'God's Message progressed and spread widely'.

Among the Woes of the period came the great famine of A.D. 46.[11] According to Luke, a Nazorean prophet called Agab had predicted this when he was at Antioch, and the Community there decided to send relief to the stricken brethren of Judea. Their bounty was conveyed to Jerusalem by Barnabas and Saul and handed over to the Elders for distribution. When they returned to Antioch they took with them John

Mark, a nephew of Barnabas. The famine must have been a particularly severe affliction, since the next year A.D. 47 to 48 was another Sabbatical Year for the land. Moreover, before the end of that year a new Roman census was due to be taken. It can well be imagined, therefore, what misery prevailed and what resentment was aroused. It required no prophetic gift to prognosticate that there was going to be serious trouble for the Roman government in this vexatious and quite insufferable part of the Empire.

NOTES AND REFERENCES

1. *Meg.* fol. 6a.
2. *Kethub.* fol. 17a.
3. Mishnah, *Bikkur,* iii. 3–4.
4. *Sotah.* fol. 41a.
5. Josephus, *Antiq.* XIX. 332–4.
6. Josephus states that while Agrippa received from his territories no less than twelve million drachmae in revenue, 'he borrowed much, for, owing to his generosity, his expenditures were extravagant beyond his income, and his ambitions knew no bounds of expense' (*Antiq.* XIX. 352).
7. Clement of Alexandria, quoted by Eusebius, *Eccl. Hist.* II. ix.
8. See above, p. 126.
9. See S. G. F. Brandon, *Jesus and the Zealots.*
10. Josephus, *Antiq.* XX. 97–8.
11. See above, p. 120.

CHAPTER 16

INTO ACTION

At the time of the great famine Claudius sent a new procurator to take charge of Jewish affairs. He was Tiberius Alexander, a lapsed Jew, son of Alexander the influential governor of Alexandria, styled alabarch. One reason for the change may have been the impending Roman census. Possibly the emperor thought that he could handle the explosive situation with more finesse than Fadus. There are indications that for an initial period, most unusually, Fadus and Alexander were conjoined in the administration, and Alexander was withdrawn once the taking of the census was concluded. In the circumstances it seems somewhat strange that Josephus does not allude to this census directly since he could have drawn a parallel with the first census of A.D. 6 to 7.[1] Then the Zealot leader Judas of Galilee had protested in arms against the imposition. Now it was two of his sons, Jacob and Simon. On the orders of Alexander they were brought to trial and crucified.

It is tempting to think that it might have been as a tribute to these two 'brigands' that the Nazoreans told of the two who had been crucified with Jesus, and that Cassius Longinus, legate of Syria at this juncture, may have been in mind in giving the name Longinus to that soldier, or centurion, who had pierced the side of Jesus with a spear.[2] Such a reflection of later persons in anterior incidents would be in keeping with legend-making practice. The links between the Nazoreans and the Zealots would incline many of them to regard the pacification measures of Longinus, Fadus and Alexander as attacks on the Messiah himself. Josephus praises these Roman officials for keeping the nation at peace; but the old Russian version of the *Jewish War* introduces at this point a passage that speaks of drastic action taken against the Nazoreans. This at least seems to reflect a very ancient tradition.

> And since in the time of those [governors] many followers of the Wonder-worker aforementioned [i.e. Jesus] had appeared and spoken to the people of their master, that he was alive, although he had been dead, and that 'he will free you from your bondage', many of the multitude hearkened to their preaching and took heed to their injunctions . . .; for they were of

the humbler sort, some mere shoe-makers, others sandalmakers, others artisans. . . . But when these noble governors saw the falling away of the people, they determined . . . to seize them . . . for fear lest the little might not be little, if it ended in the great. . . . They sent some away, some to Caesar, others to Antioch to be tried, others they exiled to distant lands.[3]

To such circumstances Eusebius may be referring when he states that 'the rest of the apostles, who were harassed in innumerable ways with a view to destroy them, and driven from the land of Judea, had gone forth to preach the gospel to all nations.'[4]

Whether the Nazoreans made a virtue of necessity, or whether they were carrying out an agreed policy, must be left an open question. Both could be true. But the evidences point clearly to a great extension of the range of their propaganda from this time onward. The Acts records that not very long after the return of Barnabas and Saul to Antioch, after they had taken relief to Jerusalem in the famine of A.D. 46, the community there was instructed 'by the holy Spirit' that the two should set out on a missionary journey. They took John Mark with them as their attendant. This move we may date early in A.D. 47, and it is possible that it owed something to conference with the Elders at Jerusalem.

Peter and other apostles will have set forth on their own travels abroad not much later. We find a tradition handed down that Jesus had commanded his disciples not to leave Jerusalem for twelve years.[5] This is more positively stated in the *Preaching of Peter,* where it is said that Jesus had told his disciples, 'If any one of Israel will repent, to believe in God through my name, his sins shall be forgiven him. After twelve years go forth into the world, that no one may say, We have not heard.'[6] Twelve years from A.D. 36 brings us to the year 48, the very time to which events in Judea point.

As it was understood at Jerusalem it was now imperative to reach all the Jews of the Dispersion. There is a hint of this in Paul's statement that responsibility for a Ministry to the Circumcision had been assigned to Peter (Gal. ii. 8-9). It was claimed that Peter had reached Rome in the reign of Claudius. Paul also indicated that Peter had his wife with him, and that some of the brothers of Jesus, similarly accompanied, were engaged in the campaigns (I Cor. ix. 5). Naturally, in the later Church the Great Commission came to be represented as applying no less to the Gentiles, as reported at the end of Matthew's Gospel; but the Nazoreans had no design to proclaim the Messiahship of Jesus to other than Jews. It seemed appropriate subsequently that Jesus should have given a mandate to the Twelve for a general and universal evangelization, as asserted in a fragment of an unknown Gospel in Coptic, bound in with a fifth-century manuscript of the Gnostic *Pistis Sophia.* Here we read:

> . . . the Just one. They went forth by threes to the four regions of the heaven and proclaimed the Gospel of the Kingdom in the whole world, the Messiah working with them by the word of strengthening and the signs and wonders which accompanied them. And so have men learnt of the Kingdom of God in all the earth and in the whole world of Israel for a testimony for all nations that are from the rising of the sun unto the going down thereof.[7]

Even with the tour of Barnabas and Saul the Message was first given out at Salamis 'in the synagogues of the Jews' (Acts xiii. 5). But in Paphos in Cyprus the Word, by official request, was proclaimed in the presence of the Roman proconsul Sergius Paullus. Thereafter, in the progress of the tour, Jesus as the Christ was announced to both Jewish and Gentile audiences. From this time Saul used the Roman name of Paul. What had happened at Paphos evidently shocked John Mark. To preach about Jesus to Rome's representatives was casting pearls before swine. We may imagine that on the voyage from Paphos to Perga in Pamphylia there was heated argument, and on arrival there Mark would go no further and returned to Jerusalem. To be an instrument for enlightening the Gentiles had been one of Paul's great dreams, and he was convinced that Jesus had assigned this task to him. He had his chance now, and he intended to seize it. From this moment he assumed leadership of the expedition and Barnabas fell into second place.

We may consider that the diffusion of the Messianic proclamation on a major scale created the first real need for written propaganda material. This had to be fairly brief to go into a traveller's pouch with a minimum of personal necessities. It would appear, according to tradition, that two documents were prepared initially, and the name of Matthew is linked with their compilation. One of these consisted of a collection of passages from the Old Testament interpreted as evidential of the Messiahship of Jesus and what would befall him. The other set down some of the things Jesus had said and done. Both these pamphlets, no longer extant, furnished sources which were utilized in the formation of the canonical Gospels.[8]

The preparation of such texts was timely in any case, since already legend was beginning to supplant memory and embroider upon it. There were now in the Nazorean Party multitudes who had never known Jesus personally, and whose spiritual affiliations were very diverse. On one wing were those of ascetic and esoteric inclination, while on the other were the pragmatists and activists. Influences were at work to accommodate the story of Jesus to concepts embraced by fraternal sects. The pressure of external events was also contributing to magnifying the image of the Man in the Sky, whose attributes had to be of an order that made him convincingly the superior of the Roman emperor who was Satan's nominee as world ruler, and which assured that the Messiah would be victorious in the coming power-struggle. Caesar might have his legions of soldiers, but the Christ would command legions of angels.

The Nazoreans could not ascribe deity to their king as the heathen could to theirs. But they could claim that he had been predesignated by God before the universe was created, and revealed to the righteous throughout the Ages, who thus were partially initiated in advance into the Messianic mystery. There were those would would go further and see the spiritual Man in the Sky as the Light-Adam, the Primordial Man, the being in whose likeness the universe and afterwards the earthly Adam had been created. In Jesus at the due time the Heavenly Messiah had incarnated, and being in this way revealed on earth and performing his mission had returned on high to abide with God until the climax of the Ages was reached. The figure of the Man (Son of Man) in Daniel lent itself to such metaphysical concepts brought out in the curious *Similitudes of Enoch,* in the Christology of Paul and the hymnology of the Zadokite-Essenes.[9] The stature of Jesus grew as the predestined king of kings and lord of lords, before whom all earthly rulers must bow down or perish in the Day of Judgment.

There followed also from such ideas an emphasis of the predestination of the righteous. They too had been chosen from the beginning of creation and their names were registered in heaven. One fate had been reserved in the providence of God for all the Children of Light and another for all the Children of Darkness. Between the companies of the Saints there was much sharing and comparing as the Signs pointed increasingly to the near approach of the Day. The time had come to go forth, to the east and the west, to the south and the north, to reach all who should be saved. And these would be a host, a multitude no man could number; for it had been promised to Abraham that his seed should be as the sands on the seashore, and as the uncounted stars of heaven.

The militant extremists also saw the need to go forth into the world. They were not content to await the Day: they were eager to hasten its arrival by organized action. The book of Daniel which spoke of the Son of Man as the world ruler also spoke of the harsh kingdom which would be the great enemy of God and the Saints. That kingdom was now clearly revealed to be Rome. Consequently it was the duty of the faithful to promote by every means the downfall of the Empire.

One method of contributing to this was by the circulation of specially composed Sibylline Oracles, writings for which the Romans had a superstitious regard. Seditious texts were prepared associating the doom of Rome with the Day of Judgment. In one of them we read:

> God's revelation of great wrath to come in the Last Time upon a faithless world, I make known. . . . On thee some day shall come, O haughty Rome, a fitting stroke from heaven, and thou the first shall bend the neck, be levelled to the earth, and fire shall utterly consume thee, bent upon thy pavements. Thy wealth shall perish, and on thy site shall wolves and foxes dwell, and then shalt thou become all desolate as though thou hadst not been. . . . Near at hand is the End of the World, and the Last Day, and judgment of immortal God on behalf of those who are both called and chosen. First of all inexorable wrath shall fall on Rome. A time of blood and wretched life shall come. Woe, woe to thee, O land of Italy, great barbarous nation. . . . And no more under slavish yoke to thee will either Greek or Syrian put his neck, barbarian or any other nation. Thou shalt be plundered and shalt be destroyed for what thou didst, and wailing aloud in fear thou shalt give until thou shalt all repay.[10]

Another Oracle declares:

> But when Rome shall rule over Egypt, though still delaying, then shall the great Kingdom of the Immortal King appear among men, and a holy king [i.e. the Messiah] shall come who shall rule over the whole earth for all the ages of the course of Time. Then shall implacable wrath fall upon the men of Latium. . . . Ah, wretched me, when shall that day come, and the judgment of Immortal God, the Great King? Yet still be ye builded, ye cities, and all adorned with temples and theatres, with market squares, and images of gold, silver and stone, that so ye may come to the day of bitterness. For it shall come, when the smell of brimstone shall pass over all men.[11]

Of great service to the Messianic activists was an old-established system which lent itself admirably to their purpose in seeking to create cells in cities with large Jewish populations, which should be the means of spreading subversive propaganda and promoting revolt throughout the Roman Empire. This system was the Apostolic system. It had long been customary for the Sanhedrin to send agents to the Jewish communities abroad, to deal with the collection of the Temple tax and convey instructions on various religious matters. The system was under Roman protection, and the Romans themselves by their lines of communication on land and sea greatly facilitated the travels of such emissaries, a fact which must have been appreciated as Divine justice by the Messianists intent on Rome's overthrow. They could utilize these routes, and the whole system, to foster rebellion and to collect funds for the work of the movement and the purchase of arms.

Many of the Nazoreans were Zealot sympathizers, and it cannot have been at all easy for the Jews of the Dispersion to distinguish at this time between non-militant religious teachers and Zealot agents. The militants did not have it all their own way, because the majority of Jews in the Provinces were loyal to the Roman regime. They enjoyed special privileges, their worship was safeguarded, and they were protected from the anti-Jewish outbursts of their Gentile neighbours. Consequently, there was considerable alarm at the arrival of envoys proclaiming Messianic doctrines in the synagogues, and anxiety to get rid of them. Luke quite fails to comprehend the cause of Jewish antagonism in the Hellenic cities towards Paul and his colleagues, even though he indicates the nature of the Jewish fears in his account of Paul's second missionary journey. The apostles were imagined to be Zealot agitators, for example, by the Jews of Thessalonica, who in self-protection took action against them, informing the politarchs that 'these subverters of the Empire have now reached here, and Jason has harboured them. All of them are violators of Caesar's decrees, and declare that there is another emperor, Jesus' (Acts xvii. 7). Several years after this Paul was indicted at Caesarea as 'a plague-carrier, a fomenter of revolt among all the Jews of the Empire, a ringleader of the Nazorean Party' (Acts xxiv. 5).

The inoffensive Paul, himself a Roman citizen, was so much of a mystic that he would seem to have been almost completely blind to what was going on. It did not appear to have dawned on him that in proclaiming the resurrection of Christ (*anastasis Christou*) he might be understood as being concerned with a 'Messianic uprising'. Moreover, he was collecting sums of money for his fellows in Judea. For what purpose were these funds intended? Might it not be for the purchase of weapons?

By around A.D. 50 the Roman authorities were alerted to a menace they were ill-equipped to counter, one which could not be pinned down and which travelled insidiously from land to land like the plague. No legions could be used against it: it was here, there and everywhere. It was elicited that the personality behind the threat to the Empire was a Jew who had been crucified in Judea as a rebel against Rome; but this could give the Romans little joy, since his followers believed that he had been taken to heaven like the deified Caesars and was now issuing his commands through dreams and visions from that unreachable region. Soon, it was reported, he would return to the earth with great power to overthrow the Empire. But no one, it seemed, could furnish information as to how and when the assault might be expected.

Claudius took what counter-measures he could that would not be too provocative. He replaced Alexander as procurator of Judea by an uncompromising Roman, Ventidius Cumanus, who no doubt was given instructions to watch for any dangerous developments. He wrote a stern letter to the Jews of Alexandria warning them not to entertain Jewish itinerants from Syria and Upper Egypt, if they did not wish to be treated as abettors of 'a pest which threatens the whole world'.[12] From Suetonius we learn that Claudius 'expelled the Jews from Rome, who were continually making disturbances at the instigation of Chrestus'.[13] Dio Cassius, however, says that the Jews were too numerous to expel from the capital without danger, but that Claudius closed the synagogues.[14] Probably it was only the foreign Jews who were expelled from Rome. The Acts reports that among them were Aquila the tent-maker and his wife Priscilla. Aquila was a native of Pontus in Asia Minor, and Paul met this couple at Corinth after they had left Italy (xviii. 2).

However, the best allies Claudius had were the Jews of the Diaspora, who for the most part refused to participate in subversive activities. It was different in the next century after the bitter blow of the Roman destruction of Jerusalem and the Temple. There were many more then who were ready to respond to Zealot propaganda. There were outbreaks in such widely separated areas as Egypt and Cyrene, Cyprus and Mesopotamia. Even though the Romans quelled the rising after bloody battles the militants did not despair. They found a notable adherent in the famous Rabbi Akiba, who personally visited the Jewish communities in Parthia, Asia Minor, Cilicia, Cappadocia, Phrygia and Galatia in a manner similar to the earlier apostles. In Media he dwelt on the sufferings of Job, pointing out how these were a prelude to better things. He recommended to the Jews there the practice of the Medes, who, 'when they took counsel, assembled in the fields, where their deliberations were less liable to be betrayed'.

In the missionary journeys of Akiba, preaching his gospel in the synagogues, proclaiming the coming Messiah, afterwards announced as Bar-Cochba, collecting funds for arms and equipment, organizing revolt, we can see a parallel to what we have described of nationalist efforts to carry the war into the enemy's camp in the middle of the first century A.D.

There was another side to the proclamation of Jesus and the Gospel of the Kingdom than Christians have imagined. Some of those engaged were not like modern missionaries bringing word of the love of God to the heathen as revealed in the death of Jesus Christ. They represented the Church Militant in a grimmer sense. They were preparing the Way of the Lord with fanatical zeal by sowing broadcast the seeds of disaffection in the strongholds of the foe.

NOTES AND REFERENCES

1. See Josephus, *Antiq.* XX. 102. He mentions that Judas of Galilee had aroused the people to revolt at the time of the first Roman census, but does not intimate that his sons were now similarly engaged. Perhaps he meant to have this inferred, deeming it unwise to say so openly. He also does not refer directly to the census of A.D. 62-3.
2. *Gospel of Nicodemus,* xvi. 7. Cp. Jn. xix. 34–5.
3. Replacing the *Jewish War,* 221f. See Thackeray's translation of Josephus, Vol. III, pp. 651–2 (Loeb Classical Library), and Eisler, *The Messiah Jesus.*
4. Eusebius, *Eccl. Hist.* III. v.
5. Quoted by Eusebius from Apollonius in *Eccl. Hist.* V. xviii.
6. Quoted by Clement of Alexandria, *Strom.* VI. vi.
7. Cp. the present ending of Mark's Gospel and Rom. x. 12–21.
8. See Schonfield, *The Passover Plot,* Part 2, ch. iv, 'Gospels in the Making'.
9. See Schonfield, *The Passover Plot,* Part 2, ch. iii, 'The Suffering Just One and the Son of Man'; also 'The Christology of Paul' in Schonfield, *Those Incredible Christians.*
10. *Sibylline Oracles,* Bk. VIII, 1–3, 37–42, 91–5, 121–9, tr. M. S. Terry.
11. *Ibid.* Bk. III, 45–60, tr. H. N. Bate.
12. See H. Idris Bell, *Jews and Christians in Egypt,* pp. 25–6. Tradition attributes the evangelization of Egypt to John Mark.
13. Suetonius, *Claudius,* xxv.
14. Dio Cassius, lx, 6.

CHAPTER 17

SOUND AN ALARM

The belief that the Roman Empire could be undermined by the machinations of a few hundred dedicated propagandists seems extremely far-fetched. Yet we well know what a reckless fanaticism is capable of achieving with quite small numbers. Rome was not loved by its subject peoples, many of whom would be ready to revolt if circumstances were favourable. There was also a vast slave population to furnish eager recruits to the cause of freedom. The prospects for a widespread seditious movement were not so unpromising that the Romans could afford to neglect the danger of which they were apprised, and which was associated with the mysterious name Christus. And it did not take long to determine that the peril had its source in Judea.

But what baffled and misled the Romans was that there did not appear to be in that turbulent country any systematic opposition to Roman rule. What were to be found there were religious factions which sometimes clashed with one another, and independent bands of brigands and guerrillas whose operations did not exclude attacks on fellow-Jews. It was necessary to exercise an iron control and keep a watchful eye on developments. But while there was no unity, no effective military leadership, nothing seemed likely to materialize that would constitute a serious risk. The Jewish aristocracy could evidently be trusted to remain loyal to Rome, and it was up to them to co-operate, since it was in their own interest, in checking the activities of fanatics and subversive elements. The same held good for the Jews in the chief cities of the Provinces.

We are not in possession of any reports of how the Nazorean and Zealot agents fared in their missionary efforts abroad. But judging by the accounts given of Paul's experiences they cannot have been too successful. The Acts tells a tale of opposition, rejection and frequent failure. There is no mention of multitudes of Jews amounting to many thousands responding to the Message, as is stated of what had been happening in Judea. Paul himself speaks of few Jewish converts. The greatest response, as might be expected, came from the Gentile God-fearers, who were much more open to Paul's peculiar doctrine which gave them entitlement to Jewish privileges without the onerous obligations imposed by the Jewish Laws. Mostly the converts were women, slaves, and freedmen who followed various trades. The communities created were frequently quite small, and in many cities easily able to assemble in some member's house.

Paul believed that he had been chosen by God as ambassador to the nations. He appears not to have distinguished between the general Jewish mission to turn the Gentiles from idolatry to the worship of the One God and the particular presentation of Jesus Christ as the instrument of salvation for each individual. He cherished the hope that if great numbers of Gentiles accepted Jesus, the Jews of the Diaspora would be provoked to jealousy and would want what the Gentiles had gained. But others might say that in magnifying his office he was putting on a bold front to minimize the paucity of his success with his own people, and that he was admitting Gentiles on condition of faith alone in order to secure a substantial following at any price, and so be able to boast of the results of his work. It also seemed to many of the Nazoreans that Paul was bent on setting up a rival schismatic organization to that of the Nazorean Party. This, however, was never his intention.

The bitter controversy which now began and raged until Paul's death has largely been misrepresented and misunderstood. Necessarily things looked very different at Jerusalem to what they did in a Graeco-Roman environment. It was at Antioch in Syria, on the termination of Paul's first missionary tour, that the question of the terms of admission to the Party of Gentile converts first became a serious issue, and we have to consider the circumstances in the light of the contemporary situation in Judea.

Tension was mounting among the faithful as they drew the conclusion from the present tribulations that the Day was fast approaching. To merit deliverance and have a place in the Kingdom the utmost diligence was called for in practising the Law and keeping free from every taint of heathenism. The loyal Jew must redouble his vigilance and use the utmost circumspection in his external relations. These were grimly critical days for Israel, and safeguarding regulations and controls had rigidly to be enforced.

Of the Zealot-Essenes we learn: 'Some of these observe a still more rigid practice in not handling or looking at a coin which bears an image, nor will they even enter a city at the gates of which statues are erected. Others again threaten to slay any Gentile taking part in a discourse about God and His Law if he refuses to be circumcised. From this they were called Zealots by some, Sicarii by others. Others again will call no man lord, except God, even though they be tortured and killed.'[1]

The temper of the people at this time may be judged by two incidents reported by Josephus. The first took place at the Passover when multitudes came to the Temple. Fearing the possibility of an uprising the governor Cumanus took the usual precaution of posting troops from the Antonia on the roofs of the Temple porticoes. On the fourth day of the feast one of the soldiers in sight of the worshippers let down his breeches and made indecent noises and gestures. The enraged crowd cried out that a blasphemy of God had been committed. Some reviled the governor, thinking him to have authorized the outrage. When they would not be pacified Cumanus unwisely ordered all available forces to the Antonia as a deterrent. The alarmed people, imagining they were to be attacked, struggled to get through the Temple exits, and twenty thousand were crushed to death.

Shortly after this some of the militants robbed a Roman government official on the road about twelve miles from Jerusalem. When Cumanus heard of this he retaliated by sending troops to plunder the villages in the vicinity and bring him their headmen in chains. At one place a soldier found a scroll of the Law, which he publicly tore up and burnt. When the news spread crowds converged on Caesarea to clamour for redress. To avoid what he believed might develop into a revolt for which he would be held responsible, the governor after consulting his friends gave orders that the soldier should be beheaded.[2] Such events played directly into the hands of the extremists and intensified xenophobia.

The atmosphere is reflected acutely in the Jewish apocalyptic literature. It has to register on our understanding that in these times the larger part of the nation in its homeland was caught up in such eschatology, living in its fantasies from day to day. The forecast is credited to Jesus that 'false messiahs and false prophets will arise and exhibit great signs and wonders, so as to deceive even the very Elect if possible' (Mt. xxiv). But how could multitudes be deceived, as they were, by impostors and madmen unless their wrongs, the violations of their religion, and the sense of supernatural forces breaking in upon events, had disposed them to entertain the wildest notions and propositions? When Josephus speaks of these things, which were known to him, he is not letting his imagination run riot.

Let us quote here from only one of our apocalyptic sources which reflects the situation.

> For that time will arise which brings affliction; for it will come and pass by with quick vehemence, and it will be turbulent coming in the heat of indignation. . . . And there will be many rumours and tidings not a few, and the works of portents will be shown, and promises not a few will be recounted, and some of them will prove idle, and some of them will be confirmed. . . . And while they are meditating these things, then zeal will arise in those of whom they thought not, and passion will seize him who is peaceful, and many will be roused in anger to injure many, and they will rouse up armies in order to shed blood. . . . And it will come to pass at the self-same time, that a change of times will manifestly appear to every man, by reason of which in all those times they were polluted and practised oppression, and walked every man in his own works, and remembered not the Law of the Mighty One. Therefore a fire will consume their thoughts, and in flame will the meditation of their reins be tried; for the Judge will come and will not tarry.[3]

The whole force of iniquity finds its incarnation in the Roman Empire.

> Its power will be harsh and evil far beyond those kingdoms which were before it, and it will rule many times as the forests of the plain, and it will hold fast the times and will exalt itself more than the cedars of Lebanon. And by it the truth will be hidden, and all those who are polluted with iniquity will flee to it, as evil beasts flee and creep into the forest. And it will come to pass when the time of its consummation that it should fall has approached, then the principate of My Messiah will be revealed . . . and it will root out the multitude of its host.[4]

The eschatological contest between Jerusalem and Rome had now begun in earnest. It was staged before a backcloth on which was depicted a lurid and confused pattern of flames and trumpets, a crimsoned moon shining out of inky skies, hurtling heavenly bodies, and struggling demonic figures. The hope of Israel lay in absolute devotion to the Law of Commandments contained in ordinances.

The work we have quoted cries: 'For we are named One People, who have received One Law from One; and the Law which is among us will aid us, and the Supreme Wisdom within us will help us.'[5] In Nazorean parlance, the Dragon incarnate in Rome is at war with the

Woman, the daughter of Zion, whose offspring is the Messiah, and his wrath is directed against 'those who observe the Commandments of God and hold the testimony of the Messiah Jesus' (Rev. xii. 13).

The Nazoreans saw themselves as in the vanguard of the struggle. As the Party of the king of Israel, soon to return from heaven, it was for them to set an example to the whole nation of devotion to the Law. The issue which arose at Antioch – which came within the jurisdiction of the Council because it was the capital of the Province of Syria in which Judea was included – had nothing to do with whether Gentiles could become Christians without observing the Law of Moses. At this period there was no Christian religion, and consequently 'Judaizing' was not the point of the controversy. The question was whether Gentiles could become Israelites without accepting the obligations of Israel, simply on the basis of faith in Israel's king and the rejection of idolatry.

When we read the arguments in Paul's letters without preconceived ideas we find that he was contending that all who are 'in Christ' are automatically thereby the seed of Abraham and heirs of the promises made to the Patriarchs. Whatever their origin they have become Israelites, members of the People of God, because the Messiah represented Israel in person. The atoning death of the Messiah had terminated the validity of the Law 'in respect of righteousness'. It sufficed, therefore, to have that kind of faith which Abraham had before he was circumcised, faith which was reckoned to him as righteousness. There was only one People of God, and that was Israel. But now this privilege had been granted by faith to those who had not before been God's People.[6]

We are not informed how word reached Jerusalem of the character of Paul's teaching. One of the channels may well have been John Mark. It would appear that when the missionaries had reported back at Antioch Peter was sent there to check on the position. According to Paul, Peter did not scruple to partake of the communal meal with the Gentile converts, and possibly Peter made some compromising reference in a communication to the Nazorean government. At any rate, coming at this particular juncture of affairs in Judea the news from Antioch caused an outburst of zealous anger. If conditions had not been so abnormal feeling might have been less intense. And if Paul had not been urging that the Gentile believers were Israelites this too could have made a difference. As it was, action had to be taken promptly and emphatically to counter a gross betrayal which could discredit the whole Nazorean cause, the cause of the Messiah himself. The Council of Apostles and Elders, however, wanted to be sure of the facts, and decided in the first instance to make an on-the-spot investigation. Armed with the authority of Jacob the brother of Jesus the commissioners set out for Antioch.

Only one side of the story is given in the New Testament, and this in two versions, that of Paul in his letter to the Galatians and that of Luke in the Acts, which differ so much that some have thought they cannot have been referring to the same events. What they represent, however, is different angles written with distinct aims in view. We have to supply the missing Nazorean version from what we know of contemporary attitudes and by reading between the lines of the extant accounts.

The author of the Acts, of course, is intent on building up Paul as the architect and pioneer of the new Hellenic Christianity which was developing in the last quarter of the first century A.D. Consequently he is concerned to tone down the bitterness of the conflict with the parent body and to convey that the issue was resolved in a manner which endorsed Paul's championship of the rights of Gentile believers. Paul himself, in another way, tries to give the same impression that he had achieved his objectives. Imperiously, he waves aside all the opposition to his position and claims that he accepted nothing compromising to the stand he had taken. But the tradition of the strict Jewish followers of Jesus will have none of this. Peter was rescued from any suggestion of laxity, and Paul was held to be the great apostate, who had done the cause of the Messiah much harm, and his name and memory were reviled and execrated for centuries.[7]

The controversy in the first place was not about whether Gentile believers could be saved if they did not become circumcised, as Luke asserts. What was insisted upon by the commission from Jacob was that only those believing Gentiles who became full proselytes to Judaism qualified for membership of the House of Israel. The Jewish people stood in a different relationship to God than all the other nations, being designated as a holy priestly nation sanctified to God by covenant and the keeping of His commandments so that they might be fitted to carry out His will in the world. Jesus as the Messiah was a true Israelite, who was obedient to that covenant and upheld the Law by his teaching and example. It was incumbent, therefore, on all who wished to be reckoned with the People of God to come within the covenant and become amenable to the Law given through Moses.[8]

The argument was cogent and made the Jewish members withdraw from the common table and take their meals apart in ritual cleanliness. Some of the Gentile believers, convinced and anxious, were ready to conform. Others were in great distress. The cleavage was profound.

Paul was deeply incensed at what he termed the hypocrisy of his eminent colleagues, which made a mockery of his gospel. If what he had taught was not true his converts were still aliens. He challenged Peter openly – so he records – with the incisive question, 'If you, born a Jew, could live like a Gentile, why do you force the Gentiles to keep Jewish ways?' But he does not give Peter's reply.[9]

The issue had to be decided officially, and a ruling had therefore to be obtained at governmental level in Jerusalem. It was agreed to send a delegation to the Nazorean Council headed by Paul and Barnabas. Paul seems to have been overruled in this matter. Clearly for him the risks were very great. He knew what he would be up against with a vast majority of ardent zealots for the Law. Unless he could gain the support of the Big Three (Jacob, Peter and John) he would not stand a chance. And once a verdict had been given against him a split would be inevitable. And what then would become of his mission? Paul was no schismatic: the cause he championed demanded a unity of the Nazorean body politic as the Israel of God with Jerusalem as its organic and spiritual centre. There could be only one community of the Messiah. A break could well destroy him and his whole life's work.

On the other hand it was impossible to refuse what appeared to be an eminently reasonable proposition without putting himself immediately in the wrong. Paul's fertile mind got to work. He would not have gone up to Jerusalem, he wrote afterwards to the Galatians (ii. 1-10) except by a revelation. There had been shown him a way in which he might come through the ordeal with a fair prospect of success.

Paul's plan, we may infer, was not to wait for the general session of the Council, but first to tackle the leaders privately and seek to reach prior agreement with them. We are given the impression that this plan worked reasonably well. The issue was really settled out of court. The subsequent assembly of the Apostles and Elders was fully under control. Everything had been arranged beforehand.

Certainly the Nazorean leaders were fully alive to the dangers of a rival movement claiming to represent the cause of Jesus as Messiah. This by its nature would have the most serious repercussions, since inevitably it would be supposed that the main body of the Nazoreans were disloyal Jews. The Party would be discredited at home, and lose all prospect of winning many of their co-religionists abroad. A solution had to be found immediately.

When the problem was tackled at top level Paul encountered in the brother of Jesus a personality as strong as his own, and a mind no less astute. It was Jacob who laid down the terms on which agreement was practicable. Paul's status as an envoy would be officially endorsed only on condition that he confined his activities exclusively to Gentiles, when the question of persuading Jews to forsake the Law would not arise. But this still left the issue of the status of Gentiles who accepted Jesus as Messiah.

Paul, as his letters reveal, made much of Abraham's faith before he was circumcised, and this was hundreds of years before the Law had been given to Moses. Very well, but as Paul was fully aware, outside and prior to the Covenants with the Fathers, other Divine Laws had been in operation, the Laws of Noah, or Primeval Laws. These laws were incumbent on all the sons of Noah from whom the nations derived if they were to be accounted righteous, and the three basic ones were 1) not to worship idols, 2) not to commit adultery, and 3) not to commit murder.[10] These laws must therefore be obeyed by all Gentile believers in Jesus if they were to be acknowledged as entitled to share in the bliss of the Age to Come. They could not, however, be regarded as members of the House of Israel unless they went on to become full proselytes to Judaism, in which case they would cease to be Gentiles. The option was open to them, since the Law was read every Sabbath in the synagogues, which all Gentiles were free to attend.

What was being proposed was in line with Jewish practice, where a Gentile who did not desire to become a full Son of the Covenant could, by declaration before three Jewish witnesses, announce his recantation of idolatry and take upon himself the Primeval Laws. His status then became that of a colleague, and he was regarded as coming under the Biblical designation of *ger-toshab* (resident alien), entitled to the same care and protection as if he were an Israelite. He was the 'stranger within the gates'. In effect, so far as the Nazorean leaders were concerned, Gentile believers in Jesus were to be treated as non-Jewish associates, resident aliens of the Messianic Community, subject only to the Laws of Noah.

This face-saving solution did not content Paul. The right of full Israelite status for the Gentile believers was refused except upon terms of acceptance of full Israelite responsibilities. But he was forced to acquiesce in this decision. He had sought this private ruling and he had got it, and it was certainly better than he might otherwise have received. No sooner was this conclusion reached than it was acted upon, and the preliminaries were duly staged before the Assembly. The extremists heard the verdict delivered by Jacob as President to which they could offer no valid objection.[11] To prevent any misrepresentation of the decision it was agreed that the judgment should be set down in writing and conveyed to Antioch by two prominent Nazoreans, Judas Bar-Sabbas and Silas (Silvanus), who would furnish verbal confirmation and explain the terms.[12]

In all the circumstances Paul had come off very well. He had received unqualified recognition of his apostolic status, and was left to do his work among the Gentiles in his own way. He had been at this juncture saved from his traducers. He had obtained an official document endorsed by the whole Nazorean Council, ratified by the testimony of two witnesses – as the Law required – from among its most respected members, which absolved the Gentile brethren while remaining Gentiles from all necessity to be circumcised and obey the Law of Moses and Israel. They would be subject only to the Laws of Noah. The Nazorean leaders could also congratulate themselves on a crisis safely passed.

The relief, however, proved to be temporary. If the Acts is to be believed, Paul himself broke the compact by continuing to preach in the Jewish synagogues everywhere he went on subsequent journeys. Equally, those who were envoys to the Jews of the Diaspora did not scruple to interfere in Paul's affairs, visiting his communities to undermine his authority and induce his converts to become full proselytes to Judaism.[13]

NOTES AND REFERENCES

1. Hippolytus, *Philosophumena,* Bk. IX, 26. The remarks represent the Fourth Philosophy in general.
2. See Josephus, *Antiq.* XX. 105–17; *J.W.* II. 223–31.

3. *Apocalypse of Baruch,* xlviii. 31–9, tr. Charles. Cp. Jas. v. 1–9; I Cor. iii. 13.
4. *Ibid.* xxxix. 5 to xl. 3. This passage and the one quoted above are from part of this work believed to have been composed between A.D. 50 and 65. See the Introduction to the edition of R. H. Charles (A. & C. Black, 1896).
5. *Ibid.* xlviii. 24.
6. The arguments are chiefly found in Galatians and Romans.
7. See Schonfield, *Those Incredible Christians,* ch. x.
8. It is pertinent to refer to the account given by Josephus of the conversion of Izates, king of the Adiabene. A Jewish merchant named Ananias had won the women of the court to become God-fearers, and they in turn helped to convince Izates (*Antiq.* XX. 34). Izates was anxious to become a full Jew, but for state reasons and because of risk to himself Ananias dissuaded the king from taking this step. However, another Jew, named Eleazar, 'who came from Galilee and who had a reputation for being extremely strict when it came to the ancestral laws', urged Izates to be circumcised. Visiting the court and finding the king reading the Law of Moses, he said: 'In your ignorance, O king, you are guilty of the greatest offence against the Law and thereby against God. For you ought not merely to read the Law but also, and even more, to do what is commanded in it. How long will you continue to be uncircumcised? If you have not yet read the Law concerning this matter, read it now, so that you may know what an impiety it is that you commit.' The king therefore decided to delay no longer having the rite performed (XX. 38–45).
9. Gal. ii. 11–14.
10. It is laid down in the Mishnah (*Aboth,* v), 'Captivity comes upon the world on account of idolatry, fornication and bloodshed.' Later rabbis pronounced that 'Any sin denounced by the Law may be committed by a man if his life is threatened, except those of idolatry, fornication and murder' (*Sanh.* fol. 64a). In the Revelation (xxi. 8; xxii. 15) 'whoremongers, murderers and idolaters' are grouped together among those who are excluded from the Tree of Life and the City of God. Paul himself excludes from the Kingdom of God those who commit these and other grave sins (Gal. v. 19–21; I Cor. vi. 9–10).
11. In his ruling Jacob cites Amos ix. 11–12, where for 'the remnant of Edom' he substitutes 'residue of men' (Adam). Edom was a term applied to the Roman Empire. We may compare the Zadokite *Commentary on Habakkuk,* where the prophet's reference to 'the residue of the peoples' is interpreted to mean the Romans (designated as the Kittim). Jacob infers from Amos that the re-erection of the fallen tent of David would be accompanied by the turning to the Lord of Gentiles from the Roman Empire.
12. See Acts xv. A version of the text of the letter is given in verses 23–9.
13. See Galatians, also II Cor. x–xi. and Phil. iii.

CHAPTER 18

THE NAZOREAN SCRIBES

Not long after the decision on the status of Gentile believers Paul was anxious to leave Antioch to visit the communities created during his first missionary tour to discover how they were getting on. He wanted Barnabas to accompany him as before, but Barnabas required that his nephew Mark should come too. This Paul point-blank refused. There were heated words between the two envoys, and they split up. Barnabas set off with Mark for his native Cyprus, and Paul took as his associate Silas from Jerusalem. This was a good move, as Silas had been one of the two delegates from the Nazorean Council sent to Antioch to confirm the terms of the Jerusalem decree. Also, from what is said in the Acts, it may be inferred that Silas (Silvanus) was a Jew holding Roman citizenship.[1]

Paul's second missionary journey, which probably began in the spring of A.D. 50, turned out to be more prolonged and extensive than was planned. It took him and his colleagues into Europe, traversing Greece to Athens, and then further west to Corinth where he made his longest stay. Altogether these travels lasted about three years.

The Acts concentrates on Paul's adventures in the course of this tour and of a third which commenced in A.D. 53 and ended in 58. Consequently, as regards this source, we lose all contact with Nazorean affairs in Judea for about eight years.

However, from the pages of Josephus we are fairly well informed about developments in the Land of Israel, and these must have affected both the thinking and activities of the Jewish followers of Jesus.

But before we address ourselves to these there are two items of interest arising from the Acts, beyond what we have already considered of Nazorean and Zealot propaganda. The first is a point of chronology. Luke equates part of Paul's sojourn at Corinth with the term of office of Gallio as proconsul of Achaia. Gallio was the brother of the famous Stoic philosopher Seneca, and it is certified from a recovered inscription that he must have been in office from July, A.D. 51, until June of the following year.

The second point affects Nazorean practice. Both at the close of

Paul's second and third tour we find him anxious to reach Jerusalem in time for a particular festival. In the last instance this is the feast of Pentecost, and we can assume that it was the same previously (Acts xviii. 21, xx. 16; cp. I Cor. xvi. 8). We have already indicated[2] the possibility that the Nazoreans followed the custom of the Essenes in holding an annual General Assembly at Pentecost, the feast of the Renewal of the Covenant. The information given about Paul may be held to offer some support to this suggestion. In this case additional light would be thrown on the relations between the Nazoreans and Zadokites.

That there was a close, and indeed intimate, relationship between the Nazoreans and the Zadokite-Essenes has emerged from a fresh study of all references to the Essenes following the discovery of the Dead Sea Scrolls. It was a revelation that between the New Testament and the Scrolls there were so many parallels of expression and ideas. But having noted the importance of the comparisons there was a tendency among certain Christian scholars to reject the implications. Thus, for example, G. R. Driver, when he wrote:

> There is an infinite difference between the doctrines sketched in the Scrolls and those in the New Testament on both the legalistic and ritual sides, even though similar moral sentiments may be found in the teachings of Covenanters and of Christians. The rigorous and esoteric legalism, the recruiting of new members and the organized life of the community at Qumran are far removed from the freedom of the Gospel; the closed religious order, living only for itself, is totally unlike the world-wide Church with its missionary enthusiasm in preaching the Gospel to all men, Jew and Gentile alike. . . . If the Scrolls are regarded as approximately contemporary with the New Testament, the probability that the authors of these two collections of Jewish works influenced one another is necessarily great; in fact, that two religious groups should live for a considerable time within a few miles of each other without affecting one another would be a cause for surprise; but that two groups, whose doctrines diverged so widely as did those of the Covenanters and Christians, should have had a common origin or should have borrowed anything essential from one another would be equally surprising.[3]

And this brings us directly to what we now have to argue further about the Nazoreans. Driver's contention implies that Christianity as we know it from the New Testament was the faith of the early Jewish followers of Jesus. Certainly that is what the later Christian Church wanted to be believed. And the truth of this is what we have to challenge. We have to be prepared on the evidence to discard the notion that the Nazoreans were Christians, as we think of Christianity. We have to look at these people quite differently and objectively, as a phenomenon, related to the Christian past and its outstanding personalities, of which we are becoming sufficiently conscious for the first time.

This kind of perception is represented by Theodor H. Gaster. In the study of the Scrolls for his English translation he traced important comparisons with the Mandaean-Nazorean literature, and also the Samaritan, which are consequential for the interpretation of Nazorean Christian expression. As regards the New Testament he found especially illuminating a comparison between the Scrolls and the Epistle of Jacob (James). This work, which Luther slightingly referred to as 'a straw epistle', is addressed to 'the Twelve Tribes in the Dispersion' and may date originally from about A.D. 50. Gaster writes:

> On the strength of these comparisons we may perhaps not unreasonably conclude that the Dead Sea Scrolls indeed open a window upon the little community of Jewish Christians clustered around James in Jerusalem. These men may have been originally the urban brethren of the hardier souls that betook themselves to Qumran and to other camp-settlements in the Desert of Judah.[4]

He goes on to refer to the description of Jacob (James) furnished by Hegesippus, and finds in the title 'the Righteous' bestowed on him 'a reflection of the title "Teacher of Righteousness" (or, True Expounder of the Law) which occurs so frequently in the Scrolls and in the *Zadokite Document* as that of the spiritual instructor of the Brotherhood'.

The Gospels, as we have already seen, wear two faces, showing that behind the view of Jesus characteristic of the time when they were composed there was another view going back to the older Nazorean literature. Attitudes which are strongly nationalistic are in contrast with others of a universalistic persuasion. In one aspect Jesus emphatically upholds the Law down to the smallest detail, and insists that his disciples preach only to Jews, while in the other he inclines to laxity and finds greater faith among Gentiles than in Israel.[5]

It is interesting here to compare one of the canonical stories with its counterpart in the lost *Gospel of the Hebrews*. In Mark, followed by Matthew, there is an anecdote of a rich man who came to Jesus asking what he should do to qualify for a place in the Age to Come.

He is told to keep the commandments, and protests that he has always kept them. Jesus then calls upon him to part with his possessions and distribute the money to the poor and become his follower. But in the Hebrew Gospel, when the rich man parades his virtues, and is given the same advice, we read that 'he began to scratch his head, and it pleased him not.' Thereupon Jesus challenges him, 'How can you say, I have kept the Law and the Prophets? It is written in the Law, Thou shalt love thy neighbour as thyself, and lo, many of your brethren, the children of Abraham, are clad in filth, dying of hunger, and your house is full of many good things, and nothing at all goes out of it to them.'[6] Not only does Jesus have a special concern for the poor of his own nation, omitted in the canonical records, he takes a position – as elsewhere – which is Essenite in the matter of riches and possessions (cp. Jas. v. 1-5). It was not without cause that Zadokites and Nazoreans bore the name of *Ebionim* (the Poor), for whose benefit Paul willingly collected funds from the Gentile believers.

We should particularly think of the period between A.D. 45 and 55 as one which left an impress on Nazorean literature. The scale of composition is not likely to have been very great since the Nazoreans had access to the wealth of documents produced by the Essene scribes; but some specific writings of their own would have existed, some account of the teaching of Jesus and Biblical testimonies relating to him, some records of the Party such as the *Ascents of Jacob*, and certain apocalyptic works of the type of the Revelation. The Nazorean scribes could also amplify and interpolate the literature of their spiritual colleagues.

We may regard it as very possible that some of the extant Jewish *pseudepigrapha*, known to have been overworked at a later date by the Christian Church, includes material which had earlier been composed or revised by the Nazoreans. Mystery surrounds the origin of that part of the Enoch collection known as the *Similitudes*, with its peculiar Son of Man doctrine answering to what may well have been Nazorean teaching. The *Testaments of the XII Patriarchs*, as we now have it, contains so much of both ideas and language that is related to the Gospels and the Acts that parts of this work may have emanated from the Nazorean scribes.[7] We find in the *Apocalypse of Baruch* a passage which appears in Papias as a teaching of Jesus.[8] The oldest section of *Baruch* has another passage which may be identified as Nazorean. This reads:

> And it will come to pass after these things, when the time of the advent of the Messiah is fulfilled, and he will return in glory, then all who have fallen asleep in hope of him shall rise again. And it will come to pass at that time that the treasuries will be opened in which is preserved the number of the souls of the righteous, and they will come forth, and a multitude of souls will be seen together in one assemblage of one thought, and the first will rejoice and the last will not be grieved (xxx).

Since Jerusalem is still standing in the earliest *Baruch* source it must have been composed well before A.D. 70 and probably between A.D. 50 and 60.[9] We have an analagous case with the book of Revelation in the New Testament where again some of the material is early, though the work as it stands belongs to the closing years of the reign of Domitian (c. A.D. 95). In the body of the text Jesus is not mentioned by name. He appears in heaven as 'a butchered lamb' identified as the Lion of Judah, the Stock of David (v. 5-6), who reveals what is to come to pass, beginning with the Woes signified by the Four Horsemen, Pestilence, War, Famine and Death.

In view of all that was happening in Israel the burden of the Nazorean writings would largely have been of an apocalyptic and eschatological nature. As with the Dead Sea Scrolls, and in the fashion of such literature, individuals were characterized instead of named. So in Nazorean apocalyptic we should not expect to find the name of Jesus. Neither should we expect doctrine plainly identifiable as Christian. This is where Christian scholars were previously misled. They looked for correspondences with the familiar Christian positions of Church teaching, and when these were not evident they sometimes labelled material as Jewish which equally could have been Nazorean, that is to say material expressing a viewpoint which could be described as nationalistic and legalistic, and where the Messiah is not intimated to be Son of God, or performing an act of atonement by his death and resurrection.

For the Pauline Church the name Jesus Christ had the worth of a God-name, since in the Graeco-Roman world these names were mysterious like the Hebrew *Sabaoth*. But in Israel there were many hundreds who bore the name of Jesus, and even the title of Messiah (Christ) conjoined would not create a sufficient sense of awe attaching to one now sitting at God's right hand. The Son of Man furnished both a prophetic and indirect form of reference, at once powerful and impressive, befitting him who was soon to return to earth in judgment and glory. The Son of Man references in the Gospels, the esoteric Adamism of Paul and the Mandaeans, as well as 'The Man' ideas of the Dead Sea Scrolls and the Enoch *Similitudes*, illustrate how this designation was coming to the fore. We find the ascetic Jacob, brother of Jesus as he was, preferring to speak of him as the Son of Man.

In the remains of Nazorean teaching surviving in Patristic reports there is much which suggests not only an attachment to the Law and to Jewish worship, but also to Essenite concern with inner mysteries disclosed only to the fully initiated. There is a distinction made between those who are 'outside' and those who are 'inside'. This too appears in Pauline teaching and in the Gospels.[10]

We have also in the Gospels certain parables of Jesus in this connection, which are explained in such a simple manner that they do not answer at all to the declaration of Jesus that such parables are Secrets of the Kingdom, whose understanding had to be revealed privately to the disciples.[11] We may perhaps infer that one of the inner Nazorean works was a book of *Mysteries of the Kingdom of Heaven.*

On the esoteric side, Paul speaks of certain information he had received, and this may well have been in written form (I Cor. xi. 23-7, xv. 3-8). The letters of Paul to the Corinthians may be dated about A.D. 55-6, so that they could reflect what we have suggested was the chief period of Nazorean literary activity. When Epiphanius denounces the Ebionites of his day for the fictitious books they have composed in the names of apostles and of Jacob the brother of Jesus, some of these writings may incorporate sources which were much more antique.

What we have represented is wholly in keeping with our knowledge of Jewish pseudepigraphic and eschatological literature. For the Nazoreans it was now a matter of urgency, a prophetic burden, to proclaim in Israel a call to repentance in face of the imminence of the Judgment to Come. We get the sense of this in the words of the epistle to the Hebrews (xii. 25): 'If they did not escape who refused to listen to him [i.e. Moses] who conferred with them on earth, how much more we who turn our backs on him [i.e. Jesus] who confers with us from heaven?'

'The Judge will come and will not tarry,' cries the seer in *Baruch.* 'Lo, the Judge stands at the door,' says the epistle of Jacob in the New Testament. For the Nazoreans the returning Messiah would be both judge and executioner, the Joshua who would give the Elect the Promised Land and also the Captain of the Lord's hosts who would smite the wicked. When they quoted from Psalm cx, 'The Lord said unto my lord, Sit thou at My right hand until I make thine enemies thy footstool,' they were not unaware of the context, 'The Lord at thy right hand shall strike through kings in the day of His wrath. He shall judge among the heathen, He shall fill the places with the dead bodies; He shall wound the heads over many countries.'

The Nazoreans spoke the same language as the Zadokites and other eclectic groups as regards the Wrath to Come. Thus the *Damascus Rule* (ii) speaks of 'power, might, and great flaming wrath by the hand of all the Angels of Destruction towards those who depart from the Way and abhor the Precept'. This is comparable to Paul's words, that 'it becomes just on God's part to repay affliction to those who afflict you . . . when the Lord Jesus is revealed from heaven with his mighty angels in flaming fire, inflicting retribution on those who do not acknowledge God and do not respond to the gospel of our Lord Jesus' (II Thess. i. 6-9). Similarly the seer of the Revelation has his vision of the returning Messiah, 'who judges and fights with justice, whose eyes are like a fiery flame. . . . Behind him on white horses followed the heavenly hosts, clad in pure white linen [i.e. like priests and Essenes], while from his mouth there projected a sharp two-edged sword with which to smite the nations. He shall herd them with an iron-shod staff, and it is he who shall tread the winepress of the wrath of God Almighty' (xix. 11-21).

What made the Nazorean eschatology more vivid and realistic, and therefore more telling, was that it could disclose the identity of the Messiah and explain how and for what purpose he was for the present in heaven. By the calling of Jesus from earth into the presence of God, the imagination of him progressively expanded. While still humanly real as a person whom many still living had known and associated with, he was increasingly invested with the unearthly attributes of his exalted position. Paul did not want to know him any more 'according to the flesh', but for the main body of the Nazoreans the Heavenly Messiah answered to all the experiences of that Jesus whose teaching and actions were still recalled. It was only that now the remembrances of him had taken on a fresh dimension which made him larger than life. He could therefore be thought of as having already when on earth exhibited the power and quality of the dignity he enjoyed when taken on high. One illustration of this is a story put into circulation which was the source of the Gospel account of the Transfiguration.

In the story the 'revelation' is made exclusively to the inner triumvirate persisting in the names of Peter, Jacob and John. Jesus takes them up a high mountain – a symbolical touch – and there 'he was transformed in their presence, and his robes became more dazzlingly white than any fuller on earth could bleach them. Then Moses and Elijah [representing the Law and the Prophets] appeared to them and entered into conversation with Jesus.' At the end Jesus instructs these disciples not to reveal what they have seen 'before the Son of Man is risen from the dead' (Mk. ix. 1-9). The incident, like certain others, is a contribution to the Jesus-saga as it was progressively being formulated in Nazorean circles.

We have clearly to recognize in the accounts given of Jesus and his teaching that upon the memories of him there were being superimposed reflections of views and conditions which arose at intervals, first among the Nazoreans before A.D. 66, and second among the Christians in the course of some four decades after the fall of Jerusalem. Thus by the critical study of the Gospel material we can discern some of the issues with which the followers of Jesus were confronted in each period, and their reactions to them. We can even in certain instances, as we have noted at various points, discover in the canonical narratives traces of historical happenings between 36 and 66 which came to be reflected back and to colour what was related of Jesus. We have parallels to this process in the Jewish *pseudepigrapha* and in the Commentaries of the Dead Sea Scrolls.

In the histories of Josephus there is a record of a major outbreak which took place in A.D. 51, of a nature which must have concerned and troubled the Nazoreans. It began with an attack by the Samaritans on the village of Ginae, the modern Jenin, on a band of Jewish pilgrims from Galilee travelling to Jerusalem for one of the festivals. Again we have two versions of the story as related by Josephus in the *Jewish War* and in the *Antiquities*,[12] so that the details cannot exactly be determined. We must therefore be content to report broadly on what took place.

One or more of the Galilean pilgrims had been killed by the Samaritans, and complaint was immediately made to the governor Cumanus. For some reason he refused redress to the Jewish notables who appealed to him, which not only incensed the Galileans but roused the ire of many of the inhabitants of Jerusalem. The Zealots were evidently behind the next move to enlist the support of the guerrilla bands under the command of a famous nationalist rebel Eleazar Bar-Deinaeus, who for many years from his mountain fastnesses had carried out numerous raiding expeditions and had successfully evaded capture by the Romans. With the co-operation of Eleazar, and led by him and a certain Alexander, a punitive attack was made on several Samaritan villages in the Acrabatene area, south-east of Shechem, whose inhabitants were ruthlessly massacred and their houses burnt down.

When the news reached Cumanus he took cavalry of a Roman corps recruited in Samaria, and perhaps infantry as well, and marched against the aggressors, slew many and captured others – though not Eleazar himself. The gravity of the situation was such at this point that the Jews were closer to open rebellion against Rome than they had ever been before, and the alarmed Sanhedrin sent representatives to calm things down. It was again a case of 'the Romans will come and take away both our place [the Temple] and our nation' (Jn. xi. 48; cp. *J.W.* II. 237). Many of the people yielded to the entreaties of the magistrates and dispersed; but Josephus remarks that from this time revolutionary outbreaks in various parts of the country were continuous. Tacitus, the Roman historian, paints an even more alarming picture of the situation than Josephus. He speaks of a number of Roman soldiers killed by the Jews, and of strong action which had to be taken to prevent a full-scale war.[13]

Quadratus, the legate of Syria, was forced to intervene after hearing the charges on both sides, and crucified a number of the prisoners taken by Cumanus, both Jews and Samaritans. Finally the chief representatives of the two nations, together with Cumanus and tribune Celer, were sent to Rome to answer to the emperor. A decision was given by Claudius against the Samaritans as the primary cause of the trouble, and Cumanus was held responsible for resorting to force before investigating the circumstances. He was accordingly sentenced to banishment, while Celer was sent back to Jerusalem, there to be dragged round the city and publicly beheaded. By these judgments a temporary peace was achieved. Antonius Felix, who was only a freedman, was appointed as the new governor of Galilee, Samaria and Judea.

Such a consequential happening could hardly fail to find some reflection in the Jesus-story, at least in Luke's version. And indeed we have a passage relating to a journey of Jesus from Galilee to Jerusalem. 'Jesus turned firmly towards Jerusalem, and dispatched messengers ahead of him. As they went forward they entered a Samaritan village to make preparations for him. But the people would not give him welcome because he was bent on going to Jerusalem. When his disciples Jacob and John saw this they said, "Master, will you have us invoke fire to descend from heaven to consume them, as Elijah did?" (II Ki. i. 10). But he turned and rebuked them, and they went on to another village' (Lk. ix. 51-6). After the words 'rebuked them' some *MSS* add, 'You do not realize the kind of spirit you represent. The Son of Man has not come to destroy men's lives but to preserve them.'

The attitude of Jesus here is non-violent, and this raises the issue of whether the same was true of the Nazoreans. Nationalistic militancy was now increasingly gaining not only popular sympathy but active support. Did the Nazoreans make common cause with the Zealot militants, or did they advocate a policy of No Reprisals? These questions have to be faced, since they govern our understanding of the Nazorean position from this time until the Jewish revolt against the Romans in A.D. 66. How far does the Sermon on the Mount reflect Nazorean convictions?

NOTES AND REFERENCES

1. See Acts xvi. 37.
2. See above, pp. 115–16.
3. G. R. Driver, *The Judean Scrolls*, pp. 582–3 (Basil Blackwell, 1965).
4. Theodor H. Gaster, *The Dead Sea Scriptures in English Translation*, Introduction, Section VI, especially p. 17 (Doubleday Anchor Books, 1956).
5. Brandon, *Jesus and the Zealots*, rightly distinguishes between the Gospel material preserved by the Jewish Christians and those elements which conflict with it and reflect the teaching of the Gentile Church.
6. The passage is found in the Latin version of the *Commentary on Matthew* attributed to Origen (now called Pseudo-Origen) at Mt. xix.
7. R. H. Charles in his edition and translation of the *Testaments* lists in Section 26 of his Introduction, 'Influence of the *Testaments* on the New Testament', the points of comparison.
8. See above, p. 138.
9. Charles, *The Apocalypse of Baruch*, Introduction, pp. lv–lviii.
10. I Cor. v. 12–13; Mk. iv. 11.
11. Eusebius, *Eccl. Hist.* iii. 39, remarks that Papias in his *Exegesis of the Dominical Oracles* had recorded 'certain strange parables of Jesus and teachings of his'. These evidently had to do to a considerable extent with the Kingdom in its Millennial fulfilment.
12. See *J.W.* II. 232–46; *Antiq.* XX. 118–36.
13. Tacitus, *Annals*, XII. liv.

CHAPTER 19

THE GATHERING STORM

The governorship of Felix was marked by mounting disorders, terrorist activities, and the appearance of false messiahs and prophets. Josephus describes this period in the following terms:

> Of the brigands whom Felix crucified, and of the common people who were convicted of complicity with them and punished by him, the number was incalculable.
>
> But while the country was thus cleared of these pests, a new species of banditti was springing up in Jerusalem, the so-called *sicarii,* who committed murders in broad daylight in the heart of the city. . . . Besides these there arose another body of villains, with purer hands but more impious intentions, who no less than the assassins ruined the peace of the city. Deceivers and impostors, under the pretence of divine inspiration fostering revolutionary changes, they persuaded the multitude to act like madmen, and led them out into the desert under the belief that God would there give them tokens of deliverance. . . .
>
> No sooner were these disorders reduced than the inflammation, as in a sick man's body, broke out again in another quarter. The impostors and brigands, banding together, incited numbers to revolt, exhorting them to assert their independence, and threatening to kill any who submitted to Roman domination and forcibly to suppress those who voluntarily accepted servitude. Distributing themselves in companies throughout the country, they looted the houses of the wealthy, murdered their owners, and set the villages on fire. The effects of their frenzy were thus felt throughout Judea, and every day saw this war being fanned into fiercer flame (*J.W.* II. 253–65).

It is a grim picture that is painted here, and while we must recognize the antipathy of Josephus to the nationalist extremists we are not entitled to say that he has completely falsified and misrepresented the situation. At the time of which he speaks he was a highly impressionable teenager who was not ignorant of what was going on around him and who was greatly interested in the Essenes. Moreover, what he tells us is supported by other sources, including the *Apocalypse of Baruch.*[1]

It is with this image in our minds that we have to take up the question of the position of the Nazoreans, and whether it was in agreement with or contrary to the non-violent teaching credited to Jesus in the Gospels.

But first we have to concern ourselves with the Zealots. We know that this Fourth Philosophy was militantly anti-Roman; but it is agreed on very clear evidence that its inspiration was religious. The Zealots obtained their name from their zeal for God and His Law. Since the discovery of the Dead Sea Scrolls and the finds at Masada, where the nationalists made their last stand in A.D. 73, scholars like Roth and Driver have argued that the Zadokites of Qumran were identical with the Zealots. But there is no real proof of this: it is only possible to say that there was a good deal of common ground between them. Conceivably, the Zadokites of the first century A.D. may have represented an offshoot of the movement initiated by Judas of Galilee and his associate Zadok. If so, they had elected to follow an Essenite course in functioning as a distinct religious order organized in camps and communities for the purpose of practising the Law in purity. They had separated from the company of wicked men, and made their principal centre in the wilderness. They envisaged a final struggle between the forces of Light and Darkness; but they would not act on their own initiative, and awaited the moment chosen by God.

We are not therefore entitled to imagine that the Zadokites would or did involve themselves in a protracted course of militancy, participating in armed attacks, forays and murderous assaults. This would have been a violation of their status as the atoning Elect, enduring suffering and persecution for righteousness' sake, and would have meant acceptance of a contamination they had gone to extreme lengths to avoid. Their attitude has to weigh with us in considering that of the Nazoreans, for there was a close affinity between them. To be zealous for the Law did not mean that necessarily one had to be a freedom-fighter employing carnal weapons. The majority of the Pharisees, as we know, did not hold with violent action to promote the advent of the Kingdom of God, and repudiated the activities of men like Eleazar Bar-Deinaeus.[2]

As regards the militant wing of the Zealots they had taken to arms initially, not because they were bellicose, but out of a sense of unendurable wrongs, of insults to their Faith and to their human dignity as free men. History has many records of their like in other times and places. We can certainly assume, as such records show, that the movement acquired numerous adherents who were not animated by the same high principles – the desperate and unfortunate, and those who chose to live by robbery and violence. The more conditions deteriorated the greater likelihood there was of such outcasts and outlaws joining in. And here we must observe that there had been brigands, robbers and desperadoes in Israel and on its borders long before the Zealot movement came into existence. Consequently there is no call subsequently to see in every band of pillagers and cut-throats a manifestation of Zealot patriotism. Some of such bands may have found it convenient to pose as ardent nationalists. And while Josephus was no doubt anxious to represent the rebels in the worst light by classing them with brigands we cannot say that his comments were wholly unjustified.

To those who followed the Way of the Lord with a pure heart the atrocities committed will have been sickening and revolting. They preached repentance from all evil deeds as the only means by which the nation's miseries would be ended and it would become fit for deliverance. For them Belial had been let loose in Israel, and his name was interpreted as *B'li-'ol,* 'without yoke', one of the great signs of his activities being the manifestation of the spirit of lawlessness. In the *Testaments of the XII Patriarchs* we read admonitions such as these:

> The spirit of hatred worketh together with Satan, through hastiness of spirit, in all things unto men's death; but the spirit of love worketh together with the Law of God in long-suffering unto the salvation of men. Hatred, therefore, is evil, for it constantly mateth with lying, speaking against the truth; for it maketh small things to be great, and causeth the light to be darkness, and calleth the sweet bitter, and teacheth slander, and kindleth wrath, and stirreth up war, and violence and all covetousness; it filleth the heart with evils and devilish poison. These things, therefore, I say to you from experience, my children, that ye may drive forth hatred, which is of the devil, and cleave to the love of God (*T. Gad.* iv. 7–v. 2).
>
> Therefore, my children, I tell you, flee the malice of Belial; for he giveth a sword to them that obey him. And the sword is the mother of seven evils . . . at first there is bloodshed; secondly, ruin; thirdly, tribulation; fourthly, exile; fifthly, dearth; sixthly, panic; seventhly, destruction. Therefore was Cain delivered over to seven vengeances by God (*T. Benj.* vii. 1–3).

The pious of the first century before Christ had foreseen the coming of a Messiah who would be righteous and taught of God, ruling a holy people. He would be one who 'shall not put his trust in horse and rider and bow, nor shall he multiply unto himself gold and silver for war, nor by ships shall he gather confidence for the day of battle. . . . He himself also is pure from sin, so that he may rule a mighty people, and rebuke princes and overthrow sinners by the might of his word' (*Psalms of Solomon,* xviii).

Quotations could be multiplied which demonstrate that the teaching ascribed to Jesus in the Sermon on the Mount was representative of all those in Israel who looked for salvation through perfection of conduct, and refused to have anything to do with deeds of shame and lawlessness. They were not the less patriotic and freedom-loving on this account, or impervious to their people's miseries. We find the later rabbis attributing the disastrous consequences of the wars with the Romans to Jewish acts of retaliation,[3] and declaring that, 'They who being reviled revile not again, who take no heed of insults, and act in love, rejoicing in affliction, of them Scripture says, "Them that love Him are as the sun when it goes forth in its strength." '[4]

We must not be deceived by a Zadokite-Essene book like *The War of the Sons of Light with the Sons of Darkness*, with all its military panoply, its battle dispositions, banner slogans and trumpet calls. This is a spiritual struggle like Bunyan's *Holy War*, and as devoid of physically violent purpose as the hymn *Onward, Christian Soldiers*. The Jewish eschatological literature, including the New Testament book of Revelation, visualizes the final showdown between the forces of Good and Evil in terms of physical warfare, with the Messiah as leader on one side and the head of the Evil Empire as his opponent. Many passages in the Biblical Prophets could be interpreted also as foreshadowing an ultimate great assault on Israel by its enemies, which would be defeated by Divine interposition. Many therefore were led to believe that the final war would be a real and bloody one, and militants were inspired to use such prognostications to justify their engagement in acts of open hostility. The sense of deep and bitter grievance at subjection to a harsh foreign power was in any case an incentive to strike at the Romans and their supporters where and when opportunity offered. But we should not then conclude that in general the Nazoreans, Essenes and Pharisees sanctioned and supported guerrilla tactics and terrorist activities, though we would expect some to be carried away by their feelings, especially as aggravation increased.

It may well be not the actual words of Jesus but a Nazorean comment on these troubled times, when we read (Mt. xi. 12), 'From John the Baptist's time until now, however, the Kingdom of Heaven is under pressure, and the violent seize upon it.'

Brandon has argued cogently that much of the pacifism attributed to Jesus in the Gospels is a reflection of the Christian attitude in the decades following the defeat of the Jews in their revolt against Rome.[5] We must certainly allow that the Christians of the Empire, who by this time were predominantly Gentiles and in a very precarious position, had good cause to urge that they had no connection with militant messianism, and consequently were anxious to stress that Jesus had been opposed to hostility and preached love and forgiveness. But there is a strong Jewishness and Hebraic structure with certain of these sayings, like those in the Sermon on the Mount, which suggest that they were not alien to the views of the Nazoreans in the period before the outbreak of the war with Rome. As we have seen, there are parallels in Jewish eclectic literature.

Perhaps no book in the New Testament more faithfully reflects a pacifistic outlook than the epistle ascribed to Jacob the brother of Jesus. The whole work counsels peacefulness and patience, the patience of Job, and echoes the Sermon on the Mount. It is fully consistent with how the saintly President of the Nazoreans is depicted by tradition, as a man of the deepest piety who spent long hours on his knees praying for forgiveness of his people. It is even possible that some of the pacific sayings of Jesus emanated from Jacob and his circle.[6]

We have pointed out that there was a spiritual quality in Zealotism, and we should be careful to avoid holding the Zealots responsible for all outbreaks of violence and insurrection, cruelty and outrage. Inevitably with worsening conditions passions intensified, as *Baruch* describes,[7] and a kind of madness took possession of ordinarily inoffensive people. Many threw in their lot with the war party, seeing no hope of remedy except by resort to arms. But we are not entitled to claim as Zealots all the personalities who in these days were moved to engage in pillage and rapine, arson and murder.

It would not make any the less patriotic the Nazoreans, or those of the Pharisees and Essenes who held similar convictions that God would intervene at the appointed time to deliver His people from their enemies, that they would experience a revulsion against senseless barbarity and refuse to countenance or condone it. Such behaviour, since it violated the Law of God, far from bringing nearer the Day of Redemption, could only serve to delay it. And those responsible would themselves be counted among the evildoers who would perish.

As Jacob's epistle expresses it, 'If you will but carry out that prince of laws in the Scripture, "You are to love your neighbour as yourself," you will do well. But if you exhibit partiality you commit a sin, and are convicted by the Law as transgressors; for whoever will keep the whole Law, yet fail in one particular, becomes guilty of all the rest. For He who said, "Do not commit adultery," also said, "Do not murder." So if you do not commit adultery, yet commit murder, you have become a transgressor of the Law. So speak, and so act, as those who will be judged by the law of liberty; for there will be judgment without mercy for him who has shown no mercy, while mercy will override judgment' (ii. 8-13).

The Message from the beginning had been associated with a call to national and individual repentance. The revolution it proclaimed was one of non-violence, of adjustment to the attributes of the Good Society in the Kingdom of God, when nation would no longer lift up sword against nation, neither would they learn war any more (Isa. ii. 4).

There is impressed upon us by Josephus that a new phase of hostility and lawlessness had commenced with the death of the Emperor Claudius and the accession of Nero. Claudius died in October, A.D. 54, which as it happened was shortly after the commencement for the Jews of another Sabbatical Year. In such years, as we have several times pointed out, the Jewish people by reason of the cessation of agricultural labour had much greater leisure to become involved politically. Josephus reports the deterioration and the infestation of the country with 'brigands and impostors who deceived the mob. Not a day passed, however, that Felix captured and put to death many of these impostors and brigands' (*Antiq.* XX. 160-1). One of his triumphs was to get the notorious Eleazar Bar-Deinaeus into his clutches by a ruse and send him to Rome.

Felix had been confirmed in office as governor of Judea by Nero. And according to the *Antiquities* one of those who had recommended him was the former high priest Jonathan son of Annas.[8] Felix was now anxious to get rid of him 'because of his frequent admonition to improve the administration of the affairs of Judea; for Jonathan feared that he himself might incur the censure of the multitude' in that he had had a hand in Felix's reappointment.[9] Josephus relates that Felix bribed a close friend of Jonathan to employ assassins to murder him apparently on the way to the Temple. We learn here in the *Antiquities* (XX. 163-6), and in the parallel account in the *Jewish War*, of the first appearance of 'a new species of banditti, the so-called *sicarii*'. They carried short curved daggers beneath their cloaks, and this gave them their name. Mingling with the crowds in the city at festival times, they struck at their victims with little risk of discovery in the press of people. They even killed some within the Temple precincts. 'The panic created was more alarming than the calamity. . . . Men kept watch at a distance on their enemies and would not trust even their friends when they approached. Yet, even while their suspicions were aroused and they were on their guard, they fell; so swift were the conspirators and so crafty in eluding detection' (*J.W.* II. 256-7).

Josephus at times distinguishes the Sicarii from the Zealots, but at others he treats them as identical, especially in the *Jewish War*. The name seems to serve him to signify the most fanatical and brutal elements among the rebels against Rome, so that by means of this opprobrious term he can hold up to execration the great many who fought against the Romans with a fervour and courage born of deep-seated conviction of the justice of their cause.

The circumstances already begin to become confusing ten years before the Jewish revolt came to a head, and they would become even more so as the decade advanced. The country was moving with increasing momentum towards a state of anarchy and internal strife, where opportunity was afforded for every kind of bold activity, whether selfish or altruistic. The storm was gathering, and its thunders and lightnings were already taking away peace with their premonitory peals and flashes.

NOTES AND REFERENCES

1. See the passage quoted above, p. 182.
2. 'This Eleazar son of Dinai is quite well known to the Mishnah, where he is mentioned as a famous "murderer", and to the Midrash, which knows him as the leader of one of the unfortunate generations who tried to force the messianic redemption of Israel before the time of God's own good will' (Eisler, *The Messiah Jesus,* p. 102).
3. According to the Talmud, *Gittin,* fol. 55b–57a, Jewish acts of reprisal brought about the destruction wrought by Hadrian's forces in the Second Revolt of 132–5.
4. *Baba Kama,* 93a.
5. Brandon, *Jesus and the Zealots,* especially ch. vi, 'The Concept of the Pacific Christ: its Origin and Development.'
6. See below, pp. 234–5.
7. See below, p. 182.
8. See above, p. 132. The Jewish 'Underground' seems to have had its spies and agents everywhere. And no doubt it was remembered that Jonathan had a hand in the first persecution of the Nazoreans.
9. Felix at this time was married to an eminent Jewess, the lovely Drusilla, daughter of Agrippa I. She had previously been the wife of Aziz, king of Emesa, but had deserted him. See also Acts xxiv. 24.

CHAPTER 20

APOSTLE CHAINED

An ugly aspect of the deteriorating situation among the Jews was the use of religion as a sanction for acts of savagery. Men of violence committed atrocities against fellow-Jews on the pretext of purifying the nation from all taint of heathenism. Many of the wealthy could be slain and their goods plundered on this score. All who gave any kind of comfort or support to the Occupying Power were stigmatized as traitors and apostates; for the Romans were not only the political enemy, they were also heathen. If the term had been in vogue the aristocracy and the rich and powerful sacerdotal families would have been denounced as 'imperialists', and enmity towards them was fostered in the traditional manner of class war. This kind of internal hostility had been building up for many years, and now was coming much more into the open. In Jerusalem the clash was between the Lower City and the Upper City, between the East-side and West-side. In earlier chapters of this book we have drawn attention to the significance of this social cleavage, especially in Chapter 10, and have quoted the kind of demo-slogans which actually relate to the time we have now reached.[1]

In A.D. 59 Agrippa II appointed Ishmael son of Pheabi as high priest, and in giving this information Josephus goes on to state:

> There now was enkindled mutual enmity and class warfare between the high priests, on the one hand, and the priests and leaders of the populace, on the other. Each of the factions formed and collected for itself a band of the most reckless revolutionaries and acted as their leader. And when they clashed, they used abusive language and pelted each other with stones. And there was not even one person to rebuke them. No, it was as if there was no one in charge of the city, so that they acted as they did with full licence (*Antiq.* XX. 180).

It is to be noted that the ordinary priests, many of whom had joined the Nazorean Party, sided with the populace. They occupied part of the Ophel south of the Temple in immediate proximity to the Nazorean headquarters on Mount Zion. The hierarchy retaliated against their offending subordinates by sending their slaves to the threshing floors to receive the tithes due to the priests, and having got possession of them refused to distribute their share to the ordinary priests. One of those particularly implicated in these harsh reprisals was Ananias son of Nedebaeus, the high priest who had preceded Ishmael. The policy seems to have continued for several years. 'So it happened,' as Josephus says, 'that those of the priests who in olden days were maintained by the tithes now starved to death.'[2]

Brandon has suggested that one of the reasons why the high priests were determined to destroy Jacob the brother of Jesus, which they succeeded in doing in A.D. 62, was because he had outspokenly taken up the cudgels on behalf of the priestly victims.[3] Certainly he is found in his epistle fulminating against the rich oppressors of the poor,[4] and when Jacob was executed it was a priest belonging to the ascetic Rechabites who intervened to try to save him.

Another aspect of the intensification of hostilities was that it stimulated xenophobia, and worsened relations at this time between Jew and Gentile in Caesarea, a city of mixed population on the coast within the territory administered by Felix and which was his normal place of residence. This was a perennial trouble spot. A quarrel arose on the subject of the equal civic rights of the two communities. The Jews contended that they had the precedence, because Caesarea had been created by Herod the Great, while the Syrians asserted that before that there had been no Jewish inhabitants of what had formerly been called Strato's Tower. Mutual abuse led to stone throwing, and the prospect of even more serious strife. Finally Felix intervened with his troops, directing their attack particularly against the Jews as the primary instigators of the conflict. He only desisted when a number of the Jewish citizens of worth and substance begged him to do so. The plea was perhaps accompanied by a considerable financial 'sweetener'.

It is against this general background that we have to view developments in Nazorean affairs consequent upon the arrival of Paul at this juncture on his last visit to Jerusalem.

Paul had been hastening to reach Jerusalem from Macedonia in time for the feast of Pentecost in June, A.D. 58. He was conveying a liberal sum of money collected for the 'poor saints' by the communities of Macedonia and Achaia, and was accompanied by seven of his associates who were notable representatives of his missionary labours. He was still at Philippi at Passover, and the speed of his journey thereafter is described graphically in the Acts (xx-xxi). Finally the company arrived at Caesarea after coasting down from Tyre via Ptolemais, and lodged with Philip, one of the original seven deacons appointed by the Apostles in the early days of the movement, who was living there with his four unmarried daughters who were prophetesses.

At intervals in the course of the journey, according to Luke, and now again at Caesarea, Paul had been warned that if he persisted in going to Jerusalem bonds and imprisonment awaited him. But he would not be turned from his purpose. What his aim was can perhaps be inferred from his letters, II Corinthians and Romans. He had been fighting a losing battle, and had been driven to desperation by the Nazorean apostles, who invaded the communities he had created to induce his converts to become full Jews and disparaged Paul as one who was quite unqualified to speak for Jesus as he had not known him or been appointed by him. The effects were so disruptive, since the Hellenic believers were in any case inclined to be factious, that Paul was compelled to seek relief from harassment by appeal to the Nazorean leadership. The funds he had been collecting would show that he had not been unmindful of his duty and that his communities had a sense of their obligations (cp. Rom. xv. 26-7), in token whereof he had brought with him representative members to pay their respects to Jacob and the Elders.

The man who had carried such heavy burdens upon his shoulders and been so assertive of his independence was prepared now to eat humble pie; but he was not conscious of how radically circumstances had changed since he was last in Jerusalem. He had not bargained for the tension and explosive conditions which now prevailed, and which made this a most unpropitious moment for his purpose.

The Nazorean Council was in a quandary. The officers were sufficiently beset with grave problems, and could have wished Paul and his companions anywhere but on their doorstep at this time. But they put as good a face as they could on the situation.

'You must take into consideration, brother,' they told him, 'how many myriads there are among the Jews who have believed. Naturally they are staunch upholders of the Law, and they have been informed about you that you teach all the Jews in Gentile lands to apostatize from Moses, telling them not to circumcise their children or conform to the customs. What is this going to mean? They are bound to learn of your arrival. Here, then, is what you must do. We have four men under a common vow. Take over these men and undergo purification with them, and pay their offering costs so that they can shave their heads. Everyone will then realize that there is no foundation whatever for what they have been informed about you, and that on the contrary you yourself conform and observe the Law. So far as Gentiles who have believed are concerned, we have communicated our decision that they should avoid what is dedicated to idols, blood, eating strangled animals, and sexual impurity' (Acts xxi. 20-5).

We can follow the narrative of the Acts fairly closely from this point,[5] as it may be held to rest on first-hand knowledge of what transpired.

The depressed Paul agreed to what was required of him without demur, but while in the Temple during the period of purification was spotted by some Jews of Asia, who seized him and raised an outcry.[6]

The whole city was set in uproar, and the people came rushing together. Those who had seized Paul dragged him outside the Sanctuary, and at once the gates were closed. They were attempting to kill him when word reached the military tribune [i.e. in the Antonia fortress] that all Jerusalem was seething. Instantly he took troops and centurions and ran down to them; and as soon as they saw the tribune and the troops they stopped striking Paul.

Coming up, the tribune took him in charge, and ordered him to be bound with two chains, and inquired who he was and what he had been up to. Some of the crowd said one thing and some another; and as he could not discover the truth because of the commotion he ordered Paul to be conveyed into the fort. When the steps were reached it was found that he had to be lifted up them by the soldiers because of the pressure of the crowd; for the mass of the people surged close behind yelling, 'Away with him!'

When they were about to enter the fort, Paul said to the tribune, 'May I have a word with you?'

'So you speak Greek?' he replied. 'Aren't you then the Egyptian who recently started an insurrection and led those four thousand Sicarii out into the wilderness?'

'I am actually a Jew,' said Paul, 'from Tarsus in Cilicia, a citizen of no insignificant city. Please allow me to address the people.'

The Egyptian referred to was one who had recently given himself out to be a prophet, and collected a large following (Josephus gives a figure of 30,000). Coming from the wilderness to the Mount of Olives, he proposed to force an entrance into Jerusalem and overpower the Roman garrison. Felix sent his heavy infantry against him, and most of the insurgents were killed or captured. But the Egyptian had managed to get away with a few of his henchmen.[7] The figure in the Acts seems more probable, since in the *Antiquities*, reporting the same event, Josephus says that four hundred were killed and another two hundred were taken prisoner.

Paul addressed the crowd in Hebrew, and on this account obtained a fairly quiet hearing. But when he came to mention that his mission had been to the Gentiles uproar was renewed. Since the tribune could not make out why the people were so incensed he decided to examine the prisoner by flogging. Paul, however, said to the centurion in charge, 'Is it right for you to flog one who is a Roman and uncondemned?'

When the centurion heard this he reported it to the tribune. 'What do you propose to do?' he asked. 'The man is a Roman citizen.'

Confirming this with Paul, the tribune remarked, 'I had to pay a pretty penny for my citizenship.' 'But I had it by birth,' said Paul.

There was no question of flogging after this. But the next day the tribune brought the prisoner before the Sanhedrin, presided over by the high priest Ananias son of Nedebaeus.[8]

The proceedings, however, were entirely nullified by Paul's astuteness in dividing the Court on a matter of doctrine before he could be questioned.

> When Paul was aware that one part of the Sanhedrin were Sadducees and the others were Pharisees, he cried out, 'Brothers, I am a Pharisee of Pharisee stock. I am being judged for the expectation of the resurrection of the dead.'
>
> By saying this he set the Pharisees at loggerheads with the Sadducees, and there was a split in the assembly. For the Sadducees say there is no resurrection, nor any angel or spirit, but the Pharisees affirm both propositions. A first-class row ensued, with some of the Pharisee scribes hotly contending, 'We find nothing criminal in this man. If a spirit has spoken to him, or an angel . . . ' The conflict here became so furious that the tribune, afraid that Paul would get torn to pieces, ordered a company down to extricate him from them and escort him back into the fort.

The following day Paul's nephew, son of his sister, overheard that there was a plot to have him assassinated, hatched with the connivance of the hierarchy. The nephew courageously went to the fort and informed Paul, who told him to repeat his information to the tribune. The tribune took this development very seriously. Cautioning the youth 'not to tell a soul what you have disclosed to me', he dismissed him. Next, having summoned two of his centurions, he issued instructions, 'Have two hundred men ready to go to Caesarea, also seventy cavalry and two hundred light infantry, this evening at nine o'clock sharp. And have a baggage train brought round to convey Paul safely to the Governor Felix.' He also wrote a letter to Felix explaining the circumstances, mentioning that he had advised Paul's accusers to bring their case before him.

The soldiers accordingly took Paul by night as far as Antipatris, when they returned to Jerusalem leaving the cavalry to go forward to Caesarea. There they delivered the letter to the governor, and also surrendered Paul to him. When the governor had read the letter he asked Paul from what Province he came. When he heard that this was Cilicia he said, 'I will hear you as soon as your accusers arrive,' and remanded him in custody in Herod's praetorium.

Five days later the high priest Ananias came down with other members of the Sanhedrin and an advocate Tertullus. When Paul had been summoned, Tertullus opened the case for his accusers as follows:

> Thanks to you, Your Excellency Felix, profound peace is our lot and law and order has been restored to our nation under your wise guidance. This we freely and fully acknowledge with deep gratitude. In order not to weary you unduly, therefore, I beg for your consideration in putting our case with the utmost brevity.[9]
>
> We have found this man a plague-carrier, a fomentor of revolt among all the Jews of the Empire, a chief agent of the Nazorean Party. When we apprehended him he was also attempting to desecrate the Sanctuary, as you can ascertain for yourself by investigating these several charges we bring against him.

Paul was then given leave to reply, and we may quote his chief defence as reported in the Acts.

> Knowing that you have had many years' experience in governing our nation I speak in my own defence with every confidence, since you can ascertain that barely twelve days have elapsed since I went up to worship at Jerusalem. They neither found me in the Sanctuary arguing with anyone, nor haranguing a crowd either in the synagogues or up and down the city. They can offer no shred of evidence to support the charges they now bring against me. . . .
>
> After an interval of several years I arrived to make charitable gifts to my nation, and also to offer sacrifices, engaged in which activities some Jews of Asia found me in the Sanctuary when I had undergone purification, with no sign of a crowd or commotion. They should have been here before you to accuse me if there had been anything against me. As they are not, let those who are here speak of what wrongdoing they discovered when I stood before the Sanhedrin, or about the one thing I cried out as I stood among them, 'Concerning the resurrection of the dead I am being judged by you today!'

Felix, we are told, was very accurately informed about Nazorean beliefs, and thereupon adjourned the proceedings, saying, 'When Tribune Lysias[10] gets down I will decide your case.'

Paul was remanded in custody under fairly decent conditions and allowed to have visitors who could bring him food and other necessities. He had another opportunity soon after this to address Felix on his convictions, and at intervals afterwards. But his case was not decided. Luke suggests, as is quite probable, that the governor was hoping to be offered by Paul a suitable bribe to set him at liberty. Paul was still a prisoner nearly two years later when Felix was replaced by Porcius Festus.

In the latter part of this period Felix had to deal with the conflict between the Jews and Syrians in Caesarea, to which we have referred. And when he was recalled by Nero the leaders of the Jewish community there themselves went to Rome to accuse Felix. He only escaped punishment through the influence of his brother Pallas and others. The verdict of Tacitus on Felix is that 'he exercised the power of a king in the spirit of a slave.'[11]

The affair of Paul was now brought to a head. When Festus went up to Jerusalem from Caesarea three days after his arrival the hierarchy made representations to him to have Paul sent to the capital. The request was refused, but Festus said they could bring charges against Paul at Casarea on his return there.[12]

The prisoner was duly brought before the tribunal, and after listening to the charges the governor asked Paul whether he was prepared to go to Jerusalem to be tried before him there. Paul wisely declined.

'I am standing now at Caesar's tribunal, where I should be tried. I have not injured Jews, as you can see quite plainly. If I am at fault and have done something that merits death I am not begging myself off from dying. But if there is no foundation for these charges they bring against me, no one is entitled to gratify them. I appeal to Caesar.'

Paul was fully within his rights as a Roman citizen, and after conferring with the accusers Festus assented. 'You have appealed to Caesar. To Caesar you must go.'

The governor must have been thankful enough not to have to deal with the case, and the hierarchy was not too dissatisfied as Paul would at least be removed far from Judea.

But there was a further development before arrangements were made for Paul to be embarked on the voyage to Italy. King Agrippa and his sister Berenice arrived at Caesarea to pay their respects to the governor, and Felix took the opportunity of speaking about Paul to the king.

Agrippa expressed the wish to hear the man, and this was arranged for the next day. Festus was only too pleased, for as he explained he was quite out of his depth with accusations on matters of the Jewish religion, which had nothing to do with the kind of crimes within his competence to judge. The prisoner had appealed to Caesar; but, said Felix at the opening of the proceedings, 'I find myself with nothing definite to write to our Lord. I have therefore brought him before you, and especially before you King Agrippa, so that after this examination I might know what to write; for it seems senseless to me to be sending a prisoner without at the same time specifying the charge against him.'

Given the king's leave to speak, Paul again told his story, and wound up by saying, 'Aided by God's providence, I continue to stand – just as I am doing at this moment – witnessing to high and low, uttering no single word beyond what the Prophets foretold would happen, yes, and Moses himself, that the Messiah would suffer, that he would be the first to rise from the dead, and thereafter bring light to our people and to the Gentiles.'

Thus the Acts, from which we may continue to quote.

When he had reached this part of his defence, Festus interjected, 'You are raving, Paul! All this study has disturbed your reason.'

'I am not mad, Your Excellency Festus,' Paul rejoined. 'I am speaking plainly matters of fact and sense; for the king, before whom I can express myself feely, well understands these things. I am persuaded that none of them has escaped his notice, for they were not done in a corner.

'King Agrippa, do you believe the Prophets? Of course you do.'

Said Agrippa to Paul, 'In next-to-no-time you will be persuading me to turn Christian.'

'I pray God,' Paul replied, 'that whether in next-to-no-time or a long time, not only you but all who hear me today will become as I am, except for these chains.'

Then the king rose, followed by the governor, Berenice, and the assembled company. When they had withdrawn they discussed the matter among themselves. 'The man has done nothing,' they agreed, 'to deserve death or imprisonment.'

'He could have been released,' said Agrippa to Festus, 'had he not appealed to Caesar.'

The affair of Paul quickly dropped out of mind, except for those who were specially interested. The governor was pressingly involved with the activities of the Sicarii, who had gained considerably in boldness and numerical strength, and with at least one fresh claimant to free the Jews from the Roman yoke.

Agrippa too had his own problems. At the Hasmonean Palace at Jerusalem he had a dining-room which from its eminence and proximity to the Temple commanded a view of the interior. He enjoyed watching what was going on while he reclined at meals. The hierarchy were offended that the sacrifices should be spied on, and erected a high interior wall to block this view. The wall, however, also interfered with observation by the Roman guards, who during the festivals were posted along the roof of the western portico. So both the king, and even more the governor, were extremely angry, and Festus gave orders for the wall to be demolished.

Instead of complying the hierarchy asked leave to send an embassy to Nero, and when this was granted sent a deputation to Rome consisting of ten of their number together with the high priest Ishmael and Helcias the keeper of the treasury.

Nero ruled in favour of the suppliants, out of favour, as Josephus declares, to the Empress Poppaea, who was a worshipper of God, and who pleaded on behalf of the Jews. The deputation was sent back to Jerusalem, but Ishmael and Helcias were for the present detained in Rome. On learning of this, Agrippa deposed Ishmael and gave the high priesthood to Joseph Cabi, son of the high priest Simon.[13] Joseph, however, held the office only briefly and was replaced by Annas (Ananus) son of the famous Annas son of Seth.[14]

The autumn of A.D. 61 marked the commencement of a Sabbatical Year, impinging at this momentous juncture on the time for the taking of the next Roman census of A.D. 62-3. The census may have had to be delayed owing to the death of Porcius Festus, which left the country temporarily without a procurator.

NOTES AND REFERENCES

1. See above, p. 116.
2. See Josephus, *Antiq.* XX. 181 and 205–7.
3. Brandon, *Jesus and the Zealots*, pp. 118 and 169.
4. Jas. ii. 6; v. 1–6.
5. See Acts xxi–xxvi. The translations given are my own from the *Authentic New Testament.*
6. One of their inflammatory statements was that Paul had brought Greeks into the Temple proper, which was forbidden on pain of death. They made

this claim, according to the Acts, because they had seen Paul in the city in company with Trophimus the Ephesian.

7. Josephus, *J.W.* II. 261–3; *Antiq.* XX. 169–72.
8. Ananias was still high priest in A.D. 58. His successor Ishmael was appointed the following year.
9. The encomium on Felix, while politic flattery, was totally unwarranted by the governor's behaviour in office. He had in fact signally failed to produce peace and law and order.
10. Claudius Lysias, named in the Acts as in command at Fort Antonia.
11. Tacitus, *Hist.* V. ix. Cp. *Annals,* XII. liv, and Josephus, *Antiq,* XX. 182.
12. According to the Acts, Paul would not have reached Jerusalem alive, since it was designed to lay an ambush to assassinate him while on the way.
13. Presumably Simon Cantheras of the family of Boethus, appointed high priest by Agrippa I in A.D. 41. The account of the embassy is given in the *Antiquities* XX. 194–6.
14. Father-in-law of Joseph Caiaphas, high priest in the time of Jesus.

CHAPTER 21

DEATH OF A SAINT

In A.D. 62 a state of affairs arose comparable to what had existed at the beginning of the year 37. There was an interregnum in so far as for a certain period the country was without a Roman procurator. In these circumstances it devolved upon the reigning high priest to exercise responsibility in the Roman interest for the maintenance of good order. Porcius Festus died in office, and there was a gap until Nero had decided to appoint Lucceius Albinus, who held a post in Egypt and had to travel from Alexandria.

It may be recalled that in A.D. 37 the reigning high priest had been Jonathan son of Annas, and that it was he who had supported the attack on the Nazoreans instigated by Paul before his conversion.[1] The high priest now was a younger brother of Jonathan who bore the same name as his father. This Annas or Ananus (in Hebrew Hanan) is described by Josephus in his more sober and responsible work, the *Antiquities*, as a man who was 'rash in his temper and unusually daring. He followed the Party of the Sadducees, who are indeed harsher than any of the other Jews when they sit in judgment' (XX. 199). Annas determined to take full advantage of the position in which he found himself to settle scores once and for all with the hostile Nazoreans, who had the ear of the people and were regarded as the spiritual backers of the Zealots, in league with the lower priests and Essenes. It was intolerable that the Nazoreans on Mount Zion should maintain what amounted to a rival Sanhedrin giving allegiance to Jesus as Messiah, under the Presidency of his brother Jacob. With his by no means unwilling colleagues, Annas formed the plan to deal the opposition a shattering blow by seizing and executing Jacob and as many of the Nazorean Elders as he could lay hands on.

Ever since the delivery of Jesus into the hands of the Romans, which brought about his crucifixion, there had been a feud between the Nazoreans and the family of Annas the Elder. For the Nazoreans the Ananites were guilty of slaying the Lord's anointed.[2]

An echo of the feud comes to us in the fateful words given in Matthew's Gospel, 'His blood be on us, and on our children.' But there the animus of the Church against the Jews has put these words into the mouth of 'all the people' (Mt. xxvii. 25). The consequences of this falsehood have lasted until the present day, and brought upon the Jews untold suffering, misery and loss of life in the name of Jesus. At long last the truth can be made plain, and it is hoped that it will register and change Christian teaching much more emphatically than was done by the Second Vatican Council.

The feud developed as nationalist feeling was intensified. Jonathan son of Annas, who was behind the vendetta against the Nazoreans in A.D. 37, was assassinated by the Sicarii in mysterious circumstances in the governorship of Felix. Annas son of Annas, who, as we shall relate, compassed the death of Jacob brother of Jesus, was in his turn in the Jewish Revolt murdered by the Idumeans whom the Zealots had brought into Jerusalem.[3] We are afforded a graphic illustration of the prolonged conflict testified to by the Dead Sea Scrolls between the Wicked Priest and the True Teacher.

It is by no means easy to get at what happened in A.D. 62 because of the paucity and diversity of the records. The account given by Josephus is straightforward, in the text of the *Antiquities* as we have it, and we may therefore quote this first.

> Possessed of such a character [i.e. for rashness and daring], Ananus thought that he had a favourable opportunity because Festus was dead and Albinus was still on the way. And so he convened the judges of the Sanhedrin and brought before them a man named Jacob, the brother of Jesus who was called the Christ, and certain others. He accused them of having transgressed the Law and delivered them up to be stoned. Those of the inhabitants of the city who were considered the most fair-minded and who were strict in the observance of the Law[4] were offended at this. They therefore secretly sent to King Agrippa urging him, for Ananus had not even been correct in his first step [i.e. convening the Sanhedrin without official sanction], to order him to desist from any further such actions. Certain of them even went to meet Albinus, who was on his way from Alexandria, and informed him that Ananus had no authority to convene the Sanhedrin without his consent. Convinced by these words, Albinus angrily wrote to Ananus threatening to take vengeance upon him. King Agrippa, because of Ananus' action, deposed him from the high priesthood which he had held for three months and replaced him with Jesus the son of Damnaeus (XX. 200–3).

Another relevant passage is attributed to Josephus by Origen and Eusebius, but this does not occur in any known manuscript of his writings. This states: 'These things happened to the Jews to avenge

Jacob the Just, who was the brother of Jesus called Christ, and whom the Jews had slain, although he was a man most distinguished for his justice.'[5] The passage, as is evident from both the writers mentioned, appeared in a context having to do with the causes of the doom of Jerusalem at the hands of the Romans.

The question has to be considered, whether this second pronouncement is genuine. And if so, where in the writings of Josephus could it have been located?

The words used are not alien to the thinking of Josephus, for he shows himself very concerned as a Pharisee with evil actions which brought retribution, particularly with respect to the destruction of Jerusalem and the Temple. Also, in the *Antiquities*, he reports that the defeat of the forces of Herod Antipas by the Nabataeans was ascribed by many Jews to the tetrarch's execution of John the Baptist (XVIII. 116). The statement is unlikely to be a Christian interpolation, since Origen is surprised that Josephus should regard the fall of Jerusalem as a punishment for what was done to Jacob rather than to Christ, which is what he should have asserted.

It is likely, therefore, that something approximating to the statement quoted was read in Josephus, and that he was responsible for it. Where, then, was it found?

The most probable work would be the *Jewish War*. In the standard text there is no reference whatever to the death of Jacob. But this text looks back in the main to a revised version made in the author's lifetime. There had earlier been in circulation an original Greek edition, which bore the first title of the work, *On the Capture* (or *Destruction*) *of Jerusalem (PERI HALOSEOS HIEROUSALEM)*. It could have been a copy based on this edition which Origen had seen.

Since the execution of Jacob took place in A.D. 62 shortly before the arrival of Albinus as governor, as described by Josephus in the *Antiquities*, the section in the *Halosis* where we should expect to find the statement would be that which covered the administration of Albinus, where it would be pertinent. Now this period is covered with remarkable brevity in the *Jewish War* (II. 272-6), in not more than a long paragraph. But the last sentence is important, where Josephus writes: 'In short, none could now speak his mind, with tyrants on every side; and from this date were sown in the city the seeds of its impending destruction (*halosis*).' Here the author is in fact, with reference to the time of Albinus, linking events with the doom of Jerusalem, and employing the term *halosis*. It is conceivable, therefore, that in the earlier Greek edition a further sentence appeared to this effect: 'Some held that these calamities happened to the Jews to avenge Jacob the Just, who was the brother of Jesus called Christ, and who at this time the judges of the nation had executed, although he was a man distinguished for his justice.'

We turn now to another version of the death of the Nazorean leader given by Hegesippus in his *Memoirs*, dating from the second half of the second century A.D., and quoted by Eusebius (*Eccl. Hist.* II. xxiii). The account of Hegesippus may well be more illuminating as it rests on information gleaned from the Gentile Church of the new Jerusalem (Aelia Capitolina) after A.D. 135. But, unfortunately, the report betrays so much confusion and ignorance that it is extremely difficult to extract from it matters of historical value. Yet there are things of worth and consequence in the narrative which call for an effort to wrestle with the extraordinary story as it has come down to us.

But first we must reproduce the narrative as it stands.

Some of the seven sects of the people, mentioned by me above in my *Memoirs,* asked him [i.e. Jacob] what was the door to Jesus. And he answered, 'that he was the Saviour'. From which some believed that Jesus is the Christ. But the aforesaid heresies did not believe either in a resurrection, or that he was coming to give every one according to his works. As many, however, as did believe, did so on account of Jacob. As there were many therefore of the rulers that believed, there arose a tumult among the Jews, Scribes and Pharisees, saying that there was danger, that the people would now expect Jesus as the Christ.

They came therefore together, and said to Jacob, 'We entreat thee, restrain the people, who are led astray after Jesus, as if he were the Christ. We entreat thee to persuade all who are coming to the feast of the Passover rightly concerning Jesus; for we all have confidence in thee. For we and all the people bear witness to thee that thou art just and no respecter of persons. Persuade therefore the people not to be led astray by Jesus, for we and all the people have great confidence in thee. Stand, therefore, upon a wing of the Temple that thou mayest be conspicuous on high, and thy words may be easily heard by all the people; for all the tribes have come together on account of the Passover, with some of the Gentiles also.'

The aforesaid Scribes and Pharisees, accordingly, placed Jacob upon a wing of the Temple, and cried out to him, 'O thou Just One, whom we ought all to credit, since the people are led astray after Jesus that was crucified, declare to us what is the door to Jesus that was crucified.' But he answered with a loud voice, 'Why do you ask me regarding Jesus the Son of Man? He is now sitting in the heavens on the right hand of Great Power, and is about to come on the clouds of Heaven.'

And as many were confirmed, and gloried in this testimony of Jacob, and said, 'Hosanna to the Son of David,' these same priests and Pharisees said to one another, 'We have done badly in affording such testimony to Jesus; but let us go and cast him down, that they may fear to believe in him.' And they cried out, 'Oh, oh, the Just himself is deceived,' and they fulfilled that which is written in Isaiah, 'Let us do away with the just, because he is offensive to us; wherefore they shall eat the fruit of their doings' [Isa. iii. 10; Gr. LXX]. Going up therefore, they cast down the Just One, saying to one another, 'Let us stone Jacob the Just.'

And they began to stone him, as he did not die immediately when cast down; but turning round, he knelt down, saying, 'I beseech Thee, O Lord God and Father, forgive them, for they know not what they do.'

Thus they were stoning him, when one of the priests of the sons of Rechab, a son of the Rechabites spoken of by Jeremiah the prophet, cried out, saying, 'Stop! What are you doing? The Just is praying for you.'

But one of them, a fuller, beat out the brains of the Just with the club he used to beat out clothes. Thus he suffered martyrdom, and they buried him on the spot where his tombstone still remains, close to the Temple. He became a faithful witness, both to the Jews and Greeks, that Jesus is the Christ. Immediately after this, Vespasian invaded and took Judea.

In examining this narrative we have first to observe that it dates from a period when Christian fiction had begun to flourish. On one hand there was a desire for more knowledge of what had happened in the past, and on the other to provide confirmation on high authority of doctrines put forward by various teachers. A crop of literature of an apocryphal nature was produced, some of it making use of floating tradition, but on the whole betraying little acquaintance with the Jewish history and practices represented.

We have something of a hotch-potch here. 'Scribes and Pharisees' had become a Christian stock phrase for the opponents of Jesus. The placing of Jacob on the Temple pinnacle, and his casting down from there, may owe something to one of the items of the temptation of Jesus (Mt. iv. 5-6), and to the tradition that Saul of Tarsus had assaulted Jacob and thrown him down the Temple steps.[7] The question, 'What is the door to Jesus?', has been held to be a mistaken translation of Hebrew words such as *'Mah petach yeshuah*?' meaning 'What is the door (or, means) of salvation?' It has also been pointed out that the concerned Jewish authorities can hardly have imagined that the leader of the Nazoreans would be willing to instruct the people not to expect Jesus as Messiah when for some quarter of a century he had been testifying to the opposite.

There are certain points of likeness to the account of the death of

Jacob given by Josephus. The allusion to resurrection, to the Temple, and once to 'Priests and Pharisees', conveys that those who acted against Jacob were in fact Sadducees. It is also agreed that there was a stoning of Jacob. But otherwise the stories are different.

We may not dismiss the story told by Hegesippus as without foundation. Garbled as it is, there are elements in it which point to a Nazorean source of information of real value.

First we have reference to the season, namely the Passover, which may well be correct since this festival commemorated the salvation of Israel from bondage and would be an occasion – especially in this Sabbatical Year of A.D. 61-2 – when the Nazoreans would be particularly vociferous in their propaganda on behalf of Jesus as Messiah. It had been at the Passover that he had been crucified through the instrumentality of the detested Sadducean hierarchy, but had been raised from the dead by God and was now at God's right hand. The Nazoreans were now loud in proclaiming that the return of Jesus was imminent, and this was having a powerful effect not only on the populace but on 'many of the rulers'. These rulers presumably included Pharisee members of the Sanhedrin. There would therefore be valid cause for the Sadducean hierarchy to take alarm, saying 'that there was danger, that the people would now expect Jesus as the Messiah', and might be inspired to engage in rebellious action.

It is conceivable that Jacob and some of his associates may have been requested to appear before a hastily convened meeting of the political Sanhedrin; and because of his known non-violent character and the veneration in which he was held by the multitude it was demanded of him – initially in a conciliatory manner – that he should address the crowd in order to pacify them. We are to imagine that Jacob consented to speak to the people; but when he was given the opportunity, whatever he may have said to call for patience under suffering and provocation (cp. Jas. v. 7-11), he would not compromise as regards his convictions, and testified to the Messiahship and near return of Jesus.

His words were greeted with cries of many acclaiming the Son of David, which incensed the hierarchy and defeated their purpose. If we are to reconcile Hegesippus with Josephus, we would have to suppose that Jacob was swiftly arrested and condemned to death in order that his execution should act as a deterrent to those who might contemplate participating in revolt against the Romans. The charge against

Jacob of breaking the Law in a manner calling for death by stoning, referred to by Josephus, must have been a trumped-up one, since no one was a more observant Jew. Josephus suggests as much in stating that the most unprejudiced and devout citizens were shocked. None of the crimes for which stoning was the penalty could have relevance to Jacob.[8] Possibly it was represented that as a colleague of the notorious Paul he was guilty of some kind of idolatry or leading the people astray to worship other gods. In the version of Hegesippus there is no mention of any Court proceedings. What exactly happened must therefore remain a mystery.

However, there are other points of interest still to be observed. There is the reference in Hegesippus to Isaiah. iii. 10. This chapter of the prophet could indeed be the source of the view that the murder of Jacob, judicial or otherwise, brought a judgment on Jerusalem. For there it is declared:

> Woe unto their soul! for they have rewarded evil unto themselves. Say ye to the *righteous* that it shall be well with him; but they shall eat of the fruit of their doings. Woe unto the wicked! it shall be ill with him; for the reward of his hands shall be given him. . . . The Lord will enter into judgment with the ancients of His people, and the princes thereof: for ye have eaten up the vineyard; the spoil of the *poor* is in your houses [cp. Jas. v. 1–6]. What mean ye that ye beat My people to pieces, and grind the faces of the *poor*? saith the Lord God of hosts. . . . Thy men shall fall by the sword, and thy might in the war.

We are reminded of the doom of the Wicked Priest in the *Commentary on Habakkuk* in the Dead Sea Scrolls, who is delivered into the hands of his enemies because of the iniquity committed against the Teacher of Righteousness and the men of his Council. The money and wealth of the Last Priests of Jerusalem would be delivered into the hands of the army of the Kittim (i.e. the Romans).[9]

We note too that it is one of the ordinary priests of Rechabite descent, who may have been a Nazorean or sympathizer, who cries to the killers of Jacob to stay their hand as he is praying for them. The prayer of this Saint is itself in line with all we know of his character, 'O Lord God and Father, forgive them, for they know not what they do.' It may be that it was from the lips of Jacob that Luke appropriated these noble words as befitting Jesus himself on the cross; for no other Gospel writer ascribes them to him, which surely they might have been expected to do if Jesus had uttered them. For the Nazoreans the death of Jacob was the greatest tragedy they had suffered. For so long he had been their leader, their wise counsellor, their guide and example. Blood-brother of Jesus, in him they had been able to see a living likeness to their absent and exalted king, the proof that their faith was not in vain. In their bereavement it was as if the Messiah had died again.

NOTES AND REFERENCES

1. See above, p. 132.
2. Acts v. 28. A garbled account of the feud is contained in the *Toldoth Jeshu,* a Jewish counter-gospel circulating in the Middle Ages which, however, rests on early Nazorean sources. See Schonfield, *According to the Hebrews.*
3. Josephus, *J.W.* IV. 305–25. Other high priests were killed by the rebels; the notorious high priest Ananias son of Nedebaeus, who had deprived the priests of their tithes, together with his brother Hezekiah were murdered by the followers of Menahem the Zealot descendant of Judas of Galilee. Also Jesus son of Gamalas, another high priest, was killed with Ananus (Annas) by the Idumeans.
4. Does Josephus here indicate the leading Pharisees?
5. Origen, *Contra Cels.* I. xlvii; Euseb. *Eccl. Hist.* II. xxiii.
6. See Eisler, *The Messiah Jesus and John the Baptist.*
7. See above, p. 127.
8. See the Mishnah, *Sanhed.* vii. 4.
9. *Comm. Hab.* ix (Vermes).

CHAPTER 22

REIGN OF TERROR

When Jesus was executed the event was attended, according to the Gospels, by prodigies of nature. The sun was blotted out, and darkness reigned for three hours. And as he passed into oblivion there was an earthquake and the veil of the Temple was rent from top to bottom. The *Gospel of the Hebrews* says that the great lintel stone fell and was shattered to pieces.[1] We have no Nazorean source which reports such prodigies at the death of Jacob, though these may well have once existed. But Josephus, who was a Pharisee inclined to Essenism and believed in such signs, records their occurrence at this time.

The first came at the Passover, the feast of unleavened bread. This may have been the same Passover, of A.D. 62, which saw the martyrdom of Jacob. At the beginning of the festival, at three o'clock in the morning, such a brilliant light shone round the altar and Sanctuary that it seemed to be broad daylight. This lasted for half an hour. During the same seven-day feast a cow brought for sacrifice gave birth to a lamb in the midst of the court of the Temple. Further, at midnight, the great bronze eastern gate which gave access to the inner court of the Temple, and which required twenty men to close because of its weight, was discovered to have opened of its own accord. 'The watchmen of the Temple ran and reported the matter to the Captain [i.e. of the Temple Guard], and he came up and with difficulty succeeded in getting it shut.' Josephus continues, 'This to the uninitiated seemed the best of omens, as they supposed that God had opened to them the door of blessings;[2] but the learned understood that the security of the Temple was dissolving of its own accord, and that the opening of the door meant a present to the enemy, interpreting the portent in their own minds as indicative of coming desolation.'[3]

Curiously, this third event and how it was interpreted by the learned is confirmed by the Talmud (*Yoma,* fol. 39b). When news of the mysterious opening of the Temple door came to the eminent Pharisee John son of Zachaeus (Johanan ben Zaccai), who had the gift of prophecy,[4] he is said to have exclaimed, 'O Temple, Temple, why dost thou frighten thyself? I know that thou shalt be destroyed. Zechariah the son of Iddo has already prophesied concerning thee (Zech. xi. 1), "Open thy doors, O Lebanon, that the fire may devour thy cedars".'

But these were only the beginning of the portents. We again quote Josephus.

> Again, not many days after the festival [i.e. of unleavened bread] on the twenty-first day of the month Artemisium [c. late May or early June], there appeared a miraculous phenomenon, passing belief. Indeed, what I am about to relate would, I imagine, have been deemed a fable, were it not for the narratives of eyewitnesses for the subsequent calamities which deserved to be signalized. For before sunset throughout all parts of the country chariots were seen in the air and armed battalions hurtling through the clouds and encompassing the cities. Moreover, at the feast which is called Pentecost, the priests on entering the inner court of the Temple by night, as their custom was in the discharge of their ministrations, reported that they were conscious, first of a commotion and a din, and after that of a voice as of a host saying, 'We are departing hence.'

Josephus concludes his stories of omens here with one which he calls 'even more alarming'. In the autumn of A.D. 62, at the feast of Tabernacles,[5] a peasant named Jesus son of Ananias, standing in the Temple, suddenly began to cry out, 'A voice from the east, a voice from the west, a voice from the four winds; a voice against Jerusalem and the Sanctuary, a voice against the bridegroom and the bride, a voice against the people.' Day and night thereafter he went up and down the alleys of the city repeating his doleful cry, until the magistrates arrested and beat him. But this made no difference. They then brought him before the Roman governor. 'There, although flayed to the bone with scourges, he neither sued for mercy nor shed a tear, but, merely introducing the most mournful of variations into his ejaculation, responded to each stroke with "Woe to Jerusalem!" When Albinus, the governor, asked him who and whence he was and why he uttered these cries, he answered him never a word, but unceasingly reiterated his dirge over the city, until Albinus pronounced him a maniac and let him go' (*J. W.* VI. 300-5).

Jesus continued his lament day in and day out, crying especially loudly at the festivals, year after year until the seige of the city by the Romans in A.D. 70. Then while going on his round he shouted, 'Woe once more to the city and to the people and to the Temple,' but added, 'and woe to me also.' Thereupon a stone from one of the Roman *ballistae* struck and killed him on the spot.

A reflection of the history of this other Jesus seems to occur in the

Gospel of John, the Gospel which is notable for its Jerusalem scenes. It is only in this Gospel that Jesus of Nazareth is said to have cried aloud in the Temple on the last day of the feast of Tabernacles. And when he is before the governor, and is asked, 'Whence art thou?' Jesus gives him no answer (Jn. vii. 37; xix. 9).

We have furnished an account of these phenomena from the pages of Josephus because they are eloquent of the superstitious awe of the ancient world, where major events were believed to cast their shadow before through prophecies, signs and prodigies of nature. The Jewish nation in its tribulations was highly responsive to the impact of the supernatural in its affairs, as we may judge not only from what has been cited but also from the number of deluded persons and charlatans whom the people were ready to heed and follow, and who were multiplied as conditions became progressively more intolerable.

One sign, certainly, the passing of Jacob the Just had represented, the ending of moderate counsels and the possibility of any peaceful outcome of the struggle between Jerusalem and Rome. In the strangest of associations the Zealots and their antagonists the Roman governors seemed to be joining in an unholy partnership to bring about the ruin of the country.

At this juncture, as ill luck would have it, the Roman census was again due with all the hostile feeling which this periodic event aroused. On the returns of the census the tribute was imposed, and the procurators had the golden opportunity, if they chose to take it, to extract more than was due to line their own pockets. The most unscrupulous and avaricious of them seized their chance with both hands, and the reign of terror which had been mounting steadily gave a license which in normal circumstances would not have been overlooked by their superiors.

Josephus does not directly allude to the census under Albinus, just as he does not to the previous one fourteen years earlier, but he does accuse the governor of 'burdening the whole nation with extraordinary taxes'.[6] In his official capacity he stole and plundered private property.

The villainy of Albinus, however, went much further, according to Josephus.

> He accepted ransoms from their relatives on behalf of those who had been imprisoned for robbery by the local councils or by former procurators; and the only persons left in jail as malefactors were those who failed to pay

the price. Now, too, the audacity of the revolutionary party in Jerusalem was stimulated; the influential men among their number secured from Albinus, by means of bribes, immunity for their seditious practices; while of the populace all who were dissatisfied with peace joined hands with the governor's accomplices. Each ruffian, with his own band of followers grouped around him, towered above his company like a brigand chief or tyrant, employing his bodyguard to plunder peaceful citizens. The result was that the victims of robbery kept their grievances, of which they had every reason to complain, to themselves, while those who escaped injury cringed to wretches deserving of punishment, through fear of suffering the same fate (*J.W.* II. 273–6).

The Nazoreans, as recommended by Jacob, like the moderate Pharisees and colleagues of the devout Elect, could only possess their souls in patience, grieving and horrified. But some of the more intrepid, especially among the young, may well have abandoned a passive attitude, and inflamed by the passions of the time have thrown in their lot with the war party. Yet those who waited and prayed must have considered that the End must now be very close at hand. Surely the signal would soon be given from the skies!

The Sicarii naturally were among those who profited from the situation. One of their exploits was to kidnap the officer of Eleazar the Captain of the Temple, son of the former high priest Ananias son of Nedebaeus. They then offered to release him if Ananias would persuade Albinus to free ten of their number who were prisoners. No doubt by a handsome gift to the governor the wealthy Ananias succeeded. This only led to further kidnappings to obtain the release of terrorists, an activity still in vogue nineteen centuries later.

Near the end of the governorship of Albinus in A.D. 64, King Agrippa deposed Jesus son of Damnaeus from the high priesthood, and gave the office to Jesus son of Gamalas (or Gamaliel). In these days of violence it also happened that the Temple, whose reconstruction had been initiated by Herod the Great, was at long last completed. This threw eighteen thousand workmen engaged on the structure out of employment. Agrippa was petitioned to sanction additional work to raise the height of the east portico overlooking the Kedron Valley. The request was refused, but instead he authorized the paving of Jerusalem with white stones.

Nero now replaced Albinus by Gessius Florus, the most criminal of all the procurators as represented by Josephus. By comparison with him, he declares, Albinus was a paragon of virtue. Albinus masked his depredations by perpetrating them in secret and with dissimulation; but Florus, on the contrary, ostentatiously paraded his outrages upon the nation.

At this point, however, we must turn from the mounting disorders in Judea to an outstanding event in Rome, which was to have dire consequences for the Nazoreans, or, as they were better known there, the Christiani. We have first to follow the experiences of Paul.

In the summer of A.D. 60 Paul had been embarked at Caesarea with some of his companions, on the way to Italy for his appeal to be heard by Nero. The journey, as it happened, was prolonged and perilous. There was a change of ship at Myra in Lycia to an Alexandrian cargo boat, but this encountered headwinds and made slow progress. The attempt was made to reach Crete and winter there; but this was frustrated by a tremendous storm and the boat was shipwrecked on the island of Malta. After three months there another Alexandrian boat conveyed the company to the Italian port of Puteoli, and the journey was continued by road to Rome. While waiting for his case to come up Paul under guard was permitted to occupy his own rented apartment.

Paul was now in the capital of the Empire he had long hoped to reach, but not as a free agent. He was to occupy his lodging for two full years, and his first action was to send for the representatives of the Jewish community. 'You see in me, brothers,' he told them, 'a prisoner from Jerusalem, who though he has done nothing against our people or our ancestral customs was handed over to the Romans. When they had examined me they proposed to set me free, as there was nothing against me to justify a death sentence. But when certain Jews opposed this I was forced to appeal to Caesar, though not because I have any grounds of complaint against my nation. My reason for asking you here is to see you and speak with you, because it is for the sake of the Hope of Israel I wear this chain' (Acts xxviii. 17-20).

His visitors informed him that they had received no communication or verbal report about him. Their acquaintance with the sect to which he belonged was meagre. They only knew for certain that it had a bad reputation, but would like to hear his views. A further meeting was accordingly arranged. An all-day session resulted, which did not turn out too well.

Neither was Paul's presence very welcome to the Nazoreans of Rome, though Luke would suggest otherwise. They seem to have kept very much to themselves after the agitation in the time of Claudius.[7] They had received Paul's letter, the epistle to the Romans, but being mainly Jews and proselytes they did not support his doctrines. Paul therefore turned to the Gentiles, his particular objective. Confined though he was he was not a man to be inactive. Very soon he was writing to the Ephesians to pray for him, 'that fluent speech may be given me boldly to make known the mystery, on account of which I am an ambassador in chains, that even so placed I may speak as boldly as it behoves me to speak (Eph. vi. 19-20). And he did speak, to good effect, to his guards, and to many who came to see him, until his message had penetrated into Caesar's household (Phil. iv. 22).

It is through the Pauline 'Prison' and 'Pastoral' letters that we make contact with developments.

> I want to tell you, brothers [Paul writes to the community at Philippi] that my circumstances have rather tended to the advancement of the News; for my letters have publicized Christ to the whole praetorium and everywhere else, and the majority of the brothers, having been fired with confidence in the Lord by my fetters, have become much more venturesome, giving out God's message fearlessly. Some of course do it out of envy and rivalry, but others proclaim Christ from goodwill. These do it out of regard, knowing that I am thus circumstanced for the defence of the News, while the former who are not well-intentioned, announce Christ in a factious spirit, trying deliberately to make trouble for me in my fettered state. What does it matter? The main thing is, that whether in pretence or sincerity Christ is proclaimed. For this I rejoice. But there is greater joy in store . . . with the earnest hope and expectation I have that I shall in no way be put to shame, but that freely and fully, now as always, Christ will be magnified in my person, whether by life or death (Phil. i. 12–20).

He speaks at times with some confidence that his appeal when heard would be successful; but one feels that this is done more to keep up the spirits of his distant flock than with any real conviction. Evidently his own evangelical zeal was causing the Nazoreans of Rome to become more active, partly to combat the influence of his heterodox teaching. The effect was to bring the followers of Jesus more prominently to public and official attention, which probably contributed to sealing Paul's fate and brought terrible suffering on the whole community.

Hostility of the Nazoreans towards Paul progressively increased. They totally disowned him. He writes plaintively to the community at

Colossae that of Jewish believers in the Messiah only three associated with him, Aristarchus a fellow-prisoner, Mark the nephew of Barnabas then in Rome, and Jesus called Justus; and none of these were members of the Rome community (Col. iv. 10-11).

We have no information about the hearing of Paul's appeal to Nero, except that apparently judgment was deferred. There seems no doubt however what the verdict was going to be. What we can glean of the circumstances has reached us through the second letter to Paul's young associate Timotheus.

I am now on the eve of peace, and the time for my discharge is approaching. I have fought a gallant contest; I have completed the course; I have kept the Faith. There remains in store for me the crown to which I am entitled, which the Lord, that honourable judge, will award me on that Day. . . .

Do your utmost to come to me quickly, for Demas, loving the present world, has deserted me and gone off to Thessalonica, Crescens has gone to Gaul, Titus to Dalmatia. Only Luke remains with me. Pick up Mark and bring him with you, for he is valuable to me in administrative work, and I have dispatched Tychicus to Ephesus. When you come bring the book-wrap I left with Carpus at Troas, also the books, particularly the parchments. Alexander the blacksmith has shown himself very ill-disposed towards me. The Lord will requite him in accordance with his actions. Watch out for him yourself, for he is strongly opposed to our views.

At the first hearing of my defence no one supported me: everyone deserted me. May it not be counted against them! But the Lord supported and strengthened me, so that through me the proclamation might ring out, and all the Gentiles might hear it; and I was saved from the jaws of the Lion [i.e. Nero].

What deferred the verdict on Paul's appeal is not known. Nero in his passion for theatrical display had taken himself off to Naples at the beginning of A.D. 64, and then crossed Italy to Beneventum. But he returned to Rome in the spring.[8] Possibly this was the reason for the delay.

It may have been the bad news of the state of affairs in Judea, which caused Nero to recall Albinus and replace him by Gessius Florus, which determined that Paul should die as a seditionist. According to a late tradition he met his end by beheading not far from the Ostian Way.

Not long after, in the summer of A.D. 64, the Great Fire of Rome broke out and raged for many days. Of the fourteen quarters of the city only four remained intact, three were totally destroyed, and the other seven were little more than a heap of ruins. It was widely suspected that Nero was responsible for this incendiarism; but it seems unlikely. What is certain is that the emperor had need of a scapegoat, and the blame was laid on the Christiani.

As a result of Paul's activities the Nazoreans in Rome, as we have seen, had lately become much more energetic in their Messianic propaganda. In this there was proclaimed the speedy return of Jesus in judgment on the idolaters and evildoers, and what was more the doom of Rome by fire.[9] The Messianists, therefore, left themselves open to the accusation of having 'in their enmity of humanity' deliberately fulfilled their own prediction. At the very least, they could be held guilty of ill-wishing Rome and the Empire. A considerable number were accordingly rounded up and barbarously put to death. Some were covered with the skins of wild beasts and torn by dogs, others converted into living torches by affixing them to crosses and covering them with inflammable material. These modes of execution agree with the Roman penalties prescribed for the practice of magic and sorcery.[10]

The dire tidings of the extermination of the community in Rome must have reached Jerusalem by September, increasing still more the conviction that the climax of Belial's persecution of the saints had come, and the End could not much longer be delayed. Either at the time of the Great Fire, or shortly after, it has been held that Peter too suffered martyrdom in Rome. So at this juncture the cause of Jesus had lost its chief protagonists. The souls of the butchered were crying out, in the words of the Revelation, 'How long will it be, holy and true Sovereign Lord, before Thou dost judge and avenge our blood on those who dwell on earth?'

NOTES AND REFERENCES

1. *Gospel of the Hebrews*, quoted by Jerome, on Mt. xxvii. 51, and in *Letter to Hedibia*, 8.
2. Cp. the reference in Hegesippus to 'the door of salvation', above pp. 219–20.
3. Josephus, *J.W.* VI. 293–6.
4. Like Josephus, John also predicted that Vespasian would become emperor.
5. This event is exactly dated by Josephus as four years before the outbreak of the war. The prophecies of Jesus son of Ananias continued for seven years and five months, until March, A.D. 70 (*J.W.* VI. 308).
6. One of the first actions at the beginning of the revolt in A.D. 66 was that a number of Jews withheld payment of tribute to Rome (Josephus, *J.W.* II. 404–5).
7. See above, p. 177. Paul had no hand in the creation of the Rome

community, which owed its existence to Judean apostles, probably Peter among them. It therefore followed the orthodox line of loyalty to the Law of Moses.

8. Tacitus, *Annals,* XV. xxxiii-xxxvi.
9. See above, p. 175. Cp. Rev. xviii. 8.
10. Paulus, *Sent.* v. quoted by E. G. Hardy, *Studies in Roman History* (First Series), pp. 53–4. On the torture inflicted on the Christians, see Tacitus, *Annals.* XV. xliv.

CHAPTER 23

THE EXODUS

The trials and tribulations which had come upon the Nazoreans, and the effect upon them both of the depredations of Florus and the unrestrained terrorism of the militants and brigands, made it increasingly difficult for the Party to preserve its cohesion. There was a sense of helplessness in the face of prevailing conditions. What policy should now be followed? Things were getting so completely out of hand that to exert any influence was becoming virtually impossible. For many within the Party inactivity was intolerable and counsels of patient waiting seemed like defeatism. There were those who were consumed with the fevers of nationalist militancy, and urged open commitment to the cause of revolt. Others were for intensifying a rigorous devotion to fasting and prayer that Divine guidance might be vouchsafed. Acrimony and heated debate threatened disruption. There were defections, and it became a question whether at the centre of events in Jerusalem, or indeed in the midst of the anarchic conditions generally throughout the country, the body of believers in the return of Jesus could endure to the End.

The year A.D. 65 was one of agony and uncertainty for the Jewish people. It was difficult to determine which was the greater enormity, the crimes of Florus or the pillages of the robber bands. They even seemed to be in league. Many who could afford to do so packed up and fled abroad.[1]

Josephus, who tells us this, accuses Florus of deliberately goading the Jews into revolt to cover up his own excesses. 'For, if the peace were kept, he expected to have the Jews accusing him before Caesar; whereas, could he bring about their revolt, he hoped that this larger crime would divert inquiry into less serious offences. In order, therefore, to produce an outbreak of the nation, he daily added to their sufferings' (*J. W.* II. 283).

At this crisis the Nazoreans were fortunate in finding a new and able leader, Simeon son of Cleophas. According to Hegesippus he was a first cousin of Jesus and Jacob, his father Cleophas being the brother of Joseph, and it must be presumed on the evidence a younger brother, since Simeon survived until early in the second century in the reign of Trajan, credited with being a centenarian. He was a member, therefore, of the Messiah's family and a descendant of King David.

We learn a little about him from Christian tradition, but, as it happens, a good deal more – though rather garbled – through Jewish channels. Indirectly it is Epiphanius who puts us on the right track. He had information that in the possession of the Jewish scholars at Tiberias in the second half of the fourth century A.D. were three 'Christian' works in Hebrew, described as the Gospels of Matthew and John, and the Acts of the Apostles.[2] Epiphanius makes many bungling statements, and it transpired on investigation that the three books in question were Nazorean documents, the *Gospel of the Hebrews* (or Hebrew Matthew), the *Ascents of Jacob* (Epiphanius' 'falsified Acts') and the *Book of John,* the Hebrew source of the Revelation. In a late Jewish source the composition of all three works is ascribed to Simeon ben Calpus, an honourable old man, stated to have been an uncle of Jesus. The uncle, of course, was Calpus (Cleophas). On the basis of such material Jewish anti-Christian propagandists created parodies, which were in circulation in the Middle Ages and later. There are several texts in existence, and as Samuel Krauss established,[3] these are not worthless as had been supposed. Through their fanciful statements, which became more confused when reference could no longer be made to the Nazorean manuscripts which had perished many centuries earlier, we are able to obtain valuable glimpses of the lost history we are seeking to recover. What we can ascertain fits in with the slender indications remaining to us from Christian records.

The passages which concern us here relate to a period specified as being thirty years after the death of Jesus. By our reckoning this would be A.D. 66. At this time the Sanhedrin ('the wise men of Israel') is disturbed by the continual strife with the 'insurgents', many of whom are followers of Jesus. The authorities decide, therefore, to seek for someone they can trust to remove the Nazoreans from their midst. The man they select is 'a certain aged man from among the Elders . . . who frequented the Holy of Holies.' He is called in one text Simeon Cepha,[4] but correctly in another Simeon ben Calpus.

In the figure of Simeon we have some reminiscence of Jacob the Just, who is said by Epiphanius to have served as high priest, and was permitted to enter the Holy of Holies once a year. Hegesippus only says of Jacob that 'he alone was allowed to enter the holy place.' But, like the *Toldoth Jeshu,*[5] Hegesippus conveys that the Jewish authorities wanted to deter the people from believing in Jesus as the Messiah, and tried to use Jacob for their purpose. His death was brought about because instead of warning the people he testified on behalf of Jesus. The underlying source would seem to be the lost Nazorean Acts.

Some of the teaching emphasized by the new leader, in the Jewish texts, comes from the Sermon on the Mount. But it is interesting to find him adding, 'In meekness Jesus showed himself, that ye might see his example of meekness, and suffer whatsoever might be done unto you. And at the Day of Judgment Jesus will cast them off [i.e. those who have rejected him]; but ye shall have hope because of your meekness. For so it is written (Zeph. ii. 3), Seek ye the Lord, all ye meek of the earth, which have wrought His judgment; seek righteousness, seek meekness; it may be ye shall be hid in the day of the Lord's anger.'

By this teaching, at the height of the strife between the sanhedrists and the insurgents, whose forces included 'brethren and kinsmen of Jesus', the Nazoreans are prevailed upon by Simeon to retire from Jerusalem and remove themselves from the midst of Israel.

While the information has reached us only in a confused manner, we are yet able to extract from this source an important addition to our knowledge, namely that Simeon son of Cleophas was chiefly instrumental in conducting at this time a substantial withdrawal of the Nazoreans from Jerusalem and Judea. There was great sense in this, apart from other considerations, since probably in no other way in the circumstances existing could the Party have been preserved relatively intact.

Both Eusebius and Epiphanius, as we shall see, report this exodus, though without direct reference to Simeon. Eusebius, however, does record that after the capture of Jerusalem by the Romans, 'those of the apostles and the disciples of our Lord, that were yet surviving, came together from all parts with those who were related to our Lord according to the flesh. For the greater part of them were still living. These consulted together to determine whom it was proper to pronounce worthy of being the successor of Jacob. They unanimously declared Simeon the son of Cleophas, of whom mention is made in the sacred volume [Lk. xxiv. 18], as worthy of the episcopal seat there [i.e. as bishop of Jerusalem].'[6]

We come to what Christian sources tell of the withdrawal. First from Eusebius we have this statement.

> The people of the church at Jerusalem, having been commanded by a Divine oracle given by revelation to men of approved piety there before the war, removed from the city, and dwelt at a certain town of Peraea called Pella. Here, those that believed in Christ, having removed from Jerusalem, as if holy men had entirely abandoned the royal city itself; the Divine justice, for their crimes against Christ and the apostles, finally overtook them, totally destroying the whole generation of these evildoers from the earth.[7]

Comparable passages occur in Epiphanius.[8] He, however, makes the warning to be given by Christ himself in his work *Against Heresies,* and by an angel in his book *On Weights and Measures.* This need not trouble us as in the Revelation Jesus communicates to the seer through his angel (Rev. i. 1; xxii. 16). Epiphanius concurs that the disciples left Jerusalem and dwelt at Pella in Peraea; but he is more definite that the flight took place just before the siege of the city by the Romans when its conquest seemed imminent.

Knowing only of the Christian tradition, S. G. F. Brandon has challenged its reliability on various counts.[9] He gives cogent reasons why the Nazoreans cannot be imagined to have left Jerusalem for Pella at any time from the summer of A.D. 66 until the final siege of the city by Titus. He also points out that Pella can be thought to be an unlikely place of refuge for devout Jews like the Nazoreans, as it was a Greek heathen city. Furthermore, it was sacked by the Jews early in the autumn of A.D. 66, and a devastated city could have offered little shelter.

But the Christian authorities are very anxious to telescope the period from the death of Jacob to the fall of Jerusalem, as if the latter came hard on the heels of the former. The time of the exodus, which the Jewish data indicate, would have been early in 66, and this would appear on other grounds to be more probable. We have no need to be concerned unduly with the statements that the Nazoreans took up residence in Pella itself. They could as well have camped in the region of Pella, in the foothills beyond. To this area the Mandaean-Nazoreans had fled in A.D. 37,[10] at the time of the persecuting activities of Saul of Tarsus, and it is in Batanea and the Hauran to the north that we find the major communities of Jewish followers of Jesus down to at least the fifth century A.D.[11]

As regards the warning revelation, one such has come down to us in the so-called Little Apocalypse (Mk. xiii, and cp. Mt. xxiv). There we read that under conditions of tribulation and internecine strife the faithful in Judea should flee to the mountains. The flight is to be hurried, with even more haste than at the going out from Egypt under Moses.

Indeed, we are reminded of that event, and of the flight of the righteous Lot and his family from Sodom before its overthrow. In the book of Revelation it is now Jerusalem which spiritually is called Sodom and Egypt (Rev. xi. 8).[12]

It is tempting to think that Josephus is referring to the year 65-6 when he relates that prior to the war 'a star, resembling a sword, stood over the city, and a comet which continued for a year' (*J.W.* VI. 289). Such a sign would be variously interpreted, as a Divine warning or as a Messianic promise of victory in terms of Numbers xxiv. 17, 'A Star shall go forth from Jacob, and a Comet shall rise out of Israel.' This scripture had long before been used by the Zadokite-Essenes to justify the physical departure from Israel of one of their leaders who went to the land of Damascus. Could the Nazoreans also have taken such a phenomenon in a literal sense as conveying that the Community of the Messiah should 'go forth' from Judea?

Whatever the prompting it was a statesmanlike move on the part of Simeon to call upon the Community to leave the city which had been its headquarters and nerve-centre for thirty years. It was no act of cowardice, and attended by no little danger. Under present conditions there was no impact which could be made to change the course events were taking, and many of the Pharisees had come to the same conclusion. If the Party was to be preserved, if it was not to collapse and disintegrate under the pressures of lawlessness, war fever and partisan strife, the People of God, as of old, must go into the wilderness. There the Elect could purify themselves from every taint and regain their calm while they waited for the Day of Deliverance.

The predictions of the prophet Hosea were very much in mind in these days with their pronouncement of judgment on the wayward nation. But also there was hope.

> Behold, I will allure her, and bring her into the wilderness, and speak kindly unto her. And I will give her vineyards from thence, and the valley of Achor for a door of hope: and she shall sing there, as in the days of her youth, and as in the day when she came up out of the land of Egypt.

. . . Afterward shall the children of Israel return, and seek the Lord their God and David their king; and shall fear the Lord and His goodness in the latter days (Hos. ii–iii).

If we are to understand the feelings and actions of the Nazoreans, just as with the Essenes, we have to acclimatize ourselves to their way of thinking and interpretation.

'About this time,' we read, 'Miriam the mother of Jesus died,' and was buried at the place where Jesus had been crucified, 'and a memorial stone was set up on the spot.' On this stone 'the kinsmen of Jesus wrote these words, "Lo, this is a ladder set upon the earth, whose top reaches to heaven, and the angels of God ascend and descend upon it, and the mother rejoices here in her children. Hallelujah."'

The information no doubt derives from the Nazorean Acts, and there is nothing historically improbable about it. We may compare what Hegesippus says of the burial of Jacob the brother of Jesus: 'they buried him on the spot where his memorial stone still remains, close to the Temple.' The 'kinsmen of Jesus' – who became known as 'the Heirs' – are familiar to us from Hegesippus, quoted by Eusebius, and from Julius Africanus. With the language of the inscription we may compare John i. 51 and the closing words of Psalm cxiii.

Here, however, we must turn to our last piece of evidence about the withdrawal of the Nazoreans. This comes to us in the strange language of the imagery of the book of Revelation, a work which as we have seen was credited in its Hebrew form to Simeon son of Cleophas. To an appreciable extent the meaning can be deciphered when we are acquainted with the technique. Chapters vii to xii have a bearing on the period up to the fall of Jerusalem and relate to the judgments upon apostate Israel.

Before the judgments begin all who serve God in faithfulness are sealed on their foreheads for preservation. The reference back is to the prophecies of Ezekiel (viii-lix) where in vision a man clad in linen with an inkhorn at his side is told by God, 'Go through the midst of the city, through the midst of Jerusalem, and set a *tau* upon the foreheads of the men that sigh and cry for all the abominations that be done in the midst thereof' (ix. 4). These are to be saved when the evildoers are slain. The letter tau in ancient Hebrew had the form of a cross (× or +). It is like the prelude to the exodus from Egypt, when the Lord spared the occupants of all houses whose doorposts and lintels were marked with the blood of the paschal lamb.

We advance to chapters x and xi of the Revelation, where again there is a reflection of Ezekiel's prophecies, the little book (Ezek. ii. 8-iii. 3) and the measuring of the Temple (Ezek. xl). On the last point we note the words of Josephus that 'the Jews, after the demolition of the Antonia fortress, reduced the Temple to a square, although they had it in their oracles that the city and the Sanctuary would be taken when the Temple should become four-square' (*J.W.* VI. 311).

The seer of the Revelation now introduces Jerusalem's two last witnesses. They have the powers of Moses and Elijah, and represent the Law and the Prophets (cp. Lk. xvi. 31). The infamy and anarchy has become such that neither is heeded any longer. They are slaughtered amidst general rejoicing. But they are indestructible, and being reanimated are taken up to heaven, where the Messiah himself is, the child of the Faithful Israel whom the Dragon, the Devil himself, had been unable to devour (xii. 1-5).

The last phase of the power of the Evil One is about to begin. He is cast down to earth, knowing that his time is short. Therefore he turns his wrath upon Faithful Israel.

> But the Woman [who had given birth to the Messiah] was given the two wings of a great eagle, so that she might wing her way to the wilderness, to her place there, where she is to be cared for for a time, times, and a half, from the presence of the Serpent. Then the Serpent spouted water after the Woman like a river, to carry her away with a flood. But the earth aided the Woman, and the earth gaped and swallowed the river which the Dragon spouted from his mouth. So the Dragon was enraged against the Woman, and went off to make war with the remainder of her offspring, who observe the commandments of God [i.e. the Law] and hold the testimony of Jesus (xii. 14–17).

Again we have a reminder of the exodus from Egypt. When Israel of old escaped they were pursued by the forces of Pharaoh to the Red Sea. There the people passed over safely on dry land, while the enemy was drowned by a return of the waters. God speaking through Moses after this tells the people, 'Ye have seen what I did to the Egyptians, and how I bare you on eagles' wings, and brought you unto Myself' (Ex. xix. 4).

We may interpret the imagery, therefore, as relating to the flight of Nazoreans to Peraea. They apparently did not reach their destination without impediment. Possibly they were pursued by hostile bands of militants. They had need to cross the Jordan by a ford, and may have found the river in spate. In this case we may infer that the waters subsided sufficiently to permit their passage. Refugees in Vespasian's campaign in Judea in the spring of A.D. 68 were not so fortunate. Trying to get across the Jordan near Jericho *from* Peraea, that is in the reverse direction, to escape the cavalry of Placidus, they found the river so swollen by flood water that it was impossible to cross. Many thousands were killed or drowned and their cattle captured.[13]

This is as much light on the circumstances of the evacuation as can be thrown at present. If we accept that it took place not later than the spring of A.D. 66, and possibly at the season of the Passover, objections such as those raised by Brandon would not seem to be of great weight. The testimonies are strong and sufficiently coherent not to be set aside except on very solid evidence to the contrary, which is not forthcoming. It does not appear to be of consequence that in the autumn of 66 Jewish bands raided and sacked a number of Greek cities, Pella among them, in retaliation for the massacre of Jews at Caesarea in September. The view we have taken is that the Nazoreans would not have been residing in Pella itself but in the country nearby towards the north-east. Neither is it of account that when Vespasian's troops advanced on Jerusalem early in A.D. 68 the commander sent Placidus into southern Peraea to crush opposition there and thus safeguard his left flank. The Nazorean emigration was not at this time, and Josephus does not indicate any Roman attack in the region of Pella at the northernmost tip of Peraea from which no danger was to be expected.

Within months of the withdrawal of the Nazoreans the horrific war with the Romans, and indeed between Jew and Jew, had effectively begun. But the die was already cast within weeks, as Josephus announces almost with a flourish, 'in the twelfth year of the principate of Nero, and the seventeenth of the reign of Agrippa, in the month of Artemisius' (c. May, A.D. 66).[14]

NOTES AND REFERENCES

1. See Josephus, *J.W.* II. 278–9; *Antiq.* XX. 256. In the latter he says that 'the ill-fated Jews, unable to endure the devastation by brigands that went on, were one and all forced to abandon their own country and flee, for they thought that it would be better to settle among gentiles, no matter where.'

It is by no means impossible that Josephus had in mind here the Nazoreans as well as many other refugees. He must have known of their departure from Jerusalem to the region of the Greek cities of the Decapolis beyond Jordan. See below, pp. 289–90.

2. Epiphanius, *Panar.* xxx. See Schonfield, *According to the Hebrews,* ch. xv. and *Saints Against Caesar.*
3. S. Krauss, *Das Leben Jesus nach Jüdischen Quellen.*
4. The substitution of Cephas for Calpus is understandable since Simeon Cephas (Peter) was better known. According to *Codex Strasburg* he was called Cepha, 'because he stood upon the stone whereon Ezekiel prophesied by the river Chebar, and on that stone there came to Simeon a voice from heaven.'
5. This was the most familiar name for the Jewish parody of the Nazorean texts; but there were others. See Krauss *op. cit.*
6. Eusebius, *Eccl. Hist.* III. xi.
7. *Ibid.* III. v.
8. Epiphanius, *Panar.* xxix. 7; xxx. 2; *De Mens. et Pond.* xv.
9. S. G. F. Brandon, *The Fall of Jerusalem and the Christian Church* (1951), and *Jesus and the Zealots* (1967).
10. See Part Three, p. 285.
11. See Part Three, p. 289ff.
12. Cp. Isa. i. 7–28, especially verse 10.
13. Josephus, *J.W.* IV. 433–6.
14. *J.W.* II. 284.

CHAPTER 24

LAST LOOKS

Spiritually and sentimentally it must have been a great wrench for the Nazoreans to abandon Jerusalem, the scene of so many experiences, the repository of such high hopes. It was not merely that suffering and hardship lay ahead in the perilous journey undertaken, and in adaptation to life in the wilderness; there was all the tragedy of a sorrowful leave-taking, a sense of defeat rather than of triumph in the thought of the miseries that were to come upon the doomed city. It needed the encouragement and strength of character of a Simeon son of Cleophas, the consolation of a vision of the New Jerusalem, to ease the pain of parting.

The most sustaining consideration was the conviction that the period of absence would be of no great length, a comfort that was destined to be denied as year succeeded year, and decade followed decade, and still he who was awaited from heaven did not return. Yet tenaciously it was clung to century after century that God must bring to pass what the Prophets had foretold. 'The vision is yet for an appointed time, but at the end it shall speak, and not lie: though it tarry, wait for it; because it will surely come' (Hab. ii. 3). In the same faith the threatened Zadokite-Essenes at Qumran, a year or so later than the Nazorean exodus, put away their significant scrolls in the caves of the rocks, and also crossed over Jordan and trekked north to the haven where Messianists could hold out until the Day.

Commenting on the words of Habakkuk, they declared: 'God told Habakkuk to write down that which would happen to the final generation, but He did not make known to him when the time would come to an end. . . . The final age shall be prolonged, and shall exceed all that the Prophets have said; for the mysteries of God are astounding.' As for the waiting period, 'this concerns the men of truth who keep the Law, whose hands shall not slacken in the service of truth when the final age is prolonged. For all the ages of God reach their appointed end as He determines for them in the mysteries of His wisdom.'[1]

It does not come within the scope of this volume to follow the fortunes of the Nazoreans in exile. Because they remained Jews, adhering to the Law and the Prophets, and could not endorse the doctrines of the new religion of Christianity which developed in a Gentile environment of thought, they remained largely in isolation. The new Judaism of the Rabbis was also uncongenial. Thus, as Jerome expressed it in the fourth century, 'while they will be both Jews and Christians they are neither Jews nor Christians.'[2] The orthodoxies which established themselves had no place for them, and discriminated against them. Yet it was they who were the repositories of the faith which had inspired the original Pentecost Revolution, the faith of Peter and Jacob and their apostolic colleagues. Their witness was not wholly extinguished, and some reflections of it have survived to the present day.

Christianity, however, owes a great debt of gratitude to the Nazoreans. If the Church had to depend on the letters of Paul it would know almost nothing of the career and teaching of Jesus. It is from Nazorean sources that there has come down to us, mediated through the Gospels, some account of the historical Christ.

If any part of Jerusalem deserves to be visited by Christian pilgrims it is that now undistinguished ridge outside the city walls which represents what has survived of the Ophel and Akra. Here where once was the City of David the Pentecost Revolution began and ended. And here was the administrative centre from which functioned the interim government of the absent Messiah.[3]

Our last looks are therefore reserved for what transpired here during the war and subsequently.

Curiously, within a few months of the departure of the Nazoreans another would-be king of the Jews came to the Ophel, but only as a fugitive. This was Menahem of the family of Judas of Galilee. Once the revolt had started he sought to become its royal leader, and came to Jerusalem with a force he had equipped from Herod's armoury in the fortress of Masada. At first his help was accepted by the nationalists, and they succeeded in occupying Herod's Palace except for the flanking towers. In the grounds the supporters of Menahem found the high priest Ananias and his brother Hezekiah, and slaughtered them. But Menahem's triumph was short-lived because his disposition was that of a tyrant. Going to the Temple in royal robes he and his followers were there attacked by the people.

Menahem fled, and took refuge in the Ophel. There he was found, tortured and executed.

In the later stages of the war, when the Romans under Titus were already encamped before Jerusalem, the Ophel with the Temple area was held by the forces under John of Gischala, who earlier had reached Jerusalem from Galilee, while the greater part of the city was controlled by a rival leader, Simon son of Gioras. Finally, in September of A.D. 70, when the Temple had already gone up in flames, the Ophel and Akra were sacked and burnt by the Roman troops. The houses and streets became the funeral pyre of multitudes who had already perished of famine.[4]

A gap here occurs in our records. Epiphanius is our sole authority for stating that there was a return of the Nazorean refugees from Peraea to Jerusalem.[5] He does not, however, give any indication of when this took place. It is unlikely to have been earlier than the reign of Trajan, in the first decade of the second century A.D. We have the evidence both of Hegesippus and Julius Africanus that the kindred of Jesus continued to rule the communities, as a kind of government in exile, down to the beginning of Trajan's reign when Simeon son of Cloephas, by then a centenarian, died a martyr.[6] It would seem that associated with him in the government were, among others, the two grandchildren of Judas the brother of Jesus. While they visited the different communities they would appear to have had their base of operations in Batanea in the Pella region and the Hauran at villages such as Nazara and Cochaba.[7] We have no indication that 'the Heirs' (the family of Jesus) ever returned to Jerusalem.

Eusebius understood from tradition, probably having obtained the information from the *Memoirs* of Hegesippus, that after the death of Simeon there were thirteen more Jewish bishops of Jerusalem. He lists their names, but does not know their respective terms of office, only that they served in each case for a very short time.[8] Since the Jewish succession terminated about A.D. 133 during the Second Jewish Revolt under Bar-Cochba the average term for each would have been about two and a half years. The point is that none of the thirteen appears to have been of the family of Jesus. It could be, therefore, that there was a change of policy, and that with Trajan's rather more liberal attitude towards the followers of Jesus some part of the Nazoreans elected to return to Jerusalem and rebuild the Community there under a series of bishops whom they chose. Epiphanius may well be correct.

Those who returned from Pella, according to Epiphanius, established a small church on Zion. It was still there in A.D. 131 when the emperor Hadrian, planning to build the new city of Aelia Capitolina on the ruined site of Jerusalem, seems to have sent there as overseer of the work a relation of his, Aquila of Sinope in Pontus. He became a disciple of Jesus, we are told, but was later expelled from the Community and subsequently became a convert to Judaism and a translator of the Old Testament into Greek.[9]

The construction of Aelia was disrupted in the following year, a Roman census year, by the Second Jewish Revolt, and Justin Martyr relates that Bar-Cochba persecuted the Christians because they would not deny the Messiahship of Jesus, and – Eusebius mentions – would not join him in fighting the Romans.[10]

When the Revolt was suppressed after a prolonged struggle, in which the Roman forces as well as their opponents suffered heavy casualties, the building of the new city went ahead. But to Hadrian's Aelia Capitolina Jews were not admitted. When a church was established there it had no Nazorean members, since they too were Jews. It was a church of the Gentiles under a Gentile bishop, Marcus.

Not until the nineteenth century was there another bishop of Jewish race in the Holy City, when in 1841 the Right Reverend Michael Solomon Alexander was created Lord Bishop of the United Church of England and Ireland at Jerusalem.

So far as our present information serves, such was the Pentecost Revolution of the Jewish royalists, who adhered to Jesus son of Joseph as their rightful and God-appointed king of the line of David.

In its character it was a revolution that had no specific undertaking beyond witnessing to Jesus as Messiah, since it was proclaimed that he was at the right hand of God, and would ere long return to establish his kingdom. There was no plan to bring the kingdom into being by direct action, as with the Zealots; only to enlist under the banner of the Messiah a community of faithful observers of the commandments of God to await the Day of Judgment and Deliverance.

There was a Jacobite flavour about the Revolution. But instead of 'the king over the water' it was for the Nazoreans 'the king up in the sky'. Yet the Jacobite song of the eighteenth century directed to Bonnie Prince Charlie could equally be the prayer of the Nazoreans.

Better lo'ed ye canna be,
Will ye no' come back again?

The Pentecost Revolution failed in so far as the prayer was to remain unanswered. It relied on what could not be proven, and on a sublime event beyond human calculation and control. It cherished a proposition beset with ifs and buts, idealistic in conception and conviction, but lacking that quality of dedicated pragmatic enterprise without which the creation of a heaven upon earth could never be more than a vision without fulfilment, a dream that could never come true.

Jacob the Just would seem to have been more aware of this than many, if the words ascribed to him are his, when he taught:

> Of what avail is it, brothers, for someone to say he has faith, when he has no deeds to show for it? Can faith save him? If a brother or sister are destitute, lacking even daily bread, and one of you says to them, 'Go in peace. Mind you keep warm and take enough nourishment,' but you give them no physical necessities for the purpose, what avails it? So with faith. Unless deeds spring from it it is dead in isolation. . . . For just as the body without the spirit is dead, so is faith without deeds (Jas. ii. 14–17).

If the story of the Pentecost Revolution has a moral it may well be an advice to all good people that, 'If you are *Waiting for Godot,*[11] remember that Godot may also be waiting for you.'

NOTES AND REFERENCES

1. *Commentary on Habakkuk*. vii. (Vermes).
2. Jerome, *Epistle to Augustus*.
3. See above, Part One, Chapter 4, and Part Two, Chapter 13.
4. Josephus, *J.W.* VI. 344–5.
5. Epiphanius, *De Mens. et Pond.* xv.
6. Simeon seems to have lost his life as a result of a 'palace plot', being denounced to the Romans by certain heretics as a descendant of David and a follower of Jesus (Hegesippus, quoted by Eusebius, *Eccl. Hist.* III. xxxii).
7. See Part Three, Chapter 29.
8. Eusebius, *Eccl. Hist.* IV. v.
9. Epiphanius, *De Mens. et Pond.* xiv–xv.
10. Justin Martyr, *I. Apol.* xxxi; Eusebius, *Chronicle,* under *Hadrian's Year 18* (A.D. 134).
11. Samuel Beckett's brilliant play.

Part Three

BEHIND THE SCENES

CHAPTER 25

LINE UP

It is characteristic of times of great crisis in human history that they should produce remarkable personalities, including religious enthusiasts giving rise to strange sects. Nature has its own way of making response to social and political pressures. The reaction against Hellenism had done this with the Jews, and the persecution by Antiochus Epiphanes had brought forward the Hasmonean brothers. But the Last-Times conviction which developed during Herod's reign was responsible for an extraordinary proliferation of movements. It is imperative to be aware of these manifestations, religio-political in the Jewish context, because they provided the seed-bed in which Christianity originated. Indeed, one may say that Christianity itself, in its original Nazorean expression, was one of them.

There is still, in general, despite a number of recent books of a fairly popular type, a lamentable ignorance of the influences affecting Jesus and his Jewish followers. It continues to be widely imagined, because the churches do not teach otherwise, that they were opposed to a rather rigid and arid religion called Judaism. In fact in those days Judaism was not so much a creed as a way of life of the Jewish people based on the Divine Laws, the Torah, laid down in the books of Moses. The dogmatic element was essentially confined to belief in the Unity of God and the claim that Israel had been chosen as the vehicle of the Divine will to mankind. Everything else was a matter of group-thinking, persuasion and interpretation.

Everyone knows that there were Pharisees and Sadducees, and also Essenes; but it is not realized that membership of these bodies numbered no more than six or seven thousand persons in each case. There were other sects and parties, as we shall see, equally of no great size. But the bulk of the population had no denominational affiliation: they were just Jews, who might favour one or other opinion as they chose, without being adherents of any of them.

The Pharisees formed a very closely knit fellowship, which had the ear of the people chiefly because they were anti-aristocratic and made a great virtue of their zeal for the Torah, which aimed at investing all daily life and conduct with sanctity. They made a fetish of paying tithes, and could often be distinguished by wearing large phylacteries at prayer and exaggerating the length of the fringe with a blue thread which Jews wore on their outer garment. The Pharisees were also a preaching and teaching fraternity, and the backbone of the synagogues. Educationally they did much good, since for them the uncultured man was he who was ignorant of the Torah. They had no use for the idle rich, and insisted on all their members following a trade. One of their most notable exemplars at this time was the great Hillel, who was a woodcutter. While they were teachers of the Law, there was no such thing among them in those days as the professional rabbi.

Partly because of antagonism to rulers who followed alien ways and were puppets of a heathen Power the Pharisees strongly espoused the expectation of a Messiah of David's line, who would be the ideal righteous king delighting in the observance of the Torah. They had a strong sense of social justice, and partly because of this they were firm believers in the Redemption of Israel and the ideal Age to Come. Hence their emphasis on the purification of national life from every taint of vice, idolatry and brutality.

The Sadducees represented an older, more exact application of the Laws of Moses. They were more of a class than a sect, and stood for conservative traditionalism with strong hierarchic and ritualistic interests. They looked back to the time when priesthood and nobility held the reins of government, and under Roman rule they were trying to the extent that was practicable to achieve a restoration of their position. Their aim was a theocracy vested in ecclesiastical authority.

In political matters the Sadducees thought of themselves as realists, who recognized that they were not living in a perfect world, but foresaw the purity of Jewish faith and the wisdom of the Jewish laws eventually winning universal regard, so that Jerusalem would become the cult centre of mankind. At one time, in the first flush of the Maccabean triumph and reformation, the Sadducees had more emphatically upheld the distinction between Israel and the nations,[1] but latterly they had tended to become more accommodating. The crudities of heathenism were still deplored, and the superiority of Judaism asserted; but it was allowable to enjoy many of the benefits of contemporary civilization. The idea of a cataclysmic Divine intervention was rejected.

Sadduceeism thus attracted the aristocracy and the well-to-do, who were often related to the chief priestly families. It found no support among the underprivileged, who while in general supporting the Temple worship, as did the Pharisees, resented the arrogance and opulence of the leading hierarchy.

From what has been said of these two prominent groups the frequent description of Jesus as a reforming Jewish rabbi is nonsensical. As the Gospels rightly and continually make clear the vast majority of the Jewish people belonged to neither group; and it was with the common people that Jesus was primarily concerned. It was the Pharisees who were the religious reformers, who sought by interpretation to mitigate the more severe applications of the Mosaic ordinances and make their performance more readily practicable under contemporary conditions. One Pharisaic school, that of Hillel, was noted for its sympathetic tolerance. The objective was not an enslavement to commandments, but the capacity to rejoice in their practice, whereby the nation would become fit for deliverance.

The former judgments of Christian divines failed to take account of chronology and the effects of contemporary circumstances on Jewish attitudes at different periods. They wrongly assumed that Rabbinical literature of a subsequent time when the Jews were deprived of national and religious liberties, and forced for survival to be more demanding in what was required to keep Jewishness alive, could be used as a guide to the character of Judaism under earlier and different conditions.

Jesus, as a man of the people, came frequently in contact with the Pharisees, but with the Sadducees hardly at all until he staged his last dramatic challenge at Jerusalem. He did not disagree with the Pharisees, but his thought was for those they did not reach, the lost sheep of the house of Israel. A kingdom divided against itself could never stand. It was the sick who needed a physician; and the first step towards national redemption must be to involve the poor, the downtrodden and the outcasts, and bring about an integration founded on the two chief commandments of the Torah, to love God and one's neighbour.

Anxiety and oppression had strained human relationships almost to breaking point. Jesus, therefore, stressed the characteristics of society as it would be constituted in a Kingdom of God environment, where there would be no hostility and fault-finding, no injustice and neglect. This was no reformation of Judaism, but an assertion of its most vital principles as enunciated by the Prophets. It was the fufilment of the Messianic Hope as it had been foretold, incumbent on the Messiah, in terms of bringing the whole Jewish people – not merely select groups of saints and pietists – within the experience of becoming a holy nation for the blessing of all mankind. This is what the Sermon on the Mount is all about.

The chief contrast of the teaching of Jesus was with that of the Essenes, who have been held up by the ill-informed as mirrors of wisdom and virtue from whom Jesus learned much. Jesus certainly learned from some of their literature, and approved of their simplicity of living and rejection of possessions, and he accepted certain of their tenets.

After he was gone Essene-type organization and thinking contributed to the shaping of the structure and outlook of the Nazorean communities. But this was largely due to new recruits.

We know very little of the origins of the Essenes or Esseans. They are believed to have derived from the earlier Chasidim with an admixture of eastern philosophy. Abbot Nilus, who flourished at the end of the fourth century A.D., considered that they were an offshoot of the Rechabites, an ancient nomadic clan who abstained from wine and the practice of agriculture. Certainly the Essenes, described by Josephus and others, had moved out of the mainstream of Jewish life, though certain of their members appeared at court and were consulted by rulers because of their prophetic gifts. They dwelt in closely-knit communities, both urban and rural, with their principle settlement near the Dead Sea. We can accept that Qumran here represented the Essene centre in the first century A.D., and that the Party of the New Covenant was at least the inheritor of the Essene teaching.

In the view of this movement Israel had so far gone astray that those who would keep the Laws of Moses strictly and in absolute purity must separate themselves from society, and preferably make their home in the wilderness. They had adherents among the priests; but for them neither the Pharisees nor Sadducees were sufficiently orthodox. They were the harshest and most inflexible of the Jewish sects, as Professor Yadin has pointed out in his discussion of the Temple Scroll.[2]

The Qumranites saw the only hope of salvation in total observance of the Torah and the avoidance of every kind of contamination. Applicants for admission to the Order had to undergo a prolonged period of probation and accept a stringent discipline. They produced many sacred books of their own, some of which were for the use only of the fully initiated. By their techniques they interpreted the Scriptures prophetically, especially in relation to their own affairs. They regulated their festivals by the old lunar calendar, and used an era related to a succession of Jubilees. They also investigated the medicinal properties of herbs and stones, claiming that the secrets of nature had been handed down to them from Shem the son of Noah.

Since the appeal of Jesus was to those who were despised and largely neglected by the self-contained and self-sufficient segments of the nation, he had no sympathy with Essene exclusiveness. Of what service to the Jewish masses was monastic seclusion, esoteric learning, and closely guarded secrets? Whatever was worth having should be public property, and what was whispered in the ear should be shouted from the housetops.

The Essenes, however, regarded themselves as the true Poor. They believed themselves to be the Very Elect who would inherit the Kingdom of God. They were the loyal and obedient remnant of Israel, who by their total purity and uncompromising faithfulness to the Torah alone qualified for the bliss of the Age to Come. Their devotion and sufferings made atonement for the desecration of the land and the iniquities of its inhabitants; so that they, the Saints, were free from all taint of guilt in respect of an evil and adulterous generation. As the Elect of God, therefore, they were the final repositories of Divine revelation, who supremely by their science knew the mysteries of the Last Times contained in the Oracles of God.

The greater part of the Jewish people, exploited and in want, did not know where they stood. They were taught to look for a deliverer who would change their condition and overthrow their enemies, not only the heathen but Jewish sinners in the seats of power, and at the same time they were filled with superstitious dread of the calamities and punishments of the Wrath to Come.

In these circumstances there was a great temptation for the bolder and more reckless spirits to join or support what Josephus calls the Fourth Philosophy among the Jews, which emerged around this time. The originators of the movement were Judas, the Galilean or Gaulanite, who came from the town of Gamala east of the Sea of Galilee, and a Pharisee named Zadok. It has been questioned, but it seems probable that Judas of Galilee is to be identified with Judas son of Hezekiah, also of Galilee, who led a rising in the north on the death of Herod the Great. His father Hezekiah had been a rebel chieftain in Galilee killed by Herod when he was governor there before he came to the throne. The objection to this identification has arisen because Josephus describes Judas of Galilee as a learned man animated by a religious impulse, who therefore was something more than the warrior leader of a pillaging band. The exploits of Judas son of Hezekiah are dated in 4 B.C., whereas Judas the Galilean came to the fore nearly ten years later at the time of the Roman census in A.D. 6. There is also the testimony of Josephus that a son of Judas of Galilee was a candidate for rulership in the revolt of A.D. 66. The latter, called Menahem, could of course have been a grandson, and in Jewish tradition he is named as Menahem son of Hezekiah. This suggests that the father of Menahem had been named after his grandfather, who had been the father of Judas of Galilee. It seems improbable that Menahem could have been an active militant when he was already in his sixties, as he must have been if Judas was his father. On the whole it seems more likely that Judas of Galilee and Judas son of Hezekiah were one and the same, and that Menahem was a grandson of this Judas.

The rebellious mood of the Jews had exhibited itself immediately after Herod's death. They saw this event as an opportunity to regain their independence of Rome, and were strongly opposed to the succession as king of Herod's son Archelaus. Not only Judas son of Hezekiah but a number of others in various parts of the country went on the war-path, some merely to exploit the breakdown of ordered government, but others proposing to set themselves up as kinglets of the people's choice. There is no indication that any of these individuals claimed to be the Messiah of prophetic anticipation. They gave the Romans a lot of trouble but were ruthlessly put down, as Rome had no intention of relinquishing her hold on the country.

The outbreak in the capital, Jerusalem, involving many of the better citizens, was more serious. It began at the Passover of 4 B.C. as a rising against Archelaus, whose troops slew some three thousand of the disaffected. When Archelaus had left for Rome to secure Caesar's endorsement of his sovereignty, Sabinus, the financial agent of Augustus in Syria, had gone to Jerusalem to take account of Herod's property, since Herod had appointed the emperor as his executor. Quinctilius Varus, legate of Syria, anticipating trouble had already left a legion in the city. And trouble there was at the ensuing feast of Pentecost when multitudes of Jewish pilgrims were in Jerusalem. It developed into an ugly struggle with the Roman forces, with some of Herod's old troops making common cause with the rebels. Many were slain, and in the course of the fighting the Romans set fire to the porticoes of the Temple and plundered its treasury. The revolt, which was gaining support in other parts of the country, was not put down until Varus with an army and Arab allies swept through the land with fire and sword. The leaders were rounded up, and two thousand of the more prominent were crucified.

So ended the War of Varus. Archelaus did not obtain the throne of Herod. Instead, Caesar made him ethnarch in the south. The rest of the country was apportioned between Herod's other sons Antipas and Philip as tetrarchs. A general supervision was exercised by Rome through the legate of Syria.

But the flame of freedom had been kindled, and was fanned again in A.D. 6 when Archelaus was deposed, and the area he had misgoverned, consisting of Judea, Samaria and Idumea, was converted into an administrative region under a Roman procurator. The whole country thus became liable to tribute, and Quirinius, now legate of Syria, ordered the census of persons and property to be taken. It was this innovation, so far as the Jews were concerned, which brought Judas of Galilee and his associate Zadok into prominence. They proclaimed that Israel could acknowledge no other lord than God Himself, and that the taxation reduced the Jews to the status of slaves.

The Fourth Philosophy has been receiving much more attention since the discovery of the Dead Sea Scrolls, because certain common attitudes are reflected, and there are also indications of some relationship between the respective parties. The followers of Judas and Zadok became known as the Galileans, and more characteristically as the Zealots. But despite the erudite efforts of Driver and Roth[3] it is going much too far to identify the people of the Scrolls with the Zealots, and the Menahem already mentioned with the True Teacher. Yet we do need to examine the sometimes confusing intimations of tradition, complicated by changes and developments in the second and third centuries A.D., because otherwise we shall have quite a wrong view of the beginnings of Christianity and of the nature of the Nazorean movement which developed under the leadership of Jacob brother of Jesus. Modern forms of Jesus-cult, and a recent book *The Secret*

Gospel by Morton Smith, have simply ignored historical causes and effects.

So far as we may gather from Josephus' revised statement in the *Antiquities* the followers of Judas and Zadok held similar beliefs to the Pharisees. What chiefly distinguished them was that the Zealots were activists with an inflexible attachment to freedom, which led them to oppose all who followed alien ways and were subservient to Rome, and finally to commit themselves to all-out war. Those who were zealous for the Lord aimed at the achievement of a democratic theocracy, which involved a purification of the national life from every taint of heathenism, and the redemption of the land which was God's special possession.

Jesus, who had at least one Zealot among his chosen apostles, made reference to what this movement represented when he is recorded to have said, 'From the time of John the Baptist until now the Kingdom of Heaven is being stormed, and men of violence take it by force' (Mt. xi. 12). The militants could not stomach waiting indefinitely for Divine intervention. Goaded by the wrongs suffered by the nation they were moved to fight the Lord's battles on His behalf.

An important point is raised by the indication in the saying attributed to Jesus of a considerable interval between the chief period of the Baptist's activities and the time at which Jesus would have been speaking. Possibly the saying was created fifteen or twenty years after the death of Jesus, when conditions had materially worsened. But there is an alternative. Matthew's Gospel, after stating that the parents of Jesus went to Nazareth when they learnt that Archelaus was now ruling Judea (end of ch. ii), continues immediately, 'In those days [presumably of Archelaus] came John the Baptist, preaching in the wilderness of Judea' (iii, i).[4]

The interpolator of the Old Russian version of the *Jewish War* believed this to be the case, since he introduces the first preaching of John the Baptist at the beginning of the reign of Archelaus, as a consequence of which he was brought before the ethnarch and the Jewish Council, the Sanhedrin. What is said of John here is significant: 'He came to the Jews and summoned them to freedom, saying, "God hath sent me to show you the Way of the Law, whereby you may free yourselves from many masters; and there shall be no mortal ruling over you, but only the Highest who has sent me." '[5]

Thus John would have begun his call to national repentance about the same time and in much the same terms as the founders of the Zealots. John refers to the Way of the Law. Now this is the very expression the people of the Dead Sea Scrolls employed of the course to which they were committed. Further, according to the *Damascus Rule,* they also denounced as fornication the taking of a second wife while the first was alive. On the same grounds John the Baptist later attacked Antipas for taking his brother's wife.

There are, indeed, a good many evidences of links between the Baptist sect, the Zealots, and the presumed Essenes of the Scrolls, some of which tie in with the beginning of the reign of Archelaus. The Clementine *Recognitions,* reflecting certain Nazorean traditions, says that the Jewish people 'were divided into many parties, ever since the days of John the Baptist. . . . The first schism was that of the so-called Sadducees, who took their rise almost in the time of John' (I. liii-liv). Because of the coincidence of names the author here confuses the Sadducees, who were long before John, with the Zadokites. A similar mistake occurs in the *Aboth R. Nathan,* where a certain Zadok is made the founder of the Sadducees. As we have seen, a Zadok was co-founder of the Zealots with Judas of Galilee.

The Zadokites of the Scrolls venerated a Zadok, and had a *Book of Zadok,* which has not been recovered.[6] We must therefore give some account of their history. This is principally disclosed by the *Damascus Rule,* first made known by the find of old manuscripts in the Karaite synagogue in Fostat (Cairo), deriving from an earlier collection of Dead Sea Scrolls which came to light at the beginning of the ninth century A.D.[7]

The first phase of the movement's existence is here traced back to an emigration from Palestine of the 'Penitents of Israel' to the land of Damascus. They were led or joined by a Student of the Law under whom they entered into a New Covenant,[8] and who laid down the code of regulations by which they were to be guided until the coming of the True Teacher of the Last Times. The emigration was an ancient one, since there is reference to several intervening generations, and through a passage in Josephus I have elsewhere dated it about 160-159 B.C., during the persecution that followed the death in battle of Judas Maccabaeus.[9] I have seen no reason to change that view.

The movement remained in the north, where it was joined by others, for a prolonged period. But when the Last Times were believed to have come the sect returned to the land of Judah to share in the final struggle of the forces of the Children of Light with those of the Children of Darkness. The three phases of the sect's history are represented by an interpretation of the words of Ezekiel (xliv. 15), 'The Priests, the Levites, and the Sons of Zadok, who kept the charge of My Sanctuary when the children of Israel strayed from Me, they shall offer me fat and blood.' The *Damascus Rule* explains: 'The *Priests* means the Penitents of Israel who departed from the land of Judah, and the *Levites* are those who joined them. The *Sons of Zadok* are the Elect of Israel, called by name, who shall stand at the End of the Days.' The Sons of Zadok phase related therefore to the time of the return.

The objective of the return is conveyed by the *War Rule* from Qumran: 'The sons of Levi, Judah and Benjamin, the exiles in the wilderness, shall battle against them [i.e. the Children of Darkness] . . . all their bands, when the exiled Children of Light return from the Wilderness of the Peoples to camp in the Wilderness of Jerusalem.'

The question is, when did the return take place? There are several clues. The first is that it was at the beginning of what were held to be the Last Times. This we have been able to show was around the close of the first century B.C., and thus about the beginning of the reign of Archelaus. The second clue is that the name Zadok now comes to the fore in the Scrolls, and the community begins to appear as the Sons of Zadok, Zadokites, which coincides with the advent of Zadok, colleague of Judas of Galilee, and with the reported manifestation of the Zadokites 'almost in the time of John the Baptist' in the first phase of his activities.

But we can go further. The archaeological and numismatic evidence from Qumran shows that the settlement there, which may have been Essene, was abandoned in 31 B.C. when it was partly destroyed in the great earthquake, and was not reoccupied until about A.D. 4. As Driver points out, nothing necessarily connects the new occupants with their predecessors, and they could have been the followers of Judas and Zadok.[10] If we infer from the term 'Wilderness of the Peoples' a connection with Galilee of the Gentiles (i.e. Nations), then the land of Damascus from which the exiles returned at the advent of the Last Times might well have been in the region north-east of the Sea of Galilee not far distant from where Judas of Galilee was born.[11] Did the Zadokites of the Scrolls then mean the area of Qumran when they said that they came back to camp in the 'Wilderness of Jerusalem'?

It was in the Judean wilderness east of Jerusalem that John the Baptist appeared, and the Zadokites required of all who joined them that 'they shall separate from the habitation of ungodly men, and go into the wilderness,' quoting in support the same text from Isaiah applied to John the Baptist, 'Prepare ye in the wilderness the way of the Lord, make straight in the desert a highway for our God.'

The range of these Last-Times manifestations extended also to Samaria, where under the name of Dositheans a sect arose which the traditions link with the Zadokites and the movement of John the Baptist.[12] Erupting in the north-east at the dawn of the Christian Era, the prophetic word spread south and south-west like a lava flow. Excitement was progressively built up until the climax of the Jewish Revolt was reached in A.D. 66. As the Talmud (T.J. *Sanh.* 29c) records, 'Israel did not go into captivity until there had come into existence twenty-four varieties of sectaries' (i.e. double the number of the twelve tribes).

Here was the authentic environment of ideas which influenced Jesus and called forth his own contribution. Here was the 'good soil' of the Gospel parable in which the seed of the Kingdom message would be sown. It was entirely appropriate that in the company of Jesus should be Zealots like Simon and Judas Iscariot, and former disciples of John the Baptist like Peter and his brother Andrew, and Philip, coming from Bethsaida at the north-eastern tip of the Sea of Galilee (Jn. i. 44).

It is this atmosphere we have to imbibe if we are concerned to obtain a true understanding, and we have far to go before we have observed and absorbed what is discoverable.

NOTES AND REFERENCES

1. The distinction is brought out in the *Letter of Aristeas,* from about the middle of the second century B.C. This work tells the story of the translation of the Bible into Greek, and the author puts these words into the mouth of Eleazar the High Priest: 'When, therefore, the lawgiver [Moses] . . . had in his wisdom considered everything, he fenced us about with impregnable palisades and with walls of iron, to the intent that we should in no way have dealings with any of the other nations, pure in body and mind, released from vain ideas, reverencing the one Almighty God above the entire creation. And hence it comes that the priests who rule the Egyptians . . . call us "men of God", a designation which does not belong to the rest of mankind, but to him only who reverences the true God. But they are men of meat and drink and raiment, for their whole nature finds its solace in these things. But with our countrymen these things are

counted of no worth, but their reflections throughout their whole life concern the sovereignty of God' (139–40, tr. St J. Thackeray).

2. The Temple Scroll, one of the lengthiest and most important of the Dead Sea Scrolls, was acquired after the Six-Day War, and Prof. Yadin's Edition was still in preparation when the present work was written. But Yadin has disclosed that the document purports to be the words of the Lord spoken to Moses at Sinai, and deals with regulations affecting the Temple and the holy city of Jerusalem as ideally seen by the Essenes.
3. See G. R. Driver, *The Judean Scrolls,* and Cecil Roth, *The Historical Background of the Dead Sea Scrolls*. The two scholars worked closely together on the thesis that the Zadokites of the Scrolls were to be identified with the Zealots. Their conclusions were not wholly unjustified.
4. Luke's nativity narrative partly reflects controversy with those Baptists who held John to have been the Messiah. The importance of John is affirmed, as also in the Gospel of John, but only as the forerunner of Jesus. The claim that Elizabeth the mother of the Baptist was a kinswoman of Mary the mother of Jesus is just possible; but that John was born six months before Jesus conflicts with other evidence and may be regarded as a propaganda device.
5. The passage quoted follows II. 110 of the *Jewish War,* and is given in full in Eisler, *The Messiah Jesus and John the Baptist,* and in the Appendix to Thackeray's translation of the *Jewish War* in the Loeb Classical Library edition of Josephus.
6. The information is given by Kirkisani, a Karaite scholar of the tenth century A.D. in his *Kitab al-Anwar*. See the Introduction to Charles's *Fragments of a Zadokite Work*.
7. The earlier great discovery of Scrolls was reported by Timotheus, Metropolitan of Seleucia, in A.D. 819. The details have been given in many books and papers dealing with the Scrolls, including Schonfield, *Secrets of the Dead Sea Scrolls*.
8. The student of the Law is described as the Star, in allusion to the passage in Numbers, 'There shall go forth a star out of Jacob.' This was interpreted by the Zadokites to mean a literal departure from the land of Israel.
9. See below, p. 280.
10. See Driver, *The Judean Scrolls,* p.47.
11. See further below, Chapter 28.
12. On the Dositheans, see for example Driver, *op. cit.* and Black, *The Scrolls and Christian Origins.*

CHAPTER 26

REFLECTED ATTITUDES

Readers familiar with the New Testament may already have noted that attitudes typical of the Fourth Philosophy in its varied expressions are reflected in the Acts of the Apostles. It would appear that the early Christians were strongly influenced by Fourth Philosophy thinking, deriving from those who joined Jesus and those who in increasing numbers were attracted to the Nazorean movement. We have therefore to look more sympathetically at the position taken by the Nazoreans, especially on those issues which brought them into bitter conflict with Paul.

Many scholars have studied the very clear evidences of the impact of Zadokite ideas, language and practices on the early Church. The kinship had already been observed by some of the Church Fathers, and one or two had supposed that the Essenes were the original Christians, at least in their Nazorean aspect. That view has been revived in modern times, particularly as regards the sect of Ebionites. It was immediately noticed when the Dead Sea Scrolls began to come to light that the Essene-Zadokites referred to themselves as the *Ebionim*, the Poor, as one of the designations of the Party of the New Covenant. The very fact that these people had entered into the pact of a New Covenant in the land of Damascus came as a surprise. There were other terms and expressions held in common. Not only so, but at first glance the life and sufferings of the Father Figure of the Party, long before the time of Jesus, the so-called Teacher of Righteousness, seemed to suggest that the experiences of Jesus were a reflection of the image of this previous Unknown. If the Christians were not the same people, what were they doing with so close a likeness?

Such extreme opinions could not be sustained; but it remained that there was an affinity between Zadokites and Nazoreans which was too circumstantial to be attributed to chance. There must have been direct contact between the Christians and the Fourth Philosophy movement. Josephus never mentions the Nazoreans, but it is at least possible that he was alluding to them when he refers to 'another kind of Essenes'.

In those passages of the Acts which relate to the Jewish followers of Jesus we have to allow for the author's aims and intentions. He was seeking to placate the Roman authorities and to modify the cleavage between the Jerusalem apostles and Paul. Even so, he keeps sufficiently close to his sources to preserve valuable scraps of information. Unfortunately there is very much which he omits, things we particularly want to know. His hero is Paul, and he relates little more about the Judean believers than will serve to illustrate the conversion and career of Paul and the proclamation of the Gospel to the Gentiles. We have to remind ourselves that the Acts covers a period of nearly thirty years, years marked by great changes in Jewish affairs and ever-mounting excitement and unrest which accentuated and intensified earlier trends. Of these developments the Acts does not make us emphatically conscious, and it is only by setting beside Luke's story the account of those years given by Josephus that we can grasp the significance of this and that fairly casually reported circumstance.

In the previous chapter we saw that there were three prominent positions taken by the Fourth Philosophy groups. They were Zealots for the Torah; they were anti-Gentile because of the contamination of heathenism; and they were opposed to Caesar or any foreigner as their ruler.

When Paul went up to Jerusalem for the last time and was received by Jacob and the elders of the Nazoreans, he was told, 'You see, brother, how many myriads there are among the Jews who have believed [i.e. in Jesus]; they are all zealous for the Law, and they have been told about you that you teach all the Jews who are among the Gentiles to forsake Moses, telling them not to circumcise their children or observe the customs.' They urged Paul to undergo purification with four of their number who were under a nazirite vow, so that 'everyone will realize that there is no foundation whatever for what they have been informed about you, and that on the contrary you yourself conform and observe the Law' (xxi. 20-4).

In the sequel Paul was spied by certain Jews of Asia, who denounced him as 'the man who is teaching everywhere against the people, and the Law, and this place; moreover he also brought Greeks into the Temple, and he has defiled this Holy Place' (27-8).

For some time on the balustrade round the Temple proper there had been placed at intervals warning notices in Greek, Latin and Hebrew, stating that, 'No stranger is to enter within the balustrade round the

Temple and enclosure. Whoever is caught will be responsible for his own death, which will ensue.'

The plain statement that the Jewish followers of Jesus were also zealots for the Torah throws light on the controversy over the reception of Gentiles into the Christian community which arose at Antioch, when 'some men came down from Judea and were teaching the brethren, "Unless you are circumcised according to the Custom of Moses, you cannot be saved"' (xv. 1). Paul says in the letter to the Galatians that the men were emissaries of Jacob the brother of Jesus.

We have to look at the Judaizing question quite differently. It was not a matter of a conservative Judaism versus a liberal and progressive Christianity. Christianity as a religion did not begin to exist until after the fall of Jerusalem in A.D. 70. The people we are dealing with were representatives of the eclectic parties among the Jews, and the Nazoreans were of their number. The times were the Last Times, when Satan was intensifying his assaults on Israel to cause them to forsake the Torah. The redemption of the nation was seen to depend on the utmost loyalty and obedience to the Law of Moses. The fiat of the Fourth Philosophy had gone out. There must be no compromise.

The attitude of the different parties concerned is brought out by Hippolytus in his *Refutation of All Heresies*,[1] where he revises and amplifies the information given by Josephus. Hippolytus thinks of all these particularist parties as varieties of Essenes. Points he makes about their attitudes stress the extremes to which they were prepared to go. There were those who would not leave their beds on the Sabbath for fear of violating its sanctity. There were those who would never touch a coin on the ground, that one should neither carry, nor look upon, nor make an image. Some would not go into a city because they might have to pass through a gate adorned with statues. Things had even reached the point where Zealot extremists, if they heard a Gentile discussing God and His Law, would lie in wait for him and threaten him with death if he refused to be circumcised.

The Mishnah and Josephus confirm the mounting fanaticism. The hero of the extremists was the Biblical Phinehas (Nu. xxv. 6-13). They would kill a man for cohabiting with a Syrian woman. If a priest served at the Altar in a state of uncleanness, the young priests who were Zealots would take him outside the Temple Court and split open his brains with clubs.[2]

The state of affairs in the fifties of the first century A.D. was moving towards a peak of emotional intensity. One of its manifestations among the Zealots, as we have seen, was the Sicarii, who assassinated those whom they regarded as lax or collaborators. Josephus reports that those he calls impostors and brigands, 'banding together, incited numbers to revolt, exhorting them to assert their independence, and threatening to kill any who submitted to Roman domination and forcibly to suppress those who voluntarily accepted servitude. Distributing themselves in companies throughout the country, they looted the houses of the wealthy, murdered their owners, and set the villages on fire. The effects of their frenzy were thus felt throughout Judea, and every day saw this war being fanned into fiercer flame.'[3]

We have an echo in the Acts from this very period, where a Zealot group of more than forty men had taken a vow neither to eat nor drink until they had killed Paul (xxiii. 12-13). It is typical of Luke's slant that he attributes this plot simply to 'the Jews'.

But in this atmosphere we do begin to understand the insistence of the Nazorean zealots that Gentile believers be compelled to be circumcised and observe the Torah. We are not surprised that they should castigate Peter for going to uncircumcised men and eating with them (Acts xi. 3).

In the fifties there were Fourth Philosophy advocates visiting all the Jewish communities of the Dispersion, seeking to enlist their support for a Messianic general rising against the Romans. The Hellenized Jews throughout the Empire could not readily distinguish between the Zealot and purely Nazorean spokesmen. At Thessalonica Paul and Silas were taken to be Fourth Philosophy agents. The local Jews, whose peace and privileges under the Empire were threatened, took alarm, informing the authorities that 'these men who have turned the world upside down have come here also, and they are all acting against the decrees of Caesar, saying there is another king, Jesus' (xvii. 6-7). We learn from our sources that the Jews were expelled from Rome by the Emperor Claudius for engaging in Messianic sedition, and the Jews of Alexandria were also warned against the itinerant preachers who constituted 'a pest which threatens the whole world'.[4] Paul himself was eventually accused of being 'a plague-carrier, an agitator among all the Jews throughout the world, a ring-leader of the sect of Nazoreans' (Acts xxiv. 5).

The Nazoreans, like the Zadokites, rejoiced in the observance of the Jewish holy days. The *Damascus Rule* declares: 'But with them that held fast by the commandments of God, He confirmed the covenant with Israel for ever. . . . His holy Sabbaths and His glorious festivals, His righteous testimonies and His true ways.' Paul found his own teaching continually threatened and undermined. He takes the Galatians to task for retreating from his doctrine: 'You observe days, and months, and seasons, and years,' that is, the Sabbaths, New Moons, Festivals and probably Jubilees according to the Zadokite lunar calendar (Gal. iv. 10). Paul admonishes the Colossians also, not to allow anyone to pass judgment on them in matters of food and drink, or with regard to a Festival, New Moon or Sabbath. They must not submit to regulations, 'Do not handle, do not taste, do not touch' (Col. ii. 16-22). Paul's position was singular: he was the odd man out, and many of his own following refused to go along with his doctrinal eccentricities and embraced the orthodox Nazorean teaching.

In all the circumstances it is little wonder that there should be a strong Zealot-Zadokite element among the followers of Jesus. They especially represented ardent, militant and revolutionary youth (cp. the story of Ananias and Saphira, Acts v. 1-11). Josephus writes of the Fourth Philosophy that 'it has been the support given to it by the youth that has caused the ruin of our land' (*Antiq.* XVIII. 9-10).[5]

The exuberant inauguration of the Nazorean community in Jerusalem is declared by Peter, according to the Acts, to be a fulfilment of the Prophecy of Joel (Joel. ii. 28-32) that 'In the Last Days, God says, "I will pour out my Spirit on all flesh. Your sons and daughters will prophesy; your young men will see visions, and your old men will dream dreams" ' (ii. 16-17). The aged would dream their dreams, but it would be the young who would see the visions and act upon them. When it all began, many of the disciples were young men still in their twenties, including perhaps the impulsive Simon Peter and the stormy sons of Zebedee. The great attraction of the Nazorean cause was its appeal to idealistic and nationalistic young Zionists.

The evidences of Zealotism among the early Christians still discoverable in the Acts, despite the aims of the book, should no less be found in the Gospels, especially Matthew and Luke.

Like the Acts, the Gospels were written after the Jewish war with the Romans, when Jerusalem and the Temple were in ruins. There were new conditions, new problems, new requirements of belief. The Gospels were designed for Gentile Christians, largely remote from desolate Judea, at a time when the Church was distinguishing itself from the Jews and evincing hostility towards them. But the Evangelists, while reflecting the changed circumstances in the image of Jesus and his teaching they presented, could not tell their story with verisimilitude without dependence on the sources available to them, for those sources gave them their only claim to authority. It was once thought that they largely availed themselves of oral tradition; but it has become increasingly clear that they relied in the main on documents now lost. They may arrange their materials differently, introduce changes and additions, but they do not depart from their sources too radically where these were available.

There was much vital information which was unobtainable, and the Gospel writers, especially Matthew and Luke, frequently left the gaps, confusions and contradictions as unresolved puzzles. They also retained from the surviving records aspects of the teaching and behaviour of Jesus with which the Church was no longer in sympathy and agreement.

Certain of the sources we are now roughly able to reconstruct, or at least discern their character. For some of them it is evident that there must have been Hebrew and Aramaic originals. The Dead Sea Scrolls and the Jewish *pseudepigrapha* point to a very considerable literary activity by the Fourth Philosophy groups. But what we are emphasizing here is that if Zealot and Zadokite attitudes were prominent among the followers of Jesus, as we have indicated, then what was held and reported about the one who would 'restore the kingdom to Israel' (Acts i. 6) must have been consistent with them. The impress of these attitudes must have been reflected in the Nazorean text-books.

The prophetic concept of the Messiah was that he would supremely exemplify the observance of the Torah. Many thousands of Jews believed that Jesus was the Messiah. This they could not possibly have done if it had been well-known that Jesus had been anti-Torah. A Jewish paraphrase interprets the words of Isaiah ix. 6, 'the government shall be upon his shoulder', as 'he has taken the Torah upon himself, to keep it'.

So we find Jesus in the Sermon on the Mount declaring, 'Do not imagine that I have come to abolish the Law and the Prophets: I have not come to abolish them, but to give effect to them. I tell you positively, until heaven and earth pass away not one iota, not a single stroke, shall be removed from the Law till everything has come to pass. So whoever would relax the most insignificant of the commandments, and teach men so, shall be treated as insignificant in the Kingdom of Heaven. But whoever both observes and teaches them shall be treated as of consequence in the Kingdom of Heaven. I tell you, therefore, unless your devoutness exceeds that of the scribes and Pharisees you will never enter the Kingdom of Heaven' (Mt. v. 17-20).

Elsewhere we find: 'Then Jesus addressed the people and his disciples, "The scribes and Pharisees sit in Moses' seat. Execute and observe, therefore, whatever they tell you; but do not act as they do, for they preach but fail to practise" ' (Mt. xxiii. 1-3).

Jesus insists on the words of the Torah, 'You must be perfect as your heavenly Father is perfect' (Mt. v. 48), 'You are to make God's kingdom and your duty to Him your first concern' (Mt. vi. 33). A merely formal keeping of the commandments is not good enough. Those who would enter the Kingdom of Heaven must ever be conscious of their implications.

The mission of Jesus is exclusively to the lost sheep of the house of Israel. The apostles, therefore, are not to go to any place of the Gentiles: they are not even to go into any Samaritan town (Mt. x. 5-6).

The question evidently arose as to whether it was permissible for the Messiah to heal Gentiles. One answer that was given would seem to have been, Yes, but only in exceptional circumstances. There had been the case of a Roman officer with a sick slave who was dear to him. This centurion acknowledged that he was no fit person for Jesus to come under his roof. He had sent elders of the local Jews to entreat the help of Jesus, and these earnestly pleaded with him that the man deserved to have his request granted 'because he loves our people, and had our synagogue built for us himself' (Lk. vii. 1-7). In fact Jesus does not enter the Gentile's house.

There had been another case of a Syro-Phoenician woman whose daughter Jesus cured. She had greeted him as Son of David, and begged him to take pity on her. He made no reply, but she kept crying after him. The disciples would have him grant her petition if only to get rid of her; but Jesus insisted that he had been sent only to Israelites. Addressing her, he said, 'It is not fair to take the children's food and throw it to puppies.' But with quick wit she replied, 'Quite so, sir. But even puppies may eat the scraps that fall from their masters' table.' 'Because you have said that,' Jesus told her, 'go your way: you will find the demon has gone from your daughter' (Mk. vii. 24-30; Mt. xv. 21-8).

In both instances a justification is found for Jesus to heal a Gentile. Otherwise, except for one of ten lepers who turned out afterwards to be a Samaritan, and two demoniacs in the Gerasa area who may not have been Jews in religion, there are no other references in the Gospels to Jesus curing non-Jews. Neither is there any record of his entering the houses of Gentiles or eating with them.

There are correspondences with Essene practice in the instructions given by Jesus to the Twelve. 'Take neither gold, nor silver, nor copper in your belts, nor a wallet for the road, nor two tunics, nor shoes, nor a staff; for the labourer deserves his keep. When you enter a town or village inquire first who in it is worthy, and stay there until you leave again' (Mt. x. 9-11).

Josephus says of the Essenes, 'On the arrival of any of the sect from elsewhere, all the resources of the community are put at their disposal, just as if they were their own; and they enter the houses of men whom they have never seen before as though they were the most intimate friends. Consequently they carry nothing whatever with them on their journeys, except arms as a protection against brigands. In every city there is one of the Order expressly appointed to attend to strangers, who provides them with raiment and other necessaries' (*J.W.* II. 124-5).

Regarding swearing, Jesus told his followers not to swear at all. 'Do not even swear by your head, since you are powerless to whiten a single hair or to turn it black again. Confine yourselves, therefore, to plain Yes or No. Anything beyond that is wrong' (Mt. v. 33-7).

To the same effect Josephus states of the Essenes, 'Any word of theirs has more force than an oath; swearing they avoid, regarding it as worse than perjury; for they say that one who is not believed without an appeal to God stands condemned already' (*J.W.* II. 135).

There are other elements of the teaching of Jesus in the Sermon on the Mount which reflect the best ethics of the Essenes. We may cite two examples. Jesus warned against anger and hatred. The Essenes said, 'Unless you keep yourself from the spirit of lying and anger, and love truth and long-suffering, you shall perish. For anger is blindness, and does not permit one to see the face of any man with truth.' And again, 'For the spirit of hatred works with Satan, through hastiness of spirit, in all things to men's death; but the spirit of love works with the Law of God in long-suffering to the salvation of men' (*Testaments of the XII Patriarchs*; Dan. ii. 1-2; Gad. iv. 7).

Similarly on the theme of adultery (Mt. v. 27-8), the Essenes said, 'he who has a pure mind in love, does not look at a woman with a view to fornication; for he has no defilement in his heart, because the Spirit of God rests upon him' (Benj. viii. 2).

The parable of the sheep and the goats (Mt. xxv. 31-46) draws on the experience of the patriarch Joseph in Egypt as reflected in the *Testaments.* Joseph there declares, 'I was sold into slavery, and the Lord of all made me free: I was taken into captivity, and His strong hand succoured me. I was beset with hunger, and the Lord Himself nourished me. I was alone, and my God comforted me: I was sick, and the Lord visited me: I was in prison, and my God showed favour to me; in bonds, and He released me; slandered, and He pleaded my cause; bitterly spoken against by the Egyptians, and He delivered me; envied by my fellow-slaves, and He exalted me' (Jos. i. 3-7).

There are many evidences in the New Testament of the use by the early Church of Essene-Zadokite literature, ideas and techniques of interpretation. The Nazoreans clearly attracted many from other groups within the sphere of the Fourth Philosophy, who contributed to Christian formulation a great deal from their writings, organization and convictions. This is only what we should expect; and it is no longer tenable that Christianity in its inception – whatever happened later – was distinct from contemporary attitudes within Judaism.

Finally, here, we come to that vital issue for the Jewish people raised by the question put to Jesus, 'Is it right, or not, to pay the tribute to Caesar? Should we pay it, or not pay?' (Mk. xii. 14-15). Jesus was intended to answer, and could have answered, either Yes or No. The question was framed as a trap. In the one case Jesus would would have acknowledged the lordship of Caesar, thus showing that he could not be the Messiah. In the other case he would openly have proclaimed himself an active rebel liable to immediate arrest and execution, and would no less have involved his followers and many others present in an outbreak of violence causing many deaths.

If the brilliant answer Jesus did give had been no more than a clever equivocation it would hardly have been preserved by the zealous among the Nazoreans. It is significant in Mark's account that Jesus asks for a Roman denarius to be brought to him to look at. It is not stated that he handled the coin himself. He then inquired whose image and superscription it bore. They told him it was Caesar's. 'Very well,' said Jesus, 'render to Caesar what is Caesar's, and to God what is God's.'

If Jesus had meant that Jews should pay tribute to Caesar the first part of his answer would have sufficed. But by introducing the second part of his reply he in effect, as his Jewish hearers would perceive, negatived the first without resort to a direct denial. Those who were puppets of the Romans could pay Caesar in his own coin, while those for whom God was paramount had no such obligation. God's sovereignty over His people cancelled out Caesar's.

It is quite clear that the collaborating Jewish authorities knew perfectly well the implications of the answer Jesus gave. For when the chief priests drew up the indictment against him, 'forbidding us to pay tribute to Caesar' (Lk. xxiii. 2) was on the list.

Thus in a variety of connections we find facets of the Fourth Philosophy breaking through the restraint and even contrary positions of the authors of the Gospels and the Acts. We begin to learn what was the real character of primitive Christianity and the reasons for its strict adherence to the Way of the Law, the Way of Freedom from all heathenism.

NOTES AND REFERENCES

1. See Brandon, *Jesus and the Zealots,* pp. 45–6, and Black, *The Scrolls and Christian Origins,* Appendix B.
2. Mishnah, *Sanhedrin,* ix. 6, tr. Herbert Danby, pp. 396–7.
3. *Jewish War,* II. 264–5.
4. Suetonius, *Claud.* xxv, and the *Letter of Claudius to the Alexandrians* (H. Idris Bell, *Jews and Christians in Egypt*).
5. Josephus had good cause to know the intense religious feeling and militancy of youth. When he was in command in Galilee the young men regarded him as much too lukewarm in the struggle for freedom. They plotted against him and circulated a report that he intended to betray Galilee to the Romans (*Life,* 127, 171–3, 185). It was probably the young rebels who, when two non-Jewish nobles sought asylum, demanded that they be circumcised as a condition of staying among Jews (*Life,* 113).

CHAPTER 27

NEW COVENANTS

An aspect of the situation we must now consider in the light of Jewish Last-Times attitudes is that which occupied itself with the Covenants of God. The idea of a New Covenant sealed with the blood of Jesus Christ is peculiarly precious to Christians. It was construed by Paul and others to mean that in Christ the Old Covenant of the Mosaic economy had been superseded as relating to salvation, and that the penalties of the Law contained in ordinances had been abolished for believers by the atonement wrought on Calvary. But this could be argued only if another element of Pauline teaching was accepted, namely that all persons of all nationalities who believed in Jesus as the Christ (the Messiah) thereby became Israelites, the true Israel of God. They thus came under law to Christ, with his perfection shaping their behaviour and changing them into new men and women.

This arose necessarily from the prophecy of Jeremiah in which reference to a New Covenant was made, since that prediction applied only to Israel and Judah.

> Behold the days are coming, says the Lord, when I will make a new covenant with the house of Israel and the house of Judah, not like the covenant which I made with their fathers when I took them by the hand to bring them out of the land of Egypt, My covenant which they broke, though I was their husband, says the Lord. But this is the covenant which I will make with the house of Israel after those days, says the Lord: I will put My Law within them, and I will write it upon their hearts; and I will be their God, and they shall be My people . . . for I will forgive their iniquity, and I will remember their sin no more (Jer. xxxi. 31–4).

The consciousness of the inward Law would make practicable the performance of the outward Law. The people would keep the Law because it had become natural for them to do so, and not because they had been so commanded. This was the interpretation the Nazoreans opposed to the position taken by Paul; and it made so much sense that a great many of Paul's converts were won over to it to his intense distress. They opted for the full implications of their acquired Israelite status instead of the uncertainty of identity which Pauline teaching gave them.

The prophecy of Jeremiah is part and parcel of a series of Last-Days visions relating to the restoration of Israel and the redemption of Zion, and its fulfilment could only be considered in that connection. The New Covenant, in fact, guaranteed the imperishability of the Jewish nation.

The Church of later times was quite happy for the most part to ignore the associations of the New Covenant affirmed by Jesus as Messiah the Son of David, and it was something of a surprise to discover from the Zadokite literature that, as the loyalists of Israel, their community had pledged itself to a New Covenant which was the Way of the Law. Yet how could those who, in the conviction that the Last Days were imminent, occupied themselves with the prophetic meaning of the Scriptures fail to take cognizance of the covenant predictions?

The great pacts of the Bible were between God and His chosen ones, with Noah, with Abraham, Isaac and Jacob, with Moses, and with David and Solomon. God by His nature could not break His promises. The covenants could only be broken by the human parties. Even so, God could not violate His word, and therefore to bring it into effect the old covenants had to be reaffirmed on the basis of new conditions which would permit of their accomplishment. 'The word of our God will stand for ever' (Isa. xl. 8). 'I the Lord do not change; therefore you, O sons of Jacob, are not consumed' (Isa. lv. 11). The new was not to supersede the old, but to create the circumstances in which the old would be operative. The New Covenant could not be to destroy, only to fulfil.

The Fourth Philosophy in all its aspects was determined to combat everything that contributed to delaying the realization of the Kingdom of God, the era of salvation and regeneration. If we possessed the Zadokite-Essene *Commentary on Jeremiah* it would be extremely revealing. But we have sufficient of the Dead Sea Scrolls and the Jewish *pseudepigrapha* to make clear that a war was being waged with the forces of Belial in respect of defilements which held back the fulfilment of three other covenants, the Covenant of the Kingship, the Covenant of the Priesthood, and the Covenant of the Land.

Of these Jeremiah had written,

> Behold, the days are coming, says the Lord, when I will fulfil the promise I made to the house of Israel and the house of Judah. In those days and at

that time I will cause a righteous branch to spring forth from David; and he shall execute justice and righteousness in the Land. In those days Judah will be saved and Jerusalem will dwell securely. And this is the name by which it will be called: 'The Lord is our righteousness.'

For thus says the Lord: David shall never lack a man to sit on the throne of the house of Israel. And the Levitical priests shall never lack a man in my presence to offer burnt offerings, to burn cereal offerings, and to make sacrifices for ever.

The word of the Lord came to Jeremiah: Thus says the Lord: if you can break My covenant with the day and My covenant with the night, so that day and night will not come at their appointed time, then also my covenant with David my servant may be broken, so that he shall not have a son to reign on his throne, and my covenant with the Levitical priests my ministers (Jer. xxxiii. 14–22).

For the Saints the fulfilment of these promises was being delayed by the sinfulness of the people and the impiety of the priesthood. It had all begun with the Hellenization of the country, and had gone on down to the time of the revolt in A.D. 66.

The Zadokites quoted Isaiah xxiv. 17, 'Fear, and the pit, and the snare are upon you, O inhabitants of the land.' These, they said, were the three nets of Belial, in which Israel was entangled. And they interpreted them as 'fornication, wealth, and pollution of the Sanctuary' (*Damascus Rule,* vi). The only thing to do was to get away into the wilderness, to abandon association with evildoers, and take no direct part in the Temple sacrifices.

In similar vein the *Psalms of Solomon* declares: 'In secret places of the earth they were doing evil; the son had connexion with the mother and the father with the daughter: and all of them committed adultery with their neighbours' wives . . . they were plundering the House of God's holiness, as if there were none to inherit and to deliver. And they were treading His Sanctuary in all their pollutions, and in the time of their separation they polluted the sacrifices as common meat: and they left no sins which they did not commit, and even worse than the Gentiles' (*Ps. Sol.* viii). Therefore, 'they that love the assemblies of the Saints fled away from them: and they flew like sparrows who fly from their nests: and they were wandering in the wilderness, in order to save their souls from evil: and precious in their eyes was the sojourning with them of any soul that was saved from them' [i.e. the evildoers] (*Ps. Sol.* xvii).

The behaviour of the chief priests in the first century A.D. had become a scandal, as all the sources agree, including Josephus and the

Talmud. They were venal, often buying the office of high priest from the Romans with gold. They were arrogant, avaricious and oppressive.

The expectation was held out that God would raise up a new priest to whom the word of the Lord would be revealed,[1] and that soon the righteous Son of David would appear. So there came into currency the doctrine of the Priestly and Davidic Messiahs, as in the *Testaments of the XII Patriarchs*[2] and the Dead Sea Scrolls.[3] The Pharisees too looked for the two Redeemers, corresponding to Moses and Aaron. The two of the Last Times would be Elijah of the house of Aaron and Messiah the son of David.[4] To this also seemed to agree the words of Zechariah, 'Behold, the man whose name is the Branch: for he shall grow up in his place, and he shall build the Temple of the Lord . . . and shall bear royal honour, and shall sit and rule upon his throne. And there shall be a priest by his throne, and peaceful understanding shall be between them both' (vi. 12-13). These personalities had been foreshadowed by Zerubbabel and by Joshua the son of Josedech, the high priest.

For the Zadokites, with their emphasis on the priestly ministry, the high priest of the new era would be superior to the monarch. For the Nazoreans, following here the Pharisees, the returned Elijah would be the priestly forerunner of the Davidic Messiah. In the Gospels they become John the Baptist and Jesus; but some, as in the Epistle to the Hebrews, would hold that one Messiah would be both king and high priest after the order of Melchizedek.[5] St Ephraim the Syrian insisted that Jesus was both king and priest, and the tradition received by Hegesippus claimed that Jacob the brother of Jesus had in fact officiated as high priest.[6] But such interpretations violate the prediction of the permanency of the Levitical priesthood.

The Zadokites applied to themselves the words of Ezekiel, 'The priests and the Levites and the sons of Zadok, that kept the charge of my Sanctuary when the children of Israel went astray from Me, they shall bring near unto Me fat and blood' (xliii. 15). 'The *Priests*,' said the Zadokites, 'are the penitents of Israel who went forth out of the land of Judah; and the *Levites* are those who joined them. And the *Sons of Zadok* are the Elect of Israel called by name that arise in the End of the Days' (*Damascus Rule*, iv). This would equally seem to be conferring a sacerdotal status on laymen; but the Zadokites appear to have had a good many priests in their ranks, and Levites as well, and in their Community they carefully distinguished the orders of Priests, Levites and Laymen.

Thus we read:

> On entering the [New] Covenant, the Priests and Levites shall bless the God of salvation and all His faithfulness, and all those entering the Covenant shall say after them, Amen, Amen. Then the Priests shall recite the favours of God manifested in His mighty deeds, and shall declare all His merciful grace to Israel, and the Levites shall recite the iniquities of the children of Israel, and their guilty rebellions and sins during the domination of Satan. And after them, all those entering the Covenant shall confess and say: We have strayed. We have disobeyed. We and our fathers before us have sinned and done wickedly in walking counter to the precepts of truth and righteousness (*Community Rule,* 1).

Always the three grades functioned in order of precedence.

During the whole 'Period of Wickedness' in Israel until the Redemption, the Zadokites refused all attendance at the polluted Temple, and their priests would not participate in its services. But they continued to send there the prescribed offerings, provided they were conveyed by a person in a state of ritual purity and were not placed on the altar on the Sabbath.[7]

The belief communicated itself to the people via the Fourth Philosophy that the alien rulers of Israel were the enemies of the true priesthood.[8] This was readily acceptable to the masses who suffered under Herodian and Roman domination, and who detested the hierarchy for being in league with the Romans, copying the ways of the Gentiles, and generally acting in a scandalous and highhanded manner. As the revolt developed there were attacks on the rich and aristocratic, and the chief priests were among the early victims. The ire of the downtrodden and oppressed was easily aroused by Zealot preachers who proclaimed that until these defilers of God's House and Throne were swept away the Deliverance of Israel could not come.

For the spiritually-minded not only had there to be a New Covenant in respect of the observation of the Divine Laws, but also a New Covenant to redeem the promises to David and the Priesthood, which had been violated by the usurpers and wrongdoers. The ministers of these New Covenants would be the ideal king and the ideal priest, who would delight to do the will of God in all purity and holiness. Since God could not break His promises, it was from the side that had broken faith that rectification was to come. Fulfilment would take place by God Himself raising up the Priestly Messenger of the Covenant who would purify the sons of Levi (Mal. i. 3) and the righteous Branch of David.

The third Covenant concerned the Land. It was not only the Promised Land, but the Holy Land, God's land and heritage (Jer. ii. 7). It was a land that 'the Lord your God cares for; the eyes of the Lord your God are always upon it, from the beginning of the year to the end of the year' (Deut. xi. 12). So too God had chosen Jerusalem, and Zion was 'His holy hill' (Ps. ii. 6).

The Covenant of the Land no less required Israel's faithfulness. If the people were obedient they would dwell in it happily and peacefully. But if they did evil plagues would come upon them, earthquakes, famine and pestilence, and foreign invasion. In the last resort they would be driven out and go into captivity.

The pious, accordingly, were ever ready when natural disasters occurred, or war and oppression, to claim these as judgments for national turpitude. Especially did they hit out at horrible iniquities in high places.[9] The militants were fully prepared to back the prophets of doom, and to affirm that foreigners were at the root of all evil. The presence of aliens with their idolatrous ways, the temptations they placed in the path of the people, brought defilement of the land. The remedy was to drive out the foreigners and compel all resident Gentiles to become Jews. Then the land would be cleansed, and Israel would regain liberty, accepting God as the only Lord. In the view of the Zealot extremists, the Kingdom of God could not be attained except by violence.

Therefore, they contended, it was essential to begin by capturing Zion and destroying those who had made it another Sodom and Egypt (Rev. xi. 8). The visions of Ezekiel with their promise of a New Jerusalem were studied with hopeful conviction. Both Nazoreans and Zadokites delighted in the future City of God. The Elect saw themselves making atonement for the land, and in this way also renewing the Covenant, by which all the promises of restoration, peace and bliss would be realized. God would fulfil the Covenant of the Land by a free pardon once the people were moved to repentance.

There were many to listen to all these propositions, to execrate Belial and his allies, and to regard the multiplying calamities of the nation as the Woes preceding the advent of the Messianic Age. The crowning evil would be the setting up of the Abomination of Desolation in the Holy Place. The present sufferings were to be regarded as the waking nightmare of the Last Times, the hour of decision and amendment. He that should turn to God and endure to the end, the same should be saved.

It is a strange atmosphere in which we find ourselves, and one to which it is not easy to adjust. But we have to make the effort, because this was the actual environment in which Christianity had its beginnings, and what it represented is not what we may hitherto have supposed.

NOTES AND REFERENCES

1. See *Testaments of the XII Patriarchs,* Levi. xvii. 10ff.
2. *Testaments,* Simeon, vii. 1–2.
3. See *Damascus Rule,* ix (Dead Sea Scrolls).
4. *Midrash Tehillim,* xliii. 1. See Schonfield, *Secrets of the Dead Sea Scrolls.*
5. The Hasmonean rulers, as high priests, took a title after the order of Melchizedek, calling themselves Priests of the Most High God. See *Testaments,* Levi. viii. 14, and Dr Charles's comment thereon in his edition.
6. Ephrem Syrus, *Gospel Commentaries,* and Epiphanius, *Panar.* lxxviii.
7. See G. Vermes, *The Dead Sea Scrolls in English,* pp. 45–6. His remarks are based on the *Damascus Rule,* vi and xi.
8. A wicked priest comes out prominently in the Scrolls, especially in the *Habakkuk Commentary,* and indeed wicked priests had long figured in such literature. Cp. *Testaments,* Levi. xiv. 5–8, 'The offerings of the Lord ye shall rob, and from His portion shall ye steal choice portions, eating them contemptuously with harlots. . . . And ye shall be puffed up because of your priesthood, lifting yourselves up against men, and not only so, but also against the commands of God. For ye shall condemn the holy things with jests and laughter.'
9. The prophecy of the Seventy Weeks of Daniel was requisitioned. 'And now I have learnt that for seventy weeks ye shall go astray, and profane the priesthood, and pollute the sacrifices. And ye shall make void the Law, and set at naught the words of the prophets by evil perverseness. And ye shall persecute righteous men, and hate the godly; and the words of the faithful shall ye abhor. . . . And because of this your holy place shall be laid waste even to the ground. And ye shall have no place that is clean; but ye shall be among the Gentiles a curse and a dispersion until He shall again visit you, and in pity receive you' (Levi. xvi. 1–5; cp. Mt. xxiii. 29–39).

CHAPTER 28

NAZARENE COUNTRY

The Jewish followers of Jesus were commonly called Nazoreans (in Hebrew *Notsrim*). It was in a non-semitic environment, at Antioch in Syria, that the nickname Christians was coined, and came to be accepted after the fall of Jerusalem by the Church in the Roman Empire. But the old name persisted in the East, where the Jewish believers continued for many centuries, as descriptive of Christians in general.

The meaning of the designation *Notsrim* is quite clear: it signifies the Keepers or Preservers, and could be explained of those who maintained the true teaching and tradition, or who cherished certain secrets which they did not divulge to others, as did the Zadokite-Essenes. The question is whether the name had also a topographical significance. Was Jesus known as the Nazorean, as Judas was known as the Galilean or Gaulanite?

We have a parallel in another sectarian context. The Samaritans (*Shomronim*), inhabitants of samaria, were not concerned to derive their name from Shemer (I Ki. xvi. 24), but regarded themselves rather as the *Shamerine*, those who guarded and kept the true Law of Moses. *Natsaraya* is the Aramaic equivalent. In the Gospel parables Jesus refers to secrets (mysteries) of the Kingdom of God made known exclusively to his disciples, but not disclosed to 'those outside' to whom is applied the saying of Isaiah (vi. 9–10) that they should see, but not perceive, and hear, but not understand (Mk. iv. 10-12; Mt. xiii. 10-17). With reference to the potters (*yotsrim*) in the book of Chronicles, the Talmud plays on the word in the sense of *notsrim* by commenting, 'These potters are the descendants of Jonadab son of Rechab, who *keep* the oath of their ancestor (Jer. xxxv. 6-8), to drink no wine, to lay out no vineyard or other plantation, nor to till the soil, nor to build houses to dwell in them.'[1] Abbot Nilus, as we have already observed, understood the Essenes to have derived from the Rechabites, and Rechabite priests were in contact with the Nazoreans.

We are on the frontiers here of one of the big problems of Christian origins, a problem both of location and association.

Let us recall some other things of which we have previously become aware. The Essenes and their Zadokite wing made a great feature of the secrets in their possession. The secrets were of many kinds. There were secrets of the correct interpretation of the Scriptures. These people claimed also to be the true *keepers* of the Divine Laws, and of the method of determining the right observation of the festivals. In considering the ramifications of the Fourth Philosophy we had also noted the sojourn of the forerunners of the Zadokites in the land of Damascus, from which 'wilderness of the peoples' they returned when they believed the Last Times had arrived.

Judas, one of the prime movers of the Fourth Philosophy in its popular Zealot expression, had come from Gamala east of the Sea of Galilee. The movements of John the Baptist at around the same time had Galilean adherents, and similarly emphasized the Way of the Law and the slogan 'No Ruler but God'. There was a Samaritan offshoot of the movement known as the Dositheans.[2]

We have pointers, therefore, to an original breeding ground of prophetic and conservationist movements in the area to the north-east and east of the Sea of Galilee. The activity fed upon elements which were a legacy from the ancient Northern Kingdom of Israel, which had retained a certain hostility to Judah and regarded its religion as corrupt. When the Last Times were believed to have begun, and it was necessary for the salvation of all Israel, the forces claiming a purer loyalty to God and His law erupted from their base and invaded the south on both sides of the Jordan.

It is these pointers we have now to pursue, because the issues are of the utmost consequence for the right understanding of the position of those who attached themselves to the cause of Jesus the Nazorean. The difficulties are great because we have to follow a number of lines of inquiry, our sources are diverse, and the Christian ones are too narrow in their representation. Some things we must now envisage change the image of early Christianity so much that instinctively many will wish to reject them. We can only present the evidences, and endeavour to make comprehension of them not too strenuous an enterprise.

Like those who constructed King Hezekiah's tunnel at Siloam, the best method seems to be to work from both ends towards a meeting place in the middle.

The region with which we are concerned lay in a horizontal band from west to east in northern Palestine. On the west was the River Jordan from its source down to the Sea of Galilee. To the north was Mount Hermon and further east Damascus. Eastward lay the desert route to the Euphrates and Babylon, and on the south was the land of Gilead. Through the territory, which embraced a fertile belt of country, ran the River Dan, a tributary of the Jordan.

Anciently this had been Amorite country, partly known as the land of Argob. It had been noted for a very tall indigenous people, the Rephaim and Anakim, a survivor of the race at the time of the Israelite conquest being Og king of Bashan, whose capital was at Edrei, and whose bed was said to be four cubits in width and nine in length (Deut. iii. 1-11). There were many caves in the region. Edrei itself had vast subterranean caverns forming a kind of underground city.

To this country, called by the Zadokites the land of Damascus and the 'wilderness of the peoples', had migrated a body of the Jewish Chasidim (the Pious Ones), seeking refuge from the persecution initiated by Antiochus IV and a place where they could keep their faith in purity. The pattern is a familiar one in religious history. We may have an indication that this migration took place about 159 B.C. after the death of Judas Maccabaeus, for Josephus records that after Judas had been slain in battle 'all the wicked, and those that transgressed the laws of their forefathers, sprang up again in Judea, and grew upon them, and distressed them on every side. A famine also assisted their wickedness, and afflicted their country, till not a few, who by reason of the want of necessities, and because they were not able to bear up against the miseries that both the famine and their enemies brought upon them, deserted their country and went to the Macedonians' (i.e. the land of the north).[3]

One of the early literary productions of the Chasidim was the book of *Enoch*, which has a special connection with the area where they settled. The book is built round the story in Genesis that before the Flood the sons of God came down to the daughters of men and had intercourse with them. The offspring of this union were the giants (Gen. vi. 1-4).

According to Enoch[4] it was certain angels of those called the Watchers (cp. Dan. iv. 13, 17) who committed this crime. There were some two hundred of them, 'and they descended in the days of Jared on the summit of Mount Hermon, and they called it Mount Hermon because they had sworn and bound themselves upon it by mutual imprecations [to cohabit with humans].' There are plays on words here. They descended (Heb. *jeredu*) appropriately in the days of Jared father of Enoch, and Hermon was so-called from the curse (Heb. *herem*) with which they bound themselves (*En.* vi. 6). The mortal women bore giants who turned against mankind. Then Michael, Gabriel and other angels cried to God about what the Watchers had done, teaching all unrighteousness on earth and revealing the secret things of heaven. The Divine fiat then went forth that the earth's evil inhabitants must be destroyed by a flood, and the offending Watchers were to be led off to the abyss of fire, condemned to torment and eternal imprisonment.

The scene of the whole story is set in the region to which the Chasidim had migrated. The angel Michael was now sent to inform the Watchers of the sentence passed upon them. They approached Enoch to assist them in drawing up a petition for mercy, which he agreed to present. We note here that throughout the book, just like the Teacher of Righteousness of the Dead Sea Scrolls, Enoch is termed the Scribe of Righteousness, or True Scribe. Enoch sits down by the waters of the River Dan to study the petition. He falls asleep, and in a dream-vision learns that there can be no forgiveness for the rebels. Accordingly, when he wakes he goes to inform them. 'And when I awaked, I came to them, and they were all sitting together with their faces covered at Ublesjael, which is between Lebanon and Seneser.' The Ethiopic text of the names is corrupt. Possibly for Seneser we should read Genesar, on the north-west shore of the Sea of Galilee.

Christian readers will be aware that the early followers of Jesus were familiar with our book, which they regarded as divinely inspired. Reference to the fallen angels is made in Jude, and there is a direct quotation from *Enoch* in verses 14 to 15. The story is also echoed in 2 Peter.

The aim of *Enoch*'s account of the punishment of the Watchers is made clear from the opening of the book, and is wholly in line with Zadokite propaganda.

It begins: 'The words of the blessing of Enoch, wherewith he blessed the elect and righteous, who will be living in the day of tribulation, when all the wicked and godless are to be removed. And Enoch answered and spake. . . . I heard everything [which the angels showed me], and I understood what I saw, but not for this generation, but for the remote generations which are to come' (i. 1-2).

The story of the fallen angels is an object lesson of what will happen in the Last Times to those who have transgressed the Law of the Lord, and have slanderously spoken proud and harsh words against His greatness. And therefore 'the years of your destruction will be multiplied in eternal execration, and ye will find no mercy. . . . But for the Elect there will be light and joy and peace, and they will inherit the earth.' It is like the Christian statement that when the Son of Man comes it will be a repetition of what happened in the days of Noah (Mt. xxiv. 37-9).

It is impossible not to see the connection with Daniel's Son of Man vision, explained to mean that 'the kingdom and the dominion, and the greatness of the kingdoms under the whole heaven, shall be given to the people of the Saints of the Most High'. And with the saying of Jesus, that the oppressed in spirit would have the Kingdom of God, and the meek would inherit the earth (Mt. v. 3-5). Similarly, in the Zadokite *Damascus Rule* it is said that, 'in the period of the wrath . . . God made to spring forth from Israel and Aaron a root of His planting to inherit His land.'

To follow up this last reference we find that the Saints in *Enoch* are called the Plant of Righteousness, or True Plant. This thinking goes back to Isa. lx. 21: 'You people shall be all righteous; they shall possess the land for ever, the shoot [Heb. *nezer*] of my planting, the work of my hands, that I might be glorified.' Again we are reminded of the words of Jesus, 'Every plant which my heavenly Father has not planted will be rooted up' (Mt. xv. 13).

We need to pay the very closest attention and keep continually in mind the interweaving of strands of thinking in the literature of all the manifestations of the Way, so that we cease to regard the original Christians as a unique phenomenon. It emerges ever more clearly that there was cross-fertilization, and that the term Nazorean covers a group of sects with strong affinities as well as certain distinguishing features. We have to set aside that Paulinism, on which what became orthodox Christianity largely rests, reflects the true position of those who were the first followers of Jesus the Nazorean. Equally, we have to abandon the idea that we can know the real Jesus through later Christian interpretation of him. Our whole perspective has now to be radically, and perhaps painfully, changed as more information comes to light.

Having now looked briefly at the far end of the tunnel, and found a line leading inwards, we may turn directly to the near end. This is so near that it is in fact contemporary.

There are two surviving clans with a long history behind them, both of which have an ancient association with the region in which we are interested, and both of which have a likeness of nomenclature.

The first is the Nusairiyeh, a mysterious people found mainly in Syria, whose ancestors belonged to the region south of the Lebanon.[5] How they originated is still uncertain. Dr Thomson, author of that popular Victorian work *The Land and the Book,* had several encounters with the Nusairiyeh. They were extremely evasive about their religion, and the good doctor could only gather that they claimed to be Christians, though not like others, honouring Moses and Jesus. Persecution by the followers of Islam had made them very wary. Their ceremonies were held in secret, and the author adds, 'Should any of their number divulge their mysteries, he would be assassinated without remorse, mercy, or delay.' The Islamic references illustrate that, like our other sect, the Nusairiyeh had absorbed ideas from various sources in the course of their history. Their existence, as well as their name, remains, however, a link with the past which should not be ignored.

These people conceivably take us back to those pre-Christian Nasarenes or Nosarenes, described by Epiphanius in the fourth century as surviving in Gilead and Bashan. By religion these Nasarenes were a kind of Jew, but more closely related in their beliefs to the Dositheau Samaritans. They held that they were in possession of the true Law of Moses, which differed from that of the Jews, just as did the Samaritans. In this respect, says Epiphanius, they were like the Osseans.

Bishop Epiphanius, who devoted himself to dealing with numerous sects in his massive *Panarion,* wrestled manfully with the problems of identification arising from a similarity of names – Osseans and Jessaeans, Nasarenes and Nazoreans – and what relationship these had to the Christians who were also called Nazoreans. There was the added complication of the Jewish devotees called nazirites. The tangle is certainly a difficult one to sort out, since all these groups were to be found roughly in the same region.

We shall return to the problem later. But confining ourselves for the moment to the Nasarenes, it could be possible that the Nusairiyeh may go back to them. Were they the people of this land? We encounter a reference in Pliny to a Nazerine tetrarchy (*Natural History* v. 81). This was adjacent to Coele-Syria. Pliny was writing in the first century

A.D. but how he picked up the name is a mystery. The only tetrarchy in the vicinity was that allocated by Augustus to Philip son of Herod the Great, which embraced Batanea (Bashan), Auranitis, Trachonitis, and part of Iturea in the region of Paneas (afterwards Caesarea-Philippi). Half a century later, with some additions, it was assigned to Agrippa II. Auranitis (the Hauran) had a reputation for being the haunt of rebels and malcontents.

Right across the region there were vestiges of the older peoples of the land, who had hung on to a certain amount of independence, and were regarded as sullen and uncommunicative. As a working hypothesis it may be suggested that the region was natively known as Nasarene or Nazarene Country (cp. the Se-neser of *Enoch* and Ge-nesar, Gennesaret) by the Sea of Galilee. Some scholars have proposed that the eastern zone of Galilee of the Nations was called Nasara of Galilee.[6] The broader area seems to be indicated in the prophecy of Isaiah that in the Last Times 'God will make glorious the way of the sea, beyond Jordan, Galilee of the Gentiles' (Isa. ix. 1-2), where the people who walked in darkness would see great light.

Was, then, the native land of Jesus the eastern zone of Galilee? And did its reputation create the Judean proverb, 'Can anything good come out of Nazareth?' (Jn. i. 46).

We are not yet ready to develop this theme, and must come to our second lead-in from the present day. This is represented by those known as Mandaeans, but who call themselves Nazoreans. For purposes of distinction from Christian Nazoreans we shall speak of them as Mandaean-Nazoreans. These survive in a rather miserable condition in the marsh land of the Lower Euphrates, and have been studied intimately and much of their literature translated by the author's friend the late Lady Drower, as well as previously by Lidzbarski and others.

Down the centuries these people have suffered so many vicissitudes that their traditions are confused, and their remaining writings are of no great antiquity. We can trace, however, that originally they were an offshoot of the movement connected with John the Baptist, which later incorporated Gnostic and certain Iranian-Babylonian concepts. According to the teaching they espoused, Jesus was treated as a false Messiah whom John at first had refused to baptize. We know from the Clementine Nazorean texts that at an early stage there was conflict between Baptists and Christian-Nazoreans as to whether John or Jesus had been the Messiah. Mandaean-Nazorean tradition is hostile to the Jews, because at the beginning in Jerusalem they had been persecuted by them. We are very interested in this tradition, because the name Nazorean links the early Mandaeans with the early Christians.

A Mandaean text discussed by Dr Rudolf Macuch[7] gives rise to the view that the persecution can be dated in A.D. 37. Matthew Black comments, 'It is possible that we have to do with a movement of Christians, emigrating from Palestine, though the date is curious.' Anyway, the claim of the Mandaean *Haran Gawaita* is that the Mandaean-Nazoreans fled from Judea – the number mentioned is 60,000, but we should probably read 6,000 – and found asylum in the Hauran (Auranitis). 'A line in the baptismal hymns,' writes Lady Drower. ' "with Hauran our garment, in Hauraran our cover" may hint that these place-names refer to geographical districts and that they once afforded concealment and cover to refugees for religion's sake.'

But why should the date A.D. 37 be curious? It does not seem to have occurred to these authorities that we here have to do with the same persecution that broke out after the martyrdom of Stephen, and which found in Saul of Tarsus an eager instrument. The Acts appears to confine the victims of the attack to the followers of Jesus; but this is not necessarily correct. The action could equally have been directed against Baptists and Zadokites, all the Last-Times groups, those of the Way of the Law, the Way of Freedom, whose ardent propaganda was regarded as highly dangerous by the pro-Roman authorities. We have been learning to think of Nazoreanism as not confined to the followers of Jesus, but having some kinship with all the Fourth Philosophy advocates. The events of A.D. 37 are given a new historical importance.

Those who were dispersed all fled to the north. Some apparently went to Samaria and up the coastal lands to Phoenicia and Syria (Acts viii. 1; xi. 19). But evidently many others crossed the Jordan near Jericho, and proceeded through Gilead and Bashan to the Hauran, to the land of Damascus, the original place of refuge of the Zadokites, where many of them must have remained.

Who was the Ananias of Damascus, who opened Saul's eyes and spoke to him about the Just One? Was he a Zadokite?

Another tradition about this persecution preserved in the Clementine *Recognitions* reports that 5,000 of the disciples went down to Jericho,[8] where secret tidings reached them that Saul had received a commission to go to Damascus and make havoc among the faithful, and that he was hastening to Damascus because he believed Peter had fled there (I. lxxi).[9] It has always been a mystery why the authorities at Jerusalem should have regarded the region of Damascus as an area of concentration of followers of the Way. The Dead Sea Scrolls and the Mandaean literature now help to explain the mystery.

But to return specifically to the Mandaean-Nazoreans: their records indicate that from the Hauran they later moved north-eastward to Haran, and so eventually made thier way down the Euphrates to their present location. In other words they were roughly following in reverse the route taken by Abraham when he came from Ur of the Chaldees to Haran, and finally on to Canaan. By much the same route the eminent Pharisee Hillel had reached Judea from Babylonia in the time of Herod the Great.[10] Indeed, as Josephus tells us, Babylonian Jews making the pilgrimage to Jerusalem customarily followed this route.

Thus from the near end of our tunnel we also move inwards, finding ourselves always reaching towards a point of junction in the same particular area. The various sects which interest us, and which so confused Epiphanius, were in contact in the sturdily independent region which gave asylum to them all.

But we have not yet done with the zealous Church Father. He affirms that the followers of Jesus were initially known as Jessaeans. This might have been due to Jesse the father of King David, having in mind the prediction of Isaiah that there should come forth a shoot (*nezer*) from the stump of Jesse (xi. 1). But then by Jessaeans Epiphanius thinks it more probably that those known as Therapeutae, familiar to Philo in Egypt, must be intended. So by Jessaeans he is signifying the Essaeans or Essenes, whom he identifies with the Christians because the Hebrew name Jesus is to be translated *therapeutes,* with the association physician or saviour (*Panar*. xxix).

With this another term comes into the picture, that of the nazirites. Epiphanius is aware that this term has nothing to do with Nazoreans. The nazirites were persons who had been dedicated to God like Samson and Samuel,[11] or who had taken either a lifetime or temporary vow. A distinguishing mark of nazirites was that they did not cut their hair and abstained from intoxicants. Jesus was decidedly no nazirite, and in the earliest pictures of him his hair is short. The nazirites, however, were not a sect, or even a special order; and because some of the sects and groups favoured asceticism, were abstainers and vegetarians, there is no call to describe them as nazirites. Some individuals among them did take nazirite vows, but so did many other Jews. The Mishnah devotes a whole section of legislation to the nazirs, both male and female.

It is not necessary to deal with other sects named and described by the Christian heresiologists. These are well known to scholars, and the details would only weary and puzzle the general reader. Suffice it to say that certain affinities existed between those which were before the time of Jesus, especially at the dawn of the first century A.D. Later, following the first and second Jewish revolt against the Romans, there was a further multiplication of sects with an even greater exchange of beliefs and practices. What is important to grasp is that it was the general area in and around what we have called Nazarene Country, which had contributed so much initially to Last-Times concerns, which saw also the shapings of its later impulses.

We are now reasonably well-prepared to come to the place of meeting on which the lines of our investigation have converged.

NOTES AND REFERENCES

1. *Baba Bathra,* 9lb.
2. See Driver, *The Judean Scrolls,* and Black, *The Scrolls and Christian Origins.*
3. Josephus, *Antiq.* XIII. 1–3. See further Schonfield, *Secrets of the Dead Sea Scrolls,* p. 20f.
4. The edition and translation of *Enoch* used here is that of R. H. Charles. Fragments of *Enoch* have been found among the Dead Sea Scrolls.
5. Some of their settlements were to be found not long ago on the southern slopes of Mount Hermon, where *Enoch's* lusting angels had descended.
6. See, for example, Burrage, *Nazareth and the Beginnings of Christianity* (Oxford, 1914).
7. Macuch, *Alter und Heimat der Mandäismus nach neuerschlossenen Quellen,* Theologische Literaturzeitung, 82. See also Black, *op. cit.* p. 68, and E. S. Drower, *Mandaean Polemic,* Bulletin of the School of Oriental and African Studies, Vol. XXV, Part 3, 1962.
8. Some of the refugees could well have sought asylum with the Zadokites at Qumran, not far from Jericho. But the community there could not have absorbed the large numbers indicated, even if tradition has exaggerated the figures.
9. This certainly gives one reason why Saul should have gone to Damascus, but what we have gone on to suggest seems more probable. Saul's own allusions in his letters (2 Cor. xi. 32–3; Gal. i. 16–17) give no account at all of his expedition, or for what reason he was in trouble with the governor of Damascus. He only tells us himself (1 Cor. xv. 8–9) that he had a

vision of Jesus, and that he persecuted the Community of God. He did go to Arabia, presumably to the Nabataean territory adjoining Trachonitis.

10. Except that one had to beware of the brigands of Trachonitis and Arabian marauders this was also one of the regular routes from Babylon to the Mediterranean seaboard, and there were Roman roads through the area.
11. And of course John the Baptist. Nazirite vows were taken by Jacob the brother of Jesus, and apparently by Paul on one occasion.

CHAPTER 29

MEETING PLACE

The Nazoreans who were the Jewish adherents of Jesus were still very active and flourishing in the fourth century A.D. when Epiphanius and Jerome were acquainted with them. Their communities and synagogues were spread out over an arc extending from the Syrian coast through northern Transjordan down into Peraea. They were in possession of, and used exclusively, a Gospel in Aramaic known to the Church Fathers as the Hebrew Matthew or *Gospel of the Hebrews.* The more sectarian Ebionites seem to have employed the same Gospel with certain variations. From quotations which have preserved parts of the text this work had correspondences with Matthew more particularly, but also with Luke. It also contained independent traditions and alternative readings to the canonical writings. Its composition cannot have been much later than the middle of the second century A.D. and some of the material could be very early and important.[1]

The Nazoreans of all kinds, including Ebionites, were to be found, says Epiphanius, in Beroea (Aleppo), in Coele-Syria, also in the Decapolis in the proximity of Pella, and generally in Transjordan, in Batanea (Bashan) at a place called Cocabe (Heb. Cochabe) which lies in the area of Carnaim, Arnemi and Ashtarothae (Ashtaroth-Karnaim). See *Panar.* xviii. 1; xxix. 7; xxx. 2.

The point about this information, as with earlier information we shall encounter, is that it largely directs us to the eastern side of the Jordan. This accords with what has already been brought to our attention. In the pre-Christian period we have the Zadokite emigration to the north-east, the land of Damascus, the wilderness of the peoples. Judas of Galilee came from Gamala in Gaulanitis. John the Baptist reflected the prophet Elijah who had been a native of Gilead. At the beginning of the Christian-Nazorean development there was a persecution which caused many of the refugees to seek asylum in the region of Damascus, and the Mandaean-Nazoreans recall that at this time their people had fled to the Hauran. Then, at the outbreak of the Jewish revolt against the Romans, Christian tradition insists that the followers of Jesus in Judea, in obedience to a prediction of Jesus or other revelation, crossed the Jordan near Jericho and established themselves in the vicinity of Pella in the Decapolis.

Western Galilee, upper and lower, does not appear in this picture as an important area of concentration, though we know that Christian-Nazoreans were to be found there because various rabbis from the first to the fourth century encountered them, and the Nazorean writings were in the library of the Rabbinical College at Tiberias, the seat of the Jewish Patriarch.[2]

This gives rise to the much debated Nazareth problem we have touched upon. It remains in doubt whether the Nazareth to which millions of Christians have directed their steps was in fact the place where the family to which Jesus belonged were settled and where he grew to manhood. Apart from a doubtful reference which may go back to the third century A.D. no mention of this Nazareth is made in any previous description of western Galilee. Cana is mentioned in this territory, so is Magdala and Capernaum, but not Nazareth.[3]

Pliny's Nazerine tetrarchy does not tie in with western Galilee.[4] We have to distinguish between a Hebrew word written with the letter *samech* (and thus *Naser* or *Nosar*) underlying Nazerine, and one written with the letter *tsadi* (and thus *Natsrath*) associated with the word netzer in relation to Nazareth. The employment of the letter 'z' in both cases is misleading.

The territory, then, to which we have chiefly been directed is that which, according to Josephus, was the ancient land of the tribe of Naphthali. This stretched from Upper Galilee as far north as Mount Libanus (Hermon), and the sources of the Jordan, right across to the east as far as Damascus (*Antiq.* V. 86). It was the northern Transjordan country which in the times with which we are concerned was the home of Jewish militants and messianists. In the war with the Romans, when Vespasian overran Galilee and occupied Tiberias, it was Jewish freedom-fighters from the east who were the backbone of the revolt. Josephus disparagingly describes them as 'a mob from Trachonitis, Gaulanitis, Hippos and Gadara, seditionists and fugitives, to whom their infamous careers in peace-time gave war its attractions' (*J.W.* III. 542). The reference supports incidentally that the Transjordan region was familiar as a place of asylum.

Let us suppose that the Nazareth of the Gospels was in the east. Does this not better fit the saying, 'Can anything good come out of Nazareth?' And does it not better fit the circumstances of the preaching of Jesus in the synagogue at Nazareth as reported by Luke?

Jesus speaks from a text in Isaiah which promises good news to the poor, release for captives, liberty for the oppressed, sentiments which evidently appealed to the congregation. He then says that his hearers may demand, 'What we have heard you did at Capernaum, do here also in *your own country.*' If Jesus is supposed to know that many of the local people were militantly nationalistic this will account for what follows. Citing the Transjordan prophet Elijah, and his successor Elisha, he reminds his audience that though there were plenty of widows and lepers in Israel these prophets were sent to the heathen, to a widow of Phoenicia and a man who was a Syrian. This was an insult which outraged national sentiment, and the congregation rose in wrath and indignation to throw Jesus out.

The speech may well be apocryphal, but if the author had read his Josephus – as there is evidence that he had – he would be well aware of the feelings and attitudes of the people in the north-east.

Elijah, and probably Elisha, were hero figures of the Fourth Philosophy groups. John the Baptist appeared in Elijah's character and garb, promising fire from heaven on the evildoers. Several of the miracles attributed to Jesus seem to have been inspired by the exploits of these prophets as related in the book of Kings, such as raising a youth to life, a widow's son (Lk. vii. 11-16), healing lepers, and feeding a multitude leaving a surplus (cp. 2 Ki. iv. 42-4).

Here we may interject a rabbinical passage about Elisha. 'It is written' (2 Ki. viii. 7), 'And Elisha went to Damascus.' Why did he go to Damascus? R. Jochanan says that he went to turn Gehazi (his servant) to repentance, but he did not repent. 'He said to him, "Repent," but he answered, "Thus have I received from thee, that whoever has sinned, and has caused the multitude to sin, is given no chance of repentance" ' (b. *Sotah* 47a, also *Sanh.* 107a).

Gehazi, who took a bribe from Naaman the Syrian, is treated with some others in the Talmud as a type of inflexible heretic. We remember too that Paul went to Damascus to arrest sectaries. The Rabbinical discussion is apt because it must have been well-known to the Jewish scholars of the third and fourth century that Jewish heretics had long been rampant in the Damascus region.

The Talmud also mentions a Ben-Netzer as a brigand chief with pretensions to kingship.[5] Who is meant has never been satisfactorily determined, but the name has a messianic connotation, deriving from the sprout or shoot from the stump of Jesse in Isaiah xi. 1. It is like Bar-Cochba, the leader of the Second Revolt in A.D. 133, whose real name Cosiba was changed to reflect the prophecy of Balaam (Nu. xxiv. 17) of the star (*cochab*) that should come forth out of Jacob.

The interesting thing is that we find the Sprout prophecy and the Star prophecy conjoined by the early Christians as a testimony to Jesus. Thus Justin Martyr, 'And Isaiah, another prophet, spoke thus, "A star shall rise out of Jacob, and a flower shall spring from the root of Jesse"' (I *Apol.* xxxii). Justin appears not to know that the first half of his quotation is from Numbers and not from Isaiah. The very same phenomenon occurs at the opening of Mark's Gospel. There a quotation from Malachi iii. 1 is immediately followed by one from Isaiah xl. 3, the whole text being ascribed to Isaiah. We meet with other instances where a prediction regarded as applying to Christ is attributed to the wrong Old Testament authority. We also discover that some of the Church Fathers in listing prophetic testimonies to Christ repeat the same errors of ascription. This seems to indicate that direct reference was not being made to the Bible, but to a collection of *Testimonia* in which passages from different books of the Old Testament were arranged under subjects leading off with the words of a particular prophet. One group would deal, for example, with the Stone texts in the Psalms, Isaiah and Daniel.[6]

Instruction in the testimonies is attributed by Luke to Jesus himself (Lk. xxiv. 44), and it is possible that in the words used we have the opening sentence of a primitive book of Testimonies: 'These are my words which I spoke to you while I was still with you, that everything written about me in the Law of Moses, and in the Prophets and Psalms, must be fulfilled' (cp. Jn. v. 46; Acts xxvi. 22-3). The recovered *Gospel of Thomas* commences in a somewhat similar manner.

The compilation of the *Testimonia* is ascribed by Papias (c. A.D. 140) to Matthew. 'Matthew compiled the Oracles in the Hebrew language, and each interpreted [or expounded] them as he was able.'[7] This could have been known as the *Gospel of Matthew,* just as a collection of sayings of Jesus could be known as the *Gospel of Thomas,* thus misleading later writers who imagined that reference was being made to canonical Matthew. This little work, an essential manual for Christian missionaries, especially in going to Jews, was arranged like the books of Moses in five books. Papias, on this basis, produced his own work in five books, and entitled it *Exegesis of the Oracles pertaining to the Lord.*

The Matthean document was known to the early rabbis, for they handed down a tradition that Jesus had five disciples, Matthai, Naqai, Netzer, Buni and Thodah. The passage in the Talmud (b. *Sanh.* 43a) is all about proof-texts put forward by the followers of Jesus, and of counter-texts used to refute them. The writer long ago pointed out that these five disciples represent the five divisions of the Testimony Book,[8] and the first name that comes up is that of the compiler Matthew (Matthias).[9] We note that the third section (*Netzer*) would presumably have dealt with the Sprout and Branch testimonies, which would explain why the prediction in Matthew ii. 23 that Jesus would be called Nazorean is ascribed to the prophets (plural). The Patristic evidence suggests that the original Hebrew work was later extended in Greek versions in order to reflect advances in Christian thinking, and that it was such a version that was used by Justin.

But we have digressed sufficiently – though perhaps usefully – from what we were observing, namely the conjunction of the Netzer and Cochab predictions in a single prophecy. In the light of Justin's reference it is necessary to remind ourselves that one of the Nazorean centres in Batanea east of the Jordan was called Cochabe or Cochaba. Tradition has it that it was in the vicinity of this place, south-west of Damascus, that Saul of Tarsus had his vision of Jesus.

Following up this clue, we might conceivably expect that not very far from Cochaba we would also discover a Netzer locality. Nor are we disappointed.

In his *Ecclesiastical History* Eusebius makes reference to the *Letter to Aristides* by Julius Africanus. In this letter, dealing with the genealogies of Jesus in Matthew and Luke, Julius records a tradition about the members of the family of Jesus who had survived the war of A.D. 66-70. They took pride in their Davidic descent, and from memory or private records composed their family tree. Julius continues: 'These coming from Nazara and Cochaba, Jewish villages, to the other parts of the country, explained the aforesaid genealogy as faithfully as possible from the book of Chronicles' (*Eccl. Hist.* I. vii).

Here towards the end of the first century A.D. we have members of the family of Jesus residing at places significantly named Nazara (Sproutville) and Cochaba (Starville). They are called Jewish villages presumably because they were in an area where there were many non-

Jews and not far distant from the Greek cities of the Decapolis. It was to Pella in the Decapolis that the Christian-Nazoreans had removed from Judea and Jerusalem shortly before the war with the Romans. If we accept the statement of Epiphanius cited at the beginning of this chapter, that Cochaba was in Batanea, then we should look for Nazara in the same district. It was hereabouts that the Christian-Nazoreans after the war appear to have set up a kind of government in exile under a cousin of Jesus named Simeon son of Cleophas. To this Eusebius refers, basing himself on the lost *Memoirs* of the second-century writer Hegesippus.

After the martyrdom of Jacob [i.e. the brother of Jesus], and the capture of Jerusalem which immediately followed, the report is, that those of the apostles and the disciples of the Lord who still survived came together from all parts with those who were related to the Lord according to the flesh – for the great part of them were still living. These consulted together to determine who was most suitable to succeed Jacob. They unanimously declared Simeon son of Cleophas, of whom mention is made in the sacred volume [i.e. Lk. xxiv. 18], as worthy of the episcopal seat there. They say he was a first cousin of the Saviour; for Hegesippus asserts that Cleophas was the brother of Joseph' (*Eccl. Hist.* III. xi).

The question then arises, when had these messianically-named villages come into existence? Had they been created by a much earlier stream of pious Jews? And then, of course, we have to ask, when the relations of Jesus are found in these villages after the war, were they returning to their ancestral homes? Was this Nazara the Nazareth of the Gospels, where – according to Luke – the family from which Jesus sprang had been settled before he was born?

This is a problem to which no clear-cut answer is possible. We have taken into account a variety of factors which point to eastern rather than to western Galilee. The initial activities of Jesus were all to the north of the Sea of Galilee, a considerable distance from the traditional Nazareth. It is not explained why from somewhere in western Lower Galilee Jesus and his family (Jn. ii. 12) should move to Capernaum at the head of the lake. But if they were coming from Batanea this would be quite natural. Among the first followers of Jesus were fishermen living at Bethsaida at the northern end of the lake, some with Greek names like Andrew and Philip. The affirmation that Jesus was the Messiah was made in the north at Caesarea-Philippi.

Some further light may be thrown on the problem by an interesting passage in Josephus. About 23 B.C. Augustus Caesar had added to Herod the Great's realm the countries of Trachonitis, Batanea and Auranitis. The reason for the grant was the behaviour of Zenodorus, who 'was perpetually setting the brigands of Trachonitis to molest the inhabitants of Damascus' (*J.W.* I. 398). The information to which we are referring, however, is given in the *Antiquities*. It appears that Herod, after gaining this territory, wished to make it safe from Trachonite incursions. We may now quote Josephus at some length.

> When Herod learned that a Jew from Babylonia had crossed the Euphrates with five hundred horsemen, all of them mounted archers, and a group of kinsmen amounting to a hundred men ... he sent for this man and his band of followers, promising to give them land in the toparchy called Batanea, which bordered on Trachonitis, for he wished to make a buffer-zone out of such a settlement, and he promised that this land should be free of taxes and that they should be exempt from all the customary forms of tribute, for he would permit them to settle on the land without obligation.
>
> Being persuaded by this offer, the Babylonian went there to take possession of the land and build on it fortresses and a village, to which he gave the name of Bathyra. This man was a shield both to the inhabitants exposed to the Trachonites and to the Jews who came from Babylonia to sacrifice in Jerusalem; these he kept from being harmed by the brigandage of the Trachonites. And there came to him many men – and from all parts – who were devoted to the ancestral customs of the Jews [*hois ta Ioudaion therapeutai patria*]. And so this land became very populous because of its immunity – a state of things which lasted so long as Herod lived. But when his son Philip succeeded to the kingship, he subjected them to taxation, though it was not much and only for a short time. Agrippa the Great, however, and his son of the same name did indeed grind them down, and yet were unwilling to take their freedom away. And the Romans, who have succeeded these kings as rulers, also preserve their status as free men, but by the imposition of tribute have completely crushed them (*Antiq.* XVII. 23–8).

It may be a long shot, but among the Jews devoted to their ancestral faith who flocked to this tax-haven in Batanea may there not have been ardent Messianists, even the devout family from which Jesus came? Does this help to explain the Jewish villages in Batanea called Nazara and Cochaba? It is at least curious that so many lines of approach should meet in the same general area.

NOTES AND REFERENCES

1. The fragments are given in James, *The Apocryphal New Testament*. See also Schonfield, *According to the Hebrews*.

2. See R. Travers Herford, *Christianity in Talmud and Midrash.*
3. See *Klausner, Jesus of Nazareth.* Josephus, who commanded the Jewish forces in Galilee, describes the country in considerable detail, but makes no reference to Nazareth. It does not follow, of course, that it did not exist.
4. The first, I believe, to point out the significance of Pliny's reference was John Lightfoot in the seventeenth century in his *Horae Hebraicae et Talmudicae.*
5. Herford, *op. cit.* There is no indication of when this Ben-Netzer is supposed to have lived. He is described as 'a king among brigands, a brigand among kings'. Can he have operated on the border of Batanea and Trachonitis?
6. See J. Rendel Harris, *Testimonies* (2 vols.).
7. Eusebius, *Eccl. Hist.* III. xxxix.
8. Schonfield, *According to the Hebrews* (1937).
9. At the beginning of the Ebionite text of the *Gospel of the Hebrews,* Jesus says, 'Passing by the lake of Tiberias I selected John and Jacob, sons of Zebedee, and Judas the Iscariot; and you, Matthew, sitting at the receipt of custom I called, and you followed me. I wish you, therefore, to be twelve apostles for a witness to Israel' (Epiph. *Panar.* xxx. 13).

CHAPTER 30

WHO'S WHO?

While dealing with the question of Nazareth we incidentally picked up the information, on the authority of Hegesippus, that the Cleopas or Cleophas mentioned in Luke (xxiv. 18) was the brother of Joseph the father of Jesus, and therefore his uncle. This Cleophas had a son Simeon, a first cousin of Jesus, who eventually became the head of the Nazoreans.

Luke only speaks of two followers of Jesus who encountered him after his resurrection, while they were on the way to the village of Emmaus. One of the two was called Cleophas. His unnamed companion could have been his son Simeon. Evidently Luke's source did not clearly identify these persons; for if it had been plain that they were near relations of Jesus it would have been even more surprising 'that their eyes were kept from recognizing him'.

One of the difficulties we have with the Gospels is that sometimes names of people are given with little or nothing said about them. To take another example from Luke, we have the reference to women whom Jesus had cured, and who travelled with his company and helped to supply his wants from their means. We are told of Mary the Magdalene, of Joanna the wife of Chuza, steward to Herod Antipas, and Susanna (viii. 3). Who was Susanna? We do not have a clue. Similarly, Mark, when he tells of Simon of Cyrene who was requisitioned to carry the cross of Jesus, adds casually that he was the father of Alexander and Rufus (xv. 21). The sons must have been of some consequence in the early Church for their names to be on record. But what part they played is unrevealed.

Problems of identification arise in connection with the family of Jesus, and even with the Twelve Apostles, which cannot be resolved on the basis of the Gospel statements. It may seem extraordinary that there should be a conflict of testimony on matters where we would expect there to be no justification for disagreement. Fortunately we are helped by information from other sources; but they cannot clear up all the confusions.

How could it happen that there would be any mystery about the

Twelve? It can only be assumed that the Gospel writers had to rely on what was in the written sources which were available to them. The effect of the devastating Jewish war with the Romans had been not only to destroy or render unobtainable a great part of the Nazorean literature, but also to sever communication between the Christians in the West and the Nazorean refugees in Transjordan, who included members of the family of Jesus and the surviving apostles. The Gospel writers were remote both in time and locality from reliable oral memory, and had largely to depend on the limited amount of material accessible to them. They were not in a position to question or seek rectification of discrepancies. Consequently much of what they set down preserved and perpetuated limitations of knowledge and statements which were not in harmony.

The difficulty experienced by the Evangelists is illustrated by the account of the women who watched the crucifixion. Among them, says Mark, were Mary Magdalene, Mary the mother of Jacob the Small and of Joses, and Salome (xv. 40). Then, it was Mary Magdalene and Mary the mother of Joses who saw where Jesus was entombed; but when the women go to the tomb on Sunday morning they are Mary Magdalene, Mary mother of Jacob, and Salome.

It is only a very minor point, but curious that Mark should speak in one place of Mary mother of Jacob, and almost immediately of Mary mother of Joses. Perhaps there was a different source for the resurrection story. Matthew follows Mark for the crucifixion scene, except that instead of Salome he makes the identification 'the mother of Zebedee's children'. But Matthew too makes a change in the resurrection story by omitting Salome. At the tomb there were only Mary Magdalene and 'the other Mary'.

Luke does not name the women who were onlookers at the crucifixion and who saw where the body of Jesus was laid. At the tomb there were several women, among them being Mary Magdalene, Joanna (Lk. viii. 3), and Mary mother of Jacob (xxiv. 10).

In John's account there were at the cross Mary the mother of Jesus, and her sister Mary the wife (or daughter) of Clopas, and Mary Magdalene (xix. 25). The other Evangelists have no knowledge of the presence of the mother of Jesus, and we could not deduce from them that the mother of Jacob and Joses was the wife of Clopas or Cleophas and related to the mother of Jesus. It is only when we bring in the testimony of Hegesippus that we learn that Cleophas was the brother of Joseph the father of Jesus. Mary the mother of Jesus could hardly have had a sister of the same name, and therefore presumably sister here means sister-in-law. In that case Jacob the Small and Joses would have been first cousins of Jesus. But Cleophas had another son, Simeon, not mentioned, who after A.D. 70 became head of the Nazoreans. Was Mary the mother of Jacob and Joses also mother of Simeon? If so, why is this not stated? Was he the son of Cleophas by a previous marriage? We simply do not know.

What emerges, however, is of considerable interest, namely that among the followers of Jesus in his lifetime were his uncle, aunt and cousins on his father's side.

Before we go further it will be well to inquire how Hegesippus came by his information. Eusebius and others who knew his *Memoirs* inferred that he was a Christian of Jewish origin. This is not certain; but he might have been half-Jewish. He was a keen archivist, visiting Christian communities in different lands and jotting down what they could tell him of their history, and any anecdotes they had preserved of distinguished persons connected with their churches. This data he later assembled in a work in five books at some time between A.D. 160 and 180. On this account Hegesippus has been called the father of ecclesiastical history.

It seems likely that his travels had taken Hegesippus to Jerusalem, then called Aelia Capitolina, where in the reign of Antoninus Pius, who succeeded Hadrian, a small church consisting entirely of Gentiles under a bishop Marcus had managed to establish itself. After the revolt of Bar-Cochba was suppressed, Hadrian in A.D. 136 had taken his revenge on the Jews and their religion by terrible edicts, which included a denial to them of all access to the Holy City and the area where once their Temple had stood. It is possible that it was from the Gentile church of Aelia, which was very anxious to claim succession to the original Christian-Nazorean community, that Hegesippus obtained what he reported of past history and traditions concerning Jacob the brother of Jesus, his cousin Simeon and others.

Simeon had been executed as a Christian and as a descendant of David early in the reign of Trajan, when he was said to have been a centenarian. At any rate he was a very old man, and cannot have been born much later than A.D. 10. When he perished no other member of the family of Jesus had held office as bishop of Jerusalem, but there had been thirteen others, all Jews, whose names are given by Eusebius, who occupied the see between approximately A.D. 104 and 134.

It is most unfortunate that except for a few quotations from it the *Memoirs* of Hegesippus are no longer extant; but we can appreciate that however garbled and partly legendary was the information given to him it did incorporate a good deal that must have rested on certain facts which had been preserved. What he could glean does therefore to some extent compensate for the reticence and ignorance of the New Testament writers.

Even so, as we have seen, we are confronted with great difficulties of identification. Certain names were extremely popular among the Jews, notably those of the progenitors of the twelve tribes of Israel, and on the female side a Mary had been the sister of Moses, the Miriam of the Pentateuch. The early commentators were baffled that two Marys should have had sons called Jacob, Joseph and also perhaps Simeon. According to Mark (vi. 3), followed by Matthew (xiii. 55-6), Jesus had four brothers, Jacob, Joseph, Judas (Judah), and Simeon (Simon), and at least two sisters. Jesus must have been the eldest because he was the firstborn of Mary wife of Joseph (Lk. ii. 7; Mt. i. 25). To safeguard the uniqueness of Jesus and the perpetual virginity of Mary, it was argued that those called brothers must have been cousins of Jesus, or were step-brothers, the children of Joseph by a former wife, also named Mary.

But this simply will not do. Mark and Matthew very clearly state that the brothers and sisters of Jesus were the children of his own mother Mary, and they are not confused at all with the children of another Mary the wife of Cleophas, who may well have been his cousins. The names, as we have said, were very common. Two sons of Judas of Galilee were named Jacob and Simeon.

Mark refers to the eldest son of 'the other Mary' as Jacob the Small, a reference to his stature, and the intention may have been to distinguish him from another disciple Jacob, who could have been Jacob the son of Zebedee and Salome. The question then is whether Jacob son of Mary and Cleophas, Jacob the Small, is the same as Jacob son of Halphaeus? And this brings us to the Apostolic Lists.

Mark's list (iii. 16-19) begins with the three chief apostles, Simon nicknamed Peter, and Jacob and John the sons of Zebedee who were nicknamed Boanerges. Then follow Andrew, Philip, Bartholomew,

Matthew, Thomas, Jacob son of Halphaeus, Thaddaeus, Simon the Cananean, and Judas Iscariot. Matthew's list (x. 2-4) is virtually identical; but he puts Andrew second as Peter's brother, and for Thaddaeus we have the alternative reading Lebbaeus (also found in Western texts of Mark). Luke has two lists (vi. 13-16, and Acts i. 13), where Simon the Cananean is correctly called Simon the Zealot; but then in place of Thaddaeus-Lebbaeus we have a Judas, who is son or brother of a Jacob. Only which Jacob?

There is no list in John's Gospel, but there is a reference to some of the Twelve in xxi. 2, Simon Peter, Thomas called Didymus (both names mean Twin), Nathanael of Cana, Jacob and John the sons of Zebedee, and two others who are unnamed. Elsewhere John mentions Philip, Judas Iscariot,[1] and another Judas (not Iscariot). So we have reference by name to eight of the Twelve. When we compare the names from John with the synoptic lists it appears likely, though we are not told this, that Nathanael is the same as Bartholomew, which simply means son of Tolmai or Ptolemy. But why do we have to guess? John seems to agree with Luke that there was a Judas among the Twelve who was not Iscariot, the one Luke calls Judas of Jacob, and who replaces Thaddaeus otherwise Lebbaeus.

But again we run into trouble. The name Thaddaeus means Breast (*Shad*) as Lebbaeus means Heart (*Leb*), and this indicates a nickname rather than a personal name. If Luke is speaking about the same individual his actual name was Judas, to be further identified as a brother of Jacob. The most likely Jacob would be Jacob son of Halphaeus. But then in Mark (ii. 14), followed by Luke, Jesus calls to him a tax-collector who is named as Levi son of Halphaeus. Levi might be equated with Leb (Lebbaeus). We would then have to suppose that Jacob son of Halphaeus had a brother Judas, who was a tax-collector, and who when he joined Jesus received the nickname Lebbi or Thaddai (Syriac). This would be fine except that in the synoptic lists we have a Matthew, who according to Matthew's Gospel was apparently the same tax-collector.

We struggle on. There would seem to be no justification, though some early and later writers have thought the contrary, for making Jacob son of Halphaeus the same as Jacob the brother of Jesus. But there is a New Testament epistle in the name of Judas brother of Jacob, like the Judas of Jacob in Luke's Gospel. Is this Judas meant to be the brother of Jacob son of Halphaeus, or the brother of Jacob who was brother of Jesus? Hegesippus records a story about the grandchildren of the latter Judas.

Now 'the other Mary' at the scene of the crucifixion was the mother of a Jacob and Joses (Joseph), not of a Jacob and Judas. This makes it difficult to claim that her Jacob was the son of Halphaeus; but surely Luke who refers both to Cleophas and independently to Halphaeus as father of Jacob would have used the same name in both instances if they had been one and the same person? Halphai was a not uncommon Hebrew name, but Cleophas or Cleopas seems to be a contraction of Cleopater or Cleopatros, the masculine form of Cleopatra. Of course the same man could have had a Hebrew name and a near-sounding Greek one.

We are not yet at the end of the tangle, for there is still Thomas-Didymus. This is a descriptive term and not a name, both words meaning Twin. In early Syriac literature, as also in the *Gospel of Thomas* from Egypt, the name is always given as Judas Thomas, Judas the Twin. But why was he called Twin, and whose twin was he? Might it not be that Judas of Jacob was the twin brother of Jacob, and therefore called Thomas? But John speaks of a Judas, not Iscariot, and also of a Thomas, as if they were distinct. There are legends that Judas Twin was so-called because he bore such a striking resemblance to Jesus,[2] and even one that Judas Iscariot was made to look like Jesus and suffered on the cross in his stead.[3] On the whole it seems improbable that among the Twelve there were three persons named Judas.

Possibly the reader may not previously have been conscious of these puzzles of names and identities, having taken it for granted that we knew who everyone was. Now that it has been shown what we are up against, we can more clearly appreciate how far removed were the Evangelists from the circumstances of which they write. There should have been no doubt whatever about the names of the Twelve Apostles, and no mystery about their relationships, if the Gospel writers had been in direct contact with those who had survived the war. It is evident that they did not have the possibility of checking and supplementing the limited resources they could command, and this qualifies the value of their testimony in other respects. We cannot treat them as authorities in their own right, only as having to a certain extent, which we have to try to determine, preserved relics of more reliable material.

However, on the issue before us, there is an important positive side to this inquiry. The very fact that we have names of otherwise unknown persons, and of others whose connections and relationships had ceased to be clear, speaks of a once very lively close-knit community which had surrounded Jesus. Some of the names of these Jewish disciples, like Andrew and Philip, are Greek, which confirms their association with an area strongly Hellenic in complexion.

The image which ignorantly has been fostered of Jesus going about with twelve disciples completely disappears. We are introduced to a travelling company of both sexes, which may have numbered some sixty or seventy people.[4] It is largely a young company, with many of the men in their early twenties, who in some instances have one or both parents with them. They are an itinerant band like a clan of Rechabites or Essenes. They have so many names in common that distinguishing nicknames are called for like Rocky Simon, Stormy John, Shorty Jacob, and Judah Twin.

We move on from here to consider how matters stood between Jesus and his family. In the canonical Gospels we are led to suppose that Jesus went to the Jordan on his own initiative to be baptized by the prophet John. But the *Gospel of the Hebrews* in use among the Nazoreans had this to say: 'Behold, the mother of Jesus and his brothers said to him, "John the Baptist is baptizing for the remission of sins. Let us go and be baptized by him." But he said to them, "In what matter have I sinned, that I should go and be baptized by him? Unless, perhaps I have committed a sin of ignorance." '[5] We do not have the context, and so do not know whether Jesus elected to go with his family, or remained behind and went by himself later. But uniquely we have the information that Mary and her other sons were also baptized.

In John's Gospel Jesus and his family do not go their separate ways; for at the beginning of the activities of Jesus we read: 'After this he went down to Capernaum, with his mother and his brothers and his disciples, and there they stayed for several days' (ii. 12). Even later, though there is disagreement on how Jesus should act, the family have not split up. Before the feast of Tabernacles, his brothers say to Jesus, 'Leave here and go to Judea, that your disciples (there) may see the works you are doing. For no man works in secret if he seeks to be known publicly. If you do these things, show yourself to the world' (Jn. vii. 4). In the event his brothers go up to the feast, and Jesus follows soon after. This is in the same vein as the *Gospel of the*

Hebrews, and we can trace other affinities with John's information.

Again, it is John alone of the canonical Gospels who reports that the mother of Jesus was at Jerusalem at the time of the crucifixion in the company of the other women who were his disciples. And since the Passover was one of the three Jewish pilgrim festivals the brothers of Jesus must also have been there. Indeed, the *Gospel of the Hebrews*, according to Jerome, claimed that Jesus' brother Jacob, who became the leader of the Nazoreans, had taken part in the Last Supper.[6] The Passover meal, as we know, was a family celebration, with a roasted lamb shared by each household. We have also seen that among the followers of Jesus were probably cousins and also an uncle and aunt on his father's side.

When the movement established itself at Jerusalem, the Acts of the Apostles tells us that at its inception there were present not only the apostles, but also the women of the company, with Mary the mother of Jesus and his brothers (i. 13-14). The total number of disciples in Jerusalem at the beginning was about one hundred and twenty. So that even if initially his family had not understood Jesus and had disapproved of his behaviour, thinking him out of his mind, as Mark in particular stresses, they had not broken off relations with him, and had come round in the end to accepting him as the Messiah. It is rarely easy for a family to acknowledge the special dignity and consequence of one of its members with whom it has been in continual intimate contact in the everyday business of growing up and sharing the same home. Jesus with his dreams, musings and fits of abstraction, must have been quite difficult to live with.[7]

Jacob, Jesus' brother next in age, was a very different type of person, if we are to judge by what Hegesippus reports. The second son of Joseph and Mary was strongly inclined to asceticism, which according to the Gospels Jesus was not. We can probably discount as an overstatement that his parents had dedicated Jacob to God as a lifelong nazirite.[8] But by all accounts he became a very austere and rigidly devout Jew, far more the Holy Man of the Elect than his brother Jesus, who was willing to consort with the most undesirable characters. For Jacob, therefore, it must have been very hard to see in his gregarious brother the lineaments of the Holy One of God. That he was finally able to do so must have occasioned a great deal of heart-searching; and it may well have been the circumstances of the last week of Jesus' life that brought Jacob to complete conviction. It was told that Jesus after his resurrection had appeared privately to his brother, who, according to the Hebrew Gospel, had sworn to take no nourishment until he had proof that Jesus had risen from the dead.

It is to be remarked that when the new community was formed in Jerusalem it almost immediately assumed a character and structure akin to that of the Zadokite-Essenes. It may well be that Jacob had some responsibility for this. Luke does not say in the Acts how the decisions were taken to organize in the manner which came into operation. At the beginning Peter is the chief spokesman, and we are given in the Acts no indication how or when Jacob was accorded the leadership.[9] It is certainly a curious omission. And it becomes more curious when Luke deals with the visit to Jerusalem of Saul of Tarsus after his conversion. He sees Barnabas, who brings him to the apostles (Acts ix. 27). But Saul (Paul) himself says that he saw Peter, and no other apostle except Jacob the Lord's brother (Gal. i. 18-19).

What kind of people were those who followed Jesus and who joined the Nazorean community in Jerusalem? They were not exactly the same in each case; but mostly they were drawn from the lower orders of society.

We have made it clear from the outset that it was a very small minority of the Jewish population which belonged to special groups like the Pharisees, Sadducees and Essenes. The vast majority had no affiliation, and consisted in the main of peasants, artisans and small shopkeepers. These were the people who suffered most – and they *were* suffering – from food shortages, taxation and oppression, and who were most ready to respond to Fourth Philosophy and Kingdom of God preaching. Of the propaganda of Judas of Galilee and Zadok it is said by Josephus, 'Since the people heard them gladly, their reckless enterprise made much progress' (*Antiq.* XVIII. 6). So with the teaching of Jesus, Mark states that 'the common people heard him gladly' (xii. 37).

It is therefore absurd to say that the Jewish people rejected Jesus: they did nothing of the kind. It was a fraction of the minority groups of Pharisees and Sadducees who initially were offended. John makes the high-ups in Jerusalem say, 'Have any of the rulers or of the Pharisees believed in him?[10] But this people – the Jewish populace which heard Jesus gladly – who are not versed in the Law are accursed' (Jn. vii. 48). It was exceptional for one of the leading men, like Nicodemus, or one of the landed gentry, like the rich young ruler, to wish to ally himself with the raggle-taggle band which depended for its sustenance on a handful of women who had means, gifts of food brought by the people, and the coins which the charitable put into the bag.

When Peter points out that he and the others had left everything to follow Jesus, it was not great mansions and estates they had surrendered, but largely hovels and small family plots and jobs which yielded little more than a bare subsistence. But what they had given up was very precious: it was their all. They were promised a hundred per cent return and no taxation when the Kingdom of God was established.

Circumstances changed somewhat when the movement got going in Jerusalem after the death of Jesus. Then some more affluent individuals joined, and a number of priests, Pharisees and educated persons. Yet essentially the Nazoreans remained a movement of the people. Christians have been all too ready to accept the anti-Jewish bias of the Gospels and Acts, so that the contradictions have not registered. If the common people had heard Jesus gladly they could not have clamoured for his crucifixion by their enemy the Roman governor. The guilty party was the collaborating hierarchy and their servants, who scorned and feared the Jewish people, and therefore did not dare to arrest Jesus openly. Fortunately Luke did not tamper too much with his sources, so that he has preserved the incongruity that not long after the crucifixion the Jewish people of Jerusalem, supposed to have sided with the chief priests against Jesus – a circumstance most improbable from what we know historically – are now found siding with the apostles against the chief priests (Acts v. 13, 26).

It was the plebs, the proletariat of the Jewish nation, the victims of Roman domination and a self-interested hierarchy and aristocracy, who saw in the Nazoreans their champions and defenders. Many were eager and ready to believe that God had wrought a miracle for the martyred king of the Jews, and that he would speedily return to deliver them.

NOTES AND REFERENCES

1. In John's Gospel Judas Iscariot is called Simon's son (xiii. 26). Could he have been the son of Simon the Zealot?
2. On the whole problem of names, and traditions and ancient explanations of them, see Rendel Harris, *The Twelve Apostles* (1927). No additional help is obtainable from the uncanonical Gospels and Acts of individual apostles, which are largely legendary.

3. This suggestion is made in the late forgery known as the *Gospel of Barnabas.*
4. The numbers must have varied at different stages of the public life of Jesus.
5. Quoted by Jerome, *Against Pelagius,* iii. 2.
6. Jerome, *Of Illustrious Men,* 2.
7. On the characteristics of Jesus, see Schonfield, *The Passover Plot.*
8. Hegesippus relates that Jacob had been consecrated to God from his mother's womb. He abstained from intoxicants, and no razor ever came on his head. He never wore woollen garments, only linen (Euseb. *Eccl. Hist.* II. xxiii).
9. The close associates of Jesus in the Gospels are Peter, and Jacob and John the sons of Zebedee. At the beginning of the Acts they still head the disciples. But by the time of this dispute over the terms of admission of Gentiles, Jacob son of Zebedee had been executed on the orders of Agrippa I, and Jacob brother of Jesus not only occupies his place, but the supreme place (Gal. ii. 9; Acts xv. 13).
10. However, in the Acts we learn that the Nazoreans had quite a number of Pharisees who believed (Acts xv. 5).

CHRONOLOGICAL TABLE

This Table is designed to summarize the sequence of events covered by this book in conjunction with reference to contemporary rulers and authorities and individuals of note. We are thus enabled to view the circumstances in their historical context, with consequent gain to our understanding. In the light of researches and discoveries it has become practicable to furnish a more reliable chronology of Christian Beginnings than could be determined previously.

Event	A.D.
Jewish Sabbatical Year	33–4
Roman Census Year	34–5
Activities of Jesus. John the Baptist imprisoned by Herod Antipas.	
Execution of John the Baptist (autumn?).	35
War between Herod and the Nabataeans (winter).	35–6
Crucifixion of Jesus by Pilate (*Passover*, spring).	36
Appearance of a Samaritan *Taheb* (early summer).	
Nazorean Community at Jerusalem established under Simon Peter (*Pentecost*, June).	
L. Vitellius, Legate of Syria, visits Jerusalem, deposes Joseph Caiaphas as high priest and appoints Jonathan son of Annas (Sept. ?).	
Pontius Pilate, Governor of Judea, leaves for Rome to answer charges against him (autumn?).	
Execution of the Nazorean Hellenist Stephen and attack on Nazoreans led by Saul of Tarsus. Many Nazoreans take refuge in Batanea and Auranitis (winter).	36–7
DEATH OF THE EMPEROR TIBERIUS, succeeded by GAIUS CALIGULA (March).	37
Vitellius at Jerusalem with Herod Antipas. He deposes Jonathan as high priest and appoints Theophilus son of Annas (*Passover*, spring).	
Damascus leased by the Emperor Gaius to Aretas IV, king of the Nabataeans.	
Saul of Tarsus, now a Nazorean, leaves Damascus for Nabataean Arabia (spring).	
Nazorean jurisdiction extended by refugees who proclaim Jesus as Messiah. Many groups formed including one at Antioch in Syria where the disciples first came to be called Christians.	37–8

Event	Year
Central Nazorean Authority created at Jerusalem under Jacob brother of Jesus.	38
P. Petronius appointed Legate of Syria by Gaius.	39
Saul returns to Damascus, escapes arrest there and visits Jerusalem. He is sent to Tarsus.	
The Emperor Gaius designs to set up his statue in the Temple at Jerusalem.	
Jewish Sabbatical Year	40–1
The Jews protest about the statue to Petronius, and in Rome King Agrippa petitions the emperor.	40
THE EMPEROR GAIUS ASSASSINATED, succeeded by CLAUDIUS (January).	41
Agrippa is made King of Judea by Claudius.	
Saul is brought to Antioch by the Cypriot Nazorean Barnabas.	
Simon Cantheras son of Boethus made high priest by Agrippa.	
Simon Cantheras replaced by Matthias son of Annas.	42
C. Vibius Marsus appointed Legate of Syria by Gaius in place of Petronius.	
Elionaeus son of Cantheras replaces Matthias as high priest.	43
King Agrippa arrests and executes the Nazorean Jacob son of Zebedee.	
Agrippa imprisons Simon Peter, but his escape is contrived (*Passover*, spring).	44
Death of Agrippa I.	
Cuspius Fadus made Governor of Judea by Claudius.	
Cassius Longinus appointed Legate of Syria.	45
Joseph son of Camei (or Camith) made high priest by Herod king of Chalcis.	
Jewish guerrilla activities suppressed by Fadus.	
Great famine in Palestine.	46
Tiberius Alexander made Governor of Judea by Claudius.	
Jewish Sabbatical Year	47–8
First missionary journey of Saul (Paul) and Barnabas.	
Roman Census Year	48–9
Tiberius Alexander acts against the Nazoreans and Zealots. Jacob and Simon sons of Judas of Galilee seized and crucified.	
Nazoreans launch missionary campaign throughout the Roman Empire.	
Ananias son of Nedebaeus made high priest.	
Ventidius Cumanus becomes Governor of Judea.	

Controversy at Antioch on terms of admission of Gentile believers in Jesus, followed by a Nazorean Council Meeting at Jerusalem to deal with this issue.	49–50
Messianist propaganda in the Roman Empire.	
Claudius expels foreign Jews from Rome and warns the Alexandrians.	
C. Ummidius Quadrantus appointed Legate of Syria.	
Paul's second missionary journey begins.	
Disorders in Judea and Roman provocations.	50–1
First Nazorean documents probably composed at this time.	
Conflict between Samaritans and Galileans. The Jews are aided by the guerrilla leader Eleazar Bar-Deinaeus, and are attacked by the forces of Cumanus. Quadratus intervenes to prevent a rebellion.	51–2
Paul at Corinth.	
Cumanus banished by Claudius, and Antonius Felix sent as Governor of Judea.	
Paul returns to Antioch after keeping *Pentecost* at Jerusalem. In early summer he begins his third missionary journey.	53
Jewish Sabbatical Year	54–5
Militants and prophets are active in Judea and are attacked by Felix.	
Nazorean zealots wage a campaign against Paul in the communities created by him.	
DEATH OF THE EMPEROR CLAUDIUS AND ACCESSION OF NERO (October).	54
Eleazar Bar-Deinaeus seized by Felix and sent to Rome.	
Appearance of the Sicarii in Jerusalem. They assassinate the high priest Jonathan son of Annas.	55
Zealots and militants turn against the rich and all deemed favourable to Rome. Faction and class war develops in Judea.	55–7
Some of the Sadducean hierarchy start to rob the poor priests of their share of the tithes.	57–8
An Egyptian Jewish prophet enlists a following in Judea planning to overpower the Romans and occupy Jerusalem. The attempt is frustrated by Felix.	
Paul, seeking relief from interference with his work, comes to Jerusalem to appeal to the Nazorean Council bringing funds donated by his converts (*Pentecost*).	58

Paul is attacked in the Temple and taken into Fort Antonia in the belief that he is the Egyptian prophet. Later he is sent to Felix at Caesarea.	58–60
Paul is kept prisoner at Caesarea.	
Ananias son of Nedebaeus deposed as high priest by Agrippa II. Replaced by Ishmael son of Pheabi.	59
Clash between the Gentile and Jewish citizens of Caesarea.	
Felix is recalled by Nero and Porcius Festus is made Governor of Judea.	60
Paul is brought up for trial but having appealed to Caesar is sent to Rome by Festus (summer).	
After a hazardous journey and stay in Malta Paul reaches Rome (spring).	61
Controversy between King Agrippa and the hierarchy about a view of the Temple interior. An embassy is sent to Rome. The high priest is detained there.	
Agrippa gives the high priesthood to Joseph Cabi.	
Jewish Sabbatical Year	61–2
Death of Porcius Festus (late autumn?).	61
Annas (Ananus) son of Annas made high priest in place of Joseph Cabi (winter).	
Jacob the Just head of the Nazoreans arraigned by Annas and executed. Protest is made to the new Governor Albinus (*Passover,* spring).	62
Annas is deposed by Agrippa after three months in office and Jesus son of Damnaeus is made high priest.	
Roman Census Year	62–3
Reign of terror in Judea, fostered by the rapacity of Albinus.	
C. Cestius Gallus sent as Legate of Syria.	63
First hearing of Paul's appeal in Rome (autumn?).	
Second hearing and condemnation. Paul is executed (spring?).	64
Great Fire of Rome. The Christians there are accused of incendiarism and put to death (summer).	
Jesus son of Damnaeus deposed as high priest and replaced by Jesus son of Gamala.	
Albinus is recalled and replaced by Gessius Florus.	
The Temple at Jerusalem finally completed. Thousands of workmen become unemployed.	65
Matthias son of Theophilus made high priest by Agrippa in place of Jesus son of Gamala.	

Florus, to cover his excesses in Judea, goads the Jews into revolt.	65–6
Simeon son of Cleophas, a cousin of Jesus, is now acting head of the Nazoreans.	
Judea in the grip of war fever. Many leave the country.	
The Nazoreans withdraw to Transjordan and remove their Government from Jerusalem to Batanea in the region of Pella (*Passover*, spring?).	66
The Jewish Revolt against Rome begins (May).	

Index